ETHICS, CRIME, AND CRIMINAL JUSTICE

Christopher R. Williams
University of West Georgia

and

Bruce A. Arrigo
University of North Carolina at Charlotte

PEARSON

Prentice
Hall

Upper Saddle River, New Jersey 07458

Library of Congress Cataloging-in-Publication Data

Williams, Christopher R., 1972–
   Ethics, crime, and criminal justice / Christopher R. Williams and Bruce A. Arrigo.
     p. cm.
   Includes bibliographical references and index.
   ISBN 0-13-171076-1
   1. Criminal justice, Administration of—Moral and ethical aspects.   2. Criminal law—Philosophy.   3. Criminal law—Moral and ethical aspects   I. Arrigo, Bruce A.   II. Title.

K18.W54 2007
345—dc22
                                                        2006039190

Editor-in Chief: Vernon R. Anthony
Senior Editor: Tim Peyton
Editorial Assistant: Jillian Allison
Marketing Manager: Adam Kloza
Managing Editor: Mary Carnis
Manufacturing Buyer: Cathleen Petersen
Production Liaison: Ann Pulido
Production Editor: Judy Ludowitz/Carlisle Publishing Services
Composition: Carlisle Publishing Services
Senior Design Coordinator: Christopher Weigand
Cover Designer: Amy Rosen
Cover Image: Comstock Select/Corbis
Printing/Binding: R. R. Donnelley
Cover Printer: R. R. Donnelley

Pearson Education Ltd.
Pearson Education Singapore, Pte. Ltd.
Pearson Education Canada, Ltd.
Pearson Education—Japan
Pearson Education Australia PTY, Limited

Pearson Education North Asia Ltd.
Pearson Educación de Mexico, S.A. de C.V.
Pearson Education Malaysia, Pte. Ltd.
Pearson Education, Upper Saddle River, New Jersey

              10 9 8 7 6
ISBN-13: 978-0-13-171076-4
ISBN-10:   0-13-171076-1

DEDICATION

To our wives, Jami and Beth, who remind us daily that we are born for virtue in both reflection and action.

CONTENTS

Part II: Metaethics and Moral Psychology 49

PREFACE

On its most basic level, this book was written as an introduction to the subject and scope of ethics, particularly as its many problems and diverse perspectives intersect with those ongoing controversies found in the everyday world of crime, law, and justice. Ethics involves the study of many different themes and issues, including concepts such as good, right, duty, obligation, virtue, freedom, rationality, and choice, as well as the ways in which each of these notions informs the dilemmas we face, the choices we make, and the actions we undertake. The themes that ethics explores underlie many circumstances we routinely confront as individuals, groups, organizations, communities, and cultures. The immediate aim of ethics is simply to encourage critical reflection on these concepts and concerns, recognizing their significance to and contemplating their value for people in various social contexts. Ultimately, if this aim is realized, ethics enables all citizens to adopt more informed beliefs, to make better decisions, to undertake healthier actions, to be better people and, consequently, to live more rewarding and fulfilling lives.

Ethics, Crime, and Criminal Justice explores, in an accessible, stimulating, and practical way, a range of value-based concepts and perspectives designed to familiarize students with their importance both within the complex world of crime and justice and outside of it. Indeed, as Chapter 1 suggests, the fundamental purpose of morality (in thought and action) is to facilitate living a good life in a just society. Accordingly, this book was conceived, written, and organized with this in mind. It is our hope that this volume's contents helps students, practitioners, and other readers achieve the essential objectives of ethical reflection, decision-making, and conduct.

ORGANIZING THEMES

The organization of *Ethics, Crime, and Criminal Justice* differs appreciably from those other texts found in the market today. For example, rather than focusing primarily on ethical issues in criminal justice, readers are introduced to a number of concepts that function as critical thinking "tools." These tools enable the student or professional to recognize and assess a host of moral and ethical concerns that arise within the study and practice of crime, law, and justice. Rather than reviewing the facts and figures pertaining to criminal punishment, for example, the problems of human freedom, choice-making, and determinism are examined (see Chapter 3). This commentary leads to a more fully informed discussion and treatment of the moral context in which criminal punishment takes place. Moreover, rather than showcasing the topic of racism in policing or in court processing, thinking and reasoning skills are featured (see Chapter 11). This includes practical advice for the criminal justice professional on how to avoid labels, categories, and stereotypes, as well as other fundamental problems that occur when constructing arguments or taking positions that can lead to misguided perspectives, biased decision making, and questionable actions.

Not surprisingly, then, the guiding organizational premise for *Ethics, Crime, and Criminal Justice* is the emphasis it places on unpacking the assorted philosophical ideas that inform various crime and justice controversies. Moreover, this emphasis includes a targeted reliance on those conceptual tools essential for evaluating thought, choice, and conduct, especially as they relate to criminal justice dilemmas. "Ethics," as it is presented throughout this volume, is not intended to tell us what to do when faced with a conflict between, for example, loyalty toward a fellow police or correctional officer versus honesty in one's work setting. Instead, the purpose of ethics is to explore more generally the relevance of duties, obligations, and principles; to encourage sound reflection on those particular explorations; and, ideally, to be better equipped to resolve any (criminal justice) situation in which conflict might arise.

To effectively identify, assess, and reach conclusions on issues of moral significance (e.g., how to balance loyalty and honestly), one must first have an adequate appreciation for the conceptual grounding that represents ethical thought. To accomplish this, *Ethics, Crime, and Criminal Justice* draws attention to those relevant and prominent ethical theories, principles, and perspectives that have emerged throughout the history of Western civilization. In doing so, it exposes students and practitioners to the foundational thought necessary for any critical reflection about ethical choice-making and moral behavior in criminal justice settings as well as any other sphere of personal or professional life.

APPROACH, KEY FEATURES, AND PEDAGOGY

The organizing themes outlined above give rise to a basic approach, several key features, and a number of unique pedagogical aids that separate *Ethics, Crime, and Criminal Justice* from existing texts of its kind. Nearly all ethics texts in the criminal justice discipline present generous amounts of information on issues that are properly ethical or moral in nature (e.g., police corruption, prosecutorial misconduct, juvenile delinquency); however, few texts present these issues in a way that meaningfully links them to the broader study of ethics and morality. The goal in writing *Ethics, Crime, and Criminal Justice* was to offer a provocative yet accessible overview of the subject and scope of ethics, with specific attention to its relevance and value in the context of crime, law, and justice. The aim was to respond to the need for a comprehensive and illustrative text: one that provides a meaningful examination of both ethics *and* ethical concerns in criminal justice. *Ethics, Crime, and Criminal Justice* not only introduces students to the field of ethics, but demonstrates how this field can inform our understanding of moral issues in criminal justice, thereby aiding the practitioner in reasoning through situational dilemmas that require thoughtful reflection and reasoned decisions.

There are several key (and unique) features to *Ethics, Crime, and Criminal Justice*. The most noteworthy of these include the following:

> ***Comprehensive overview of ethical concepts, principles, and theories and their relevance to crime, law, and criminal justice.*** Many existing books on ethics and criminal justice provide limited treatment of the concepts and theories that constitute the foundations of ethical thinking, choosing instead to focus primarily or, in some cases, exclusively on criminal justice issues and dilemmas. While not excluding concerns of crime, law, and justice, *Ethics, Crime, and Criminal Justice* offers an informed and relevant exploration of the theoretical and conceptual foundations of ethics—foundations that, in turn, allow for the problems and concerns of criminal justice to be more thoughtfully and critically deliberated.
>
> ***Emphasis on reasoning and critical thinking skills.*** Throughout the text, the importance of reasoning and critical thinking in ethics and criminal justice is emphasized. Particularly in the final chapter, *Ethics, Crime, and Criminal Justice* challenges students to overcome common obstacles to good ethical thinking and to approach ethical issues and moral dilemmas critically and intelligently. In addition to the final chapter, which is dedicated entirely to exploring the importance of reasoning and critical thinking in ethics and criminal justice, many of the in-text illustrations and boxed inserts throughout each of the chapters are designed to encourage students to thoughtfully entertain issues and dilemmas of significance to ethics and criminal justice.
>
> ***Unique treatment of metaethical and moral psychological concerns of significance to crime, law, and justice.*** The concerns of metaethics and moral psychology—free will and determinism, relativism, self-interest, moral motivation, and development—are topics that are not only crucial to ethics, but also to understanding many of the issues and controversies in criminal justice (e.g., lawmaking, criminal punishment, unethical professional behavior). Notwithstanding their significance to the study of crime, law, and justice, many existing texts on ethics and criminal justice offer very little—and oftentimes no—attention to these key issues. *Ethics, Crime, and Criminal Justice* treats them as central concerns that must necessarily be addressed and contemplated for meaningful discussion about

moral issues and dilemmas to occur. In Part II of the text ("Metaethics and Moral Psychology"), we dedicate entire chapters to exploring many of these central issues and to examining their impact on and importance for crime, law, and justice.

Integrative approach. A key organizational feature of *Ethics, Crime, and Criminal Justice* is its integrative approach. Most books on criminal justice ethics dedicate one or more chapters near the beginning of the text to exploring ethical and moral concepts, and utilize the remaining chapters to examine ethical issues and dilemmas in criminal justice. As the issues and dilemmas explored later in the text often require utilization of the concepts presented at the beginning of the text, this approach typically has the effect of forcing instructors and students to *refer back* to the conceptual chapters throughout the course. In contrast, we have attempted to integrate criminal justice issues, conflicts, and dilemmas into the substantive conceptual chapters. Rather than including separate chapters that address issues or categories of issues in criminal justice (e.g., ethics and law enforcement, ethics and corrections), presentation and discussion of these issues occur throughout the text. This approach allows for the issues and dilemmas to be better illuminated and more thoughtfully examined in relevant conceptual contexts.

Examination of practical issues and/or controversies relevant to careers in criminal justice, the "helping" professions, and justice studies. Most books on ethics and criminal justice are directed toward current and future criminal justice professionals. As such, they tend to dedicate the majority of their content to exploring issues or dilemmas that might arise within the context of a criminal justice career. Although dedicating ample space to these sorts of concerns, *Ethics, Crime, and Criminal Justice* is written to be of value to anyone concerned with law, crime, and justice. Consequently, the book's content is relevant to those pursuing careers ancillary to criminal justice. Examples of these related professions include social work, counseling, public policy, public administration, and forensic science.

Additionally, *Ethics, Crime, and Criminal Justice* offers numerous pedagogical features. These instructional devices enable students to think critically about the twin subjects of ethics and criminal justice and the many contentious points on which they intersect. These features include:

- Lists of key terms and concepts
- Questions for review and discussion
- Lists of further suggested readings
- Ample illustrations, examples, and counterexamples throughout the text to clarify concepts, ideas, and applications of concepts and ideas
- Boxed inserts that encourage reflection on the *application* of ethical concepts and principles to "real-life" issues and scenarios in criminal justice
- Boxed inserts designed to encourage students to *critically reflect* upon controversial ethical themes, topics, arguments, and scenarios in criminal justice
- Boxed inserts that offer *case studies* of people and/or events from the world of crime, law, and justice

ORGANIZATION OF THE TEXT

Ethics, Crime, and Criminal Justice consists of eleven substantive chapters organized into three primary parts or sections. In each of the three sections, a fundamental domain of inquiry within ethics is explored, and in each chapter a substantive issue within that domain is reviewed. Consistent with the underlying focus on ethics in criminology and criminal justice, the text addresses key issues mindful of their importance for crime, law, and justice. Wherever relevant, practical illustrations and useful examples drawn from the field of criminology and criminal justice are strategically located throughout each chapter.

Part I of the text is entitled "An Invitation to Ethics." It contains two chapters. The commentary here introduces students to the field of ethics by emphasizing its value, subject, and scope, particularly in light of criminal justice concerns. Chapter 1 explains the role and importance of morality and the value of ethical inquiry, both within and outside of the criminal justice context. Additionally, routine questions about why ethics is needed—especially given the existence of laws and professional codes of conduct that outline moral ideals and standards—are both raised and addressed. Highlighting several key problems with laws and codes of conduct, the need for morality and ethical inquiry for criminal justice practitioners and nonpractitioners alike is discussed. Moreover, specific concerns impacting the three main "spheres" of criminal justice (laws and lawmaking, social justice, and criminal justice practice) are described and the special moral requirements placed on professionals within the system of criminal justice are reviewed.

In Chapter 2, a more thorough introduction to the field of ethics is provided. Focusing on the importance of choice-making, readers are encouraged to reflect upon their responsibility for making ethically responsible decisions. With this in mind, the role that values play in the choices that we make is considered. This includes outlining types of moral values and problems that can arise when values are in conflict. Chapter 2 concludes with a brief introduction to the three primary categories of ethical inquiry (meta-, normative, and applied), as well as to the domains of normative ethical inquiry (character, intentions, actions, and consequences). Given that Parts II and III of this volume explore these categories and domains, this latter segment of the chapter helps situate and organize the balance of the text.

Part II of the book is entitled "Metaethics and Moral Psychology." Several crucial metaethical concerns that inform issues of crime, law, and justice are examined. When most people think of ethics, they consider its normative domain. This domain considers what we *should* do or how we *should* live, whether in the context of individual decision-making and behavior occurring in personal or professional settings, or in the context of organizational and institutional policy and practice. Interestingly, however, there are a number of important assumptions and concerns about human nature and social conduct that must be addressed before doing any meaningful thinking about what we should do and how we should live. Included among these concerns are questions about: (1) human freedom and the determination of human behavior; (2) the relativity of moral values and the possibility of moral objectivity and universality; (3) the degree to which self-interest necessarily informs our decisions; (4) the age-old question of why we should be moral, and (5) the psychological question of how morality develops.

The first three of these concerns—freedom, relativity, and self-interest—can be thought of as obstacles or challenges to thinking and decision-making in ethics. As such, Chapters 3, 4, and 5 examine these challenges and their relevance, especially in relation to criminal justice. The latter two concerns—those of moral motivation and moral development—are often categorized as themes originating from moral psychology. Concluding Part II of *Ethics Crime, and Criminal Justice*, Chapters 6 and 7 review and discuss the psychological dimensions of ethics and morality. Once again, the manner in which these concerns intersect with those of crime, law, and justice are featured.

Part III is entitled "Normative Ethics: Theory and Application." This section investigates the normative domain of ethical decision-making. As the chapters in this portion of the book make clear, normative ethics attempts to formulate guidelines, standards, and/or principles of right and wrong, good and evil, and to provide answers to questions such as, "What should I do?" and "How should I be?" Of course, these questions do not lend themselves to easy or patented answers. In fact, moral philosophy has collected over two thousand years worth of responses to these and similarly complex concerns. And while a review of all such perspectives is unnecessary in the context of a text such as this, an examination of several of the most influential and widely discussed replies is worthwhile. These responses or, more accurately, "theories" or frameworks, function as "tools" with which to assess various types of policy- and practice-based concerns in criminal justice, ideally yielding both reasoned judgments and informed solutions.

Typically, normative ethics is broken down into three basic frameworks. These frameworks consist of consequentialism, deontology, and virtue-based ethics. Part III of *Ethics, Crime, and Criminal Justice* dedicates a full chapter to each of these perspectives. The objective over the course of these three chapters is to explore the merits of weighing consequences, duties, and character when faced with moral issues and ethical dilemmas. Chapter 8 examines the importance of considering the effects—the likely benefits and costs—of our decisions and actions. Chapter 9 explores those perspectives that place less emphasis on the consequences of our actions and, instead, focuses on whether our actions themselves conform to relevant duties, principles, and obligations. Chapter 10 addresses the importance of developing good moral character and a healthy sense of integrity. Once again, relevant illustrations from law, crime, and justice are utilized to help demonstrate how these philosophical ideas and topics routinely operate within the discipline of criminal justice.

Each of these three general frameworks (consequentialism, deontology, and virtue ethics) has many variations. Several of these variations are discussed in the respective chapters throughout Part III. However, what is perhaps most important is the degree to which the theoretical frameworks offered by normative ethics represent useful templates for critical reflection and decision-making on matters of morality. To this extent, the chapters that comprise Part III offer students and professionals a number of essential "tools" to interpret their everyday experiences and to direct their work-related practices in ways that are consistent with ethically sensible decision-making and conduct.

The final chapter of *Ethics, Crime, and Criminal Justice* serves as a "guide" to thinking about ethics and for living a virtuous life. Chapter 11 showcases a range of fundamental ideas about reasoning, thinking, and judgment that foster careful reflection on moral beliefs and values. These ideas can assist students and practitioners when making moral choices about complex crime and justice problems. Admittedly, this guide is not exhaustive; however, this is not the chapter's purpose. Instead, readers are exposed to a number of sensible, though informative, points and directives about *how* to engage in sound reasoning and critical thinking, particularly as they respond to situational dilemmas in criminal justice as well as in their personal and professional lives. To this extent, then, Chapter 11 provides direction not only in how to pursue and maintain thought, choice, and conduct that is ethical, it outlines a workable series of strategies for how to live virtuously and bring about justice in one's own life, those of others, and in society.

ACKNOWLEDGMENTS

The authors wish to thank the following reviewers: Dr. Susan Brinkley, University of Tampa, Tampa, FL; Dr. Lois Presser, University of Tennessee, Knoxville, TN; and Beverly Strickland, Fayetteville Technical Community College, Fayetteville, NC.

ABOUT THE AUTHORS

Christopher R. Williams, Ph.D., is Associate Professor of Criminology within the Department of Sociology and Criminology at the University of West Georgia. His books include, *Law, Psychology, and Justice: Chaos Theory and the New (Dis)Order; Theory, Justice, and Social Change: Theoretical Integrations and Critical Applications;* and the edited volume, *Philosophy, Crime, and Criminology.* Dr. Williams has also published numerous scholarly articles and book chapters, most confronting issues and controversies in social and criminological theory, the sociology of deviance, the philosophical foundations of crime, law, and justice, and the sociological and legal dimensions of mental health and illness. He did both undergraduate and graduate work in psychology before pursuing doctoral studies in psychology, law, and public policy within the Institute of Psychology, Law, and Public Policy at Alliant International University in Fresno, California. Dr. Williams currently resides in Villa Rica, Georgia, with his wife Jami.

Bruce A. Arrigo, Ph.D., is Professor of Crime, Law, and Society within the Department of Criminal Justice at the University of North Carolina at Charlotte. He holds additional faculty appointments in the Psychology Department, the Public Policy Program, and is a Faculty Associate in the Center for Professional and Applied Ethics. Dr. Arrigo received his Ph.D. from the Pennsylvania State University in the Administration of Justice and holds master's degrees in psychology and sociology. His recent books include *Theory, Justice, and Social Change* (2004); *The Female Homicide Offender* (2004); *Psychological Jurisprudence* (2004); *Introduction to Forensic Psychology (2nd ed.)* (2005); *Police Corruption and Psychological Testing* (2005); *Criminal Behavior* (2006); *Philosophy, Crime, and Criminology* (2006); *The Psychology of Lust Murder* (2006); and *The Terrorist Identity: Explaining the Terrorist Threat* (2006). Professor

Arrigo has also authored more than 125 journal articles, book chapters, and scholarly essays on the normative, theoretical, empirical, and policy dimensions of various criminal justice and social welfare problems. Professor Arrigo is an elected Fellow of the American Psychological Association (2002) and the Academy of Criminal Justice Sciences (2005). He currently lives in Concord, North Carolina, with his wife and two children.

Part I

An Invitation to Ethics

Chapter 1

CRIMINAL JUSTICE AND THE STUDY OF MORALITY

Criminology and criminal justice are disciplines that spark interest in almost everyone. The problems and issues as well as people and personalities associated with crime, law, and justice arouse our feelings, inflame our passions, and provoke our thoughts. In a word, the subject of crime and criminal justice is fascinating. The front page of the daily paper is commonly littered with accounts of crime and justice; the evening news frequently reports stories about terrorism, murder, arson, and high-profile court cases; and many of the most popular television programs, theater films, and computer games are crime-driven dramas. But what is it that makes these problems, issues, personalities, and stories so appealing to so many people? What is it about crime and criminals, policing and violence, courts and corrections that evokes such widespread and persistent interest? In short, what makes the phenomenon of crime and justice so sensational?

Part of the answer is that our attraction to such scenes, characters, images, and issues is steeped in *morality*. In fact, crime, law, and justice cannot be separated from morality. Unlike most other academic disciplines, criminology and criminal justice are, from their very foundation through their elemental and daily operation, inherently moral subjects. By contrast, the debates and concerns of other fields, such as computer science or geology, have appeal only to limited segments of society. The plain truth is, despite their fascination for some individuals, not everyone is significantly invested in computer technology or geological advances. Moreover, when the general public does exhibit more than passing enthusiasm for these matters, the events that draw us in are those that typically infringe upon the boundaries of morality. To illustrate, consider recent controversies over the influence of Internet technology on the growth of hate groups, child pornography and abduction, terrorism, and the availability of bomb-making instructions.[1] Each of these topics has elicited attention from governments, industries, law enforcement communities, and several other invested constituencies from around the globe. Additionally, each of the above stated mmas lies squarely at the intersection of computer technology and morality (and, ell, are matters involving crime and justice).

However, in contrast to many other disciplines, criminology and criminal justice are quite different. The subjects on which the field is constructed are based on matters of personal and social responsibility, free will and choice-making, reasoned judgment, and moral accountability. Not surprisingly, then, the topics that concern the discipline are personally meaningful, extremely provocative, and altogether engaging for more than just a few individuals. Indeed, if you have ever had a discussion on the death penalty, abortion, flag burning, war, racial profiling, or terrorism, you already know how these subjects present a clash of values whose conceptual underpinnings entail conflicting views about morality. For example, everyone (it seems) has a position on abortion—some are so committed to their position that they take part in protests, lobby politicians or, in the extreme, commit acts of violence (i.e., terrorist bombings against abortion clinics) to make their point. The same strongly held convictions surround other matters of life and death, such as that of capital punishment. Go to the sight of nearly any execution, anywhere in the country, and you will see tens if not hundreds (perhaps even thousands) of professionals and everyday citizens alike zealously voicing their position: some resistant and oppositional; others compliant and supportive. In both cases, however, people are expressing their *moral sensibilities.*

To be "for" or "against" abortion, to denounce or endorse capital punishment are commitments that are thoroughly moral in nature. Some of us may oppose abortion because, on a moral level, it is wrong to take a life; some of us may oppose the death penalty because, on a moral level, it is wrong to take a life. However, for those of us who make such claims, we are putting forth what we believe to be a valid and desirable *moral principle.* At the same time, some of us may support abortion given our conviction that people should be free to do as they see fit with their own bodies; that is, to enjoy some sense of privacy, control, and self-determination when it comes to that which is most private and most uniquely "ours." Again, though, we are invoking (knowingly or not) the language of morality when proclaiming the value and desirability of one's "rights," "autonomy," and "choice-making."

Still, the matter at hand is complicated. To illustrate, which values and whose principles are, in fact, valid and desirable in these and other contexts? Should the value of life take precedence over the right to privacy and self-determination? If so, under what specific conditions should this occur? Should the value of life supersede the value of what some define as "just" punishment? Not only do questions such as these further our regard for criminology and criminal justice, they fundamentally direct our attention to matters of *ethics.* However, as we will see shortly, ethics is not limited to the types of social and political issues thus far described. Ethics is equally about how we should live; that is, the decisions we should make and the actions we should take as we confront a variety of personal and professional scenarios over the course of our lives.

ETHICS AND MORALITY

While the subject and scope of ethics will be explored in more detail in the next chapter, it will be useful to offer some preliminary observations on its relationship to morality. At its most elemental level, **ethics** can be defined as *the philosophical study of morality*. More specifically, ethics can be described, in part, as:

- The study of what is morally "right," "wrong," "good," "bad," "obligatory," and "permissible."
- An effort to understand and justify moral concepts, principles, and theories.
- An effort to establish (justified) principles of moral behavior that can serve as guides for individuals and groups.[2]
- An investigation into the values and virtues that are important—even necessary–to leading and living a (or the) "good" life, as individuals and as societies.

Morality is typically understood to refer to *people's beliefs about right and wrong, good and bad, and the choices they make and the actions that they take as a result of those beliefs.* Ethics is an investigation into or critical consideration of such beliefs, choices, and actions. Yet, ethics is not simply the study of morality. While anthropology, sociology, and other social sciences routinely study morality, ethics is better understood as a certain way of studying morality. On the one hand, social sciences such as anthropology are interested in **descriptive** accounts of morality; that is, in characterizing the moral beliefs and practices of a given society or culture. On the other hand, ethics is largely **prescriptive**. In other words, it attempts to evaluate moral beliefs, principles, practices, and so forth, and it makes normative statements about what should be or should not be done in light of its evaluations. Thus, unlike anthropology or other social science disciplines, ethics is not the study of what *is*, but of what *should* or *ought* to be.[3]

To illustrate the distinction between prescriptive and other forms of inquiry, let us consider the example of laws prohibiting murder. If we approached the issue of homicide through the study of criminal law, we would endeavor to understand what is. We would be interested in ascertaining the existing state of the criminal law with respect to murder—how, precisely, this crime is defined; what exceptions, if any, apply to the general rule; what punishments are ascribed to the act of murder; and other considerations that allow us to better grasp what murder is and how it is understood from a legal perspective. As soon as we begin to entertain questions such as what punishments *should* or *ought* to apply to murder, whether murder *should* be legally prohibited, whether there *should* be exceptions to the general rule, and whether existing exceptions are morally justifiable, we step into the realm of ethics (see Box 1.1). In a way, ethics is interested in "taking a step back" from common beliefs and practices, subjecting them to critical examination, and reaching normative conclusions about what *should be* the case rather than what *is* the case.

Part of the significance of ethics, especially within criminology and criminal justice curricula, is that it encourages students (and teachers) to reflect critically on matters that are all too frequently taken for granted. Definitions of crimes and corresponding punishments; the rights of citizens, suspects, and incarcerated criminals; and law enforcement techniques and tactics for apprehending persons who have (or are thought to have) violated the law are examples of topics that people encounter over the course of their criminal justice and/or criminology education. Most often, however, students are simply asked to learn these things in their existing everyday forms (e.g., facts, techniques), rather than more deeply contemplate what *should* be. Thus, ethics challenges us to experience a deeper understanding of what crime and justice are or could be, directs our attention to the "rights" and "wrongs" of the criminal

BOX 1.1
The Moral Problem of Punishment

While we often entertain *practical* questions of criminal punishment, we less often consider the moral underpinnings of those practices. Why do we punish? When do we punish? What is the appropriate amount of punishment for a given infraction? While each of these questions can be answered in a practical sense, they also have moral foundations that require our critical consideration.

Utilitarian philosopher Jeremy Bentham once argued that, "all punishment is evil"—"evil" being anything people do not want inflicted upon them. He was not, of course, suggesting that we not ever practice the punishment of criminal offenders. Rather, he was simply stating an often overlooked moral reality that punishment involves the infliction of pain, the causing of suffering, and/or the infliction of deprivation—all actions that, morally, we ought to avoid wherever possible. Beyond simply being an evil in this sense, punishment is an evil that we *intentionally* inflict upon other human beings.

If we accept the notion that all punishment is evil and, further, agree that evil generally should not be caused and evil actions not done, we recognize the ethical problem of punishment. "If the infliction of evil ought not be done under most circumstances, how can we justify the infliction of evil on criminal offenders?" Outside the context of criminal justice operations, depriving persons of things that they value and/or inflicting pain and suffering upon persons is often grounds *for punishment*. Yet within the system of justice, these pains and deprivations represent the operative mode by which "justice" is often carried out. How, then, can we *justify* intentionally inflicting evil upon other human beings? What justifications can you think of for punishing criminals? What justifications might exist for dealing with criminal offenders in ways *other than* punishment?

Source: Igor Primoratz, *Justifying Legal Punishment* (New Jersey: Humanities Press, 1989), pp. 1–9.

justice system, and invites students to consider what their (potential) roles should be as current or future practitioners within the field.

Never Kill an Innocent Human Being

In the examples used near the beginning of this chapter, several values and principles were mentioned as common justifications for opposing or supporting abortion and capital punishment. In everyday discourse, we usually make judgments as to the "rightness" or "goodness" of behavior by referencing values or principles that we hold to be important. The values and principles that ethics investigates are not that different from those that factor into our own moral decision-making and judgment (e.g., honesty and fairness, duty and obligation). However, ethics removes these notions

from everyday discussions and subjects them to careful scrutiny. The goal is to identify values and construct principles that are sound, worthwhile, and applicable in a
number of situations or contexts (including those that occur within criminal justice
contexts). Consider the following questions that could be raised in response to the
idea (i.e., principle) that we should *never kill an innocent human being*:

- Is the idea that we should never kill an innocent human being a worthwhile
  principle?
- Does it apply to all situations or are there exceptions? If there are exceptions,
  what are they and why? What makes these exceptions legitimate?
- What if the principle of never killing an innocent human being conflicts
  with other principles also considered important? Can we rank-order
  principles such that some "trump" others when there is a conflict? If so, who
  decides this and by what process?
- What if, for example, killing an innocent human being can save the lives of
  ten other innocent human beings? Is this killing ethically justified?
- What is a "human being"?
- What constitutes innocence?
- What constitutes life and therefore "killing"?

You probably had an easier time with the first question than those that followed.
Despite the fact that most people would probably agree that not killing innocent human beings is a valid moral principle worth following, they would likely run into
some difficulties with one or more of the subsequent queries. Exceptions to this principle could be many and varied. For instance, in times of war military forces routinely
kill innocent human beings (both citizens of other countries and, on occasion, their
own civilians). Could we argue that citizens of other countries, by virtue of supporting their governments, are somehow less "innocent" and therefore exempt from the
principle? During the terrorist attacks of 9/11 in New York, would it have been
morally justifiable for the United States military to shoot down the hijacked
aircrafts—thereby killing dozens of innocent citizens on board—in order to prevent
these planes from reaching their targets? In other words, which innocent lives were
expendable, those in the commandeered planes or those in the World Trade center
towers? Under what ethical principle(s) would this be determined?

Defining the contours of moral values and principles can be more difficult than
often imagined. The same is true when describing the specific situations in which
these values and principles do or do not apply. Even something as seemingly straightforward as defining "human being" can be a matter of significant moral contention.
Is an unborn fetus a "human being" by moral standards? If so, at what point does it
become a human being? Historically, entire groups of people have been exempt from
human status. For instance, Nazi Germany subscribed to something similar to the
above principle that we should never kill an innocent human being. However, Jews
and certain other citizen groups (e.g., gays, various ethnic constituencies) were not
legally regarded as fully human. Therefore, killing persons within these collectives was
not a violation of the accepted principle within Nazi Germany.[4]

Ethics examines and encourages us to consider these sorts of questions. It seeks
to develop valid principles that can be used by individuals, groups, organizations,
communities, and even entire societies as guides along the path of life. Some issues

(e.g., what constitutes innocence?) may seem academic and of little relevance to our everyday realities. However, investigating such questions forces us to reflect profoundly upon our own values and beliefs, as well as why we have them and how we can or should apply them in our personal and professional lives.

THE ROLE OF MORALITY AND THE VALUE OF ETHICAL INQUIRY

Given this very provisional understanding of morality and ethics, we can begin to consider not only what both are, but what they *do*; that is, why we need morality and why the study of morality (i.e., ethics) can be of value to individuals, professionals, institutions, cultures, and societies. What role does morality play in cultural settings and in social contexts? What value does morality bring to us as individuals—both in our personal and professional lives? Why do social institutions such as law or the criminal justice apparatus (as well as their component parts) need to function in a moral fashion?

Overall, we might say that the purpose of morality is to *enable us to live a good life in a just society*. Though morality has many more specific purposes, almost all of them tend either to enable us to live good, fulfilling lives as individuals, or promote the kind of society, social conditions, and human relationships that allow all citizens to experience the same. Among other things, morality plays a significant role in preventing and reducing harm and suffering, enhances human and nonhuman well-being, provides the necessary tools to resolve conflict fairly and orderly, and encourages people to recognize and attend to the needs of others.[5] All of these things, in turn, contribute in some way to the development and sustenance of a just society—to conditions and relationships that allow us to be well and to flourish as individuals, that allow others to be well and to flourish as citizens, and that promote the greater health of the community and of society.

All of this may seem rather vague. This is because ethics—the study of morality—is not as simple as concluding that we need morality to enable us to live good lives in just societies. Ethics forces us to reflect more deeply upon what, exactly, we mean by "goodness," "justice," and how and why they are important in a social context. Even if we begin with the basic idea that morality enables us to live a good life in a just society, ethics then forces us to further address related questions and concerns:

- What is "justice" and a "just" society?
- What is a (or the) "good" life?
- How, exactly, does morality function to promote justice (or fail to do so)?
- How does morality further our interest in living a good life? A happy life? A fulfilled life?

Unfortunately, these questions do not lend themselves to easy or straightforward responses. You may be distraught to learn that despite more than two thousand years of moral philosophy—of critical reflection, argumentation, and analysis—ethical inquiry has not produced definitive, irrefutable answers to these sorts of questions. To be clear, this is not a consequence of limited efforts or misguided attempts. Moreover, a variety of provisional answers to these very questions are discernible and they are worth considering (indeed, several of them will be entertained over the course of this book). However, the point is that ethics is not something to be undertaken with the intent of finding all possible solutions. Unlike scientific and social scientific inquiries that provide factual (descriptive and explanatory) information, ethics primarily encourages us to question, to develop our own answers, and then to question some more.

Fortunately or otherwise, ethics is not an exact science. It is not an exercise in learning and applying rules and principles (such as the law). Additionally, ethics does not tell us exactly how we should lead our lives or what we should do in every situation. While ethics certainly encourages us to think about principles and to think about how they might apply in specific, concrete instances, it is perhaps best thought of as an ongoing process of critical reflection. Part of what ethical inquiry is—and part of what it means to be moral—concerns this *process* of thinking and rethinking, developing provisional answers only to recognize their limitations and reflect a bit more. How will studying ethics help you in your personal and professional life? Not, as you might think by providing solutions but instead, by encouraging you to continually reflect upon the questions themselves.

The Examined Life: What Does It Mean to Be Moral?

The Greek philosopher Socrates (469–399 B.C.E.) is reputed to have once said that, "the unexamined life is not worth living."[6] What he meant is that it is important to critically reflect upon our own lives, the principles by which we live them, the values we cherish, and the cognitive and affective (i.e., emotional) forces and processes that inform our decisions and actions—in short, the people we are, have been, and want to be. Socrates also instructed his students to be true to themselves; that is, to "know thyself" (a now familiar philosophical slogan reputed to have been inscribed on the temple of Apollo in ancient Greece). Thus, ethics not only asks that we reflect upon the issues and/or controversies that we encounter in our personal and professional lives, it also asks us to examine ourselves. Another way of saying this is that ethics asks that we live *mindfully*—to take some care in how we act, what and how we feel, what we think and believe.[7] Morality is not possible without self-knowledge; and "knowing thyself" requires the kind of critical, self-searching introspection that ethics encourages us to undertake.

In a way, then, we can understand morality as "*the self-conscious living of life.*"[8] To be moral is to have knowledge about one's self; that is, what you are about and, thus, what you are doing and why you are doing it. Searching ourselves—coming to "know ourselves"—brings us to one of the most important functions of morality in the context of our personal existence as individuals: *Morality gives meaning to and provides purpose in our lives.* Knowing one's self in the way that Socrates advocated is ultimately what enables us to experience a sense of identity, meaning, purpose, direction, and motivation. To illustrate, if we selfishly strive for money and power lying and exploiting others for our own benefit, we not only live a less-than-moral life from the perspective of others, but lack something important: a personal sense of virtue and goodness. Meaning and purpose come from being in touch with our values and principles and from being aware of and motivated by things beyond ourselves. In short, having a sense of goodness and justice serves as a way of measuring ourselves—where we have been, where we are, and where we are going—and as a guide for our decisions and actions.

If our lives are directed by a deeper sense of goodness and justice, arguably we live more complete, satisfying, and fulfilling existences. Part of what Socrates meant when he proclaimed that the unexamined life was not worth living was that a relationship could be discerned between ethics, morality, and happiness—between being moral and living a fulfilled life. Socrates, Plato, Aristotle, and other early Greek philosophers each, in their own way, suggested that being moral *was* being happy and well. In other words, when people lead good lives, notwithstanding difficulties or inconveniences they may bring to themselves because of it, they embrace happier, more fulfilling existences. This reasoning may be somewhat difficult for us to accept, especially when being moral seems often to result in unhappiness or, at least, inconvenience. However, the temporary frustrations and nuisances that can follow from setting aside our own pleasures, wants, and interests are not contrary to being well and to leading a good life. Indeed, on a deeper level, the inconveniences directly contribute to our own well-being and to that of others, as well as to the general health of the community and society of which we are a part. In other words, they directly contribute to living a good life in a just society.

WHY ETHICS WHEN WE HAVE LAWS?

Like many students of criminology and criminal justice who come upon ethics for the first time, you may be asking yourself, "don't we already have laws that serve to create and sustain a just society in which we can lead good lives?" Isn't this precisely their purpose? And, if so, why do we need to bother with ethics at all?[9]

Let us consider the example of drugs and society as a basis to examine this matter. Whether as students or teachers, both authors of this volume have discussed the phenomenon of illicit substance use/abuse and crime on a number of occasions. Invariably, when the class discussion focuses on drug decriminalization or legalization, some very strong sentiments in favor of or opposed to this policy are voiced. Eventually, after some considerable classroom debate, a student typically weighs in and says emphatically that, "It's against the law, period!" When pursuing this position with students who express such deeply held convictions, often (although not always) they are persuaded that the law is, in and of itself, sufficient justification for their views concerning illicit drug use. In other words, for them the mere fact that something is against the law is itself an indicator that further discussion on the matter is unwarranted. The question becomes whether such a position or argument is sound? Does the fact that something is against the law mean that subjecting it to critical scrutiny is pointless? That is, does the legality or illegality of a certain behavior "end the argument," so to speak?

In our joint experiences within the field of criminology and criminal justice, there are literally thousands of students who question the need for critical discourse around issues such as illicit drugs (other than, perhaps, how to control them and the people who sell and use them). In relation to ethics, the question might be asked, "why do we need to study ethics, particularly in the context of a profession that relies heavily on laws, codes of professional conduct, and the like?" Why, one might ask, do we need ethics when we already have laws and guidelines in place to *tell* us how we can and cannot act and what we should and should not do? Why study the moral dimensions of drugs, abortion, euthanasia, prostitution, gambling, rape, arson, robbery, and even murder when other people have already done so and codified (written into law) their conclusions? Why waste time on these matters when it is quicker and easier to rely on the answers that legislators and judges have already provided and that, ultimately, we must abide by anyway?

Laws Are Not Infallible

There are several important considerations that arise in response to these and similar questions. First, we might ask ourselves how and by whom laws are made. It is always important to remember that *laws are made by people*, generally through a process of ethical reasoning that involves moral considerations. More specifically, statutory laws are created by local, state, and federal legislators, regulatory law is created by administrative agencies, and case law is created by judges and justices. In all instances, it is important to remember that laws, policies, rules, guidelines, codes, and so on etc. are made by *fallible* people who are subject to the same sorts of biases, pressures, conflicts, and errors in reasoning as the rest of us (though to a lesser degree, we would hope). To illustrate, simply because state legislators conclude that gambling is harmless and remove it from the list of prohibited acts, does not mean that gambling *is* harmless or that it *should* be removed from the list of prohibited acts. Further, even if state legislators legalize gambling, they do so for what they believe are valid *reasons*. Of particular interest to us should be *what reasons* and whether they represented *good reasons*.[10] For instance, if economic considerations played a role in the state's legalization of gambling, then increased revenues, jobs, commerce, and so forth were likely identified as more important than those factors weighing against the decision. These types of considerations make the legalization of gambling a decidedly *moral judgment*.

Laws Can Be Immoral

Concerns of law and lawmaking will reappear throughout subsequent chapters. For now, what is important is that we understand the value of and need for ethics even when we have law. In short, we need ethics—even if we have laws—because *law is not possible without ethics*.[11] In making laws, legislators, judges, and others with lawmaking power are invariably making decisions that are moral in nature or have moral implications; they are arriving at conclusions about what is right and wrong based on what they believe, at the time, amount to good reasons or sound justifications. These reasons and justifications, in turn, may or may not be suspect. Laws may or may not be moral; they may or may not promote moral behavior.

Consider, for example, the **Nuremberg laws** under which the persecution of Jews in Nazi Germany was legal, or the keeping of slaves in the pre–Civil War United States—a practice that was legal both under state law and under the U.S. Constitution at the time. Persecuting Jews and the keeping of slaves are today acts that most of us would agree are less-than-moral by nearly all standards. Yet they were also acts that were legal at one time. What can we learn from these examples? Simply put, *legality does not necessarily equal morality;* and, likewise, *morality does not necessarily equal legality*. Ethics may determine that some laws (e.g., those permitting slavery or those

BOX 1.2

Jury Nullification

Jury nullification occurs when jurors return a verdict that is consistent with their own sense of justice, but inconsistent with the law. Often, this occurs when a verdict of "not guilty" is returned despite evidence that the defendant is legally guilty of the crime for which she or he is charged. In effect, the jurors determine that the existing law is immoral or has been wrongfully applied in a particular instance and decide the case on the basis of their own *moral* standards rather than applicable *legal* standards. Jurors may, for instance, refuse to find a defendant guilty of a "mercy killing," despite overwhelming evidence that the killing was in violation of criminal law (e.g., the cases of Jack Kevorkian).

- Given the problems with law outlined in this chapter (e.g., that laws can be misguided, outdated, immoral, unjust), do you feel that jury nullification could be morally acceptable in some situations? If so, under what circumstances and for which types of crimes/criminals? Keep in mind that the role of jurors is not to make or change laws, but to judge cases on the basis of legal facts with which they are presented.
- Is jury nullification a desirable part of criminal justice? Does it promote or interfere with justice? Keep in mind that it was not long ago that juries in the South regularly returned "not guilty" verdicts for white offenders who were charged with crimes against blacks, notwithstanding strong evidence of guilt. Similarly, black defendants were regularly found "guilty" on the basis of very little evidence.

Source: M. Levine and L. Wallach, *Psychological Problems, Social Issues, and the Law* (Boston: Allyn & Bacon, 2002).

promoting or maintaining discrimination on the basis of class, race, gender, etc.) are *immoral*. There are many acts that are legal, yet immoral by many standards; and, at the same time, there are many practices that were, are, or might be illegal, while being moral by at least some ethical standards (see Box 1.2) For instance, some environmentalists drive spikes into trees to prevent them from being harvested by the lumber industry (if the trees are then harvested, the spikes break the expensive saws in the lumber mills).[12] Are such practices ethical? Despite questions of legality, the principles that drive environmentalists are unquestionably moral in nature.

Right Does Not Always Make *Good*

These discrepancies are an important reason for studying ethics and morality even when we have laws to guide us. It is always important to keep in mind that even if we "do the right thing" by legal standards, we are not necessarily acting morally. Similarly, even if we do the wrong thing by legal standards, we are not necessarily acting immorally. Throughout your studies of crime and justice, politics, society, and life more generally, always keep in mind that *right* does not equal *righteous*. That is to say, just because something is a *legal* right does not make it a *moral* right. These are two very different uses of the term "right." While my friend Sara may have the "right" to have an abortion, this certainly does not mean that it is morally "right" for her to do so. Similarly, simply because it may be morally wrong for her to do so, this does not necessarily mean that it is or should be legally wrong. The relationship between morality and law is one that is as complex as it is important. While we will have occasion to return to it, for now we simply should recognize that law and morality—though arguably interrelated—are not one and the same. We cannot and should not abandon our study of ethics simply because we have laws. Laws are not definitions of morality; rather, laws are *subjects* of ethical scrutiny in the same way as everything else.

Law Is Not Inclusive of All Moral Concerns

While morality is closely linked with law, they are not one and the same. Law and morality are similar in that they are both intended to promote well-being, resolve conflicts, and generally enhance social harmony.[13] As the previous section attempted to clarify, however, there are some important differences between law and morality. In addition to laws not always being moral, and morality not always being legal, there is at least one other difference that is worth noting. The second major difference between morality and law is that *some aspects of morality are not covered by law.*[14] Most all of us would agree that lying is, in most instances, morally wrong. Yet other than those laws prohibiting perjury, various forms of fraud, and a few other situations, there are no specified laws against lying. It would be perfectly legal to live our lives lying whenever we could reap some personal gain from doing so. Yet in so doing, we would certainly not be leading moral (or, at least, morally virtuous) lives. Being a good person and doing the right thing are not equivalent to being a law-abiding citizen and avoiding illegal acts. In short, there is much more to morality than law.

It Is Not Enough to Do the Right Thing

Another important reason to study ethics is that, just as lawmakers have good (and sometimes not-so-good) reasons for passing laws, people need to have good reasons for acting one way or another, thinking one way or another, and believing in one thing or another. It is not enough to simply do the right thing; rather, we must *know why it is right*. This applies not only to laws, policies, and codes of conduct, but to all standards of conduct—whether they be professional, legal, religious, or merely social. All legal systems and all religious systems have some form of prohibition against the taking of life. Can we say that we are moral simply because we follow God's commandment not to kill? The short answer is, "no." To be moral people, we must not only follow moral rules, but *understand why* the conduct in question is moral or immoral. We must reflect upon *why* it is wrong to take life. We must, in a sense, reach the same conclusions that lawmakers, religious authorities, professional organizations, and the like have reached by reasoning through principles, scenarios, arguments, and so forth for ourselves. Some would argue, for instance, that the Christian God prohibits killing *because* it is wrong. In other words, even God has good reasons for asking us not to kill. What is important is not simply that we know *that* we should not kill and lead our lives accordingly; rather, what is important is that we know *why* we should refrain from killing.

MORALITY, ETHICAL INQUIRY, AND CRIMINAL JUSTICE

Morality, then, assumes an important role in our own lives, as well as the lives of the communities and societies of which we are a part. As valuable as morality and ethical inquiry are for human social and personal existence, most of you are probably reading this book (and/or taking this course) not because of a deep interest in ethics, but because of an interest in criminology and/or crime and justice studies. Thus, in the remainder of this chapter, it will be helpful to look more closely at the role of morality in this context, as well as the value of ethical inquiry for students and practitioners of criminal justice.

We might begin by laying out the role of ethics and morality in relation to what could be termed the **spheres of criminal justice**. Ethics is applicable to a number of different (but interrelated) levels, or spheres, that collectively make up crime and the behavior of the criminal justice system: criminal justice practice, laws and lawmaking, and social justice.[15] Each of these spheres always exists in relation to the others. Consequently, we should not regard them as mutually exclusive, but as interrelated and interdependent. Changes in law, for example, impact the practice of criminal justice as well as broader concerns of societal well-being, and changes in the practices of the criminal justice system impact the form and content of laws as well as have a more far-reaching effect on larger social concerns such as race, class, and gender relations. In light of these interactions, it is important to approach ethical inquiry in criminology and criminal justice from the perspective of each of these spheres, attending equally to concerns that emerge from within and between all of them. Throughout this volume, many ethical concerns of criminal justice practice, law and lawmaking, and social justice are featured. Here, we offer some preliminary observations on each of these spheres of criminal justice.

Criminal Justice Practice

Ethics is not limited to considerations of prominent moral and political issues such as abortion, capital punishment, and euthanasia. Ethics is equally relevant to other significant realms for criminologists and criminal justicians. Specifically, many students of criminal justice ethics are likely to be current or future *practitioners*. Criminological and criminal justice ethics encourages practitioners to confront not only contentious moral and legal issues, but also to assess their personal behavior as members of a profession. These are matters of *professional ethics*. **Professional ethics** is interested in utilizing ethical values, principles, obligations, and so on, in applying them to particular issues and practical scenarios that emerge within the context of a given field or occupation. Thus, medical ethics, business ethics, legal ethics, and police ethics are each efforts to understand the moral dimensions that characterize these professions and to formulate principles that might serve as guides for individual behavior within the context of these professions. For example, what principles do we want police officers to practice with regard to honesty or integrity? Is it ever morally acceptable for officers of the law to be dishonest? Does the context matter? What if being less than virtuous helps to achieve the aims of policing as a profession?

Each of these is a question of fundamental importance to criminal justice. Collectively, they are questions of police practice; that is, *how* police officers should go about achieving the aims of the profession. At the same time, though, they are inescapably moral concerns. *How* we behave, be it in our personal or professional lives, always has a moral dimension. Indeed, whether we realize it, nearly everything we do has some ethical relevance. Moreover, as discussed in the previous section, part of the value of studying ethics is to recognize the various ways in which our lives unmistakably possess ethical dimensions and moral significance. Once we come to this realization, we are in a position to consider how to make good ethical choices, both as everyday citizens and as stalwart professionals.

The practical sphere of criminal justice is composed of the choices and behaviors of each individual working within the system—from police dispatchers to jury members to death row executioners. We can further subdivide the ethics of criminal justice practice into three primary components. These include police, courts, and corrections. Each of these components includes unique moral dimensions that fundamentally characterize it. Similarly, each one of these subsystems encompasses concerns shared with the other two. Again, it is important to recognize that these three components of the criminal justice system are interrelated, and, as such, so are the moral concerns that emerge from within them. To illustrate, whether a police officer fully respects the legal rights of a suspect has ramifications for courts and, potentially, corrections as well.

We cannot, however, engage in any meaningful discussion about moral concerns linked to criminal justice practice without first having had some introduction to and having engaged in some critical reflection on ethical values, principles, and beliefs, more generally. We will examine the various facets of ethics, as well as practical concerns with which they intersect, throughout the remainder of this text. For now, consider the following list of questions as a way to acquaint yourself with the kinds of issues and controversies that characterize the practical aspects of criminology and criminal justice:

- Does a defense attorney have a moral obligation to defend her or his client's interests, even if in so doing a guilty person will likely be acquitted?
- Should illegally obtained evidence be excluded from trial—even if it clearly suggests that, without a doubt, the defendant is responsible for the crime(s) in question?
- Under what, if any, circumstances should law enforcement officers be permitted to use deceptive methods or techniques to gain consent for searches, to obtain evidence, to apprehend suspects?

Laws and Lawmaking

The sphere of law and lawmaking encompasses both substantive and procedural criminal law, as well as family, civil, and other types of legal decision-making that have a direct or indirect influence on crime and justice. In the context of substantive criminal law, ethics encourages us to confront not only the moral dimensions of specific statutes and cases, but also invites us to reflect upon some of the foundational questions of criminal law: What should constitute a crime? How should we treat persons who offend existing criminal laws? What are appropriate punishments for culpable offenders? What defines culpability or criminal responsibility? What moral principles should be codified into law, both as crimes and as rules that practitioners of criminal justice must follow? What relationship does morality have in general to criminal law in particular? What relationship *should* morality maintain with criminal law?

Much of what the three main branches of the criminal justice system do revolves around criminal law. In large part, the practice of policing entails upholding or enforcing substantive criminal laws in ways that are consistent with existing procedural guidelines or laws. Courts try persons accused of violating criminal laws according to the principles of criminal procedure. The correctional sphere is responsible for dealing with persons convicted of violating such laws, again doing so in a manner that conforms to the standards and regulations set forth through procedural laws and relevant court decisions. Yet, what moral values and principles are embedded in these laws? What moral values and principles are relied upon in the process of arriving at legal decisions, be they at trial or appellate levels? Perhaps more importantly, what moral values and principles *should* be relied upon and thereby embedded in the various dimensions and types of law?

In the context of criminal justice, the importance of law cannot be overstated. Consequently, it becomes that much more significant to reflect upon the moral foundations of law and lawmaking, as well as the ways in which the law impacts the moral dimensions of criminal justice practice.

Social Justice

"Social justice" is a term that routinely surfaces in sociological, criminological, political, and social philosophical discourse. However, it is a concept that is rarely defined to any satisfactory degree. In part, this is for good reason. Social justice is not easily definable, and its contours tend to change depending on the perspective from which it is approached. This being said, there are several considerations that may help us better understand what is meant by social justice and how and why it is relevant to morality, crime, law, and justice.

In his book, *Social Justice/Criminal Justice*, Bruce Arrigo defines **social justice** as a, "perspective of justice that evaluates how a society provides for the needs of its members and the extent to which it treats its subgroups equally."[16] Social justice concerns the laws, policies, programs, and practices of various societies as they pertain to the distribution of and access to housing, health care, education, employment, and other social goods. It may, however, be easier to define or at least provide instances of social injustice than to describe social justice itself. To illustrate, most of us regard racism, sexism, and poverty as social problems. As such, social justice might entail promoting minorities, women, and the disenfranchised, thereby eliminating discrimination or significantly reducing it in an effort to improve the life circumstances of everyone. What each of these problems has in common, however, is that they are *social* rather than individual concerns. If criminal justice seeks to achieve justice through its decisions and practices as they pertain to criminal offenders, then social justice is more concerned with the conditions within which both criminal offenders and criminal justice practitioners live and operate. Thus, an ethical focus on social justice does not ask whether a given court decision (i.e., outcome) is just or fair; rather, it examines the various conditions (e.g., legal, political, economic, religious) that exist that shape and give rise to the court outcome, fostering (or failing to foster) a climate of fairness, opportunity, and access to comparable social resources that are necessary for pursuing the "good life" for all.

The concerns of social justice, then, are best understood as macro-level or large-scale interests that impact both lawmaking and the practice of criminal justice. As an example of how and why these issues are of relevance to lawmaking and criminal justice, consider the phenomenon of theft. In the context of law and lawmaking, significant moral concerns arise with regard to what we consider to be theft and how we should go about dealing with persons accused and/or convicted of thievery.[17] However, what if society on the whole was organized such that the ways in which property was distributed was itself unjust? If so, then we might query whether the very laws against theft were similarly unjust. In fact, laws that protect or maintain the existing distribution of property may reproduce, aggravate, or intensify injustices that already exist. Consequently, we need to consider that criminal justice policy and practice can only be as "just" as the social organization and the institutional dynamics that they seek to maintain.[18]

While social justice and the issues that contribute to its daily functioning are not a focal concern of this book, they will arise on occasion—and in some instances only implicitly. However, we should keep in mind that almost everything about crime, law, and criminology is in some sense linked to matters involving social justice.

THE SPECIAL MORAL REQUIREMENTS OF CRIMINAL JUSTICE

By now you should have some indication of the role and importance of morality in personal, professional, and social contexts. In addition to what has already been said, there are several reasons why morality takes on even greater significance within the criminal justice field than in most other professions. Those occupations that compose the profession are in many ways unique when compared with most other fields of endeavor. To illustrate, many of the things that make the occupation of police and prosecution work unique is that those individuals employed in these areas are expected—even required—to exhibit an increased level of moral character and to exercise a heightened degree of moral judgment than we might expect of persons employed in many other professional contexts. While it is unrealistic to expect criminal justice practitioners to be perfect moral agents, it is not unreasonable to expect that they display a commitment to and strong respect for the moral dimensions inherent in their professional work. For a number of reasons, agents of criminal justice should be and commonly are held to *higher moral standards* than the general public. Though there are certainly many examples of and reasons for this, several such considerations include the following.

Authority, Power, and Discretion

Practitioners within the criminal justice profession carry with them *authority* and *power*, as well as considerable *freedom of choice* and *discretion* to impose authority and employ force in various situations.[19] Along with power comes an increased *responsibility* to use it in appropriate ways. This includes methods that are consistent with the aims of the profession, that benefit a given community and society more generally, and that promote the larger concern of justice. Earlier in the chapter, we briefly examined the ethical principle of "never kill an innocent human being." However, principles such as this assume an entirely different form when the persons to whom the notion applies have the authority and (to some extent) the discretion to take lives under specified conditions (see Box 1.3). Additionally, it is one thing to say that we should not steal; however, a different level of moral character is required to refrain from stealing when, given the routine circumstances of a profession, practitioners find themselves surrounded by things that are "there for the taking" and find that their possible apprehension is essentially eliminated. In short, with the presence of increased power, discretion, and thus opportunity, the need for morality increases considerably. Because of the power that prosecutors, defense attorneys, judges, juries, police officers, and members of parole boards have, it is especially important that such persons exhibit a heightened sense of morality, making ethically sound choices and engaging in morally responsible behavior.

Criminal Justice Agents as Public Servants

Criminal justice agents are servants of the public. The authority and discretion they enjoy is entrusted to them by those whom they serve and exercised in the name of that public; that is, in the interest of protecting and serving others.[20] Socrates would have suggested that agents of criminal justice are in many ways like teachers or educators. Thus, legislators, judges, attorneys, police officers, correctional personnel, and nearly all other persons employed in a criminal justice context have a responsibility not only to fulfill the functions of their respective jobs, but must do so in ways consistent with serving as "role models" for others. When considering laws, policies, and practices operating within criminal justice, it is always helpful to ask the following: "What messages are we sending and to whom?" If police officers, politicians, and other public officials routinely engage in dishonesty, what point are we making on behalf of the general public about the importance of honesty?[21] On a more controversial note, some criminologists have argued that the practice of capital punishment sends an irresponsible message to the American public; namely, that violence is acceptable—at least in some circumstances—as a means of dealing with our social and economic problems.[22] When considering laws and policies, as well as individual choices and behaviors, it is always helpful to ask: "Are we setting an example that we would want others to adopt?"

Individual Behavior Reflects Institutional Morality

The behavior of individuals within criminal justice not only reflects the personal character of the acting agent, but also the character of the institution of which the individual is a part. When police officers are accused of brutality or corruption, most citizens

BOX 1.3
Police Use of Force

Policing is one of the few professions in which the use of force can be a necessary part of the performance of one's professional duties. As well, it is one of the few professions in which practitioners are granted the legal right and discretion to employ force for those purposes. For these reasons, the use of force in policing is one of the more controversial topics in literature on police behavior. Whereas most would agree that the use of force by police officers is in some circumstances justifiable and not morally-problematic, there is far less agreement about what those circumstances are. What constitutes necessary and unnecessary force? What constitutes excessive force?

Police scholar John Kleinig has identified several factors that he feels are important in determining the appropriateness of the use of force. He argues, for instance, that the use of legitimate force is not morally-problematic if the officer believes it is necessary for purposes of restraining a suspect and if an appropriate amount of force is employed solely for that purpose. In contrast, the use of force becomes a moral concern where officers employ it as a means of punishment, or where its use is excessive in relation to the purposes for which it is needed. The *intention* of the officer is crucial to distinguishing ethical from unethical use of force. As well, force used should be *proportionate* to the seriousness of the offense and/or to the threat present in the situation. The type and amount of force legitimately used against a jaywalking suspect will be different from that of a fleeing robbery suspect who is believed to be armed and dangerous. A final implication is that force used should be the *minimal amount necessary* to achieve the aim for which it is employed.

- In what circumstances do you feel law enforcement officers can justifiably use force? In what circumstances do you feel law enforcement officers can justifiably use *deadly* force?
- At what point or in what circumstances does the use of force become morally-problematic? Why?
- How might emotions such as anger, hatred, intolerance, frustration, and fear impact an officer's decision to use force or the amount of force used in a given scenario? What might be done to minimize this impact?

Source: John Kleinig, *The Ethics of Policing* (New York: Cambridge University Press, 1996).

do not recall the particular officers involved; rather, they identify the instance of violence or dishonesty as indicative of a larger set of unethical behaviors attributable to the institution of law enforcement. Thus, the individual officers involved are often faceless and nameless (without any personal characteristics that distinguish them), symbolizing the system itself and calling it into question or disrepute when ethical concerns arise. Similarly, many people speak of "the law" rather than the individual justices, judges, or politicians who make or contribute to the interpretation/formation of the laws. In short, although criminal justice is practiced by people, the institutions to which those individuals are connected are significantly implicated in their actions. Consider, for instance, the events surrounding President William Jefferson Clinton, who was criticized for his private, though morally questionable, sexual behavior with Monica Lewinsky and his publicly dishonest comments concerning this relationship when subjected to questioning in a professional context. Although President Clinton—like the rest of us—is "only human," his mistakes became far more consequential than they would have for most others similarly embroiled in an inappropriate sexual relationship. Because his choices and behaviors were much like a mirror reflecting on the institution of the presidency, most Americans expected that he exhibit higher moral standards—choices and behaviors that positively reflected on government, politics, civility, and so forth.

WHAT ABOUT PROFESSIONAL CODES OF CONDUCT?

Thus far we have considered the crucial role morality plays in our personal, professional, and social well-being; that law itself is not sufficient for ensuring that individuals make good moral choices, acting on them accordingly; and that the professions within the criminal justice system demand an even higher level of morality than most other professions. Yet you may still be wondering whether the agencies and organizations that compose the system have their own ethical standards that obligate employees, specifying how they must conduct themselves professionally. Moreover, if the do, why is it necessary to study ethics in the classroom?

Over the years, the criminal justice professions have developed increasingly sophisticated *codes of conduct*. In fact, most corporations and organizations in nearly every field of endeavor have some code of ethics. These codes are intended to articulate the values and commitments identified as important for members or employees to embody. **Ethical codes** are sets of standards designed to regulate the ways in which participants or workers pursue their activities as professionals. They also educate and guide individuals along their professional path. For example, the American Correctional Association's (ACA) code of ethics includes the following:

- Members shall respect and protect the civil and legal rights of all individuals.
- Members shall treat every professional situation with concern for the welfare of the individuals involved and with no intent to personal gain.
- Members shall refrain from allowing personal interest to impair objectivity in the performance of duty while acting in an official capacity.[23]

Each of these elements of the ACA's code of ethics is offered as a guideline by which members of that organization (many of whom are correctional practitioners) *should* pursue their profession. Similar to questioning the need for ethics in a society that has an intricate system of law, the same can be asked about the necessity of ethics in criminal justice when the system's various agencies already have their own professional codes of conduct or moral guidelines. For now, we note that while codes have their workplace value, they also possess their situational limitations. It is thus important to understand the need for ethics despite the existence of professional value systems and codes of conduct. Moreover, while there are significant differences in ethical codes across agencies, several noteworthy concerns are generally applicable to all of them.

The Problem of Enforcement

Think for a moment about the number of times over the course of your college career that you had knowledge of cheating by a friend or classmate. In how many of those cases did you report the violation(s) to the professor or to someone else in a position to impose appropriate sanctions? If you elected to report it, why did you? The requirement that college students do honest work is not entirely unlike the provisions of many professional codes of conduct. Codes express organizational values and ideals; they reflect what the organization has determined to be the desirable character traits of and/or appropriate behaviors for its members. Yet violations of these values and ideals are almost certain to occur. The question, then, is whether those violations are reported and enforced.

Similar to college guidelines regarding academic honesty, the provisions found in professional codes are not easily *enforced*. This is true for several reasons. Assuming that, for at least some people, no deep motivation exists for being moral; that is, for following specified laws and codes, these individuals will likely adhere to them only if penalties are imposed when failing to follow them.[24] However, two concerns are worth noting here. First, violations of both laws and professional codes routinely go unnoticed. Second, even when violations of professional codes are detected, they are unlikely to be reported and even less likely to be met with (serious) disciplinary sanction. This is because within most professional communities, there exists a general unwillingness to report peer and colleague infractions, and there is an even greater unwillingness to testify against those who have breached workplace standards. This is especially true in occupations such as policing and corrections where informal rules (e.g., the "blue wall of silence") often override formalized codes.[25] Thus, much like the criminal law, we cannot expect that because rules or guidelines exist, people will abide by them. In other words, without a deeper appreciation for ethics, the impact and thus value of codes will be of negligible utility.

Minimalism

When we think of persons of exceptional moral character—perhaps Jesus the Nazarene, Gandhi, or Mother Teresa—we tend to think of people who have gone above and beyond what is asked of them by law, custom, or convention. Consequently, we do not regard the person who pays her taxes as embodying exemplary moral character because of this activity. She may have other admirable moral qualities; however, contributing in tax dollars what is required of her by law is certainly not one of them. On the other hand, persons who pay their taxes *and* devote additional portions of their time and/or income to charitable organizations or the needs and interests of other people *are* often regarded as demonstrating commendable moral character. Why is this?

We tend not to equate morality or moral character with simply meeting duties, obligations, ideals, and responsibilities that are expected of us. Rather, embodying exemplary moral character demands, at least in some instances, that we go beyond mere expectations or requirements. The danger here, however, is that when laws, duties, and ideals are set forth, they may be read not as minimal expectations or requirements, but as portraits of moral character and conduct.

The idea of **ethical minimalism** is that when rules or standards are in place to guide our behavior, people may be inclined to adopt a "minimalistic" or nominal attitude toward morality, doing only what is dictated by the rules and standards in place and nothing more.[26] In other words, we may believe that as long as we follow the laws, rules, or standards set forth, we are doing all that is expected of us and, thus, all that is necessary. However, persons of good moral character often do not simply meet minimum moral standards or requirements. They routinely go above and beyond what is necessary and expected. Laws and codes are intended to be minimum guidelines for conduct; however, the provision of nominal standards is not the same as saying that we should adopt a minimalistic attitude toward them. Thus, we should be careful to understand professional codes not as *replacements* for ethical inquiry, but as supplements and, perhaps, points of departure for engaging in integrity-based reasoning, decision-making, and behavior.

Codes Are External, Ethics Are Internal

One of the most important statements that can be made about morality—and one that will resurface on several occasions throughout this book—is that our reasons for being a certain way or doing a certain thing must be *our own*. In our previous discussion of law, we saw that doing the right thing was not sufficient for expressing genuine morality. This is because our reasons for being moral must come from within us—they must be representations of our moral character rather than efforts to abide by laws, codes, guidelines, and so forth. In other words, morality should be an *authentic* expression of the self—of our own beliefs, values, virtues, and moral sensibilities.

John Kleinig observes that moral worth "attaches to conduct not just by virtue of the good that it does or the evil that it prevents, but because it was done for certain kinds of reasons or was expressive of a certain kind of character."[27] Morality is not simply about *what* we do, but more importantly it is about *why* we do what we do. Unfortunately, laws and codes tend to *externalize* morality. In this way, morality appears to be imposed upon us from above and, consequently, conformity functions as a requirement rather than as a reflection of our virtuous character. While in some sense we are required to conform to laws, codes, and other codified versions of morality, our moral decisions and actions should ultimately come from within us. As we will see in chapters 6 and 7, our motivation to make good choices and to engage in right action should come from within rather than from without. Our empathy toward others should reflect our compassionate character rather than a law or standard that requires us to be compassionate. Our honesty should reflect an honest character and an underlying integrity—one that stems from recognition of the value, worth, and importance of honesty and integrity. Codes are generally well-intended; however, it is important that we internalize moral values and principles, making them part of who we are as people rather than endorsing them as mere followers of rules.

Generality and Moral Dilemmas

Similar to the law, professional codes of conduct do not provide answers to all moral dilemmas or situations we will encounter in our professional lives. In fact, most professional codes tend to suffer from the problem of **generality**. They consist of broad guidelines rather than specific solutions to ethically charged scenarios. Sometimes applying these general principles to concrete instances can be complicated, especially if the guidelines do not appear to perfectly fit the situation at hand or if there are other circumstances that need to be considered but are not specifically addressed by the professional code in use. Consider the following guidelines on discretionary decision-making, drawn from the Schererville (IN) police department's code of conduct:

> *Discretion*—A police officer will use responsibly the discretion vested in his [or her] position and exercise it within the law. The principle of reasonableness will guide the officer's determinations, and the officer will consider all surrounding circumstances in determining whether any legal action shall be taken. Consistent and wise use of discretion, based on professional policing competence, will do much to preserve good relationships and retain the confidence of the public. There can be difficulty in choosing between conflicting courses of action. It is important to remember that a timely word of advice rather than arrest—which may be correct in appropriate circumstances—can be a more effective means of achieving a desired end.[28]

The value and intention of this statement notwithstanding, the limits of its practical utility—particularly in a number of "real-life" situations—are quite apparent. To illustrate, the "principle of reasonableness" and "consider[ation] of all surrounding circumstances" will minimally help officers resolve the manifold and diverse dilemmas they encounter while on patrol. Indeed, while it is certainly important to abide by these (and similar) guidelines, what is being recommended on the issue of discretion is, in effect, that police officers should use professional *judgment* when dealing with practical situations. Honing one's skills regarding judgment—that is, considering all circumstances, values, and principles, and making sound and prudent choices in the face of them—is a good part of what the study of ethics attempts to accomplish.

Consequently, professional codes of conduct often have limited practical utility. In fact, they tend to be of minimal value in those situations where they are most needed.[29] When discretionary judgments are called for, or where conflicts arise between equally important moral values, duties, or responsibilities, reliance on professional codes for precise guidance typically yields limited direction. Most often, codes fail to prioritize values and principles. Thus, workers/employees do not know what is most important when encountering various types of conflict. Moreover, codes frequently fail to identify exceptions to general principles, and they do not account for all situational factors that might deserve consideration in diverse instances.

SUMMARY

Morality and ethical inquiry are relevant to all personal, social, and professional spheres of human existence. More specifically, the concerns of morality—and those of crime, law, and justice—are not only intriguing but essential for our individual well-being and for our collective, indeed global, sense of social cohesion. Consequently, ethics asks not simply that we entertain questions and dilemmas of a moral nature; rather, it asks that we do so responsibly, attending to and examining the many points, principles, values, and questions that underlie any moral issue or situational ethical dilemma. This requires living mindfully, examining and continually reexamining one's self in the interest of living a good life—and assisting others in doing the same—within a just and civil society. However, as we have tentatively explained, laws, codes, rules, and other guidelines for professional conduct can be problematic and, consequently, insufficient for this purpose. As such, morality should be thought of as something other than or, at least, in addition to these things. While each law, code, and rule has value and assumes an important function in the workplace or elsewhere, there is considerably more to being moral than learning about and abiding by formal norms and conforming to social expectations. As well, there is substantially more to ethics and ethical inquiry than simply learning moral standards and principles. Over the next several chapters, a more specific treatment of what ethics is, of what morality entails, and of the notable problems and pitfalls that arise in these contexts will be entertained. Chapter 2 initiates the examination of these matters, providing a more thorough assessment of the subject and scope of ethics.

KEY TERMS AND CONCEPTS

codes of conduct (ethical codes)
descriptive versus prescriptive inquiry
ethics
jury nullification
minimalism (ethical minimalism)
morality
Nuremberg laws

problem of generality (and ethical codes)
problem of enforcement (and ethical codes)
professional ethics
social justice
spheres of criminal justice

DISCUSSION QUESTIONS

1. What is the relationship between ethics and morality? How are they related, and how are they distinct? Give an example from your own experience that illustrates the relationship between ethics and morality.
2. What is the purpose of morality? How does ethics increase the likelihood that the purpose of morality is fulfilled?
3. According to Socrates, "an unexamined life is not worth living." What did Socrates mean by this? When ethics asks that we live mindfully, how does this notion advance Socrates' observation about living life?
4. Some people question why we need ethics when we have laws. What is your position on this? Please list and explain the five limitations of law.
5. Generally speaking, how are ethics and moral inquiry relevant to criminal justice? Give an example from the field of criminology/criminal justice to support your position.
6. How are criminal justice practice, law and lawmaking, and social justice linked to ethics? Be specific!
7. According to the chapter, agents of the criminal justice system (police, court, corrections personnel) are held to higher moral standards. In view of the power invested in agents of criminal justice and the discretionary nature of much criminal justice work, explain why such higher standards are necessary.

8. What are professional codes of conduct/ethics and how are they problematic in the criminal justice system? In what ways might they be beneficial to criminal justice practitioners?

SUGGESTED READINGS

Kleinig, John. (1996). *The Ethics of Policing.* Cambridge: Cambridge University Press.

Kramer, Matthew. (2004). *Where Law and Morality Meet.* New York: Oxford University Press.

Monique, John. (2002). *The Origins of Justice: The Evolution of Morality, Human Rights, and Law.* Philadelphia, PA: The University of Pennsylvania Press.

Pojman, Louis. (2001). *Life and Death: Grappling with the Moral Dilemmas of Our Time* (2nd ed.). Belmont, CA: Wadsworth.

Ruggiero, Vincent. (2001). *Thinking Critically About Ethical Issues* (5th ed.). New York: McGraw-Hill.

ENDNOTES

[1] John Douglas and Stephen Singular, *Anyone You Want to Be: A True Story of Sex and Death on the Internet* (New York: Pocket Start, 2004); Max Taylor and Ethan Quayle, *Child Pornography: An Internet Crime* (New York: Brunner-Routledge, 2003); David Wall, *Crime and the Internet* (New York: Brunner-Routledge, 2001).

[2] Louis Pojman, *Life and Death: Grappling with the Moral Dilemmas of Our Time,* 2nd ed. (Belmont, CA: Wadsworth, 2000), p. 2.

[3] John Hospers, *Human Conduct: An Introduction to the Problems of Ethics* (New York: Harcourt, Brace & World, 1961), p. 4.

[4] Gunter Grau and Claudia Shoppman, *The Hidden Holocaust: Gay and Lesbian Persecution in Germany 1933–1945* (Fitzroy Dearborn Publishers, 1995); Clarence Lusane, *Hitler's Black Victims: The Historical Experience of Afro-Germans, European Blacks, Africans and African Americans in the Nazi Era* (New York: Routledge, 2002).

[5] Louis Pojman, *Life and Death,* p. 2.

[6] Plato, *Apology,* 38A. In *Euthyphro, Apology, Crito,* F. J. Church (trans.) (Indianapolis: Bobbs-Merrill, 1956), p. 45.

[7] Anthony Weston, *A Practical Companion to Ethics,* 2nd ed. (New York: Oxford University Press, 2002), p. 2.

[8] Warner Fite, *Moral Philosophy: The Critical View of Life* (Port Washington, NY: Kennikat Press, 1925), p. 2.

[9] Vincent Ruggiero, *Thinking Critically About Ethical Issues,* 5th ed. (Boston: McGraw-Hill, 2001).

[10] Vincent Ruggiero, *Thinking Critically About Ethical Issues,* p. 5.

[11] Ibid.

[12] Ibid.

[13] Louis Pojman, *Life and Death,* p. 2.

[14] Ibid.

[15] Cf. Jeffrey Reiman, "Criminal Justice Ethics." In Paul Leighton and Jeffrey Reiman (Eds.), *Criminal Justice Ethics* (Upper Saddle River, NJ: Prentice Hall, 2001), pp. 16–18.

[16]Bruce Arrigo, *Social Justice/Criminal Justice: The Maturation of Critical Theory in Law, Crime, and Deviance* (Belmont, CA: Wadsworth, 1999), p. 282.

[17]Alfonso Gomez-Lobo, *Morality and the Human Goods: An Introduction to Natural Law Ethics* (Washington, DC: Georgetown University Press, 2002), p. 78.

[18]John Monique, *The Origins of Justice: The Evolution of Morality, Human Rights, and Law* (Philadelphia, PA: The University of Pennsylvania Press, 2002).

[19]Jeffrey Reiman, "Criminal Justice Ethics."

[20]Ibid.

[21]See, e.g., Erich Fromm, "The State as Educator: On the Psychology of Criminal Justice." In K. Anderson and R. Quinney, *Erich Fromm and Critical Criminology: Beyond the Punitive Society* (Urbana, IL: University of Illinois Press, 2000).

[22]Robert Bohm, *Death Quest II: An Introduction to the Theory and Practice of Capital Punishment in the United States* (Cincinnati, OH: Anderson Publishing, 2003); Christopher Williams, "Toward a Transvaluation of Criminal Justice: On Vengeance, Peacemaking, and Punishment," *Humanity and Society,* 2002, 26 (2), 100–116.

[23]American Correctional Association, Code of Ethics (adopted August 1975 at the 105th Congress of Correction) http://www.intech.mnsu.edu/davisj/aca_ethics.htm, retrieved November 2, 2005.

[24]John Kleinig, *The Ethics of Policing* (Cambridge: Cambridge University Press, 1996).

[25]Ibid.

[26]Ibid.

[27]John Kleinig "Ethics and Codes of Ethics." In P. Leighton and J. Reiman (Eds), *Criminal Justice Ethics* (Upper Saddle River, NJ: Prentice Hall) p. 247

[28]Schererville (IN) Police Department's Code of Conduct. Available at http://www.ci.schererville.in.us/police. Accessed 26 July 2004.

[29]John Kleinig, *The Ethics of Policing* (Cambridge: Cambridge University Press, 1996).

CHOICES, VALUES, AND THE SCOPE OF ETHICS

Imagine that you are awakened one morning by the sound of a ringing telephone. Choosing not to answer the call, you roll out of bed, put on some sweatpants and a T-shirt, make your morning coffee, and begin to go about your daily business. To most people, your morning thus far could be considered uneventful and hardly worth discussing—certainly not in the context of ethics, anyway. Yet in the context of ethics, our everyday, seemingly inconsequential choices become more than just mundane details. In fact, nearly everything you did during your hypothetical morning routine can be seen as having ethical or moral significance. To begin with, each of your actions (and nonactions) involved a choice. Each of us, every waking hour of each day, selects options. While we do not always make purely conscious or rational choices, we nevertheless exercise choice in nearly everything that we do.[1] Further, every choice that we make reflects the things that we *value*. Perhaps because you value a few minutes of peace and quiet in the morning, you chose not to answer the telephone. Your decision was a seemingly simple one. Many of our everyday choices, in fact, are as simple as deciding what time to awaken, what to wear for the day, or what to eat for lunch. Other choices, however, are much more complex and far more consequential. We may have to choose whether to lie to our best friend to protect that person's feelings. We may have to choose whether to spend the remains of our next paycheck on a night out or, instead, to use the money to make a charitable contribution. Or we may have to choose whether to "rat on" a fellow police officer whom we have discovered is involved in illegal drug activities.

In fact, every choice that we make—even the simple ones—is consequential. To suggest that all of our choices are consequential is to indicate that each of them made over the course of our everyday lives has consequences. Sometimes the consequences of our choices are good, direct, and intended; other times, they are bad, indirect, and unintended. Some of the options we select affect—or *appear* to affect—only ourselves. Other times, however, the choices we make directly or indirectly affect others in significant ways. Most of the time, as we will see, our choices seem to impact only ourselves while, in fact, they affect countless others in innumerable ways. This fact alone imbues what seem to be simple choices of personal preference with ethical and moral relevance. Returning to your hypothetical morning for a moment, consider the following choices that were made and some of the potential consequences of those selections:[2]

- The phone call that you chose not to answer was from a friend in desperate need of advice and counseling. That same friend shortly thereafter made a very poor decision that you probably could have prevented had you only chosen to answer the phone. Do you have any moral responsibility for the consequences of your friend's decision?
- The sweatpants and T-shirt that you put on were made in a sweatshop in a foreign country by 8-year-old children who work for ten cents a day. By previously purchasing and continuing to wear the items, you are contributing to the ongoing exploitation of children and, additionally, to their malnourishment, disease, and death as a result of their physical and emotional mistreatment.
- The coffee that you chose to make and consume was grown in a country with a dictatorial government that is hostile to the United States and to its own people. By purchasing and consuming that particular brand of coffee you have, again unknowingly, contributed to the economic well-being of that country and, consequently, sustained the dangers faced by both the United States and the citizens of that country.

In each instance, your choice has affected or potentially affected far more people in far more serious ways than you might ever have imagined. Though ethics does not require us to thoroughly analyze every choice that we make, it does encourage us to think more carefully, indeed critically, about what we do, when we do it, and, most importantly, why we do it.

The choices that we make represent the "stuff" of ethics. More specifically, ethics concerns the *choices that we make that affect other people.*[3] As we have seen, however, it is not always easy to determine which of our choices affect only ourselves and which choices impact others. Further, it is not always easy to determine in what ways our choices impact others—even when we can determine who they will affect. It is precisely because we do not and cannot always easily grasp which choices affect others and what consequences our choices have for others that we might say that our entire lives—our choices, the actions that follow from those choices, and the consequences that follow from those actions—are the "stuff" of ethics.

ETHICS, ACTION, AND CHOICE

A significant part of ethics involves the study of good and bad—moral and immoral—decisions or conduct. It asks what sorts of conduct we value and, subsequently, evaluates behavior in relation to the criteria it establishes for good and bad conduct. To be subjected to moral judgment, however, conduct must be voluntary.[4] To say that our conduct is **voluntary** is to say that *we have made a choice between two or more alternatives and that our action reflects that choice.*[5] Most of our conduct in the context of our everyday lives can be considered voluntary in that it follows from decisions that we make. We may not always make rational decisions, we may not always take time to reflect before or after making decisions; and we may not even be consciously aware that we have made a decision. Nevertheless, we cannot act without first deciding to act, and the fact that we decide to act presupposes a choice between alternatives. Any act that is not based in some voluntary choice cannot be said to be moral or immoral (see Box 2.1).[6]

BOX 2.1

Voluntariness and Criminal Defenses

The requirement of voluntariness as a prerequisite for judging conduct is evident in our system of law and justice. Criminal law recognizes a number of justifications and excuses for criminal activity on the basis of involuntariness. Involuntary acts are not subject to criminal punishment. **Duress** (or **coercion**), for example, is a legally recognized criminal defense in which the defendant is excused from criminal conduct because she or he was acting under the threat of immediate, serious bodily harm from another person and had no other possibility of escape. **Necessity** or the "choice of evils" is a criminal defense whereby a defendant argues that she or he engaged in criminal conduct to prevent some greater evil. In such cases, the conduct may be considered voluntary in some sense, yet in another sense the only alternative courses of action would have brought about greater harm.

- You take part in a bank robbery because someone has kidnapped and threatened to kill your child (or mother, sister, etc.) if you fail to do so. Have you made a fully voluntary choice? Remember that choice requires the presence of alternative courses of action. In this instance, could we rightfully say that you *had* such options? If so, what were they? How might the consequences of those alternatives been different from the consequences of the actions you took? Should you be exempt from criminal responsibility and your actions exempt from criminal punishment?

- You have recently received your amateur pilot's license and are making the three-hour flight to your sister's to attend her birthday party. Halfway through the flight, you experience engine failure and are forced to make an emergency landing in the mountains. Eight hours later, there is still no sign of rescue and you are very cold, very hungry, and fear that you will not be able to survive much longer. As you begin to search the area around you, you come across a small cabin. The cabin is locked and the owners have clearly not been there in some time. Would you be justified in breaking into the cabin, sleeping in the bed, and eating the stored food? If you did, would your actions be entirely voluntary? Are there any alternative courses of action you could have taken that wouldn't have involved violating the law?

Actions, then, are of concern to ethics if they are *voluntary choices.* The study of ethics and the answers to ethical questions such as, "What should I do?," are premised upon both the notion of voluntariness and that of choice. Without both voluntariness and choice, ethics is a futile endeavor. Most often, however, we do have and make voluntary choices. What ethics is concerned with is presenting principles, ideals, and/or models to inform the choices that we make in determining: what actions are right or wrong, what we should do when faced with a given scenario, and how we are to evaluate the actions of both ourselves and those of others.

In many cases, the choices with which we are faced involve conflicts. Interests can and often do conflict; the same can be said of desires, values, ideals, and obligations. Most of us probably value human freedom *and* human life. Yet these two values seem to conflict when applied to issues such as abortion, euthanasia, and suicide—we cannot have it both ways! How are we to choose between the alternatives available in these instances? Which do we and should we value more? These are the sorts of questions and dilemmas that make up the stuff of ethics. To be clear, ethics does not answer the questions for us; however, it does provide many of the tools necessary for us to reach our own conclusions and come to our own decisions.

At other times, the dilemmas or conflicts inherent in our choices are less obvious to us. In other words, we oftentimes are ignorant of, overlook, or choose to ignore the conflicting interests, values, or principles located within our decisions. We may choose to do something that promotes our own interests—perhaps by making us "feel good"—without being aware of the ways in which our choice affects others. We may be unaware that there *are* alternatives, that our actions have certain consequences, or that there are other ways of looking at a particular situation. These sorts of "hidden conflicts" are common when we are simply doing what we want or desire to do, or when we make choices solely on the basis of preformed beliefs or opinions.

For example, the choice to execute a convicted murderer may seem like an easy choice if we unreflectively support capital punishment. Perhaps we were raised in a conservative political environment in which those who influenced us the most believed wholeheartedly in the ethical soundness of the death penalty. Although we may be absolutely convinced that capital punishment is the "right" policy, we may be failing to consider the possibility that our own beliefs and opinions are flawed. The same argument follows for those who unreflectively oppose capital punishment. Failing to be mindful; that is, neglecting to evaluate the hidden conflict(s) concerning the death penalty and our commitments pertaining to this criminal justice controversy, makes us uninformed and calls into question our choices, actions, and ethics.[7]

In addition to offering us guidelines for ethical decision-making, then, ethics also challenges us to confront our own preexisting beliefs, opinions, and values. You may well be surprised at just how much your own views may change when rationally considered and evaluated against other perspectives. Throughout this book, criminology/criminal justice issues with ethical implications are prominently featured. When confronted with such examples, ask yourself how your perspective on a topic fairs when subjected to ethical analysis. While the arguments and criticisms presented are not intended to change your beliefs or values, they are intended to encourage you to engage in a process of critical reflection. Some people even become offended when their core beliefs are challenged. However, keep in mind that those beliefs and opinions we feel most strongly about and which, consequently, bring out the most intense emotional reactions from within us, are usually those that are most in need of critical reflection.

CHOICES AND OTHERS

Morality does not simply entail choices; rather, it involves choices that we make that affect other people.[8] In this regard, however, morality is much broader than is often thought. Typically, we assume that many of our choices do not affect others. In fact, coming to understand how *all* of our choices impact others in some way is a point of departure for ethics.[9] The question, "What sorts of choices do and do not affect others?" is hardly even a relevant notion. Admittedly, such thinking is often used as a basis for arguments of personal liberty—that is, "I should be able to do this or do that because it only affects me" (see Box 2.2). However, ethics teaches us that this line of thinking is not accurate. This is *not* to say that ethics cannot confirm individual liberties or support them above and beyond the interests of others in given situations. In fact, some schools of ethics suggest that our own interests are all that *should* be important in our decision-making (see, for example, *ethical egoism*).[10] In Part II of this text, we will more closely examine these schools of ethics and the degree to which our own interests should factor into our decision-making. For now, it is important to recognize that we commonly fail to appreciate the moral implications inherent in the choices we make and the ways in which all of those choices affect others.

Because every action we take has consequences, our entire lives are endowed with moral significance. Not only does every action have consequences, but every consequence has further effects, and these effects have their own consequences, and so forth. While the immediate consequences of a given action (for example, a teenager using a nonprescribed sleeping pill on school grounds that results in her passing out during class and her eventual suspension from school) may affect only the individual, the fallout of those consequences often extends far beyond the person (now, the child's parents have to rearrange their work schedule to take their daughter to an alternative school that does not provide bus transportation, causing them lost income). What is important ethically is our awareness of these more generalized consequences.

Consider the case of pornography. We may believe that purchasing and watching pornography are choices that affect only ourselves. We may therefore claim that it is not a "moral" decision at all, but merely a matter of how we elect to spend our time and money. We might recognize that pornography itself is a moral and political issue, yet even in recognizing this we may feel that our *personal* choice to purchase and watch sexually explicit material (so long as it continues to be legal) is not so much of a moral concern. However, with some critical reflection, we would soon find that our personal choice may have significant social and, therefore, moral implications. Feminist critics of the adult film industry, for instance, have pointed out that pornography is an expression of patriarchy and male dominance over women. Each time we purchase or watch a pornographic film, we are contributing to the continued exploitation of women and perpetuating gender inequality.[11] As well, watching pornography may have an impact on men's personal relationships in that exposure to the exploitation of women in adult films may "carry over" into the viewer's relationships with women

---

BOX 2.2

Personal Freedom and Consequences to Others

Ethics challenges us to confront common situations in which our personal liberties seem to conflict with the interests or well-being of others. It is commonly argued by supporters of personal freedom that such behaviors "only affect me." Yet ethics encourages us to realize that nearly *none* of our choices and actions affects only ourselves. Consider the following:

- Most states require drivers and passengers in automobiles to wear seatbelts. Yet many people still refuse to wear seatbelts, claiming that seatbelts are uncomfortable and they should have the freedom to do what they wish with their bodies when the consequences only affect themselves. Yet every one of us feels the burden when others are injured or killed in automobile accidents. Wrightsman, Nietzel, and Fortune point to such consequences as: lost wages and taxes, higher medical insurance premiums, welfare payments to the dependent family members of the deceased. They cite current estimates that suggest that motor vehicle accidents cost society as much as $90 *billion* per year. How does considering these consequences affect your position on seatbelt laws?
- What are the potential consequences and costs of other choices involving the personal freedom to: have an abortion, consume illegal substances, own a handgun, and commit suicide?
- Can you think of other "personal freedoms" that have significant consequences for other people and society as a whole? Should these freedoms be limited by law?

Source: L. Wrightsman, M. Nietzel, W. Fortune (1994). *Psychology and the Legal System* (3rd ed.). Belmont, CA (Wadsworth).

---

in his personal life.[12] The "ethics" of pornography is thus more than a mere political or religiously inspired debate. It entails a consideration of the consequences of our choices and behaviors for ourselves, for our family and friends, and for society as a whole. While we are not suggesting that pornography is immoral or that it cannot be defended on moral grounds, we should again recognize that when we are ignorant of the social and moral implications of our choices, we can potentially contribute to evil without even recognizing that we are doing so.[13]

The Involuntary Nature of Evil?

In some ways, the potentially harmful consequences of such acts as purchasing and watching pornography are what Socrates had in mind when he said that *no one ever voluntarily chooses evil.*[14] According to Socrates, we can never *choose* evil—*if*, that is, we know good.[15] This last part is obviously significant, as the first seems to fly in the face of everything we believe we know about people. Surely, we think, there are many instances of people choosing evil over good? Socrates would not argue that people make choices, and that those choices sometimes lead to evil actions and/or evil consequences. His point, however, is that those choices are made in *ignorance*.[16] Anytime we act from choice, we are pursuing some chosen end. All of our actions are intended to bring about certain consequences. If we are acting in order to bring about those consequences, Socrates would say, we must at least *believe* the consequences to be good or desirable. How could we ever want anything if it appeared to be bad or painful? Even in those situations where we intentionally bring ourselves pain (e.g., going to the dentist), we do so in pursuit of some end that we perceive as desirable (e.g., taking care of our teeth). In other words, our actions are always aimed at something that we *perceive* to be "good."

For Socrates, leading a "good" life required knowledge of goodness. If we have knowledge of what is good, our actions will automatically follow from that knowledge. If we *know* what is good, our choices and subsequent actions will also be good. We might think of this argument as follows:

> All of our actions are aimed at something we perceive to be good.

> If we know what is truly good, our actions will be aimed at what is truly good.

> Similarly, if we are ignorant of what is truly good, our actions may well be aimed at what we believe to be good, but is truly evil.

This, then, is what Socrates had in mind when he said that no one can ever voluntarily choose evil. While people sometimes pursue evil ends, it is because they see some good in it—yet they are wrong in believing that whatever good they see is *actually* good. Had their knowledge been more complete, they would have chosen otherwise. No one who *fully* knows the negative consequences of his or her actions can possibly choose those actions.[17] A conspiring bank robber who knows he will be caught and sentenced to twenty years in prison, for example, cannot possibly choose to rob that bank (unless, of course, he had no choice to begin with). If he did, Socrates would say, he would be intentionally choosing something bad. Such a choice would not, of course, make any sense. He robs the bank only because he perceives there to be some good in it (probably for himself).

What Socrates suggested more than two thousand years ago has dramatic implications for how we understand morality in relation to both ourselves and others. It is quite common for us to believe that evil is the result of "evil people" who have voluntarily chosen a life of wickedness. The evil of the world, we may feel, results from the conscious choices of a seemingly increasing number of "bad people." Certainly you and I are excluded from this category. Yet what the study of ethics encourages us to realize (or at least reflect upon) is that we—you, I, and the "bad people"—sometimes make evil choices and contribute to the evil of the world without even being aware that we are doing so. In the words of Socrates, most of us are ignorant of the evil we regularly do. Ethically, then, we cannot regard evil as an outcome of the conscious choices of "evil people." *The majority of evil in the world results from the ill-considered choices of everyday people going about their everyday lives.* The consequences of our actions are often so far-reaching that we cannot even begin to attain a full appreciation for them. We can, however, begin to reflect more thoughtfully on the likely implications of much of what we choose—both personally and professionally.

Recognizing that our decisions and actions have consequences or effects does not necessarily imply that they directly and by themselves *caused* those consequences. The emergence of any given effect or consequence requires the "coming together" of a number of factors—each of which contributes to the eventual manifestation of that consequence. Any given action which I undertake cannot directly—and by itself—cause something else to occur. Instead, a given consequence requires my action *plus* any number of additional actions, events, or circumstances.

Nevertheless, it is important to consider for moral purposes that my actions are *contributing factors* to consequential effects (even if I am "ignorant" of these effects or of the link between them and my own decisions and actions). A certain effect might not have occurred (at least in the way that it did) had it not been for the contribution of my decision or action. Others, in turn, may well have happened anyway. How morally responsible am I for contributing to events or states of affairs that would persist even if I cease to contribute? While, for example, my failure to recycle aluminum may not cause environmental destruction, I certainly do contribute to it in some minor way. If I do begin to recycle, I will probably not make a significant remedial contribution to environmental improvement. What, then, is my responsibility to the environment?

Universal Responsibility

It might be helpful to think of every choice we make as having a universal aspect. In other words, every choice we make and every action we undertake has consequences—however small—that are felt by other people. These other people may be family members, friends, colleagues, individuals in our community, or even the people of cultures thousands of miles away from us. Think of actions as a "link" in an endless chain. In many ways, our choices and actions are influenced by what immediately preceded them. In other ways, our choices and actions influence what comes immediately after them. What comes immediately after them, in turn, influences what comes after that, and so on. The "link" we have secured in the chain by choosing a certain action becomes a small, but meaningful, part of a continuing chain of events. Changing our actions—and thus the consequences of our actions—can potentially change the ways in which that entire chain of events unfolds.

Consider the following somewhat unlikely (though not necessarily improbable) scenario. Suppose you are driving to work this morning and, as you are peacefully making your way through traffic, a seemingly inconsiderate motorist cuts you off. You have done nothing, of course, to bring this on. Nevertheless, you *do* have an impact on what has yet to occur. Consider the choices you have available to you at this point: You may, for example, simply curse the disrespectful motorist in your head while continuing about your drive; you may lay on your horn while verbally cursing at the motorist out your window; you may speed up, pass the motorist, and then cut him off in retaliation; or, perhaps, you might wave at him in a friendly, understanding manner. Let us suppose that you allow your emotions to get the better of you and, consequently, you choose to lay on your horn and curse the man. Now, let us further suppose that the man (inconsiderate, perhaps, but initially merely in a hurry) becomes angry at you for your retaliatory actions. Though nothing seems to come of it immediately (you both drive off on your separate paths), the now-angry man is so disturbed that upon arriving at work, he curses his boss. In return, he is fired. Now, let us suppose even further that, having been fired, the man becomes even more emotionally unstable (imagine how you might feel!). He peels out of the parking lot at his place of employment and, not being very attentive, hits an unsuspecting pedestrian. The pedestrian is killed immediately.

Most of us—including lawmakers—would be in agreement that the man is responsible for the death of the pedestrian and will most likely face charges of vehicular manslaughter, reckless manslaughter, or whatever the applicable offense is in that particular state. Perhaps you see the story on the local news that night, thinking to yourself, "that's the jerk who cut me off today—someone like that deserves whatever he's got coming." Indeed, most of us would feel sympathy for the victim and the victim's family and a corresponding anger toward the inconsiderate (and "dangerous") motorist. Yet most of us would probably *not* stop to reflect upon our own responsibility for the unfortunate events. How responsible are *you* for the death of that innocent pedestrian?

This is not to suggest that you be held legally responsible for what has occurred. But the question here is about ethics and choices. Clearly, the motorist failed to control his emotions, acted recklessly, and is legally responsible for the harm he caused. The purpose of the preceding scenario, however, is to encourage you to reflect upon your own contribution to the events. We might imagine that, had you not responded to the man as you did when he cut you off, he would not have become so angry, cursed his boss, been fired, peeled out of the parking lot, and killed the pedestrian. There is little doubt that the circumstances leading to the death of the pedestrian were only possible because of the choice you made that morning—several hours before the event in question. Had you reacted differently, it is quite likely that the pedestrian would still be alive. What has happened is that, by choosing one course of action over another, you set in motion a chain of events that ultimately ended tragically. The tragic event need not occur immediately following your action. All that is necessary is that—at the time of your choice of actions—you made some seemingly insignificant contribution to this unfolding of events. This is precisely why we typically fail to consider the consequences of our choices. If we do not *see* the *immediate* negative consequences, we go on about our lives assuming that nothing bad or troubling has come from our choice. Again, it is important to point out that our choice of actions did not necessarily *cause* the later events. In this sense, the image of a "chain" may not be entirely realistic. Nevertheless, it is sufficient to recognize that we did meaningfully participate (although unknowingly) in the events that subsequently unfolded.

The notion of **universal responsibility** can be applied to any host of social issues or problems. Indeed, we can think in much the same way about our contribution to environmental pollution and destruction, poverty in other countries, child labor practices, international and domestic terrorism, and all forms of person-on-person and property crime. Though we are not individually responsible for these problems, our choices can and do have an important impact. The necessity of understanding the consequences of our choices—both immediate and long-term, direct and indirect—should be apparent. While I may have a *right* to free speech, should I not consider the consequences that my words might have before expressing them? While I may not find any reason to regard my shopping at certain retail stores as a moral issue, should I not at least consider that my doing so may impact children working in foreign sweatshops to make the products I am about to buy? And, before I choose to purchase and watch pornography, do I not have a *responsibility* to consider the impact of my choice on what some would regard as the continuing exploitation of women and the absence of love and genuine intimacy in sexual relationships?

Your answers to these and similar questions may vary. Certainly, there are numerous considerations. This is precisely why moral issues are *issues*. If there were no controversy or disagreement, there would be no reason to write this book or to study ethics. First and foremost, ethics encourages us to be aware of and to reflect on these sorts of questions. As well, ethics provides us with the concepts and the language necessary to better understand and evaluate these questions and issues. By encouraging critical awareness and providing conceptual "tools" for reflection and evaluation, ethics can ultimately assist us in making better choices in the face of such concerns.

ETHICS AND VALUE

We have thus far discussed the centrality of the role played by our choices in ethical inquiry. Yet, ethics concerns not only choice, but also how we come to select the courses of action that we pursue. Every conscious choice and intentional action has some basis in our thoughts and/or feelings. Whether we are aware of it, each of us likely has a system of thoughts, beliefs, and *values* which informs our choices and actions. Such a system might be called our "personal philosophy." Because the thoughts, feelings, beliefs, and values that we have and/or hold form the basis of our choices and actions, our study of ethics must ultimately pass through the realm of values.

Consider the following list of values and what they have in common:

happiness, pleasure, justice, equality, fairness, courage, loyalty, human dignity

If we understand that each of the above-listed values is similar in one significant respect, we begin to comprehend what values are and the role they play in our choices and actions. Importantly, to "value" something is to advance it as a consideration with regard to our choices and actions.[18] One of the most important commonalities between the values listed above is that each of them, for at least some people some of the time, is used as a basis for making a certain choice, pursuing a certain course of action, or judging the choices or actions of others. If we value pleasure, chances are that many of the choices we make and the actions we take will be intended to advance this value (i.e., bring about pleasure or enjoyment). If we value courage, chances are that we will be inclined to take courageous actions or, at least, hold those who do in high esteem.

Values, then, "point out" the things we should pursue in life. They give our lives a sense of meaning and purpose. Yet we should keep in mind that not all values are *moral* values. While we may value physical strength, for example, it cannot be regarded as a moral value. We may appreciate or admire physical strength and seek to embody it in our lives, though it is wholly unnecessary for moral behavior. In contrast, **moral values** are those characteristics or states of affairs that we regard as *necessary to morality*. Respect, responsibility, humility, and the reduction of pain and suffering are examples of moral values in that, if pursued, they contribute to leading a good life and creating a just society in which others can do the same.

The Study of Value

Simply categorized, ethics is a branch of philosophy. More specifically, we could also say that it is part of a broader field called axiology. **Axiology** refers to the study of *values*.[19] Within axiology we find several different—though often interrelated—branches of analysis: *aesthetics* or the study of artistic and creative value; *political philosophy* or the study of social value; and *ethics* as the study of moral value. Our **values** reflect those things, qualities, or ideals to which we assign importance. When we "value" something, we regard it as desirable, having worth or importance. Similarly, when we *evaluate* something, we judge it to be right or wrong, good or bad, according to our values or some system of values to which we are referring.[20]

Aesthetics, for example, is interested in determining what sorts of artistic achievements or creations are "good" in the sense that they reflect truth, beauty, or are appealing to the senses, intellect, or our emotions. We may value realism in art and, subsequently, evaluate art in terms of how realistically or "true to life" it portrays its subject matter. Other aesthetic perspectives may value the capacity of art to elicit certain emotions. In this case, we might evaluate art in terms of whether or to what degree it embodies that capacity or tendency.[21]

More important to criminology are the political and ethical branches of axiology. Political philosophy is interested in studying social values.[22] It responds to questions such as, "What do we value in society?" Subsequently, it is interested in evaluating laws, policies, and other political decisions in terms of the degree to which they promote or fail to promote those values. One such value might be *equality*. To say that we value equality is to say that we have determined it to be important, worthwhile, desirable, and "good" for society. As such, the decisions that are made at the level of politics should further the goal of equality, given the considerable value we assign to it. Other social values include such concepts as "freedom or liberty," "democracy," "rights," "justice," and "public good." Each of these values, as we will see, is of fundamental importance to criminology.[23]

The same processes of valuation and evaluation that inform aesthetics and political philosophy play a fundamental role in ethics and moral behavior. Ethics includes consideration of social values, but is more generally interested in moral values as they inform our personal, professional, and social lives. For example, while the freedom to have an abortion concerns *both* social and moral values, the freedom to break a promise made to a friend is a more personal moral concern. Ethics asks questions such as, "What should I do?," "What is good?," and "What kind of person should I be?" Of course, what is "good" for us personally and what is "good" for society are, in practice, intimately connected. As we have seen, *all* of our decisions and actions, in some sense, have an impact on other people. Your decision to have an abortion, for example, concerns your own "good," but many will argue that it also concerns the "good" of society as a whole. In this sense, abortion could be approached as both a personal moral concern and a public social concern.

Both ethics and politics are interested in *what we should do*. Neither is concerned with things that merely happen to us—situations in which we have no *choice*. To study ethics or politics is to study human decision-making and how best to arrive at "good" outcomes when faced with two or more alternatives. As previously noted, this process of arriving at good decisions is informed by values. If we value equality, our political decisions will be such that we intend them to bring about or further equality; if we value human life, our political decisions will be such that the actions based on those decisions will intend to protect human life. Issues of importance to criminology such as abortion, affirmative action, gun control, and the death penalty all lay squarely at the crossroads of ethics, politics, and law. With this in mind, this book's assessment of ethics, criminology, and criminal justice will often place the relationship between ethics, law, and politics at the forefront of its considerations. This is because many of the issues that are of importance to law, crime, and justice are political and legal issues with ethical foundations.

Types of Moral Values

Have you ever found yourself wondering what happiness is *for*? Not what it *is* or how to achieve it, but what happiness is used for or what its purpose is? Chances are you haven't. The reason you probably haven't thought about happiness in this way is that happiness is not *for* anything. Rather than being a means to some other desired end, happiness is what philosophers refer to as an *end-in-itself*.[24] Some values, like happiness, are ends-in-themselves. Others, in turn, are "good" because they serve as a *means to an end*. Moral values are commonly characterized in one of these two ways; those that are ends-in-themselves are categorized as *intrinsic* values, while those that are *means to an end* are referred to as *instrumental* values (see below). Depending on how we characterize a value, we will place a different degree of importance on it. Further, the more importance we place upon a value, the more that value factors into our choices and actions. Consequently, understanding the difference between these two types of values is essential to good ethical reasoning and decision-making.[25]

Intrinsic values are pursued for their own sake. The "goodness" of intrinsic values comes *from the value itself*—not from any desirable consequences that the value might bring about. In this respect, intrinsic values are described as ends-in-themselves rather than as means to an end. Intrinsic values are desirable *as is*, without any consideration for what they help us accomplish, achieve, or for their use. Ancient Greek philosophers, for example, regarded happiness as intrinsically valuable. In fact, not only did the ancient Greeks regard happiness as intrinsically valuable, but they believed that happiness was the *only* intrinsic value.[26] All other values were good or valuable only so far as they helped bring about happiness. So, for example, while the ancient Greeks valued health, humility, and courage, these values were good only because they served as a means for bringing about happiness.

In contrast to intrinsic values, **instrumental values** are valuable or good for what they can get us. Instrumental values allow us to achieve other things that we regard as valuable or good. Things like wealth, status, and respect are valuable, but only because they help us attain things that are intrinsically valuable. Failure to appreciate this distinction can have profound implications for how we live our lives—for what we pursue, the kinds of people we try to be, the choices that we make, and the ways in which we spend our time.

To illustrate, in the contemporary United States many people mistakenly regard wealth as intrinsically valuable. Many of us know people for whom wealth seems to be the most important thing in life. What many of these people fail to consider, however, is that wealth is only valuable to the degree that it allows us to get other things

BOX 2.3
Intrinsic and Instrumental Values

Generate a short list of values that you consider to be: (a) intrinsic and (b) instrumental. Briefly discuss why they are intrinsic or instrumental.

- Do you agree with the ancient Greeks that happiness is the only intrinsic value? Do you agree that all other values and goods in life are merely means of bringing about happiness? If so, why? If not, why not?
- Take a moment to reflect upon the things that you value in life. Do these things have intrinsic or instrumental value? If, for example, you value family and friends, is it because family and friends bring about happiness or pleasure?
- Using the list you generated for the preceding exercise, attempt to generate a rank-ordered list of things that you value in life, from most valuable to least valuable. Briefly describe *why* certain things are more valuable to you than others.
- Remember that our sense of morality and the choices we make are often a reflection of the things we value most. Try to think of at least three examples of choices that you have made in the recent past. How have these choices been influenced by values? Based on your rank-ordering of values, were your decisions ultimately informed by your most important values? In reflecting upon your list and those decisions, do you still feel that you made the right choice?

such as health, knowledge, and, ultimately, happiness. This is not to suggest that wealth is not or cannot be valuable to some degree. However, if the value or good of wealth is to allow us to achieve or attain other things, then these other things must be more valuable than wealth. Imagine, for example, being the wealthiest person on earth, yet having to live alone on a deserted island. For most of us, wealth would suddenly lose all of its value. Wealth and money more generally are thus valuable only in an instrumental sense; that is, they are valuable only to the extent that they allow us to pursue or attain those things like health and knowledge that are intrinsically valuable. This example illustrates the importance of distinguishing different types of values and the role they play and should play in our decision-making (see Box 2.3).

ETHICS, VALUES, AND CRIMINAL JUSTICE

Like those of academia, the corporate world, or any other professional environment, the institutions and organizations of the criminal justice system are characterized by select values that are deemed crucial to their functioning and that are intended to serve as official guidelines for professionals. As we saw in Chapter 1, codes of ethics typically outline these official or formal values, identify desirable traits of character and promote moral decision-making on the basis of these core values. Law enforcement organizations, for instance, typically promote values such as justice, fairness, equal treatment and avoidance of discrimination, commitment to serving the community, respect for law, avoidance of decisions based on self-interest, and character traits such as courage, honesty, and self-discipline. Ideally, individual practitioners will commit themselves to these values and look to them as a basis for making morally-sound decisions.

Of course, practitioners in policing and other criminal justice organizations do not always make choices on the basis of values that have been formally identified as desirable. On the one hand, individual practitioners bring their own personal system of values with them into their professional careers. As we have seen, personal values can and do influence the decisions we make and the actions we take in both our personal and professional lives. At times, personal values may contrast with organizational values, creating a scenario in which an individual practitioner may be inclined to make choices and take actions that are consistent with her or his personal system of values but inconsistent with those promoted by the profession.

In addition to personal value systems, one of the most widely discussed challenges facing law enforcement and other criminal justice professions is the existence of organizational or institutional *subcultures.* In addition to formal value systems that are promoted by codes of ethics and other official documents, criminal justice organizations are also characterized by *informal values.* "Rookies" learn the nature and content of these informal norms and values as they are socialized into the profession. Problematically, in many cases informal values may contrast with those identified and promoted as desirable and important by the organization (e.g., those found in official codes of ethics). In both policing and corrections, for instance, formal values such as integrity, honesty, and respect for the rights of suspects or inmates are deemed central to the goals of those professions, yet dishonesty and ignoring the rights of suspects may be informally understood as necessary given the realities of the job.

The informal **police value system,** for instance, has been characterized by several prominent themes. Lawrence Sherman suggests that, through socialization, police officers come to understand that loyalty to other officers is central and that the public as well as police administrators are the enemy. More specifically, Sherman suggests that the core values of police work that emerge through training, interactions with other officers, and on-the-job experience include the following:[27]

1. Decisions about whether to enforce the law "should be guided by both what the law says and who the suspect is." Demographic variables such as the race, class, and age of the suspect, as well as the suspect's demeanor, attitude, and level of cooperativeness, should all be taken into consideration.
2. Disrespect for the police should always be met with arrest or the use of force. Even when no law violation has occurred, the officer should find a way to impose punishment—even if this means making an arrest on fake charges.
3. Officers should not hesitate to use force—including deadly force—against those who "deserve it" or where it might otherwise be an effective means of solving a crime. When she or he can get away with it, the officer should employ "as much force as society should use on people like that—force and punishment which bleeding-heart judges are too soft to impose."
4. Due process exists only for the sake of protecting criminals and should be ignored wherever the officer can get away with it. Ignoring Miranda rights,

illegal searches and interrogations, and the use of physical force to coerce confessions are all acceptable ways to achieve the goal of fighting crime.

5. Dishonesty—lying and deceptive methods—is "an essential part of the police job." Even perjury should be used if necessary to protect oneself or to get a conviction. Lying in court, to drug dealers, prostitutes, muggers, and burglars are legitimate means of investigating crimes and catching criminals.

6. "You cannot go fast enough to chase a car thief or traffic violator nor slow enough to get to a 'garbage' call; and when there are no calls for service, your time is your own." Hot pursuits are necessary to catch those who challenge police authority, social-work problems such as domestic disputes are not important, and when there are no calls, one can sleep, visit friends, or anything else one can get away with.

7. It is acceptable to take any extra rewards the public wants to offer an officer. Policing is dangerous work done for low pay, so free meals, gifts, regular payments for special treatment, taking money for not giving a traffic ticket, etc. are legitimate forms of additional compensation.

8. Protecting fellow officers is the "paramount duty"—even if it means risking your own job or life. An officer should do everything she or he can to protect fellow officers, including never cooperating in an investigation against another officer and never "blowing the whistle" by informing on an officer who has taken a bribe, used excessive force, etc.

The informal values of *police subculture* have been linked with a variety of forms of **police deviance,** including the abuse of discretion and authority, use of dishonesty as a tool, accepting bribes and payoffs, brutality and the use of excessive (or unnecessary) force, and perjury. As is the case in other professions, socialization into the informal values of an organization can force a professional to abandon previously-held ethical standards or, at the very least, make it difficult to uphold personal moral ideals as well as the formal values of the profession.

The prevalence and strength of informal organizational values reinforces the suggestion in Chapter 1 that the existence of formal values in criminal justice organizations is often not enough to ensure good moral decision-making. Equally—if not more—important is the development of our own *internal* moral sensibilities. Just as values point out things we should pursue in life and provide our lives with a sense of meaning and purpose, they also point out the things we should pursue and provide meaning and purpose to our professional lives. The study of ethics helps us understand the importance of making good decisions, and as decisions are often made on the basis of things we value, ethics emphasizes the importance of critical reflection on moral values and how they do and should impact the choices we make.

Meta-, Normative, and Applied Ethics

Contemporary ethics is typically divided into three general categories or subject areas: (1) normative ethics, (2) metaethics, and (3) applied ethics.[28] When most people think of "ethics," they are thinking of its *normative* element. Much like sociology and anthropology, ethics is interested in the *norms* or guidelines that structure human personal and social behavior. Unlike sociology, anthropology, and other social sciences, ethics is not primarily interested in describing or explaining norms or behavior in relation to norms.[29] Rather, to say that ethics is "normative" is to say that it is interested in *setting, establishing,* or *recommending* norms or guidelines for human behavior. **Normative ethics** attempts to arrive at conclusions concerning moral standards, principles, and guidelines of "right" and "wrong," thereby posing *answers* to questions such as, "What should I do?" and "How should I live my life?"[30] While sociology, for example, might be interested in describing given social norms and explaining how social behavior is structured by those norms, ethics is interested in critically assessing whether those norms are "right" or "good" in the moral sense.

This is not to suggest that ethics has no use for descriptions and explanations of norms or human behavior; rather, such descriptions and explanations are valuable only in the sense that they are used to support given ethical conceptions of what *should* be or *ought* to be the case. If, for example, biology provides strong evidence for a process of human evolution, ethics can employ such evidence as a reason why what we should do is a matter of living in accordance with the evolutionary process. *Evolutionary ethics* argues that the purpose ("meaning") of human life is the continuation of the process of evolution.[31] Because the process of evolution is built upon the component process of natural selection, what we *value* in human life should be a matter of human "fitness." Consequently, the choices that we make should reflect the value of fitness and the survival of those people or those human characteristics that are most "fit."

Evolutionary ethics is but one of many normative ethical positions—and not a very popular one at that. The point, however, is that we will often find normative ethics making use of evidence from biology, sociology, anthropology, psychology, and elsewhere. However, to be clear, the role of such descriptive or explanatory evidence is limited to that of reasons for normative arguments about what we should do or ought to do.

While normative ethics is what people most often think of when they think of ethics, there are other questions and concerns of an ethical nature that have direct bearing on normative issues. Normative ethics cannot proceed with arguments and prescriptions concerning what *should* be the case or what moral principles and guidelines we *ought* to follow without first addressing several challenges posed by **metaethics.** *Meta* is a Greek prefix usually translated as "above," "after," or "beyond." Metaethics, in a sense, stands "above" normative ethics in overseeing or evaluating the specific claims and arguments made by its normative counterpart.[32] Metaethics is interested in answering such questions as:

- Where do our moral principles and frameworks come from?
- Do we really have choice concerning our actions, or are our actions (and/or thoughts and feelings) determined by forces beyond our control?
- Are our ethical frameworks socially constructed and, therefore, relative?
- Are all of our actions necessarily self-interested?
- What is the specific meaning of "good," "right," or "should" as they are used in normative arguments?

In some respects, metaethics might be thought of as asking the "bigger questions" that need to be answered for normative ethics to have any value. While normative ethics describes and argues for choices that we should make, metaethics is "behind-the-scenes" asking whether human beings even have any choice or whether our actions are partially or entirely determined by forces beyond our control. Similarly, while normative ethics might argue for the value of altruism or charity, metaethics might ask whether this value is even possible. In answering this question we may find that it is only possible (psychologically) to be altruistic or charitable if there is some corresponding gain in the act for ourselves. If this is the case, we need to reconsider the normative argument that we should or ought to be altruistic or charitable.

The final general category of ethics is applied ethics. **Applied ethics** is that area within ethics that assesses specific moral issues (e.g., war, capital punishment, abortion).[33] It is applied ethics to which many people are initially drawn. Most of us find controversial moral issues inherently interesting and may wish to begin our study of ethics by examining arguments for and against abortion, for example. We may find metaethical questions and normative theories to be dry and seemingly insignificant for purposes of our everyday personal and professional lives. In the latter case, at least, we would be misguided.

This is because the controversies that make up the area of applied ethics cannot be resolved or even argued without making use of the concepts or "tools" provided to us by normative ethics. We may well be able to argue against abortion by referring to our personal opinions, emotions, religious convictions, experiences, and so forth. Most of us, in fact, probably do resolve everyday arguments and dilemmas by relying on these things. If so, we are not engaged in ethical reasoning; we are not presenting ethical arguments; and we are probably not considering the issue in all of the various lights in which we should consider it. To reach an ethically sound resolution to a dilemma, controversy, or tough decision, we should be making use of more than two thousand years worth of normative concepts and theories that are awaiting our consideration. In other words, as you may have already found in courses such as research methods, criminological theory, and others, we must first have a sufficient understanding of the theory and concepts of a discipline to serve as the foundation or point of reference for our more practical (or *applied*) endeavors.

The defining feature of applied ethics is that it answers *practical* ethical questions as opposed to theoretical ethical questions.[34] By **practical ethical questions,** we mean *those matters for which the answer is an action.*[35] Both normative ethics and metaethics are regarded as categories of ethical *theory:* normative ethics consists of theories regarding how we should live and what we should do; and metaethics consists of theories about the theories of normative ethics. The purpose of ethics is not merely to learn theory, however—it is to help us become "good" people, make "good" decisions, and act to promote "good" consequences. Ultimately, then, ethics is a practical discipline. Practice, however, requires theoretical grounding. Imagine, if you will, a medical doctor treating patients with no theoretical understanding of how the human organs function. Or, perhaps, a psychologist treating clients without any theoretical grounding for what she or he says, does, or the methods she or he uses over the course of the psychologist's interventions. Ethics works in much the same way and is subject to the same sorts of concerns.

Thus, answering practical questions and engaging in practical activity without first having the necessary tools would be, not only futile, but potentially damaging. A medical doctor who performs surgery without an understanding of the human body will not only fail to heal the patient, but will almost certainly make the patient far worse than she or he was prior to the ill-performed surgery. In this respect, the theoretical grounding for our ethical considerations is essential. The practical questions that will likely be of most concern to your everyday personal and professional lives are answered through applied ethics. Yet applied ethics requires reasonable moral values and principles with which to generate reasonable moral answers. When we begin asking what sorts of values and principles are reasonable, we enter the domain of normative ethics. Torbjorn Tannsjo offers the following basic model for applied ethical inquiry:[36]

ETHICAL VALUES AND PRINCIPLES
+
FACTS OF THE SITUATION
= PRACTICAL CONCLUSION (MORALLY RIGHT CHOICE OR ACTION)

THE NORMATIVE DOMAINS OF ETHICAL INQUIRY

"Ethics" derives from the Greek *ethos*, often translated as "character." For ancient Greek philosophers such as Plato and Aristotle, the role of "character" was fundamental to the human project. As such, character was the foundation of any conception of ethics, morality, happiness, or the "good life" more generally. A moral person was understood to be virtuous, and ethics—as the study of virtue and character—helped human beings in their struggle to become virtuous people living virtuous, worthwhile lives. In asserting that character was fundamental to the "good life," the ancient Greeks were making a normative argument. In fact, early normative ethics was almost exclusively concerned with character and character formation.[37] Though the notion of character has continued to be an integral component of Western ethics for more than two thousand years, normative ethics has broadened considerably.

In its contemporary form, the subject of normative ethics can be broken down into four interrelated **domains of ethical inquiry**: (1) acts or actions, (2) consequences of actions, (3) character, and (4) motives or intentions.[38] Each of these domains carries *evaluative* weight in ethical theorizing. For example, ethics is not only interested in human actions, but in *evaluating* human actions as right or wrong in light of some standard(s). The standards used to make such evaluations constitute a significant portion of the world of ethics. In this regard, ethics is interested in how we determine whether an action is right or wrong. This aspect of ethics represents a systematic endeavor. Its goal is to understand moral concepts and to justify moral principles.

Ethics, then, is interested in analyzing right and wrong, good and evil, virtue and vice. In doing so, it seeks to establish portraits of good character, principles of right conduct, and frameworks for evaluating consequences that can serve as guides for human decision-making. By clarifying which character traits, which values, and which states of affairs are necessary and/or desirable, ethics seeks to provide direction to our everyday personal, professional, and social lives. By "direction," we mean that ethics attempts to guide us in those everyday dilemmas—whether big or small—that begin with the timeless question: "What should I do?"

The Domains of Ethical Inquiry[39]

Actions:	right, wrong
Consequences:	good, bad
Character:	virtuous, vicious
Motives (intentions):	good will, evil will

We will see that different moral philosophies have attached different weight to each of the domains of inquiry described above. Some ethical perspectives attach the greatest weight to our actions—irrespective of whatever consequences they may produce or contribute to. Other perspectives place primary importance on the consequences of our actions, irrespective of the inherent "rightness" or "wrongness" of the action itself. Still other perspectives insist that we be "good" (i.e., virtuous) people, regardless of whether our actions *or* consequences are right or good.

Ethics, then, involves notions of good and evil, right and wrong, and good and bad in terms of characters, motives, actions, and consequences. Yet different ethical perspectives concentrate on one or more, rather than all, of these notions. If you were to browse your school library for books on ethics, you would find that many such books have one of two foci: doing or being. The first group of theories can be referred to as **theories of doing,** or **action-based theories.**[40] These theories focus primarily on right conduct; that is, what actions we *should* undertake when given a choice of alternatives. Perspectives that focus on consequences of actions are also generally subsumed under this category. On the other hand, a second group of theories focus primarily on character or virtue. These theories can be referred to as **theories of being,** or **character-based theories.**[41] Unfortunately, theories of one sort will often neglect contributions from those of the other sort. Character, intention, actions, and consequences, however, are intimately related. When contemplating ethics, we should keep in mind that how we "are," what we "do," and the consequences of what we do are often—if not always—interrelated. Therefore, none of the four domains of ethical inquiry should be regarded as inconsequential. One could argue, for instance, that each of the four domains builds upon the other such that our character provides the basis for our intentions, our intentions provide the basis for our actions, and our actions produce or contribute to certain kinds of consequences.

SUMMARY

The scope of ethics is perhaps much broader than we might initially imagine. Nearly everything we do has moral significance. More specifically, it is the choices that we make and the actions we take (or not) as a function of those choices that is the "stuff" of ethics. Part of the value of ethical inquiry is that it encourages us to recognize the ways in which just about every choice that we make affects or can potentially affect others. On what basis do we make choices? How can we determine what a "good" choice is? These are questions that implicate moral values and principles—the "tools" that we use, knowingly or otherwise, to make decisions in our personal and professional lives. The subcategory of ethics that studies these tools is referred to as *normative ethics.* We will look more closely at normative ethics in Chapters 8, 9, and 10. Over the next several chapters, however, we need to look in more detail at some problems that arise within *metaethics* and *moral psychology*. We begin our examination of meta-ethical concerns in the next chapter with an examination of an issue that plays a crucial role in both ethics and in crime, law, and justice: that of *determinism*, or the problem of freedom.

KEY TERMS AND CONCEPTS

action-based theories (theories of doing)
applied ethics
axiology
character-based theories (theories of being)
domains of ethical inquiry
duress (or coercion)
instrumental values
intrinsic values
involuntary Nature of Evil

metaethics
moral values
necessity defense
normative ethics
police deviance
police value system
practical ethical questions
universal responsibility
values
voluntariness (voluntary conduct)

DISCUSSION QUESTIONS

1. How do the choices we make affect other people? Are the consequences emerging from our actions always good? Always intended? Always obvious? Please explain your response.
2. What does it mean to say that our conduct is or can be voluntary? How does the field of ethics help us understand the moral implications of voluntary and involuntary conduct? Use an example from policing, law, or corrections to substantiate your answer.
3. According to the text, no one voluntarily chooses evil. Where choices seem motivated by evil, they are better regarded as stemming from ignorance. Please explain this. How would you reconcile this position with persons who engage in extreme forms of repeated criminal conduct (e.g., a serial rapist, child molester, or murderer)?
4. Can you think of a criminal justice example of "universal responsibility"? Please explain how universal responsibility works. Do you agree with this concept?
5. What is the relationship between values and ethics? What does it mean to say that a value can be instrumental or intrinsic? Police officers and prosecutors value discretion. Is this value a means to an end or an end-in-itself within the criminal justice system? Explain your response.
6. Explain the differences between meta-, normative, and applied ethics.
7. According to the text, we can understand that actions, consequences, character, and intentions (or motives) are interrelated. Do you agree? Provide an illustration from personal or professional experience to support your analysis.

SUGGESTED READINGS

Arrigo, B. A., and Williams, Christopher R. (Eds.). (2006). *Philosophy, Crime, and Criminology.* Urbana-Champaign, IL: University of Illinois Press.

Christman, John. (2002). *Social and Political Philosophy: A Contemporary Introduction.* New York: Routledge.

Fieser, James. (1999). *Metaethics, Normative Ethics, and Applied Ethics: Contemporary and Historical Readings.* Belmont, CA: Wadsworth.

Foot, Phillippa. (2003). *Virtues, Vice, and Other Essays in Moral Philosophy.* New York: Oxford University Press.

McDowell, Banks. (2000). *Ethics and Excuses: The Crisis in Professional Responsibility.* Westport, CT: Quorum Books.

ENDNOTES

[1] Charles Baylis, *Ethics: The Principles of Wise Choice* (New York: Henry Holt and Company, 1958), pp. 1–2.

[2] Adapted from David Ingram and Jennifer Parks, *Understanding Ethics* (Indianapolis, IN: Alpha Books, 2002), p. 4.

[3] Charles Baylis, *Ethics: The Principles of Wise Choice.*

[4] Stephen Pepper, *Ethics* (New York: Appleton-Century-Crofts, 1960).

[5] Ibid, pp. 3, 12–35.

[6] Ibid. See also, Joseph Heath, *Communicative Action and Rational Choice* (Cambridge, MA: MIT Press, 2001).

[7] Hugo A. Bedau and Paul G. Cassell, *Debating the Death Penalty: Should America Have Capital Punishment? Experts on Both Sides Make Their Case* (New York: Oxford University Press, 2005); Robert J. Lifton and Greg Mitchell, *Who Owns Death?:Capital Punishment, the American Conscience, and the End of the Death Penalty* (New York: William Morrow & Company, 2000); Lloyd Steffen, *Executing Justice: The Moral Meaning of the Death Penalty* (New York: Pilgrim Press, 1999).

[8] Bernard Williams, *Morality: An Introduction to Ethics* (Cambridge, MA: Cambridge University Press, 1993); Bernard Williams, *Ethics and the Limits of Philosophy* (Boston, MA: Harvard University Press, 2004).

[9] Rushworth M. Kidder, *How Good People Make Tough Choices: Resolving the Dilemmas of Ethical Living* (New York: Harper, 2003).

[10] Terrence C. McConnell, *The Argument from Psychological Egoism to Ethical Egosim* (Melbourne: Australasian Association of Philosophy, 1978); Jan Berg, *Self and Others: A Study of Ethical Egoism* (The Netherlands: Springer, 1988).

[11] Diana Russell, *Dangerious Relationships: Pornography, Misogyny, and Rape* (Thousand Oaks, CA: Sage, 1998).

[12] Ibid.

[13] Paul Ginsborg, *The Politics of Everyday Life: Making Choices, Changing Lives* (New Haven, CT: Yale University Press, 2005), p. 181.

[14] Plato raises this issue in his dialogues *Gorgias* and *Protagoras.* See John Cooper (Ed.), *Plato: Complete Works* (Indianapolis, IN: Hackett, 1997).

[15] Richard Taylor, *Good and Evil* (Amherst, NY: Prometheus), p. 62. See also, Russ Shaffer-Landau, *Whatever Happened to Good and Evil?* (New York: Oxford University Press, 2003).

[16]C. C. W. Taylor, R. M. Hare, and Johnathan Barnes, *Greek Philosophers: Socrates, Plato, and Aristotle* (New York: Oxford University Press, 2001).

[17]Taylor, *Good and Evil.*

[18]Ingram and Parks, *Understanding Ethics;* Daniel Kahneman and Amos Tversky (Eds.), *Choice, Values, and Frames* (Cambridge, MA: Cambridge University Press, 2000).

[19]Donald Palmer, *Does the Center Hold? An Introduction to Western Philosophy*, 2nd ed. (Mountain View, CA: Mayfield, 1996); Hugh P. McDonald, *Radical Axiology: A First Philosophy of Values* (Amsterdam, The Netherlands: Rodopi, 2004); Nicholas Rescher, *Value Matters: Studies in Axiology* (Heusenstamm, Germany: Ontos Verlag, 2005).

[20]Ingram and Parks, *Understanding Ethics*, p. 19.

[21]Noel Carroll, *Philosophy of Art: A Contemporary Introduction* (New York: Routledge, 1999); George Dickie, *Introduction to Aesthetics: An Analytic Approach* (New York: Oxford University Press, 1999).

[22]John Christman, *Social and Political Philosophy: A Contemporary Introduction* (New York: Routledge, 2002).

[23]Bruce A. Arrigo and Christopher R. Williams (Eds.), *Philosophy, Crime, and Criminology* (Urbana-Champaign, IL: University of Illinois Press, 2006).

[24]Robert Spitzer, *Healing the Culture: A Commonsense Philosophy of Happiness, Freedom and the Life Issues* (Fort Collins, CO: Ignatius Press, 2000); Anton Vetroff, *Practical Philosophy of Happiness: The Ultimate Philosophy* (North Hatfield, MA: Troubador Press, 2005).

[25]Ingram and Parks, *Understanding Ethics*, pp. 21–22.

[26]M. Andrew Holowchak *Happiness and Greek Ethical Thought* (London: Continuum International Press, 2004).

[27]Lawrence Sherman, "Learning Police Ethics," *Criminal Justice Ethics*, 1 (1), 10–19 (1982).

[28]James Fieser, *Metaethics, Normative Ethics, and Applied Ethics: Contemporary and Historical Readings* (Belmont, CA: Wadsworth, 1999); Shelly Kagan, *Normative Ethics* (Boulder, CO: Westview Press, 1997).

[29]Cf. Louis Pojman, *Life and Death: Grappling with the Moral Dilemmas of Our Time*, 2nd ed. (Belmont, CA: Wadsworth, 2000), pp. 2–4.

[30]James Fieser, *Metaethics*; S. Jack Odell, *On Consequentialist Ethics* (Belmont, CA: Wadsworth, 2003); Torbjorn Tannsjo, *Understanding Ethics* (Edinburgh: Edinburgh University Press, 2003).

[31]Matthew H. Nitecki and Doris V. Nitecki (Eds.), *Evolutionary Ethics* (Albany, NY: SUNY Press, 1993); Paul Thompson (Ed.), *Issues in Evolutionary Ethics* (Albany, NY: SUNY Press, 2005).

[32]James Fieser, *Metaethics.*

[33]Torbjorn Tannsjo, *Understanding Ethics* (Edinburgh: Edinburgh University Press, 2003); Larry May, Sharri Collins-Chobanian, and Kai Wong, *Applied Ethics: A Muticultural Approach*, 4th ed. (Upper Saddle River, NJ: Prentice Hall, 2005).

[34]Torbjorn Tannsjo, *Understanding Ethics*, p. 3.

[35]Ibid.

[36]Ibid., p. 4.

[37]David Roochnick, *Retrieving the Ancients: An Introduction to Greek Philosophy* (New York: Blackwell, 2004).

[38]Louis Pojman, *Life and Death*, p. 5.

[39]Ibid.

[40]Joram Haber, *Doing and Being: Selected Readings in Moral Philosophy* (Upper Saddle River, NJ: Prentice Hall, 1992).

[41]Ibid.

Part II

METAETHICS AND MORAL PSYCHOLOGY

How Free Are We? The Challenge of Determinism

As described in the previous chapter, ethics can be divided into two general categories of inquiry: those that are theoretical in nature; and those that are applied or practical in nature. Theoretical ethics can be further broken down into two general types of questions: normative concerns; and those that are typically grouped under the heading of "metaethics." The first of these categories—normative ethics—involves consideration of what we *should* do or how we *should* live, both as individuals in personal or professional settings, as well as how organizations and institutions (including criminal justice agencies) *should* make decisions. Normative ethics is interested in answering questions about right and wrong, good and bad, and the values and principles by which we should make these distinctions. In doing so, it attempts to provide a referential basis for the applied or practical concerns that arise over the course of our lives. Crucially, however, normative arguments or theories rest upon a number of assumptions about human nature and individual/collective behavior. Among these assumptions are the following:

- ethics assumes that we have some *freedom* to think, choose, and act in certain ways as opposed to others;
- most ethical perspectives assume that morality can be objective and universal—that there is or can be some level of agreement about *what is* morally right/wrong, good/bad, good/evil, etc.; and
- most ethical perspectives argue that we should, and therefore *can*, at least occasionally set aside *concern for ourselves* in the interest of doing the "right" thing.

It is one thing, for instance, to make the normative claim that we should always be honest. Yet in putting forth such a principle we are assuming: (1) that we can always be truthful in the sense that we can always make a rational, free choice to be honest that is unrestricted by the influence of factors beyond our immediate control; (2) that being truthful is objectively desirable in the sense that everyone can agree that honesty is a desirable value; and (3) that it is reasonable to suggest that we can and should be truthful either when dishonesty can bring us great reward, or where being truthful stands to cause us considerable pain or discomfort. However, isn't it possible that instances of dishonesty are not always the product of free, rational choice? Moreover, isn't it possible that dishonesty may be the best policy, at least for some people and/or in some situations? Finally, isn't it possible that the value of the principle of honesty is or should be contingent upon cultural or even situational factors (see Box 3.1)?

Entertaining these assumptions brings us into the second of our two realms of theoretical ethics—*metaethics*. While metaethics is the least precisely defined of all fields of ethical inquiry, there are several identifiable concerns that commonly arise in metaethical discourse. In part, metaethics includes inquiries that address the methods, language, and arguments of normative ethics.[1] More importantly for our purposes, metaethics also raises questions about and attempts to address deeper concerns of human nature, psychology, and behavior that influence and often stand as challenges to normative ethics—challenges to the very possibility of morality and moral decision-making.[2]

There are several subcategories of inquiry or types of issues within metaethics. These include: (1) metaphysical concerns, (2) psychological issues, and (3) linguistic concerns. Though linguistic issues (i.e., those of the language of ethics) are certainly important components of any comprehensive study of ethics, our primary concern over the next several chapters will be with matters of metaphysics and moral psychology as they relate to issues of criminology and criminal justice. These include such matters as moral relativism, the problem of self-interest, moral motivation, and moral (and psychological) development. However, our focus over the remainder of the present chapter is with the *metaphysical* concern of *free will*.

Metaphysics is a subfield of philosophy that asks such questions as, "What kinds of things exist?" and "What is the nature of those things?" In the context of morality, metaphysics is interested in entertaining questions regarding the existence of morality and the nature of moral values, as well as questions of human nature as they relate to choice-making and behavior. For instance,

- Does morality exist independently of human consciousness?
- Are there eternal moral values, or are all moral values merely human constructions that vary by time and place?
- Do human beings, by nature, enjoy the sort of freedom that is necessary to make moral choices?

The first two questions raise the issue and challenge of *relativism* in ethics—an important concern not only within ethics, but also within the realm of crime, law, and justice (see Chapter 4). The third question concerns the challenge that *determinism* presents for the study of ethics and human behavior more generally. We begin our consideration of metaethical issues in criminology and criminal justice with the challenge of determinism—otherwise understood as the problem of freedom.

BOX 3.1

Is Honesty Always the Best Policy?: The Case of Protection Against Harm

During times of war, accountability for individual behavior must be weighed against difficult and trying circumstances. If a person is caught behind enemy lines and is taken prisoner, what can we expect ethically of this individual, especially if the person is responsible for classified information that, if disclosed, could jeopardize military operations in the region and the lives of countless other soldiers? Most people would likely expect the person in question to do everything humanly possible to prevent such information from being released to our country's enemies. However, what if the person's life was threatened? What if the person was tortured? What if other fellow soldiers were captured with this individual and the person in question was forced to watch as they were executed for her or his refusal to cooperate with the enemy?

In extreme circumstances such as these, the choice of whether to reveal sensitive information and thereby aid the enemy, or conceal that information and thereby cause harm to oneself and/or others may be difficult. On the one hand, one's "duty" to one's country is a paramount ethical concern; on the other hand, protecting oneself and others from harm or even death may be an equally important ethical imperative. Not only does this scenario present an interesting ethical question, but it also raises questions about the limits of human freedom. How much "choice" can one be said to have when being tortured? When watching others being tortured or executed for one's failure to cooperate?

- One question that emerges from this scenario is whether honesty is always the best policy in all situations. While honesty is generally considered morally-desirable and dishonesty morally-undesirable, might this general principle be subject to situational factors? In other words, might general moral principles such as those that commit us to truthfulness be best *disregarded* in certain circumstances? If so, what are those circumstances?
- Does the prevention of harm to oneself and/or others justify otherwise immoral practices such as dishonesty or violating duties of confidentiality or loyalty? If so, under what circumstances and for what types of harms? Does this logic apply only in extreme cases such as prevention of torture or death? What if the "harm" that may come to oneself or others is financial? Emotional?

THE PROBLEM OF FREEDOM

Throughout much of the Middle Ages, dominant explanations of criminal behavior centered upon the notion of supernatural intervention in human affairs.[3] Notably, criminals were often regarded either as having made a "pact" with the devil or having been involuntarily "possessed" by demons that subsequently assumed control of their thoughts, feelings, and behaviors. In cases involving the former, witches and other heretics were subjected to various modes of torture and often punished by death. In cases thought to involve involuntary possession by demons, however, persons were often "treated" through exorcism and other religiously inspired methods of intervention. In such cases, "possessed" persons were not presumed to be *responsible* for their deviant conduct; rather, their actions were *caused* by the demonic forces that inhabited their bodies. Those who had made a "pact" with the devil, in turn, were presumed to have made a voluntary *choice* to join forces with evil. Consequently, they were held to be fully responsible for their conduct and were punished accordingly.[4]

While theological explanations of criminal behavior are no longer appealing to the majority of criminologists, several facets of these explanations continue to have relevance in our understanding of human behavior (both deviant and otherwise). Most importantly, **demonological explanations of crime and deviance** centered on the notion of *choice*. In the previous chapter, we spent some time examining the role of choice in ethics, morality, and in our everyday lives. Each of us is faced with having to make countless decisions in navigating our personal, social, and professional worlds and carrying out our day-to-day activities. Should we spend what little free time we have studying, working to pay bills, or improving our social lives? Should we vote for a Republican political candidate who promises to reduce crime or for a Democratic candidate who promises to reduce poverty? And in our professional lives, we are or will be faced with innumerable decisions that affect not only ourselves, but the people with whom we work, as well as our families, communities, and society more generally.

Choice, it could be argued, is the very cornerstone of ethics and morality. At its core, ethics encourages us to think about our choices in the right way, to make the right choices, and to engage in the right actions as a result of these choices. As you might imagine, if we were to challenge the possibility of choice, we would be challenging the very purpose and possibility of ethics. The fundamental question of ethics, "What should I do?" presupposes that we are able to choose between different alternatives in a given situation. In other words, the question "What should I do?" presupposes a certain underlying answer to the question, "What *can* I do?"

Whenever we speak of "shoulds" and "oughts," in ethics, criminal justice, or other facets of social life, it is important to remember that *should implies can*. In ethics, we assume that we *can* choose between alternative courses of action and proceed to ask what courses of action are desirable. In criminal justice, we assume that persons who have violated the criminal law chose criminality over alternative lifestyles or courses of action and we proceed to ask what form and degree of punishment is called for with reference to the crime. We assume, in other words, that such persons *had* a choice with which to begin. If, however, we remove the possibility or weaken the power of choice, we remove the possibility or weaken the notion of right choices and right actions based on those choices. Morality requires that we have the necessary *freedom* to be moral—to make morally responsible or desirable choices and, subsequently, to engage in morally responsible or desirable actions. It is precisely this assumption about the freedom, possibility, and power of choice that is challenged by determinism.

The freedom in question is often referred to as **free will**, or the *power to make choices and engage in actions that originate with ourselves.*[5] As we have seen, authorities in the Middle Ages recognized this distinction between freedom and lack of freedom—between free will and determinism—as a basis for explaining human (deviant) behavior, ascribing moral and criminal responsibility, and for assigning punishments. Those who had "given in" to evil had made a voluntary choice and, consequently, were understood to be morally blameworthy and legally accountable. Those who had been "possessed," in turn, were not held to be fully responsible for their actions. Because demonic forces had assumed control over their bodies and souls, they had not made a voluntary choice to do wrong. Rather, their behavior was understood to be a product of influences or forces that were beyond their control.[6]

While contemporary discussions of free will tend not to center around supernatural forces, the question of whether we are always completely free to choose and act as we desire remains a central question in ethics and criminology alike.[7] Indeed, recent research on human behavior has endeavored to discover the biological, psychological, and sociological bases of our choices and actions.[8] To the degree that these bases exist, they serve as support for the notion that mental events such as thoughts and feelings and physical (behavioral) events are not—or at least not always—completely free or voluntary. At every moment of our lives we are subject to a variety of influences acting upon us—from our genetic makeup, to the balance of chemicals in our brains, to our intelligence, personality structure, and social environment. By way of these influences, our capacity for free will is substantially limited.

The threat inherent in this idea is that the kind of freedom necessary for each of us to make moral choices and to engage in moral behavior is either nonexistent or significantly weaker than what we often believe. *If* our choices and actions are not completely voluntary and *if* we lack the freedom to choose and act, both ethical inquiry and our efforts to make moral decisions in our everyday lives (and to act in a moral fashion accordingly) will be largely futile. This, then, is the challenge of determinism—that what we *should* do is more a matter of what we *will* do.[9] While most of us certainly *feel* and *believe* that we are free to choose and act as we desire, the problem of determinism is not as simple as what we feel or what we believe.

DETERMINISM AND INDETERMINISM

The doctrine of **determinsim** holds that everything is predetermined to happen *as it actually does happen*—including our thoughts, feelings, and behaviors.[10] Why? In its simplest version, determinism merely states that *every event has a cause*.[11] Our thoughts, our feelings, our desires, and our behaviors all have causes. While the idea that everything that happens has a cause was once linked to theology (often referred to as *divine determinism*), contemporary discussions of causation and determinism find grounding in modern science. Over the past several hundred years, science has discovered substantial evidence that many of the events of the natural world are subject to the laws of causation. Clouds form because water vapor condenses in air that is cooled below its saturation point. Things do not "fall off of" the earth because the force of gravity keeps them in place. The same law of gravity determines that rain should fall to the ground from clouds rather than remain in place or move upward into the atmosphere. But what does this have to do with morality and human behavior?

Applied to human thoughts, feelings, and behaviors, determinism implies that human beings are simply part of the natural world. If the objects and events of that world are governed by cause-effect relationships, then human beings must also be governed by such relationships.[12] If you have a stomachache, that stomachache has been caused by something (e.g., undercooked food, a virus). If you twist your ankle violently during a tennis game, it will break. Your broken ankle was caused by your twisting it beyond its limits of comfortable, flexible movement. In these examples, we have some event or condition that is caused by some other event or condition (or, more accurately, some combination of events and conditions). Determinism, as understood through modern science, argues that nothing, on any level of reality, happens beyond the influence of these causal forces. Nothing happens that is not caused to happen by some other event, condition, or set of events and/or conditions. If we do not understand or cannot find the cause(s) of something, we are simply *ignorant* of those causes—they are nonetheless there, waiting to be discovered.[13]

In more precise terms, the idea of **causation** is that every event is connected to preceding events in such a way that *if the first events had not occurred, the second would not have occurred.*[14] What this implies is that every event—including not only human behavior, but also human choice—is not freely brought about but caused to occur by events, and conditions that preceded it. The choices that we make are a product of our thoughts and feelings, and our thoughts and feelings are connected both to our present circumstances and things in our immediate and distant past in such a way that if our present circumstances and/or our past were in some way different, the choices we make today *could not have occurred.* Perhaps more importantly for ethics, the idea of causation also implies that if these circumstances, events, and conditions do and did occur (whatever they may be), our thoughts, feelings, desires, choices, and behaviors at present *must* occur *as they do.* If, in turn, all of these things must happen as they actually do happen, then we cannot be said to think, feel, choose, and act from free will. Taken to the extreme, determinism implies that the course we follow is the course we *must* follow.

Where many people have a problem with this idea is not in its logic, but in its moral and legal implications. Not only does free will become limited (if not eliminated) under determinism, so too does moral *responsibility.* How then are we to refute this position? What are the alternatives? The perspective opposing determinism is often referred to as *indeterminism.* **Indeterminism** is the notion that there are *at least some* (or, at least *one*) events that occur for which no previous event is necessary.[15] The most important of such events for our purposes is the event of human choice. Indeterminism does not deny that events in the *natural* world are caused or determined. Rather, indeterminists argue that simply because the laws of causation are active in the natural world, this does not mean that those same laws operate on human thought, feeling, and behavior. There is a difference, as existentialist philosopher Jean-Paul Sartre (1905–1980) argued, between human beings and other "things" in the universe.[16] While non-conscious objects may be subject to the laws of causation, conscious human subjects are knowing, willing, choosing subjects or beings. We create ourselves through the choices that we make and, while those choices may be *influenced* by factors beyond our control, our choices and actions themselves ultimately are always of our own volition. Consequently, any human action *could have been otherwise* if the acting agent *chose to do otherwise.*

What evidence do we have to support the idea that we choose and act of our own volition? The unfortunate reality is that while determinism has scientific research to back its claims, there exists no solid evidence in support of free will. We can *believe* that we have free will and continue to live our lives as if we do, but we will find very little in the way of grounds to support our claim. A commonly cited reason in support of free will is simply the **feeling of freedom**, which suggests something as follows: When we make choices, we *feel* that have freely chosen—we *feel* that we could have chosen or done otherwise if we had wanted to—and, consequently, if we feel that we have made a choice, then we must have freely made that choice.[17] The problem with the "feeling of freedom" is that we may be mistaken or simply ignorant with regard to the forces acting upon us. While you may feel that you chose to watch television rather than to read a book last night, it may be the case that you were nonetheless determined to make that choice and are simply unaware of the influences that led you to that choice. The issue is not so much whether we choose our actions, but whether we *choose our choice.* How can you be certain that your choice to watch television was not a function of biological, psychological, and sociological circumstances that, together, predetermined the choice you would eventually make?

CAUSALITY

It is important to recognize that part of the reason that we do not have a causal explanation for everything in the universe is that the process of causation can be prohibitively complex. When we argue that something is *caused*, we are not necessarily arguing that it has *a* cause. Rather, causation is best understood in other, more complex terms. For example, we cannot accurately say that smoking cigarettes causes lung cancer. If this were true, then everyone who smoked cigarettes would develop lung cancer. Because, in turn, we know that not everyone who smokes cigarettes develops lung cancer (at least not after the same length of time or number of cigarettes), we can conclude that there must be other factors that need to be considered. Perhaps smoking cigarettes *in conjunction with* a genetic predisposition to develop cancer leads to lung cancer? Perhaps continual inhalation of cigarette smoke *interacts* with the continual inhalation of polluted air that, through this interaction, encourages cancerous cells to develop? Or, perhaps, there are additional factors that should be considered, such as the effects of stress and anxiety, vitamin and mineral consumption/deficiency, exercise, diet, and others. In any case, the link between smoking and lung cancer—though very much supported by medical research—is not as simple as we might assume.

As an example from within criminology, consider the phenomenon of gang involvement. What, we might ask, *causes* youths to become involved in gangs? Chances are, if you were to research this question you would be led to entertain a number of important factors, including: low self-esteem, family conflict, weak attachment to parents, underachievement in school, the need for identity, the need for security, socializing influences of the neighborhood within which one is raised, early socializing influence of relatives and peers, and many others.[18] None of these factors can accurately be said to cause, by itself, gang involvement. Instead, it is likely that involvement in youth gangs depends on the influence of various factors working in conjunction with one another and/or influencing one another that collectively contribute to a protracted process that leads youths toward gang behavior.

For our purposes, the point of both of the above examples is that the process of causation is not always as simple as "A causes B." We should recognize that most often causality is a complex process that includes multiple factors and forces that interact with one another, mutually affect one another, and should be understood only as small pieces of an ongoing dynamic by which the effect or phenomenon in question is produced. This, of course, is not necessarily to be regarded as evidence that all things—including choice—are caused. It is, however, to suggest that while some things seem not to have identifiable causes, it may simply be that the contributing influences and causal dynamics are sufficiently complex that we do not yet understand them. This is the argument posed by determinists—what we believe to be a product of free will may be attributable to a collection of biological, psychological, and social and cultural forces that are too complex to be fully comprehended.

Free Will as a Basis of Behavior

Contrary to the notion that human choice and behavior are determined (i.e., caused by some force or combination of factors) is the idea that the choices we make and the behaviors in which we engage are, ultimately, deliberate, voluntary products of human will. If we subscribe to the idea that human choice and behavior are a product of free will, we are suggesting that the choices we make and the actions we undertake are willful, voluntary products of human reasoning. They are not caused in the true sense of the term, but emerge as rational responses to a variety of wants, needs, and desires. And while some of these needs and desires may not be purely voluntary, the ways in which we choose to respond to them are. The reasons we might have for choosing to be moral or immoral are innumerable. To illustrate, consider the following motives that have been constructed to account for instances of immoral or deviant behavior:

- To satisfy our curiosity
- Because it is fun, exciting
- To relieve feelings of boredom
- To relieve stress, tension, pain, or anxieties
- To establish or further our identity
- To avoid responsibility
- To obtain financial rewards
- To obtain nonfinancial goods or services
- To achieve status or earn prestige
- To "fit in" or, alternately, to "stand out"
- To fulfill expectations (e.g., from culture, religion, parents, friends)
- To live up to ethical or religious beliefs and values
- To experience power over ourselves or others[19]

Though there are certainly many other possible motives, what each of these has in common is that they represent reasons why one might freely choose immoral alternatives. Many, of course, could apply equally as motivations for *moral* behavior. Importantly, the choices and behaviors that stem from these potential motivations are understood *not* to be caused. To suggest that a person lies from free will to obtain financial rewards is to suggest that that person could have done otherwise, but chose dishonesty as a means of achieving what was desired. To apply a reason to his or her behavior is not the same as saying that it was "caused" in the sense that causation is being used here. Consider, however, if we were to learn that this same person has a personality disorder that compels him or her to lie. Or, perhaps, that his or her ill child is in desperate need of unreasonably expensive medication without which the child would soon die. Given these circumstances, would we be just as willing to describe the individual's choice and behavior as purely a product of free will? Or, on the other hand, would we be inclined to argue that freedom of choice and action in this case is substantially limited, if not altogether eliminated? If so, we are acknowledging the existence of biological, psychological, and cultural and social bases of human choice and behavior.

BIOLOGICAL, PSYCHOLOGICAL, AND SOCIOLOGICAL BASES OF BEHAVIOR

We have seen that determinism argues that nothing happens that is not caused to happen. In the context of human choice and behavior, what exactly are these causal forces supposed to be? There are a variety of forms of determinism, each concentrating on certain types of causal forces. Broadly speaking, variations of determinism can be categorized as *internal* or *external*. **Internal determinism** locates the process of causation at events and conditions that take place inside our bodies and/or minds, while **external determinism** suggests that our thoughts, feelings, choices, and subsequent actions are largely determined by influences acting upon us from outside of ourselves. Internal determinism can be furthered divided into *biological* determinism and *psychological* determinism, with causation being located either in biological or psychological processes, respectively. The causal forces of external determinism include social, cultural, political, and economic conditions, as well as aspects of an individual's physical environment.

Internal Determinism

The subcategories of internal determinism—biological and psychological determinism—each claim that our choices and behaviors are largely a product of events and conditions that occur or exist *within* us. Each, however, differs in terms of how it understands the nature and dynamics of those events and conditions. While biological and psychological models are not necessarily mutually exclusive, they differ with respect to what it is within us that shapes our ways of thinking, feeling, and behaving. It should also be noted that not all biological and psychological models are purely deterministic, and those that are come in a variety of forms. While it is not necessary for our purposes to look in detail at the variety of theoretical models employed in biology and psychology, it may be helpful to briefly examine what we mean by biological and psychological determinism.

BIOLOGICAL DETERMINISM

As a general example of biological causation to which most people can relate, consider the feeling of sexual desire. Imagine, for example, a moral prohibition against *experiencing* sexual desire. As much as we may wish to control such desires, they will inevitably arise periodically. Sexual desire is a universal biological element of human life. We are biologically "programmed" to have sexual desires and, in fact, the experience of such desires is necessary on a broader biological level for the continuation of the human (and other) species. Sexual desire is not a "choice" at all. Rather, it is an event that is internally determined to happen by virtue of our being alive and by way of the biological makeup of our species.

Yet **biological determinism** goes beyond looking simply at the biological makeup that is common to a given species. In some ways, we are all biologically similar because we are all human beings. In important other ways, however, each individual has a unique biological constitution that makes her or him distinct as a member of the human species. Because of this, each individual's thoughts, feelings, choices, and behaviors will be somewhat different from those of other people. Contemporary biological research, for instance, has tended to place a great deal of emphasis on genetics.[20] One implication of this research is that we all think, feel, and behave as we are genetically "programmed" to behave. Our genes essentially map out a course for us, and we follow that course accordingly. The choices that we make have, in a sense, already been made by the genetic "instructions" that define and dictate who we are and what we do.

Other hypothesized causal forces or biologically deterministic influences include: intellectual deficits, XYY chromosomal patterns, brain disorders or defects, biochemical imbalances, hormonal imbalances, blood chemistry disorders, allergens, as well as vitamin and mineral deficiencies and dietary concerns.[21] In recent years, researchers in the natural and social sciences have looked at each of these in an effort to understand various forms of deviant (and presumably immoral) behavior, including crime, homosexuality, and mental disorder.[22] Locating such behaviors and conditions in human biology has a variety of important implications, not the least of which is that if these behaviors and conditions are a product of biological forces, then they are not or are not exclusively a product of free will (i.e., they are not freely chosen). Consequently, as we will discuss shortly, we are forced to rethink traditional understandings of personal and social responsibility, as well as reward and blame for one's conduct.

PSYCHOLOGICAL DETERMINISM

The logic of **psychological determinism** is similar to that of its biological counterpart. The idea is that our choices and subsequent actions are largely determined to occur as a function of our particular psychological makeup and tendencies, and/or mental events and processes that occur beyond the level of conscious awareness and over which we have no (or very little) control.[23] Our psychological makeup and tendencies are typically discussed as **personality**, or the collection of traits, characteristics, and patterned ways of thinking, feeling, and behaving that define us as individuals. Our personalities, in turn, are thought to be determined by a variety of interrelated events and conditions, some of them biological (e.g., the balance of chemicals in our brains), and some of them social and environmental (e.g., parenting practices, the influence of significant people in our lives, our education). For some personality theorists, our characters (or identities) are more or less set very early in the lifecourse.[24] They are shaped or structured by the interaction of biological characteristics and early childhood experiences. Moreover, they consist of essentially *permanent* traits and tendencies that dictate how we think, feel, choose, and act. We of course choose neither the characteristics nor the experiences. In the extreme, we might argue that we are predetermined to think, feel, and react in certain ways about and to particular things, and we are predetermined to make specific choices in certain situations. The thoughts and feelings we have and the choices we make are not products of free will or rational decision-making, but are *caused* by our existing psychological makeup.

Many current ideas concerning psychological influences on choices and behaviors stem, in some fashion, from the seminal work of Sigmund Freud (1856–1939). For Freud, many of the mental events and processes that influence our thinking, feeling, and acting happen on an *unconscious* level. That is to say, at any given moment there is much happening within our minds of which we are unaware and over which we have no control. These events and processes, in turn, have a profound, deterministic influence on what happens consciously. For Freud and many others working within the psychoanalytic tradition of psychology, free will is nothing more than an illusion—our personalities are formed *for us* very early in our lives, and the mental events and processes that influence us happen unconsciously, beyond our control. What makes psychological determinism on the whole similar to biological determinism is that ideas such as personality structure and unconscious mental processes are references to influences that affect us in ways that significantly limit our capacity for free will. Much like we cannot choose our genetic makeup or the balance of hormones in our bodies, we also cannot choose our parents, the economic environment in which we were raised, the quality of teachers we had over the course of childhood, the workings of our unconscious minds, and or forth. Arguably, each of these things has a profound impact on our unique way of thinking, feeling, choosing, and acting, yet none of them is a result or function of conscious choices that we deliberately have made.

External Determinism

In contrast to internal variations of determinism, external determinism looks to influences *outside* of us that shape and influence our thoughts, feelings, choices, and behaviors. These external influences are many and varied. They can be socializing influences such as parenting, education, religion, and peer influence; they can stem from cultural dynamics such as stereotypes, discrimination, prejudices, social role expectations, and the various demands made by norms, beliefs, and values of cultures and subcultures. Additionally, we can be influenced by structural or institutional forces and behaviors including the media, the system of education, or the economy. Finally, ecological forces such as the neighborhood in which one lives, population density, and even the weather are external variables that serve to influence our everyday thoughts, feelings, and behaviors. If, as researchers have suggested, there is an important correlation between population density and aggressive/violent behavior (see Box 3.2), does living in overcrowded conditions limit expectations of self-control? If instances of urban violence were shown to be a product of overcrowded living conditions, would

BOX 3.2

Territoriality, Critical Mass, and Prison Violence

As an example of the ways in which human behavior might be influenced by biological, psychological, and sociological forces, consider the hypothesized importance of *interpersonal space*. In the mid-twentieth century, research on "territoriality" raised some important questions about the relationship between space and animal behavior. Some animals characteristically establish a "territory"—an area of personal space which they will instinctively and aggressively defend if violated by unwelcome others. Researchers found that rats, having been enclosed in a cage with other rats, would instinctively seize areas of the cage (i.e., personal territories). As more and more rats were introduced into the cage, the rats already in the cage became less willing to give up portions of their space. Importantly, when a certain level of crowding was reached, the rats reacted *aggressively*. What was suggested by this area of research is that there exists a *critical mass*—a sort of maximum occupancy for a given space. Once critical mass is reached, any additional rats (or, theoretically, people) will tend to respond with aggression and violence.

Although the implications of territoriality and critical mass for human behavior are less clearly established, this research is commonly referenced in studies examining the effects of *urban overcrowding*. Hypothetically, the absence of sufficient personal space and lost sense of personal control and freedom that accompanies living in overcrowded conditions contributes to physical and psychological deterioration, and perhaps to increased levels of aggression and violence (almost universally, for instance, rates of physical violence are highest in geographical areas that are most heavily crowded).

With the hypothesized link between critical mass and aggressive behavior in mind, consider the setting of prisons. When prisons are filled beyond their capacity—both in terms of the numbers in the general population and within individual cells—correctional administrators worry about increases in aggression and violence. In fact, both overcrowding and violence are among the most significant problems facing many correctional institutions today. Connecting the research described above with the noted correctional problems, think about the following:

- If human beings are, like many other animals, biologically inclined to react defensively and aggressively to invasions of personal space, how might territoriality and critical mass help account for the problem of *prison violence*?
- What implications might this research have for establishing and maintaining *control* within prisons and jails?
- What implications might this research have for establishing and maintaining *humane conditions* within correctional settings?
- If violence and other correctional problems are at least partly a function of overcrowded conditions, what—if any—moral responsibilities do policy-makers and prison administrators have for reducing overcrowding?

we be willing to agree that such offenders were less morally and, thus, criminally responsible for their actions?

Generally speaking, the idea of external determinism encourages us to recognize that there are numerous external factors that work to structure or shape our personal lives, thereby limiting our behavioral alternatives (and, consequently, freedom). Additionally, it is important to keep in mind that these various factors can work simultaneously, in combination within one another, or in conjunction with biological and/or psychological factors. Mental illness, for instance, is a commonly cited psychologically-deterministic influence that can significantly limit free will. We know, however, that poverty, unemployment, and other social factors are strongly correlated with the development of mental illness, such that persons living under these conditions are significantly more likely to develop a mental disorder (and more serious mental disorder) than persons whose living circumstances are more conducive to good mental health and well-being.[25]

Moreover, consider how state underfunding of education may result in the recruitment, hiring, and retention of teachers with minimal qualifications. This practice, in turn, can lead to poor school performance, the absence of quality mentoring, pessimistic future outlook and, ultimately, students dropping out of school and turning to street crime. This is not to suggest, of course, that street crime is directly *caused* by the state's underfunding of education; instead, it simply suggests that crime might be better understood as a complex interplay of forces, variables, pressures, and so forth than a simple expression of free will. Whether this limits free will to the extent that we are willing to concede that behavior is determined and less subject to moral condemnation remains a matter of debate. Even though the influence of such circumstances and conditions may not suggest that free will is eliminated, it perhaps does suggest that we should pay more than passing attention to the ways in which choices and actions can be shaped and constrained, as well as the implications of such constraints for moral and legal responsibility.

Hard and Soft Determinism

We have thus far discussed two competing claims with regard to free will: an extreme version of determinism which argues that everything, including our thoughts and feelings, is caused to happen by influences beyond our control; and a version of indeterminism which holds that, despite the workings of causation in the natural world, human beings are somehow different from nonconscious objects and, thus, have the capacity for (free) choice. However, many philosophers and social scientists prefer the ground that lies in between these two extreme claims. Most determinists do not want to give up the idea of free will altogether, and very few people would claim that biological, psychological, and social forces do not, to at least some extent, influence the choices we make and the actions in which we engage.

In response to the problem of determinism, there are several possible positions one can adopt. The two positions we have examined thus far are positions consistent with what is referred to as *incompatibilism*. **Incompatibilism** argues that we cannot *both* be free *and* determined.[26] Consequently, there are only two possibilities: hard determinism and libertarianism.

Hard determinism is the idea that natural and human worlds are entirely subject to the laws of causation and, consequently, nothing happens that is not a product of some causal influence or influences.[27] Under hard determinism, we cannot be said to be free in any meaningful sense. If all choices and actions are determined to happen by way of a causal link to biological, psychological, and/or social states or conditions that immediately precede them, then we have no free will and, consequently, no moral responsibility for our choices or actions.

The second incompatibilist position on the problem of freedom is that of libertarianism. **Libertarianism** (metaphysical, not political) stands at the opposite extreme from hard determinism, positing that determinism is not true.[28] There may be any number of reasons for our choices and actions, libertarians suggest, but *reasons are not causes*. Because reasons are not causes, we may be able to explain our choices and actions by referring to various influences, but we cannot say that they were caused in the sense that determinism implies. Instead, human beings have absolute free will and, consequently, have full moral responsibility.

Incompatibilism		*Compatibilism*
↑	↑	↑
Hard Determinism	Libertarianism (Free Will)	Soft Determinism

With regard to the problem of freedom, some would argue that it is not necessary to adopt either of the incompatibilist positions. Between the extremes of hard determinism and libertarianism lies the notion of **compatibilism**, which holds that we can be *both* determined *and* free (i.e., free will and determinism are conceptually *compatible*).[29] Often referred to as **soft determinism**, the compatibilist position argues that while many elements of our world are determined, we are nevertheless free in other respects. Compatibilists do not deny that the laws of causation are operative in the natural world, or even to some degree in the human world, but that the reality of causation does not eliminate the existence of free will. The compatibilist position is one that has been constructed in the interest of recognizing the importance of causal influences, but maintaining a perspective on human nature and behavior that allows for the existence of free will and moral responsibility.

Many philosophers and social scientists who subscribe to soft determinism assume that we have some freedom of choice and action, but that choices and courses of action can be *limited* in some important ways. To illustrate, a person with an I.Q. of 60 cannot become a world-renown physicist.[30] However, *within limits of what is physically, psychologically, and socially possible*, human beings enjoy the freedom to choose and act among several alternatives. Thus, in any given instance, we have whatever *breadth* of choice is granted by our biology, psychology, culture, social background and position, environmental circumstances, and the intricacies of the situation at hand. This breadth can be greater or lesser, depending upon any or all of these factors. However, what becomes important for determining moral responsibility is the *degree of influence* specific causal forces had and the extent to which free will was constrained in a given situation as a consequence of these influences. Importantly, though, proponents of soft determinism maintain that the phenomenon of *choice* is always subject to *some* freedom and thus never completely preordained. While our biological and psychological constitutions, as well as our social background and environment, have a significant impact on our patterns of thinking, feeling, choosing, and acting, we maintain at least some capacity to shape our moral character and to make morally responsible and desirable choices. This capacity to shape our moral character, to be good and engage in right action, is central to morality. As well, the presumption of at least some degree of free will is what provides justification for the study of ethics.

Free Will, Determinism, and the Criminal Justice System

The moral significance of determinism derives from the *lack of freedom* it implies. Morality clearly involves concepts such as choice, voluntariness, intention, and responsibility. However, if hard determinism is true, our thoughts, feelings, and behaviors are not freely chosen; rather, they are determined by prior conditions and events either within us, outside of us, or some combination of the two. Hard determinism eliminates the possibility that we could have selected an alternative course of action than what we did. The choices we make and the actions we take are the *only* ones we *could* have made or followed in light of the influences acting upon us. Even if we *feel* that our choices are voluntary and our actions are intentionally chosen, harder versions of determinism hold that the intentions that lead to our choices are themselves determined and, thus, the choice itself is determined. Simply put, under more extreme variations of determinism, our behavior is largely *beyond our control*.

Being able to choose, however, is an essential component of moral responsibility. If determinism were true in its more extreme form, none of us could act or can act other than the way we did or will. In this regard, none of us can be held morally responsible for our choices or actions because we could not have done otherwise—our choices and actions happened *to us* rather than being a product of intention and choice. How, we would have to ask, can any person be held responsible—morally, legally, or both—for actions the individual undertook based on choices the individual was predetermined to make? What about choices and actions that may not have been necessitated, but were significantly influenced by biological, psychological, and/or social forces acting upon the person who made or engaged in them (see Box 3.3)? These questions are not only central to ethics and morality, but are also a focal point of criminal law.

Criminal Responsibility

Since antiquity, responsibility, blame, and punishment have been reserved for voluntary actions.[31] Criminal law determines guilt and innocence on the basis of a person's intentions, rather than solely on the basis of his or her actions (although the latter are necessary for a crime to have occurred). **Mens rea** ("guilty mind") is a necessary element of criminal responsibility. It requires that a person knowingly and intentionally commit a legal offense. In the United States system of jurisprudence, we do not blame or punish

BOX 3.3

The Case of Aileen Wuornos

Aileen Wuornos was raised by her grandparents, Britta and Lori Wuornos. She believed that they were her biological parents until, at the age of 12, she was told otherwise. During her early childhood, she was often ridiculed by her grandfather. He claimed that "she was no good"; that "she didn't deserve to live in the Wuornos household"; and that "she was stupid." Aileen's grandmother was very cold and distant, displaying little warmth and affection toward her granddaughter. Several reports of sexual abuse at the hands of Aileen's grandfather and her brother, Keith, were also noted. By all accounts, Aileen experienced no positive attachments, no secure bonding, with either of her parental figures.

At the age of 9, Aileen began prostituting herself to a number of neighborhood boys for loose change and cigarettes. This continued for several years into early adolescence. During this time, Aileen was frequently truant or tardy at school, got into fights with other children, and was generally disruptive. Early alcohol and marijuana use occurred during this period as well. Eventually, Aileen left school for good. She found herself increasingly involved in criminal activity including stealing, grand theft auto, forging bad checks and, ultimately, murder. In fact, she was convicted of murdering seven men. Aileen alleged that she was the victim of sexual abuse in each of these instances. Aileen Wuornos was executed in Florida in 2002.

■ Given her life circumstances, would you argue that Aileen's behaviors were ultimately a product of free will? If so, to what extent could we claim that her freedom was at least limited by factors beyond her control? To what extent might her "choices"—to be promiscuous, to engage in underage drinking, to act criminally—have been determined for her, given the sexual and verbal abuse to which she was subjected as a child?

■ If Aileen's behaviors were, at least in part, a product of her early life experiences and formative development, should she still be regarded as morally blameworthy and legally accountable for her actions? If so, should she be sentenced and punished in the same manner as all other murderers? How would you respond to the ethical question posed by the possibility of *executing* her?

Source: Stacey L. Shipley and Bruce A. Arrigo, *The Female Homicide Offender: Serial Murder and the Case of Aileen Wuornos* (Upper Saddle River, NJ: Prentice Hall, 2004).

people for accidents, for (most) self-defensive actions, for crimes committed under duress, or for crimes committed by persons incapable of making rational choices—of knowingly and willingly choosing and acting (e.g., the legally insane, children).

The assumption underlying the idea of criminal responsibility is that any "guilty" offender *could have done otherwise.* We assume that persons freely chose to commit the offenses that were performed and that such persons did have alternative courses of action that they could have chosen to follow. Crimes, then, are thought to reflect situations in which offenders "could reasonably have been expected to have conformed [their] behavior to the demands of law."[32]

Criminal law allows for a variety of circumstances under which *mens rea* is thought not to be present; that is, conditions or circumstances under which persons could not reasonably have been expected to conform to the law. In other words, criminal law recognizes that for some people acting within some circumstances, free will is largely absent or, at least, sufficiently diminished so as to reduce legal responsibility. In a sense, criminal law has always subscribed to a version of soft determinism whereby it presumes and is founded upon the existence of free will and the presumption of freely chosen actions, but nonetheless recognizes the ways in which causal influences can at times constrain free will. The most recognized (and widely accepted) of these influences include circumstances that require a person to choose or to act a certain way in a given situation, and biological/psychological factors that substantially limit or entirely eliminate the possibility of free choice and/or self-control.

Most often, these circumstances or conditions are raised as part of a criminal *defense* that seeks to absolve the defendant of moral and legal responsibility for the individual's actions. Defenses are sometimes grouped into two distinct types: (1) the criminal law recognizes a number of **justifications** for violating legal prohibitions—circumstances that *justify* otherwise wrongful and morally blameworthy actions; and (2) a number of **excuses**, or circumstances under which we *excuse* an offender from her or his criminal conduct.

Justifications include self-defense, defense of others and property, and the notion of necessity that we were exposed to in the previous chapter. Embedded within each of these justifications is the assumption that there exist some situations that may require or compel a person to violate the criminal law, often in order to avoid some greater evil that may result from not doing so. For example, can a person engaged in self-defense from imminent harm truly be said to have a "choice" as to how to react to the situation? If free will is not eliminated under these types of circumstances, most of us would agree that it is at least constrained to the degree that the person is considerably less blameworthy on moral and, thus, legal grounds than if the constraint were not present.

However, excuses are of a different nature. The assumption underlying excuses for criminal conduct is that, although the person violated the law, there is some condition or circumstance in light of which we should not hold the person morally and legally responsible, including circumstances or conditions such as age and soundness of mind. We do not, for instance, hold children morally and legally responsible for criminal acts because they do not have sufficiently developed cognitive capacities for moral decision-making. Other recognized excuses include mistake of fact (e.g., genuinely mistaking someone else's coat for your own and, consequently, "stealing" it), involuntary intoxication (e.g., acting under the influence of alcohol or drugs that were not voluntarily consumed), and what is perhaps the most notable excuse—insanity.

In other cases, the criminal law allows for biological, psychological, and/or social influences to be considered when making determinations as to the appropriate type or amount of punishment to assign to a given offender. Sometimes referred to as **mitigating circumstances**, the criminal law recognizes the possibility that certain circumstances surrounding the commission of a crime can reduce moral responsibility and, consequently, can reduce the severity of punishment. In such cases, defendants may have acted under duress, may have been influenced by other persons, may suffer from a disabling mental illness, or may experience other emotional limitations. Significantly, the presence of mitigating circumstances, though important for reducing moral responsibility, does not eliminate guilt. What is presumed is that while these determining influences were present, the criminal act itself was ultimately a freely *chosen* action. The notion of mitigating circumstances is also very much consistent with the assumptions of *soft determinism.*

In sum, the criminal law requires that to be subject to punishment, an act must have been carried out under the guidance of free will; and in practice, the legal system tends to presume that criminal behavior *is* the product of "a free agent confronted with a choice between doing right and doing wrong and choosing freely to do wrong."[33] To the degree that determinism is true, this reasoning becomes problematic and this presumption should be questioned. Although the criminal law currently recognizes a number of limitations on free will, there are perhaps many other biological, psychological, and/or social conditions and circumstances that arguably restrict free will and for which the law permits no diminished responsibility. As former appellate judge David Bazelon suggested, we would have to consider "whether a free choice to do wrong can be found in the acts of a poverty-stricken and otherwise deprived black youth from the central city who kills a marine who taunted him with a racial epithet," one who steals food to feed his family, or the drug addict who buys drugs only to fulfill the demands of his addiction.[34]

Treatment, Punishment, and Implications for Criminal Justice Policy

The free will versus determinism debate has implications not only for criminal responsibility, but for how we respond to persons who violate the criminal law and for the approaches or strategies we take to reduce crime. The former entails a consideration of treatment and punishment and their respective effects on offender recidivism. The latter involves an assessment of the type of criminal justice policy that should guide decision-making.

Addressing the questions regarding (1) what measures to take to reduce crime (i.e., criminal justice policy) and (2) how best to respond to criminal offenders (recidivism), in part is a function of whether we generally subscribe to the notion that those who violate the law freely choose to do so, or whether we generally understand human behavior to be determined by personal and/or social characteristics. One noted implication of free will is that reducing or preventing crime might best be achieved by making criminal behavior a *less attractive alternative* than its law-abiding counterpart. If we presume that people freely choose their actions from among a number of alternatives, then making crime less attractive would function to encourage law-abiding choices.

Traditionally, questions of how best to make crime less attractive have received considerably more attention than how to make legality more appealing. Early social and legal philosophers such as Cesare Beccaria (1736–1794) and Jeremy Bentham

(1748–1832) were among the first to offer recommendations along these lines. For instance, Beccaria suggested that criminal punishments be made more certain, swift and, to a minimally necessary extent, severe in an effort to ensure that the costs of criminal activity outweigh its benefits.[35] More recent criminologists working from within rational choice and economic models of crime have made similar arguments, presuming that criminal behavior is a product of free, rational choice and, consequently, that it can be *deterred* by instilling in potential lawbreakers a fear of consequences.[36] **Deterrence** refers to an attempt to instill in citizens (either individual lawbreakers or the public at large) a fear of the consequences for violating the law. The fear of consequences (i.e., legal punishment), in turn, is thought to reinforce compliance with the legal order.[37] What is important is the policy assumption—founded on the notion of free will—that we are more likely to *choose* the moral and/or legal alternative if we are sufficiently afraid of what might happen to us if we do not.

Interestingly, some argue that all of this ignores or neglects to consider the possibility that crime is not simply a function of rationally-calculated choice. Indeed, many other philosophers and criminologists have contended that there are a variety of both internal and external influences that can significantly limit either our rationality or the choices we have available.[38] Consequently, following this line of analysis, efforts to prevent crime through deterrence will be largely ineffective for a significant portion of the population. Even among those for whom deterrence is generally effective, it will likely not be so in all situations. In other words, even those who avoid criminal behavior because, for example, of a fear of going to prison, getting a ticket, or attending drug court may at some point be faced with circumstances or situations in which stronger influences will prevail.

Social scientists who subscribe to a deterministic conception of human behavior acknowledge various limitations on free will and generally argue for the futility of attempting to alter behavior through rewards and punishments (i.e., efforts to make certain choices more attractive). In the context of crime and justice, these arguments translate into suggestions that crime control policies aimed at reducing transgressions through reforming the criminal justice system (e.g., tougher penalties, more police, or growing prisons) are equally futile. Instead, determinism implies policies that seek to resolve the underlying causes of crime. Specific policy implications will of course vary depending on whether those causes are presumed to be biological, psychological, sociological, or some combination of them. Proponents of biological determinism, for instance, have advocated everything from extreme measures such as selective breeding, surgical procedures, and **selective incapacitation** (i.e., identifying and incapacitating future criminals before they have an opportunity to break the law) to less invasive techniques such as dietary therapy or drug therapy. Advocates of psychological determinism, in turn, have been more supportive of treatment and rehabilitative efforts such as educational training, vocational training, therapy, substance abuse counseling, and other methods that address the underlying psychological causes of criminal behavior. Finally, social determinism implies the necessity of larger and more widespread social and institutional reforms that seek to promote equal opportunity, the end to prejudice and discrimination, the revitalization of neighborhoods and communities, and other efforts intended to rectify underlying social and economic causes of crime.[39]

SUMMARY

This chapter reviewed the way in which determinism and freedom inform ethical behavior. These matters are central, not only to understanding the metaphysical underpinnings of ethics, but to policy, practice, and decision-making in criminal justice. However, more than identifying several important philosophical principles as a basis to understand these doctrines (e.g., choice, causality, free will, incompatibilism), this chapter explained the sort of tensions that are inherent in ethical issues impacting the police, court, and correctional systems, including the problem of responsibility within the criminal law. In the next chapter, we further our review of metaphysics by paying particular attention to the problem of relativism. As we will quickly learn, thorny debates and controversies in criminal justice—especially those impacting the police, court, and correctional systems—require some careful evaluation of the ways in which moral subjectivism impacts choices made by actors and agents of these complex organizations. This is a fundamental matter of human nature that deeply affects the ethical basis of individual and collective behavior.

KEY TERMS AND CONCEPTS

biological determinism
causation
choice
compatibilism
demonological explanations of crime and deviance
determinism
deterrence
excuses
external determinism
feeling of freedom
free will
hard determinism

incompatibilism
indeterminism
internal determinism
justifications
libertarianism
mens rea
metaphysics
mitigating circumstantces
personality
psychological determinism
selective incapacitation
soft determinism

DISCUSSION QUESTIONS

1. Police officers typically are called upon to exercise discretion when on patrol. Given the chapter's observations on choice and free will, in what ways or in what situations might the choices of officers be constrained?
2. Please explain the difference between determinism and indeterminism. How is the notion of causality related to these concepts? Do you believe that the choices you make as a student, employee, boyfriend/girlfriend, etc., are determined? Mindful of the determinism versus indeterminism distinction, are the choices of those who break the law different from your own? If so, how?
3. Please list four examples of internal determinism and four examples of external determinism. Do you believe that "biology" or "psychology" determines the

choices that people make? If so, to what extent? Using the example of gang membership, how might biological or psychological determinism help account for this choice?

4. Incompatibilism holds that we cannot both be free and determined. Explain this. What is "libertarianism" and how does it address the problem of incompatibilism?

5. How does the concept of "soft determinism" help us understand *mens rea* and criminal responsibility?

SUGGESTED READINGS

Einstadter, Werner, and Henry, Stuart. (1995). *Criminological Theory: An Analysis of Its Underlying Assumptions*. Fort Worth, TX: Harcourt Brace.

Honderich, Ted. (2002). *How Free Are You?: The Determinism Question*. New York: Oxford University Press.

Popper, Karl Raimund. (1992). *The Open Universe: An Argument for Indeterminism*. London, UK: Routledge.

Sartre, Jean-Paul. (2003). *Being and Nothingness*. Hazel E. Barnes (trans.). New York: Routledge.

Watson, Gary. (Ed.). (2003). *Free Will* (2nd ed.). New York: Oxford University Press.

ENDNOTES

[1] James Fieser, *Metaethics, Normative Ethics, and Applied Ethics: Contemporary and Historical Readings* (Belmont, CA: Wadsworth, 1999).

[2] Donald Borchert and David Stewart, *Exploring Ethics* (New York: Macmillan, 1986); Shelly Kagan, *Normative Ethics* (Boulder, CO: Westview Press, 1997).

[3] Christopher R. Williams and Bruce A. Arrigo, "Philosophy, Crime, and Criminology: An Introduction." In B. A. Arrigo and C. R. Williams (Eds.), *Philosophy, Crime, and Criminology* (Urbana–Champaign, IL: University of Illinois Press, 2006).

[4] Stephen Pfohl, *Images of Deviance and Social Control: A Sociological History* (New York: McGraw-Hill, 1985).

[5] Ted Honderich, *How Free Are You? The Determinism Problem* (New York: Oxford University Press, 2002), p. 2; see also, Gary Watson (Ed.), *Free Will*, 2nd ed. (New York: Oxford University Press, 2003).

[6] Werner Einstadter and Stuart Henry, *Criminological Theory: An Analysis of Its Underlying Assumptions* (Fort Worth, TX: Harcourt Brace, 1995).

[7] Christopher R. Williams, "Engaging Freedom: Towards an Ethics of Crime and Deviance." In B. A. Arrigo and C. R. Williams (Eds.), *Philosophy, Crime, and Criminology* (Urbana–Champaign, IL: University of Illinois Press, 2006).

[8] Bruce A. Arrigo, *Criminal Behavior: A Systems Approach* (Upper Saddle River, NJ: Prentice Hall, 2006).

[9] Borchert and Stewart, *Exploring Ethics*, p. 30.

[10] Ted Honderich, *How Free Are You?: The Determinism Problem* (New York: Oxford University Press, 2002).

[11] John Hospers, *Human Conduct: An Introduction to the Problems of Ethics* (New York: Harcourt, Brace & World, 1961), p. 502; see also, Borchert and Stewart, *Exploring Ethics*, p. 34.

[12] Ted Honderich, *How Free Are You?: The Determinism Problem*, pp. 5–10.

[13]John Hospers, *Human Conduct*; Borchert and Stewart, *Exploring Ethics*.

[14]Borchert and Stewart, *Exploring Ethics*, p. 35.

[15]Borchert and Stewart, *Exploring Ethics*, p. 35; Timothy O'Connor, *Agents, Causes, and Events: Essays on Indeterminism* (New York: Oxford University Press, 1995); Karl Raimund Popper, *The Open Universe: An Argument for Indeterminism* (London, UK: Routledge, 1992).

[16]Jean-Paul Sartre, *Being and Nothingness*, Hazel E. Barnes (trans.) (New York: Routledge, 2003).

[17]Borchert and Stewart, *Exploring Ethics*, pp. 35–36.

[18]Bruce Arrigo, *Criminal Behavior: A Systems Approach*, pp. 168–189.

[19]Stuart Henry, *Degrees of Deviance: Student Accounts of Their Deviant Behavior* (Salem, WI: Sheffield, 1990), pp. 145–146.

[20]Ted Peters, *Playing God?: Genetic Determinism and Human Freedom*, 2nd ed. (New York: Routledge, 2002).

[21]Einstadter and Henry, *Criminological Theory*, p. 84.

[22]Richard J. Hernstein and James Q. Wilson, *Crime and Human Nature: The Definitive Study on the Causes of Crime* (New York: The Free Press, 1998).

[23]Adrian Raine, *The Psychopathology of Crime: Criminal Behavior as a Clinical Disorder* (San Diego, CA: Academic Press, 1993).

[24]See, e.g., Susan C. Cloninger, *Theories of Personality: Understanding Persons*, 4th ed. (Upper Saddle River, NJ: Prentice Hall, 2003).

[25]Jennifer L. Bullock and Bruce A. Arrigo, "The Myth That Mental Illness Causes Crime." In Robert M. Bohm and Jeffrey T. Walker (Eds.), *Demystifying Crime and Criminal Justice* (Los Angeles, CA: Roxbury Press, 2006), pp. 12–19.

[26]Ted Honderich, *How Free Are You?*; Robert Young, "The Implications of Determinism." In P. Singer (Ed.), *A Companion to Ethics* (Malden, MA: Blackwell, 1993).

[27]Robert Young, "The Implications of Determinism." In P. Singer (ed.), *A Companion to Ethics* (Malden, MA: Blackwell, 1993).

[28]Ibid.

[29]Ibid.; Ted Honderich, *How Free Are You?*

[30]Charles A. Baylis, *Ethics: The Principles of Wise Choice* (New York: Henry Holt & Co., 1958), pp. 28–33.

[31]Christopher R. Williams and Bruce A. Arrigo, "Philosophy, Crime, and Criminology: An Introduction." In B. A. Arrigo and C. R. Williams (Eds.), *Philosophy, Crime, and Criminology*. (Urbana-Champaign, IL: University of Illinois Press, 2006), pp. 3–15.

[32]David Bazelon, "The Morality of Criminal Law." In Paul Leighton and Jeffrey Reiman, *Criminal Justice Ethics* (Upper Saddle River, NJ: Prentice Hall, 2000), p. 31.

[33]Ibid., p. 31.

[34]Ibid.

[35]Cesare Beccaria, *On Crimes and Punishments*, Henry Paolucci (trans.) (Indianapolis, IN: Bobbs-Merrill, 1963).

[36]See, e.g., Liliana Pezzin, "Earning Prospects, Matching Effects, and the Decision to Terminate a Criminal Career," *Journal of Quantitative Criminology*, 11, 29–50 (1995); Robert A. Rosenthal, "Economics and Crime." In S. Guarino-Ghezzi and A. Javier Trevino (Eds.), *Understanding Crime: A Multidisciplinary Perspective* (Cincinnati, OH: Anderson Publishing, 2006), pp. 61–90; James Q. Wilson, *Thinking About Crime* (New York: Vintage Books, 1983), p. 260.

[37]Daniel Nagin and Greg Pogarsky, "Integrating Celerity, Impulsivity, and Extralegal Sanction Threats into a Model of General Deterrence: Theory and Evidence," *Criminology,* 39, 865–892 (2001).

[38]See, e.g., Teresa J. Neyhouse, *Positivism in Criminological Thought: A Study in the History and Use of Ideas* (New York: LFB Scholarly Publishing, 2002).

[39]Bruce A. Arrrigo, *Social Justice/Criminal Justice: The Maturation of Critical Theory in Crime, Law, and Deviance* (Belmont, CA: Wadsworth, 1999); Michael J. Lynch, Raymond J. Michalowski, and Byron Groves, *The New Primer in Radical Criminology: Critical Perspectives on Crime, Power, and Identity,* (3rd ed.) (New York: Willow Tree Press, 2000); Martin D. Schwartz and Suzanne E. Hatty, *Controversies in Critical Criminology* (Cincinnati, OH: Anderson Publishing, 2003).

Chapter **4**

IS MORALITY RELATIVE?
THE VARIABILITY OF
NORMS AND VALUES

Suppose, for a moment, that you support the following practices:

- Mass executions, without trial, of known terrorists
- Using torture as a means of extracting military secrets from enemy soldiers during times of war
- In times of need, stealing from those who have more than enough
- Assisting in the suicide of terminally ill friends and relatives
- Polluting the environment, undertaken by major corporations, to save money and thus to ensure greater profits for stockholders and employees
- Polygamy (i.e., marrying multiple partners)

Now suppose that another person, having learned of your support for these practices, accuses you of being immoral or, at least, of supporting immoral practices. Would she or he be right? If so, on what grounds could we claim that you or the practices you support are immoral? By most people's standards, many (perhaps all) of the above-mentioned practices could be regarded as immoral if not criminal. Yet "most people's standards" are not necessarily *truth*. Most often, they are simply reflections of *convention*. Convention, in turn, reflects the values and beliefs of the people of particular cultures or subcultures at particular points in history—socially constructed truths that are created by such peoples in the interest of making life more livable, agreeable, and convenient. What makes these socially constructed truths problematic is that it could be argued that they have merit only within those groups—only within the cultural and historical locations within which they were developed and within which they exist or existed.

Following this logic, in order to judge the above-mentioned practices as "wrong," we would have to make reference to the values and principles that "we" believe to be morally desirable. The values and principles that we feel to be morally desirable, however, may differ significantly from those that other people (e.g., those of other cultures, subcultures, geographical regions, historical eras) believe are acceptable or desirable. Arguably, practices such as punishment without trial, torture, euthanasia, polygamy, and others commonly understood to be immoral can only be judged as such from *within a framework of moral convention*. Again, however, convention does not equal truth. Simply because certain values, principles, and standards of behavior have been adopted by a majority of people does not necessarily make these values, principles, and standards "right" in the absolute sense. It does, of course, give the opinion of the majority a stronger voice and, therefore, more *power* in determining what values, beliefs, principles, and standards are embedded in social convention and codified into formal laws and regulations. Consequently, your support of torture or polygamy may result in your being ostracized, verbally abused, and even imprisoned. However, *none* of your beliefs, some would argue, could be judged "wrong" in any objective or absolute sense.

If you agree that in none of the above-cited instances could the positions and practices you support be judged wrong in any absolute sense, you might share in the perspective known as *relativism*, including one or more of its several forms. If this logic seems troublesome to you, then you are not alone. Relativism is one of the most critical challenges facing ethics and morality today.[1] Difference—especially differences in values, beliefs, and practices—is a characteristic feature of the human social world. However, to what degree and in what respects are such differences desirable? Beneficial? Harmful?

OBJECTIVISM AND UNIVERSALISM IN ETHICS

The key ethical question derived from the idea of relativism is whether there are absolute moral values and universal moral principles, or whether moral values and principles are relative to time, place, and, perhaps, person.[2] The challenge for ethics is to justify the claim that at least some moral values and principles are applicable to everyone, everywhere. Like determinism, relativism stands as one of the most provocative challenges to ethics. **Relativism** argues that morality is relative to particular cultures, time periods, and even subcultures within cultures and time periods. To suggest that morality is relative is to acknowledge that morality *varies* from culture to culture, time period to time period, and that the morality of one culture at one time is or should be applicable only to members of that culture at that time. What culture "A" believes to be moral *is* moral; and what culture "B" believes to be moral *also is* moral—even if the two beliefs contradict one another. Because different social groups have different normative beliefs, "moral" actions are simply those that are in agreement with the norms of a given social group.[3]

Before looking at the claims of relativism in more detail, it might be helpful to first consider several other concepts against which it is often contrasted. Relativism can be contrasted with *ethical objectivism* (or *ethical absolutism*) and *ethical universalism*.[4] The first two terms are often used interchangeably, and the third follows from the others. The claims made by ethical objectivism and universalism may shed some light on why relativism has been so attractive to a good number of people—both in philosophical and social scientific circles, as well as within the general public.

Ethical Objectivism

The claim of **objectivity** is a *knowledge* claim. To say that something is "objective" is to say that its quality or character lies within itself and, consequently, can be "uncovered" by any observer who knows where and how to look. Typically, when we say that something is "objectively true," we are making a claim that "true" knowledge of that thing is possible and, further, that everyone should be able to agree on that truth. Objectivity is contrasted with the idea that different observers may have different perceptions, thoughts, feelings, or experiences with something. For example, if I were to say that it is "objectively true" that the desk I am sitting at is brown, I am making a claim that it actually *is* brown and that everyone else who perceives the desk *should* also agree that it is brown. If a different observer perceives the desk to be red, she or he is simply wrong. This is because the "true" color of the desk lies *within the desk itself*, rather than in the perception of the people who are looking at it. It is possible, of course, that everyone who looks at the desk perceives it to be red when it is actually brown. In that case, we would all be wrong. All objectivism suggests is that the desk has a "true" or actual color and that it is an unchanging property of the desk itself.

Ethical objectivism takes the argument just used to describe the color of the desk and applies it to morality. To suggest that certain acts are *objectively wrong* (i.e., immoral) is to suggest that the quality of evil or the immorality of that act lies *within the act itself*. That is to say, the *act* is wrong regardless of who is doing it and when, where, and how it is being done. Another way to say that something is objectively wrong or evil would be to say that it is *inherently* wrong or evil. Much like the color of the desk might be regarded as inherently brown, according to ethical objectivism certain acts are, by nature, right or wrong; that is, they "carry" this quality with them wherever and whenever they go. In this sense, certain behaviors *always have been and always will be* wrong, evil, or immoral. Regardless of how different people *perceive* these behaviors, they are *either* right or wrong—they cannot be both!

This is not to say that certain types of behaviors cannot be morally neutral. Rather, it is simply to suggest that *if* a certain behavior is given moral status (i.e., if it has moral relevance), it must always and forever be either right or wrong, following ethical objectivism. The same behavior cannot be right in one situation or for one group of people, neutral in another situation or for a different group, and wrong for yet another situation or another group of people. If such a behavior is perceived differently in different circumstances by the same observers, or perceived differently in the same circumstances by different observers, at least some of these observers must be wrong about the moral status of that behavior.

Let us consider the example of prostitution. Given the doctrine of ethical objectivism, if one culture condones prostitution while another condemns it, they cannot both be right. If there is a conflict of values concerning the morality of prostitution, at least one of the cultures must be wrong. This follows from the fact that prostitution is *either* right *or* wrong, but not both. By the same token, lying, cheating, and stealing cannot be regarded as acceptable in some situations but not in others. These actions are either inherently wrong, or inherently acceptable. The "truth" about the morality of lying, cheating, and stealing exists—waiting to be "uncovered" and applied to human behavior.

Ethical Universalism

Universalism makes a claim very much related to, and following from, the argument of objectivism. While objectivism holds that "true" knowledge of something is possible, **ethical universalism** holds that knowledge can and should be *applied* to everyone in every similar situation. To say that something is "universal," is to say that it is—or at least should be—true of all cultures and all time periods. Something that is not universal, in contrast, would be bound in one or more ways (e.g., applicable only to a given culture, time period, situation, person). The notion of universality follows from the idea that things have true, knowable properties or characters. Because the character of something is inherent in its nature, it has the same character regardless of the individual instance in which it is applied. Every individual instance of something, though seemingly different in many respects, can still appeal to the same general rule that governs or should govern each of those instances. For example, if incest has the property of being morally wrong, then the prohibition against incest is a general rule that is applicable to every situation. Incest practiced two thousand years ago is no different from incest practiced today; incest practiced within a very small Asian culture is no different from incest practiced within the much larger and very different United States culture. Incest has the inherent property of being morally wrong and, as a general rule, we can *apply* that property of "wrongness" to all people in all situations.

If morality or certain moral principles are universal, we are obligated to treat alike all cases in which that moral principle is relevant. If something has a universal character, that character supersedes all other situational factors. A potential problem with universal notions of right and wrong is that they depend on the extent to which cases are, indeed, alike. To illustrate, we may make a universal claim that "killing is morally wrong." In doing so, however, we are making a claim that applies equally to all of the following situations: killing animals for sport, killing animals for food, capital punishment, killing in a time of war, killing in self-defense, abortion, euthanasia, and others. It might seem, then, that the view, "killing is wrong," cannot or should not be a universal moral principle. In this case, we must either allow for situational differences (which defeats universalism) or refine our moral principle so that it is applicable in all situations.

Importantly, ethical universalism holds that there are objective moral principles and that such principles can and should be applied equally to everyone. The biggest difficulty, perhaps, lies in identifying those objective moral principles. A second difficulty or, perhaps, criticism involves the source of those principles. In other words, whose principles are they? Where do they come from? What makes a particular source of principles an "authority"? If, for example, 99.9% of the population believes that abortion is morally wrong, is the fact that 99.9% of the population agrees enough to argue that abortion is objectively wrong? Is that population itself to be regarded as an authority or collective "expert" on matters of morality? Elsewhere in this chapter (see the section on pragmatic relativism), we will demonstrate that the majority opinion can be, and oftentimes is, mistaken or ill-informed, especially on matters of ethics and morality. If we cannot rely on majority opinion, where do we turn to find the "objective truth" about the morality, say, of abortion, capital punishment, flag burning, rape, and incest?

At this point, it may be tempting to turn to theological or religious interpretations of right and wrong to settle the dispute. However, we should keep in mind that we would then have to justify what makes one religion "more right" than another or, even further, what makes any religion "more right" than a belief that is not founded upon religious authority. You should begin to see, then, that both ethical objectivism and ethical universalism run into some formidable difficulties. It is precisely these difficulties that make relativism such a provocative and attractive alternative when addressing ethical decision-making throughout much of Western civilization (see Box 4.1).

BOX 4.1

Crimes *Mala in se* and *Mala Prohibita*

In discussions of criminal law, wrongful acts are sometimes classified as **mala in se** ("wrong in themselves") or **mala prohibita** ("wrong because they are prohibited"). Crimes that are wrong-in-themselves are objectively and universally wrong—they have always, everywhere been wrong and will continue to be that way. Behaviors such as murder, rape, cannibalism, and incest are common examples of crimes *mala in se*. In contrast, other behaviors are considered wrong only because a given society has defined them that way. Crimes *mala prohibita* are those that are not objectively or universally recognized as wrong; rather, their wrongfulness varies by time and place. Common examples of behaviors that are wrong only because we have defined them that way include gambling, prostitution, underage drinking, and other so-called *victimless crimes*. The idea that there is nothing inherently or objectively wrong about these types of behaviors implies that they may be acceptable for some people in some places.

- Do you agree that there are some behaviors that are objectively and universally wrong or evil? Other than those suggested above, can you think of other examples of crimes *mala in se*? Can you think of situations or circumstances in which murder, rape, or cannibalism would be *acceptable*? Are there any ways in which culture, time period, or even specific situations might make them less objectively wrong?
- Consider the practice of homosexuality. Twenty-five years ago, intercourse between two same-sexed and consenting adults was considered criminal. It was also recognized as a diagnosable mental disorder. Today, it is not considered criminal, nor is it a diagnosable mental disorder. How does the notion of moral relativism assist us in understanding how the wrongfulness of behaviors can be defined differently at different points in the history of a culture? Why might cultural conceptions of homosexual practices have changed? Do you believe that homosexuality represents behavior that *should* be defined as *mala in se*? Why or why not?

CONTEMPORARY ETHICAL RELATIVISM

With regard to objective, absolute, and universal moral sensibilities, relativism asks us to consider the possibility that there *are no* "true," "absolute," "objective," or "universal" moral principles, right or wrong actions, good or evil characters, and so fourth.[5] No moral sensibilities exist or can exist in unchanging, cross-cultural form. Similarly, we must abandon any search for an ideal ethical system, made up of ideal ethical principles. Rather than appreciating the morality of characters, intentions, actions, and consequences in their own right, it is necessary for us to understand the historical, cultural, subcultural and, perhaps, personal context within which these all occur. What we find is that while one set of moral values may be "right" in a given time period or within a given culture, these same moral values may not be "right" in a different time period or within a different culture. Yet relativism does not simply acknowledge historical and cultural differences, it suggests that such differences are *ordinal*. In other words, they are merely different without being "better" or "worse" than one another. It may be the case, then, that all morality is nothing more than *convention*. Consequently, if we are to say that morality is purely conventional, we are saying that there is no "right" or "wrong," only what *is* and what *is not*. The distinctions made between right and wrong actions, good and evil intentions, are nothing more than an agreed upon set of values and norms that were created by human beings in a particular cultural and historical context. If this is indeed the case, then we cannot *judge* other moral frameworks. Instead, we must merely seek to understand morality as a framework of artificially created conventions that are true to a particular group of people at a given time or moment.[6]

If morality can be understood as a set of rules by which human conduct is guided, we must acknowledge that such rules are not the same across time periods, cultures, subcultures, and so on.[7] Previous cultures, for example, have engaged in many practices that, by our present standards, would be judged immoral: the ancient Egyptians practiced incest; the ancient Romans practiced infanticide; and Americans practiced slavery. In each case, the people of those cultures were not performing acts that would have been considered immoral by their own standards. Such practices were perfectly in keeping with the beliefs of the practicing people and, in that sense, were perfectly "moral." In the contemporary United States, racism and sexism were (and, to some degree, still are) common attitudes based on shared beliefs, giving rise to consensual practices.[8] As immoral as such attitudes and practices appear for many of us today, chances are that we, too, would have shared popular sentiments concerning these matters had we been exposed to and raised within the cultural climate that existed fifty or more years ago. What these examples suggest, then, is the possibility that not only do different "rules" exist, but that we might not be able to impose moral judgments on any of these rules.

For purposes of clarity, we need to distinguish several of the claims made above. In particular, we noted: (1) the factual claim that morality differs from culture to culture, time period to time period; (2) that, consequently, there is no objective sense of moral right and wrong; and (3) that because of (1) and (2), we should not judge the beliefs and practices of other cultures and time periods. Ethical relativism generally holds to each of these three beliefs. Importantly, however, these beliefs do not necessarily follow from one another. To distinguish these claims and their implications for ethics, we need to address several types of relativism as each makes a slightly different claim. Claim (1) is associated with descriptive relativism; claim (2) with meta ethical relativism; and claim (3) with normative relativism.[9]

Descriptive Relativism

Moral values and practices can and do vary—sometimes significantly—between cultures. Relativism is founded upon the simple notion that there are fundamental differences between the moral values of different people and cultures.[10] This simple claim is not entirely disagreeable. In fact, there exists ample anthropological and sociological evidence that the moral value attached to different forms of behavior can vary considerably from one culture to the next.[11] This recognition that differences exist between cultures, time periods, and even subcultures within the same culture is commonly referred to as **descriptive relativism.** Descriptive relativism can be thought of as that aspect of or argument within the broader philosophy of relativism that merely acknowledges and describes the presence of moral differences between groups of people. In doing so, descriptive relativism points to the cultural variability of norms, beliefs, and moral values.[12]

The factual claim made by relativism is an appeal to the existence of **cultural variability.** Relativism points out the sometimes dramatic differences or *variations* that exist in the norms, customs, habits, spiritual beliefs, and general moral climate of different cultures.[13] Much of this evidence comes from anthropological studies of both primitive and contemporary cultures. In addition, relativists turn to history in suggesting that such dramatic differences also exist within the same cultures in different historical periods.[14] Yet it is not necessary, relativists would point out, to look to other cultures or even history for evidence of this variability. We find significant variability in beliefs, values, and general moral sensibilities simply by looking within our own culture in our own time period. There is a good deal of sociological evidence to affirm that people within different social groups show variability in their norms, values, expectations, and way of life. Race, gender, social class, and subcultural affiliation all impact our sense of morality, as does the region of the country in which we live and whether we live in an urban, suburban, or rural environment (see Box 4.2).

To illustrate, consider the differences in beliefs, values, and way of life that might exist between a lower-class family living in rural Georgia and an upper-class family living in suburban Los Angeles. Perspectives on family, work, education, religion, politics, and leisure, do vary significantly even within our own society. Such variations exist because our moral values tend to reflect those of our own social group and our own time period. This, in turn, results from the fact that we are not born with moral values, but learn them through interaction with our social environment. We internalize the norms and values that exist within our own social environment and, because social environments differ, we would expect norms and values to differ as well.[15]

Descriptive relativism serves as a premise, reason, or foundation for accepting the broader and more controversial claims of metaethical and normative relativism. The descriptive claim of relativism draws attention to the absence of any universally recognized values or principles of right conduct. Because of abundant historical and cross-cultural evidence supporting this claim, we might simply accept that there are no universal moral principles and accept that social groups differ. To this degree,

BOX 4.2

Cultural Variability and the Case of Colin Ferguson

On December 7, 1993, Colin Ferguson (a.k.a. the Long Island Railway Gunman), shot several train passengers on a commuter line in New York City. Six passengers were killed; 19 others were wounded. Upon his arrest, Mr. Ferguson, a 35-year-old Black Jamaican immigrant, alleged that he was the victim of racism. Indeed, during the course of his trial (a case in which he ultimately represented himself), Ferguson argued that his actions were the result of "Caucasian, Asians, 'Uncle Tom Blacks' and many other 'racist' people and organizations." Mr. Ferguson's "Black Rage" defense was unsuccessful and he was convicted of the crimes for which he was accused. But the question of Mr. Ferguson's defense and the basis of his opinions remain the source of speculation, especially in the context of cultural relativism and the descriptive context in which the Long Island Railway Gunman understood what had happened to him.

Ferguson was able to identify several instances as a bank teller, as an employee at an alarm manufacturing company, as a complainant in a workers' compensation case, and as a college student in which, from his description and perspective, he was subjected to repeated acts of blatant racism and discrimination. Interestingly, Ferguson's storytelling was seen as part of a delusional belief system—one that did not comport with reality. His recounting of elaborate conspiracy theories and his deep-seated distrust and paranoia were enough to cause concerns about his *competency to stand trial*. Before trial, both the prosecution and defense raised such concerns. His delusional belief system notwithstanding, Colin Ferguson was ultimately judged competent or fit to stand trial.

■ Given that Colin Ferguson was a Black Jamaican immigrant, how might cultural variability and cultural difference help us understand his beliefs and behaviors? How might they have played a role in the court's assessment of his "delusional" mental state?

■ More generally, given that beliefs vary widely between cultures, religions, geographic regions, and along racial, ethnic, and class-based lines, how might these differences produce *behavioral* variations? If differences in beliefs and behaviors can be attributed, in part, to variability between cultures, religions, races, etc., in what ways might this impact police, court, and correctional subsystems? What, if any, responsibility do the criminal justice system and practitioners within the criminal justice system have for recognizing, understanding, and working with these differences?

Source: Mark C. Bardwell and Bruce A. Arrigo, *Criminal Competency on Trial: The Case of Colin Ferguson* (Durham, NC: Carolina Academic Press, 2002).

descriptive relativism is regarded by proponents of relativism as supporting evidence for the metaethical and normative relativist positions.

In response, critics of relativism argue that simply acknowledging differences in moral sensibilities is not equivalent to saying that differing practices are equally "right" in the moral sense. Do conflicts between moral values exist simply because disagreement is an inevitable aspect of human social life? Or, perhaps, could such differences be resolved by way of demonstrating that the beliefs and practices of one group of people are somehow more "right" or more "wrong" than those of another (or many others)? It does not *necessarily* follow, then, that simply because differences exist that no "right" answer exists.

At one point in history nearly all people were certain that the earth was flat. We now believe the earth to be round. Should this difference of opinion merely be regarded as a distinction when it follows that neither belief is more "right" than the other? Most likely, our answer will be "no." Clearly, the previous belief that the earth was flat was *shown* to be wrong and our current belief that the earth is round (or, more accurately, spherical) is more "right" than the former belief. However, there is an important difference that should be addressed in this regard. While the earth can be *empirically* shown to be of a certain shape, *moral* beliefs, values, and practices are very different than this. How, for example, is one to show that polygamy is wrong in the same sense that we can show that the earth is round? The shape that the earth assumes can be regarded as objective in that its shape is not dependent upon human perception and, consequently, can be discovered with appropriate techniques of measurement. The shape that the earth assumes can also be regarded as universal in the sense that all people can (and should) agree that it is roughly round.

That the earth is not flat is an instance of a belief changing as a result of scientific advancement. While scientific explanations, for example, can appeal to a certain set of facts, there seem to be no such "objective values" to which moral arguments can appeal. The principles of mathematics, for example, can be regarded as objective and universal because they *are* largely objective and universal. This is not, however, the case with morality.

Mathematics and science offer explanations that are based on observation and measurement. Such observations and measurements provide evidence for the truth of such explanations.[16] While we can visually observe that one-plus-one equals two or that the earth is roughly round in shape, we cannot visually observe the "rightness" or "wrongness" of moral beliefs and practices. Torturing animals, for example, is cruel by nearly all standards. Yet by what values do we judge such behavior to be cruel? Even if we are to agree that, by definition, an act is cruel, by what standards are we to judge cruelty itself to be immoral? In our everyday lives, of course, many such judgments may not entail practical consequences. That is to say, certain actions—such as torturing animals—seem simply to be cruel and are not subject to widespread disagreement. Nevertheless, other sorts of actions admit to less agreement. In any event, it seems possible that there are no objective and universal standards by which we can judge *any* action.

Metaethical and Normative Implications

When considering moral issues, we need to separate *factual* claims from prescriptive or normative claims. The two are distinguished in that factual claims make statements about aspects of the world or states of affairs that are either true or false. Moral or pre-scriptive claims, by contrast, are statements about how aspects of the world *should* be. It may be factually correct to acknowledge that one culture condones polygamy while another condemns it. This is not, however, the same as saying that either or both be-liefs are "right" in the moral sense. Consequently, we can accept the facts of cultural and historical variability without necessarily accepting the arguments of metaethical and normative relativism.

Metaethical relativism argues that, given the presence of cultural variability, there is no objective sense in which "right" and "wrong" can be discussed.[17] Its chal-lenge to ethics lies in its claim that a singular ethics does not and cannot exist. For ex-ample, rather than searching for universal moral principles, we should seek merely to acknowledge, respect, and, perhaps, understand existing variations. This last point is a normative claim with important and highly controversial implications.

When considering relativism as a moral philosophy, we are referring to what we *should* or *ought* to do in response to the factual reality set forth by descriptive rela-tivism. This **normative** or **prescriptive relativism** (i.e., *prescribing* a certain morality that *should* be accepted) moves beyond its descriptive variant. Prescriptive relativism argues that since differences in practices and beliefs do exist between groups of peo-ple, this is enough to signify an absence of any objectively right answer and, further, that the absence of any objective or universal morality is enough to *prohibit us from judging* the beliefs and practices of others. Because differences do exist and, further, because we have no means of showing or proving that any one set of beliefs or prac-tices is more "right" than any other, we *should* modify our own beliefs and practices to account for the recognition that no other belief or practice is necessarily more "right" or "wrong" than our own (see Box 4.3).

What are the consequences of such a position? Perhaps most importantly, rela-tivism is often interpreted as a strategy in support of *tolerance* with regard to the beliefs and practices of others. In other words, we should "live and let live." The problem, however, is that pure relativism implies that *intolerance* should be tolerated as well. That is to say, intolerance is no more "wrong" than tolerance and, therefore, we should simply acknowledge that some people are intolerant of others and place neither moral approval nor condemnation on such attitudes.

Several examples may come to mind. Consider the conflicting beliefs concerning slavery that played an important role in the American Civil War; the conflict over apartheid as practiced for many years in South Africa; and, more recently, the efforts of the United States to "free" the "oppressed" Iraqi people from tyrannical rule. In its extreme version, relativism cannot regard slavery, apartheid, or oppression in any form as objectively "wrong" in the moral sense. Rather, each concerns the beliefs and practices of a different group of people that may be morally disagreeable to many, but not morally "wrong." Furthermore, our efforts to end slavery, apartheid, and various oppressive practices *are themselves immoral.* In "Operation Iraqi Freedom," for exam-ple, the actions of the United States could be judged immoral on many levels. While several differing justifications were given for the United States' invasion of Iraq, the one that concerns us here is that of freeing what we believed to be oppressed peoples. In the context of relativism, such actions display a demonstrable lack of tolerance for the beliefs and practices of other cultures. Rather than intervening and attempting to change the beliefs and practices of other cultures to bring them into line with what

BOX 4.3
Sex Crimes and Normative Relativism

In the sociological literature and in popular opinion, "deviant" sexual acts typically include everything from bisexuality, nudism, topless dancing, and fetish behavior to more extreme acts such as *pedophilia* (sex with children), *zoophilia* (sex with animals), and *necrophilia* (sex with dead persons). However unconventional, most sexually-deviant acts are not defined as crimes (in all places and circumstances, at least). On the other hand, more extreme forms of sexual deviance such as sex with children, animals, and dead persons are more universally regarded as unlawful. However, a strict interpretation of relativism would suggest that even these actions, no matter how despicable, could not be defined as categorically immoral—or, for that matter, "criminal." Depending on the persons involved, the culture, time period, circumstances, etc., they may be morally acceptable.

- Using the insights of relativism and objectivism discussed in this chapter, on what basis could you argue that these deviant sexual practices should always, everywhere be "criminal"? On what basis could you argue that they should *not* be? Can you think of specific situations in which sex with children, animals, or dead persons might be acceptable or excusable practices?
- When comparing illegal sexual behaviors with those that are not, what is it about the behaviors in each group that makes them more or less morally reprehensible? In what ways, for instance, do Internet sex, the use of legal pornography, and legal public nudity differ from pedophilia, zoophilia, and necrophilia?
- One of the commonalities shared by the three sex crimes discussed above is that, unlike nude dancing or sadomasochistic behaviors that are consensual acts with no identifiable "victim," children, animals, and dead persons are unable to offer voluntary and knowing *consent*. When it comes to sexual practices, is consent a desirable basis on which to judge something legal or illegal? Can you think of any consensual sexual acts that should be considered immoral and/or illegal? Can you think of any nonconsensual sexual acts that should not be considered immoral and/or illegal?
- How might the observations regarding the distinction between *mala in se* and *mala prohibita* (see Box 4.1) assist you in differentiating between different forms of sexual deviance and in identifying sex *crimes*? What, if any, types of sexual behaviors would you consider wrong-in-themselves? Why?

"we" believe to be "right," the appropriate course of action (following normative or prescriptive relativism) would have been no intrusive action at all.

The normative implications of relativism are, of course, difficult for many people to accept. For this reason, as well as others, relativism has been a hotly contested subject in moral philosophy. Nevertheless, the belief that we *should*, for example, intervene to end practices of slavery *requires* an appeal to some objective standard of right and wrong. We must be able to offer some acceptable justification for identifying slavery as morally "wrong"—something more, of course, than merely our feelings, unsupported opinions, or conventional practices. The challenge that relativism presents is that of finding an adequate source of moral authority by which to justify our beliefs and subsequent practices.[18] Various moral philosophies have responded to this dilemma in manifold ways: by appealing to theological sources; by appealing to the best interests of the people involved; by appealing to universal rules derived from logical argument. We will explore several of these potential sources in some detail in later chapters. However, before we conclude our discussion of relativism, it is worth considering one further variation: pragmatic ethical relativism and, relatedly, sociological functionalism.

PRAGMATIC RELATIVISM

Protagoras (c. 490–c. 420 B.C.E.) is often recognized as one of the earliest proponents of—and by some accounts the "father" of—what we now refer to as relativism. His famous epigram, "Man is the measure of all things . . . ," succinctly summarizes his position. For Protagoras, there is no "natural" morality, truth, justice,and so on.[19] Rather, the laws and moral rules governing human behavior vary from time to time and from place to place. Further, none of these variations is "more true" or "more right" than any other because none is objectively true or false. When faced with conflicting sets of moral standards, we often want to ask, "Which is right?" Yet to judge a set of practices, laws and customs as more moral than another requires an objective set of moral standards with which to compare them. The difficulty is that such standards do not seem to exist. Though we often mistake convention and majority opinion for truth, these things are not truth. This certainly does not mean that we do not *believe* that one set of standards (typically those of our own time period, culture, religion, etc.) is more right than another. Yet Protagoras and later relativists suggest that none actually *is* more right.[20]

Protagoras did, however, say that some beliefs and practices were "better" in light of their *consequences*.[21] To be clear, the implication is not that what is "better" is "right" or even "more right" than any other belief or practice. What Protagoras was acknowledging was simply that if everyone else agrees that today is Friday, it would be in my best interest to also agree with (or "go along with") the popular and conventional belief that today is Friday.[22] My life will certainly be easier and not subject to any of the potential negative consequences that might result from my dissension. In the context of an orderly social world, perhaps that dissenting "truth" is not as important as simply finding points of agreement to which we can refer in order to make life more predictable and, in that way, more smooth.

To illustrate, it may not be the case that sixty-five miles per hour is the "right" speed limit on the interstate near my home. Given individual differences in driving ability, differences in the quality and safety of automobiles, and the relative traction effects with various highway road surfaces, it certainly may not be the "right" speed limit for all cars and all individual persons on all interstates. However, it does create a point of agreement and a point of reference to which we can all refer in determining how fast to drive on that particular highway. In other words, imposing a speed limit of sixty-five miles per hour on the interstate, while not necessarily the "correct" velocity by any objective standard, makes driving predictable and orderly. In this regard, setting a speed limit is beneficial or "good" in its *consequences* or in the *practical value* that it has for social life.

In referring to "practical value," we come across a potentially important idea in ethics or any other field of study; namely, *pragmatism*. **Pragmatism** comes in a variety of forms, though the basic idea of each is that the purpose of anything—values, beliefs, laws, research—is not to uncover or represent the truth, but to allow us to more effectively and/or comfortably live our lives. The function of lawmakers, for example, is not to find the "right" law for a particular purpose, but to develop an *effective* law for that purpose. In other words, a good law becomes a law that *works*.[23] If, for instance, our goal is to achieve and maintain social order, then law and practices of law enforcement that serve that purpose—those that *work*—are good laws and practices. We cannot rightfully judge behaviors, customs, beliefs, and laws, except by reference to their context and effectiveness (or **functionality**) within that context.

So what are the implications of Protagorean philosophy for ethics? In short, it means that our search for objective and universal standards of truth, justice, goodness, beauty, and so forth, is futile and pointless. We should discard accounts of absolute truth and, further, abandon any related pursuits we might subsequently undertake. Moral laws do not exist, at least in any objective or "natural" sense. Social reality consists merely of human constructions that are not "right" nor "wrong," but *functional* for a given culture at a given time. "Justice" is what is believed to be "just" by a certain group of people, and what therefore works for that group of people within that historical period. "Killing" cannot be objectively wrong, yet prohibitions against killing can be functional. A culture which did not have prohibitions against killing—at least many forms of killing—would be a culture that was not primed for survival. A culture in which it was customary for men to have five wives might eventually run into practical problems if there were considerably more men than women living within that culture. By contrast, polygamy might function positively in a culture where there were considerably more women than men.

Thus, while it is quite natural for us to think about killing and polygamy as moral issues, if Protagoras is correct, we should cease judging the morality of practices and beliefs and begin seeking to understand the practicality and functionality of those practices and beliefs. This, in turn, requires abandonment of philosophical thinking about ethics and a turn toward investigating the beliefs and practices of social groups or collectives *sociologically*. What is functional for a group of people is a purely sociological question, void of any deeper moral philosophical content.

Consider the following two examples—the first pertains to cultural variability and its relation to a pragmatic conception of relativism; the second is a functionalist sociological perspective on an often-debated social and legal issue:

- European explorers discovered that Inuit (Eskimo) tribes regularly engaged in practices very different from their own. In particular, the Eskimos seemed to practice *infanticide* and a crude form of *euthanasia*. Female babies were sometimes killed off, and elderly members of the tribe were sometimes left out in the cold to die. What may have initially seemed to Europeans to reflect a remarkable lack of moral sensibilities, however, were discovered to be sensible practices. Later explorers would recognize that the Eskimo people were a nomadic tribe, traveling constantly in search of new food sources.

As hunters and food gatherers, males were far more likely to die prematurely. If all female babies were to survive, the number of female adults would quickly far outweigh the number of healthy males, thereby jeopardizing the well-being of the tribe. Further, some of the elderly members of the tribe were simply too frail to keep up. Leaving them behind to die was less a moral matter, and more a matter of doing what was necessary to ensure the survival of the group. As James Rachels suggests, "[t]he Eskimos' values are not all that different from our values. It is only that life forces upon them choices that we do not have to make."[24]

- In a much-discussed article, sociologist Kingsley Davis argued that *prostitution* is "good" for society in that it serves the overall function of maintaining the social system by performing several smaller functions.[25] Prostitution: (1) satisfies sexual desires without the associated expenses of dating or marriage and without the often-required emotional investment; (2) maintains the institution of the family by relieving wives of the necessity of satisfying the "perverse" sexual desires of their husbands, thus enabling husbands to continue to respect their wives; (3) allows a small number of women to satisfy the needs of a large number of men, including those who have difficulty finding conventional outlets for those needs; and (4) allows prostitutes themselves to earn considerably more money than they would in most other occupations.

In both of these examples, we are faced with a controversial moral issue: the first concerning life and death; the second concerning human sexuality. In the first instance, many would be quick to point out the assumed immoral nature of infanticide or allowing elderly persons to die. However, what would seem to most of us today as a profound disrespect for life and a cruelty of character might be better regarded as a practice conducted within the context of a certain cultural reality. Approached in this way, it may seem less morally reprehensible and, perhaps, even acceptable as a practice necessary (functional) for group survival. We could say the same for the second case as well: Prostitution may be morally reprehensible, yet it could also be understood as a practice that meets the needs of a large group of people within a given society. In neither case do we necessarily commit ourselves to accepting the practice as *moral*. Rather, what seems initially to be a moral question becomes a pragmatic question when viewed in a different light.

THE VALUE OF RELATIVISM

Relativism has brought mixed blessings to ethics and morality. In one sense, it represents a serious threat to the very idea of morality, as well as ethical inquiries into morality. In another sense, it alerts us to some common faults in our own thinking about moral issues. Some would argue that it is only a short step from relativism to an "anything goes" attitude in which morality can no longer serve as a foundation or point of reference for social health, happiness, and relations more generally. At the same time, others contend that a failure to recognize the diversity of moral values that exists within and between cultures (and the corresponding benefits of that diversity) can lead us to potentially more dangerous ways of thinking and potentially harmful laws, policies, and practices emerging from those ways of thinking. What are the dangers of relativism? What are the dangers of *not* taking relativism into consideration?

A significant consequence of accepting a purely relativistic ethics is that it requires us to abandon our common practice of judging other people and cultures and the often accompanying practice of attempting to change those same people and cultures by imposing our own values onto them. For relativists, this consequence is not entirely detrimental to human relations. Different laws, rules, customs, practices, and beliefs, may be entirely at odds with one another and yet work equally well for different groups of people. We should keep in mind that historical development, economic and social conditions, educational standards, and so forth of different groups of people can vary tremendously. Thus, while a given common practice may work quite well for one culture, region, or subculture, it may be devastating for another. Recognizing these differences does not require us to abandon our own sense of morality. Rather, it asks that we not be so quick to judge and impose ourselves in every situation in which there exists a conflict. It might be possible to differentiate between moral principles that are legitimately universal and moral practices that are legitimately variable.

If we subscribe to some variation of relativism, we would have to concede that practices such as capital punishment cannot be judged moral or immoral. From a pragmatic standpoint, we might better ask whether the death penalty "works" or serves some greater purpose for which it is intended.[26] Assuming that capital punishment has practical or pragmatic value as a deterrent, then executing convicted criminals would be morally acceptably and desirable so long as it fulfilled this purpose. On the other hand, if it failed to fulfill its intended function, we would have to judge the practice of capital punishment to be morally undesirable and unacceptable. Most of us, however, are probably a bit uncomfortable with the idea that practices such as capital punishment are not moral or immoral, but could be either depending on where and when the act is undertaken and who is engaged in undertaking it. Must there not be some standard or principles by which we could say conclusively that certain laws, policies, or practices are *either* moral *or* immoral?

As unsettling as it may be for some, most people do tend to think of morality as relative—at least to situational circumstances. Thus the act of killing is generally regarded as immoral, but could be moral if done in a time of war or as part of a heroic effort to prevent some greater evil. Some philosophers and social scientists (including criminologists) suggest that even if we cannot say conclusively that certain laws, policies, or practices are right or wrong on a moral level, we *can* make judgments concerning the underlying *reasons* for them. For instance, while we may not be able to make a determination one way or the other about the morality of war, we may be able to make moral judgments about the underlying reasons for going to war. Starting or entering a war in an effort to satisfy an underlying desire for vengeance against another country or our hatred for that country may be objectively less moral than if motivated by a desire to improve the well-being of the general public (consider, for example, the recent U.S. war in Iraq). Additionally, while we may not be able to conclusively say that stealing is immoral, we can say conclusively that stealing for personal material gain is immoral—leaving open the possibility that some reasons for stealing (e.g., feeding a starving family) may be socially undesirable, but not necessarily immoral.

One of the benefits that the notion of relativism provides is that it encourages us to be more open-minded and considerate of perspectives other than our own when faced with moral issues and scenarios.[27] Most people, for instance, tend be ethnocentric. **Ethnocentrism** refers to a way of perceiving the world and all aspects of the world from the perspective of one's own culture or social group.[28] From an early age, a respect for our own culture is instilled in us. This respect is not based on any experience or objective knowledge we have acquired concerning the values and practices of our culture or those of any other; rather, we are simply socialized such that we come to have this respect. The danger of ethnocentrism lies in the sequencing of thought and action that is commonly made: perceiving the world from the perspective of one's own social group (a more or less inevitable phenomenon), to believing that that perspective is the "right" one. In other words, when respect for one's own culture turns into a belief in the *superiority* of one's own culture, we endanger our capacity for open-minded reasoning.

In relation to morality, ethnocentric persons believe not only that there are objective moral values, but that their own moral values *are* the objectively right ones. Ethnocentric morality, then, entails a belief in the moral superiority of one's own culture or social group. Ethnocentrism often affects people such that they reject the possibility that their own values are wrong and that those of another culture or social group *might* be right or in some ways "better." It is only another small step from believing that the moral sensibilities of one's own group are correct to judging the moral values of other groups and attempting to change those other groups so that they are consistent with one's own culturally-bound views.

What makes ethnocentrism problematic is that it often can lead to *dogmatism* and *intolerance.*[29] **Dogma** refers to a belief or belief system that is held unquestioningly and with absolute certainty. **Dogmatism** refers to the refusal to entertain criticisms of or challenges to those beliefs.[30] Often, such beliefs are not justified or backed by sound reasons— they are merely held as unquestionable truths. Dogmatism leads to narrow-mindedness (rather than open-mindedness) and an unwillingness to reconsider one's own values and beliefs even in light of contrary evidence. As well, a dogmatic stance can lead us to reject beliefs that are inconsistent with our own without ever considering them for what they are or might be worth. The problem, of course, is that our own beliefs may well be false or, at the very least, may be capable of improvement or refinement.

Moreover, dogmatism prevents one from assuming an objective perspective on one's own moral beliefs and values, as well as those of other people. If we are certain that our own beliefs are true— even without evidence to support them—we can easily become intolerant of the beliefs and practices of others who do not share in our value-based perspective. Because tremendous diversity exists both within and between cultures with regard to moral values, beliefs, and practices, conflict becomes inevitable. Dogmatism prevents agreeable resolution to such conflicts because both parties believe themselves to be absolutely right and the other to be absolutely wrong. Thus, each party or faction will try to force the other to adopt its perspective. Of course, this does not necessarily mean that either party is, in fact, right or wrong; rather, it simply means that neither is willing to consider the perspective of the other.

While much has been said (both in support of and opposed to) the virtue of tolerance, we should keep in mind that the kind of openness implied by relativism is not necessarily one that advocates tolerance of *all* values, beliefs, and practices. Instead, we should think of tolerance as a willingness to *understand* the perspectives of others and to not make judgments until we have done so. Tolerance or acceptance of this sort suggests that we should make some effort to keep an open mind and reserve judgment until we are able to do so in light of all relevant information. Thus, the value of tolerance is perhaps best understood as a means of *avoiding intolerance*.

On the whole, relativism reminds us that we are *fallible*—as much as we may cling to certain values and beliefs, our own moral sensibilities are not necessarily absolute truths that should be applied to everyone and in all situations. As well, becoming familiar with difference and diversity can help us recognize and understand the moral perspectives of other persons, groups, and cultures in various situations and utilize this understanding before passing judgment or imposing solutions in those involving conflict. Although recognizing the relativity of moral values and norms does not mean that we should abandon our own values or adopt an "anything goes" attitude, it does encourage us to refrain from thinking in "black-and-white" terms and to maintain a willingness to understand and even learn from other perspectives.

Recognizing the variability of moral values and norms and maintaining a certain degree of open-mindedness not only seems necessary for anyone living in a complex and diverse society such as the United States, but is especially important for current and future criminal justice practitioners. Agents of criminal justice are exposed to difference and diversity of cultural and subcultural values routinely, whether through the policing of different communities, the guarding of a diverse population of prison inmates, or through representing the interests of diverse clients in a courtroom environment. In fact, most formal codes of ethics in law enforcement, correctional, and court-related professions emphasize and promote equal treatment and the avoidance of prejudice and discriminatory treatment—values that would seem to demand a certain level of understanding and respect for group and individual differences.

RELATIVISM AND THE CRIMINAL JUSTICE SYSTEM: THE MORALITY OF CRIMINAL LAW

Over the course of this chapter, we have seen that moral values and norms can and often do vary—even within the same society or culture, from region to region, religion to religion, along group, class, racial and ethnic lines, and between subcultures. We have also been exposed to the argument that, because of this variability, there is no "true" morality or, at the very least, that "true" morality is not immediately evident and therefore we should not be so quick to pass judgment on those whose values and practices differ from our own. These ideas have important but often overlooked implications for crime, law, and justice. Within the criminal justice context, the relativity of moral values—as well as the idea that morality should not be imposed on others—perhaps poses the greatest difficulties and dilemmas within the sphere of lawmaking. In this final section, we look briefly at some of the dilemmas that relativity of moral values poses for the practice of lawmaking.

When lawmakers create laws, they often cannot escape the influence of moral interests. Even when moral interests are not specifically stated, laws almost always have a moral dimension. Yet many advanced industrial societies such as the United States are characterized by moral diversity and conflict over key moral (and legal) issues. Almost universally, citizens cannot murder, rape, or rob other citizens—behaviors that directly harm the person or property of others. There tends to be a strong *consensus* among the public concerning the wrongfulness of these behaviors and the desirability of prohibiting them. Other forms of behavior, however, are less a matter of public consensus. Gambling, the sale and distribution of sexually-explicit materials and alcoholic beverages, and the possession and use of various substances are, for example, behaviors over which there has always been and continues to be moral disagreement. Where conflict over moral values and appropriate behavior exists, it is law that ultimately must supply "working answers." Importantly, laws are not written to apply only to those people who happen to agree with them or share in their underlying moral values; rather, laws are created to apply to all people, everywhere within a given jurisdiction. In other words, the nature of lawmaking is such that certain values *must* be imposed upon citizens.

Within criminal law, the existence of moral diversity and conflict is perhaps most evident is discussions about *what should be a crime.* In the United States, as in other civilized countries, citizens are not free to do whatever they wish. Federal, state, and local governments place various restrictions on individual liberties by passing laws that prohibit some forms of behavior and require others. Debate arises, however, when we begin to ask *which* behaviors should be subject to restrictions. Further, we might ask, on what grounds can we justify restricting or criminalizing some behaviors but not others? How and why is it that certain behaviors are determined to be "crimes" while others—irrespective of how harmful, immoral, or offensive they may be to some—are not? On what basis can we justify governments defining appropriate behavior and forcing citizens to comply with moral standards that they might find objectionable or disagreeable?

In his widely discussed four-volume work, *The Moral Limits of Criminal Law,* Joel Feinberg explores four principles that might be used to determine whether the government can legitimately prohibit or criminalize certain forms of behavior: the harm principle, paternalism, legal moralism, and offensive conduct. In the remainder of this section, we briefly explore each of these principles and conclude with an exercise in applying them to contemporary controversies in law and society (see Box 4.4).

The Harm Principle

One of the most commonly discussed justifications for the prohibition of certain types of behavior is the **harm principle,** derived from John Stuart Mill. The harm principle is also commonly used as justification for *not* criminalizing certain forms of behavior. In short, the question to which Mill responds is, "When is it morally acceptable for governments to coerce people through law?" To this question, he suggests a simple principle: Governments can legitimately prohibit or require certain behavior when it is necessary to *prevent people from harming others*—and *only* when it is necessary for this purpose. In Mill's own terms,

> . . . the only purpose for which power can be rightfully exercised over any member of a civilized community, against his will, is to prevent harm to others. His own good, either physical or moral, is not a sufficient warrant. . . . Over himself, over his own body and mind, the individual is sovereign.[31]

Clearly, the harm principle would justify the government passing and enforcing laws against murder, rape, robbery, theft, driving under the influence, and other forms of behavior that either cause objective harm to others or have a strong likelihood of doing

BOX 4.4
Justifying Legal Prohibitions

Moral values and norms tend to vary across and within cultures and over time. There are many behaviors about which there is a lack of moral consensus. Conflict and disagreement over which behaviors should be criminalized is reflected in the fact that laws concerning these behaviors often vary over time and from place to place at a given time. In other words, criminal law is, to some extent, *relative*. How, then, do governments determine which behaviors should be subject to legal coercion?

As we have seen in this section, over the course of his four-volume, work, *The Moral Limits of Criminal Law*, Joel Feinberg suggests that there are four principles that might be used to determine whether the government can legitimately prohibit certain forms of behavior:

1. *The Harm Principle.* Behavior can be legitimately prohibited if it causes or has a high risk of causing serious harm to other people.
2. *Paternalism.* Governments can legitimately prohibit behavior that might cause serious harm to the acting agent, even if no one else might be harmed.
3. *Legal Moralism.* Governments are justified in prohibiting behavior that is immoral, even when it does not harm or offend anyone.
4. *The Offense Principle.* Behavior can be legitimately prohibited if it seriously offends others.

As a concluding exercise, consider how the above principles might *justify* or *fail to justify* legal prohibition of the following behaviors. For those behaviors that are currently illegal, consider whether and how any of Feinberg's four principles might justify their legalization.

- Physician-assisted suicide
- Abortion
- Burning the American flag in public
- Possession and use of marijuana
- Buying and selling sex
- Buying and selling sexually-explicit material
- Owning weapons, including automatic weapons and grenades
- Polluting the environment
- Gay marriage
- Sunbathing nude in public
- An employer refusing to hire women or African Americans
- A therapist having sexual relations with his or her clients
- Treating mentally ill persons by medicating them against their will

so. Where laws prohibit nonharmful behaviors, Mill would suggest, the government is crossing boundaries that it has no moral right to cross.

For Mill, *liberty* is a key feature of human existence and wherever possible should not be limited by government. Harm or the possibility of harm to others is the only morally-legitimate reason for placing limitations on liberty through the passing and enforcing of laws. Importantly, the harm principle suggests that people should be free to do anything else they may choose—even if their actions harm themselves, offend others, or are regarded as immoral. Advocates of *decriminalization* of so-called victimless crimes often appeal to the harm principle in support of their position. Arguably, behaviors such as personal recreational drug use, paying for sex, and gambling may be regarded as immoral by some but do not create any objective harm for anyone other than those who are voluntarily involved in the behavior. So long as the participants are competent adults, *consent* negates any wrongfulness. As such, citizens should enjoy the freedom to legally engage in such behaviors.

Appealing to the harmfulness or harmlessness of certain behaviors as justification for criminalization or legalization begs an important question: namely, "What counts as harm?" Aside from obvious instances of harm that result from violent behavior, there are numerous ways in which citizens harm one another physically, emotionally, and financially. As we saw in Chapter 2, most everything we do has some effect, however small it may be, on others. In many cases, the harms we do to others are not obvious, direct, or immediately experienced. One could argue, however, that they are harms nevertheless. Thus one of the biggest difficulties in applying the harm principle—as well as in the making of laws—is determining what types of "harms" warrant legal coercion.

To this question, Feinberg suggests that the Harm Principle justifies coercive government action where behaviors harm people's *basic welfare interests*, including "continued life, health, economic sufficiency, and political liberty."[32] Wearing a T-shirt with a radical political message may cause anger and disgust, but is not likely to jeopardize the basic interests listed above. On the other hand, driving while intoxicated carries a significant risk of harming others' interests in continued life and physical health and the government may therefore be justified in prohibiting it.

Paternalism

In his description of the harm principle, John Stuart Mill suggested that laws are designed to protect people from *one another*, not from themselves. Of course, laws sometimes *are* intended to protect people from themselves, and governments *do* use coercion for this purpose (e.g., seatbelt laws, laws prohibiting the possession of dangerous drugs). When governments seek to protect citizens from themselves, this is called **paternalism**. In its most general sense, paternalism refers to a relationship of giving or aiding others in which an authority (e.g., government, organization) relates to those in need as a father would to his dependent children (*paternal* = "fatherly"). In the context of social policy, paternalism is evident where governmental power brokers assume responsibility for the (presumed) needs of its citizens, taking action through law or policy (e.g., penal, psychiatric) to meet those needs.

As a principle, paternalism holds that it is justifiable and morally permissible for the government to use law and policy to coercively protect people from themselves. Many would agree that persons who are *incompetent* (e.g., children, those with developmental disabilities) should be subject to paternalistic treatment. Feinberg, in fact, suggests that the government has a moral *duty* to intervene in such situations. However, protecting competent, rational adults from themselves is another matter. As Feinberg writes, doing so is "arrogant and demeaning." When involving competent adults, paternalism implies that "there are sharp limits to my right to govern myself . . . that others may intervene . . . to 'correct' my choices and then (worst of all) justify interference on the ground (how patronizing) that they know my own good better than I know it myself."[33] As most of us value *self-determination* or our capacity to find our own way through life and to make our own choices in everyday encounters, paternalistic laws can seem offensive and degrading—especially since these actions suggest that people are incapable of caring for themselves and need to be looked after by those who presumably "know best" or, at least, know better than they do.

A contemporary controversy involving paternalistic government policy is the practice of **civil commitment** or involuntary hospitalization for persons deemed mentally ill (though not necessarily legally incompetent) and presumed to be in need of psychiatric treatment. In such cases, the state confines a person to a hospital against that individual's will because it has judged the person to be: (1) mentally ill *and* (2) a "clear and present" danger to others, a danger to self, or "grossly disabled" and unable to adequately care for oneself. Where civil commitment is intended to protect the public from presumably dangerous persons, it might be justified by the harm principle. However, where it is used to protect people from themselves and impose psychiatric care on those who are judged unable to care for themselves, it is paternalistic in nature. Problematically, to some persons with mental health issues, the deprivation of liberty and the infringement on self-determination that accompanies such hospitalization is greatly resented. With this in mind, we might ask, "Is it morally permissible for governments to deprive persons of basic interests in liberty and self-determination for purposes of treating them when they are not a danger to others and do not want psychiatric treatment?"[34]

Legal Moralism

Legal moralism is a position which holds that governments can and should pass laws to prohibit behaviors *if those behaviors are considered to be immoral*—even if they do not cause harm to self or others. When grounded in the perceived immorality of the behavior, laws that prohibit forms of private, consensual sexual behavior are examples of legal moralism. For example, sexual behaviors collectively referred to as "sodomy" were illegal in some states until relatively recently in U.S. history. Sodomy laws were not created to protect individuals from themselves or one another, but in the interest of preserving the moral integrity and tradition of communities.

It is this perceived need to preserve certain ways of life that is often used as a justification for legal moralism. The question, however, is whether the majority—or those with the power to create laws or influence the lawmaking process—have a moral right to force others to conform to their moral standards. In what, if any, cases does a group of people have a moral right to impose laws (and thus moral values) on other people who do not agree with them and have not consented to living by those rules and values?[35]

Legal scholar Joel Feinberg argues that every community needs certain core moral values by which all of its members should live. These core values are necessary for the well-being of the community and the survival of its members (e.g., those that prevent people from harming one another). Outside of these few, basic values, however, Feinberg suggests that communities are made *stronger* by leaving room for *diversity*. On this note, Emmett Barcalow offers the following observations:[36]

- History has demonstrated that forcing people to comply with rules with which they do not agree often produces resistance—sometimes of the violent, revolutionary type.

- Recognizing and accepting a certain degree of moral relativism within communities may be necessary for social cohesion.
- Communities change and, "it is futile and probably dangerous to try to block all changes to a community's way of life."
- Some ways of life are oppressive and immoral. Consider the keeping of slaves of the American South and the subordination of women and racial/ethnic minorities. Preserving certain ways of life is not desirable if those ways of life are morally-questionable.
- Behavior which might be regarded as immoral or offensive is not usually "contagious." If homosexuality is tolerated or even accepted, for instance, most people will still be heterosexual; if prostitution were legalized, most people are still not going to seek out and solicit the services of prostitutes. Tolerating moral diversity will not likely produce significant changes to a community's way of life, as most members will remain committed to conventional values and behaviors.

Offensive Conduct

All of us are occasionally negatively affected—perhaps "harmed" in some sense—by others' rudeness, insensitivity, loud music, offensive body odor, distasteful clothing, and so on. According to Feinberg, however, these behaviors cannot rightfully be classified as "harmful":

> Not everything that we dislike or resent, and wish to avoid, is harmful to us . . . [E]xperiences can distress, offend, or irritate us without harming any of our [physical, psychological, or financial] interests. They come to us, are suffered for a time, and then go, leaving us as whole and undamaged as we were before.[37]

In other words, Feinberg argues that while experiences such as those listed above might cause temporary "unhappy mental states," they should not count as harms for legal purposes. While your body odor may cause me a brief unpleasant sensation, your insult may for a short time wound my pride, hurt my feelings, or cause me anger, and your T-shirt may momentarily shock my sensibilities, I have not been "harmed" in such a way that your behavior should be criminalized or otherwise prohibited or restricted by law. While I may experience temporary physical and psychological discomfort as a result of your behavior, you have not had any substantial negative effect on my basic interests. While many would agree that the effects of these behaviors are not "harmful" enough to justify legal intervention, they are nonetheless *offensive*. The question becomes, "Is the government morally justified in prohibiting behavior that *offends* others even if it produces no substantial harm?"

While Feinberg describes "harms" as those behaviors that impose upon others basic interests, "offensive" behavior "produces unpleasant or uncomfortable experiences—affronts to sense or sensibility, disgust, shock, shame, embarrassment, annoyance, boredom, anger, fear, or humiliation."[38] As examples, he suggests behaviors such as: playing loud music in public; vomiting in public; using the American flag as a handkerchief; copulating in public; and wearing an ethnically, racially, or religiously-derogatory T-shirt. While most people would agree that some offensive conduct should be prohibited, the question remains which such behaviors are sufficiently offensive to warrant legal prohibition?

In response to the above question, Feinberg suggests that some offensive behavior may be considered a violation of people's *right to privacy* when it invades private space. If people have a moral right to be protected from certain experiences, the offensive behavior could be considered wrongful where it "deprive[s] . . . unwilling spectators of the power to determine for themselves whether or not to undergo a certain experience."[39] As well, the *seriousness* of the offense must be considered. Seriousness depends on the intensity and duration of the unpleasantness or discomfort, the number of people offended, as well as how much inconvenience would be caused in order to avoid or escape the experience.

Feinberg also notes that we should consider the social utility of the offensive behavior. Loud trains rumbling through our neighborhood at 2:00 A.M. or the smell of manure from a nearby farm may be offensive, yet both serve important social purposes. Their social utility may outweigh any unpleasant experience that we may be forced to endure. As well, we need to consider the importance of offensive behavior to those who engage in it. Some behaviors are important parts of people lives and prohibiting them may stand to cause significant harm to their interests. The sight of an interracial or gay couple may offend some people, but the importance of love and friendship to those couples may outweigh the offense it (temporarily) causes others.

Finally, Feinberg tells us that the *intentions* of the actor must be considered. There is clearly a difference between conduct that is intended to be offensive and that of which offending others is not the primary purpose. For instance, wearing an offensive T-shirt for the mere purpose of offending others may be less permissible than wearing the same T-shirt because one is making a political statement. As well, it is easy enough for spectators to avoid looking at an offensive T-shirt.[40]

SUMMARY

We have now spent some time exploring two significant issues in metaethics: determinism and moral relativism. The former was explored in Chapter 3; the latter was reviewed in the present chapter. Clearly, both determinism and relativism present ethical challenges that warrant careful attention before doing any meaningful thinking about other moral concerns. This includes issues within the criminal justice system or those that otherwise involve criminal behavior.

Specifically within this chapter, the notion of moral relativism was contrasted with ethical objectivism and ethical universalism, and contemporary ethical relativism was examined mindful of its descriptive, metaethical, and normative variants. Finally, pragmatic relativism was considered. In part, this included commentary on the ways in which sociological functionalism helps account for ethical decision-making and whether these choices should be guided by the extent to which actions, laws, or policies fulfill (or fail to fulfill) their stated and useful purposes.

The implications of moral relativism raise enduring questions about ethnocentrism, dogmatism, and the role of tolerance in reaching ethical outcomes. Perhaps more importantly, the dilemma of relativism leads us to ask why be moral in the first place? This concern is explored more fully in Chapter 6 (and, to a lesser extent, in Chapter 5 as well). The concern for why we should be moral, however, assumes that we *can* be moral. Both of these issues raise questions about *moral psychology*. It is to these issues which we turn next.

KEY TERMS AND CONCEPTS

civil commitment	harm principle
cultural variability	legal moralism
descriptive relativism	*mala in se mala prohibita*
dogma	metaethical relativism
dogmatism	normative relativism
ethical objectivism	objectivity
ethical universalism	paternalism
ethnocentrism	pragmatism
functionality (of moral beliefs and practices)	prescriptive relativism
	relativism

DISCUSSION QUESTIONS

1. Relativism argues that morality is linked to culture, historical time periods, and even subgroups. Explain what this means. How do the doctrines of ethical objectivism and ethical universalism contrast with the notion of relativism?

2. Using the example of "victimless" crimes (e.g., gambling, prostitution, drug use), explain how descriptive relativism provides an ethical basis for their decriminalization or their legalization. Do you believe that descriptive relativism is a sensible basis to propose the decriminalization or legalization of these offenses? To what extent does the notion of cultural variability assist you in your analysis? Justify your response.

3. Do you believe there is an objective sense in which "right" and "wrong" can be identified? What does the notion of metaethical relativism say about this? If there is no objective ethical basis by which behavior can be deemed "right" or "wrong," what are the implications for criminal justice practice (consider law enforcement, court administration, and correctional work, specifically)?

4. Explain the doctrine of pragmatic relativism. In what way is sociological functionalism related to it? How does the doctrine of pragmatic relativism (and sociological functionalism) operate in everyday criminal courtroom deliberations? In decisions linked to probation or parole? In decisions to waive (or not) juveniles to the adult system?

5. How might ethnocentrism and dogmatism impact police decisions to stop and arrest suspects? Consider the phenomena of racial and criminal profiling. Ethically

speaking, how would you reconcile the presence of ethnocentrism and dogmatism in criminal justice with decisions to arrest, convict, and sentence the undocumented, foreign nationals, or those who live in the United States but whose values, beliefs, customs, and practices differ from those found within mainstream culture?

6. Identify a recent criminal case in which cultural variability was an important component of determining how the criminal justice system functioned. Do you believe that the criminal justice system is obligated to demonstrate tolerance and open-mindedness when confronted with behavior deemed unlawful? Why or why not? Justify your response.

SUGGESTED READINGS

Billet, Brett L. (2005). *Cultural Relativism in the Face of the West: The Plight of Women and Children*. New York: Palgrave MacMillan.

Harman, Gilbert, and Thomson, Judith. (1996). *Moral Relativism and Moral Objectivity*. London: Blackwell.

Mackie, J. L. (1977). *Ethics: Inventing Right and Wrong*. New York: Penguin.

Nagel, Thomas. (1986). *The View from Nowhere*. New York: Oxford University Press.

Sterba, James. (2001). *Three Challenges to Ethics: Environmentalism, Feminism, and Multiculturalism*. New York: Oxford University Press.

Streiffer, Robert. (2003). *Moral Relativism and Reasons for Action*. New York: Routledge.

ENDNOTES

[1]Robert Streiffer, *Moral Relativism and Reasons for Action* (New York: Routledge, 2003).

[2]Gilbert Harman and Judith Jarvis Thomson, *Moral Relativism and Moral Objectivity* (London: Blackwell, 1996).

[3]Donald Borchert and David Stewart, *Exploring Ethics* (New York: Macmillan, 1986), pp. 68–69.

[4]Ibid.; Harman and Thomson, *Moral Relativism and Moral Objectivity*.

[5]Paul K. Moser and Thomas L. Carson (Eds.), *Moral Relativism: A Reader* (New York: Oxford University Press, 2000).

[6]Gilbert Harman and Judith Jarvis Thomson, *Moral Relativism and Moral Objectivity*.

[7]Brett L. Billet, *Cultural Relativism in the Face of the West: The Plight of Women and Children* (New York: Palgrave MacMillan, 2005); Samuel Fleischacker, *Integrity and Moral Relativism* (Boston: Brill Academic Publisher, 1997).

[8]See, e.g., Lisa Heldke and Peg O'Connor, *Oppression, Privilege and Resistance: Theoretical Readings on Racism, Sexism, and Heterosexism* (New York: McGraw-Hill, 2003).

[9]David Wong, "Relativism." In P. Singer, *A Companion to Ethics* (Malden, MA: Blackwell, 1993).

[10]Robert Streiffer, *Moral Relativism and Reasons for Action*.

[11]Jane K. Cowan and Marie-Benedicte Dembour (Eds.), *Culture and Rights: Anthropological Perspectives* (Cambridge: Cambridge University Press, 2001).

[12]David Wong, "Relativism."

[13]Donald Borchert and David Stewart, *Exploring Ethics* (New York: Macmillan, 1986), pp. 69–70.

[14]Mary Fulbrook, *Historical Theory: Ways of Imagining the Past* (New York: Routledge, 2003), p. 22.

[15]Borchert and Stewart, *Exploring Ethics*, pp. 75–76; Dennis Chong, *Rational Lives: Norms and Values in Politics and Society* (Chicago: University of Chicago Press, 2000).

[16]Larry Laudan, *Science and Relativism: Some Key Controversies in the Philosophy of Science* (Chicago: University of Chicago Press, 1990).

[17]David Wong, "Relativism."

[18]Lawrence E. Hazelrigg, *Social Science and the Challenge of Relativism: Claims of Knowledge* (Tallahassee, FL: Florida State University, 1989).

[19]Richard Taylor, *Good and Evil* (Amherst, NY: Prometheus, 1999), p. 56.

[20]Mi-Kyoung Lee, *Epistemology After Protagoras: Responses to Relativism in Plato, Aristotle, and Democritus* (New York: Oxford University Press, 2005).

[21]Richard Taylor, *Good and Evil*, p. 59.

[22]Ibid.

[23]Ibid.

[24]James Rachels, *The Elements of Moral Philosophy* (New York: McGraw-Hill, 1986), pp. 13, 20–21.

[25]Kingsley Davis, "The Sociology of Prostitution," *American Sociological Review*, 2, 746–755 (1937).

[26]Hugo Bedau and Paul G. Cassell, *Debating the Death Penalty: Should America Have Capital Punishment? The Experts on Both Sides Make Their Best Case* (NY: Oxford University Press, 2006).

[27]James Rachels, *The Elements of Moral Philosophy*, pp. 23–24.

[28]See, e.g., Kwame Anthony Appiah, *Ethics and Identity* (Princeton, NJ: Princeton University Press, 2005).

[29]James Davidson Hunter, *Culture Wars: The Struggle to Define America* (New York: Basic Books, 1992).

[30]Anthony Weston, *A 21st Century Ethical Toolbox* (New York: Oxford University Press, 2001), pp. 11–14.

[31]John Stuart Mill, *On Liberty* (Indianapolis, IN: Hackett, 1978), p. 5.

[32]Joel Feinberg, *Harm to Others* (vol. 1 of *The Moral Limits of Criminal Law*) (New York: Oxford University Press, 1984), p. 45; quoted in E. Barcalow, *Moral Philosophy: Theories and Issues*, 2nd ed. (Belmont, CA: Wadsworth, 1998), p. 236.

[33]Joel Feinberg, *Harm to Self* (vol. 3 of *The Moral Limits of Criminal Law*) (New York: Oxford University Press, 1986), p. 23.

[34]See, e.g., Bruce A. Arrigo, *Punishing the Mentally Ill: A Critical Analysis of Law and Psychiatry* (Albany, NY: State University of New York Press, 2002); Judith Lynn Failer, *Who Qualifies for Rights: Homelessness, Mental Illness and Civil Commitment* (Ithaca, NY: Cornell University Press, 2002); Elyn R. Saks, *Refusing Care: Forced Treatment and the Rights of the Mentally Ill* (Chicago: University of Chicago Press, 2002).

[35]Emmett Barcalow, *Moral Philosophy: Theories and Issues*, 2nd ed. (Belmont, CA: Wadsworth, 1998).

[36]Ibid, pp. 244–245.

[37]Joel Feinberg, *Harm to Others*, p. 188; quoted in E. Barcalow, *Moral Philosophy*, p. 239.

[38]Joel Feinberg, *Offense to Others* (vol. 2 of *The Moral Limits of Criminal Law*) (New York: Oxford University Press, 1984), p. 5; quoted in E. Barcalow, *Moral Philosophy: Theories and Issues*, 2nd ed. (Belmont, CA: Wadsworth, 1998), p. 239.

[39]Joel Feinberg, *Offense to Others*, p. 23.

[40]40 E. Barcalow, *Moral Philosophy*, p. 241.

Chapter 5

CAN WE BE MORAL?
THE PROBLEM OF
SELF-INTEREST

In Chapters 3 and 4, we examined the *metaphysical* concerns of determinism and relativism, respectively, and their corresponding (and significant) relationships to crime, law, and justice. However, over the next three chapters, we turn our attention to several crucial *psychological* aspects of ethics. The study of psychological issues within ethics is sometimes referred to as *moral psychology*. **Moral psychology** principally evaluates the psychological assumptions, attitudes, and principles (as well as developmental matters) associated with morality.[1] Some ethical questions stemming from the application of moral psychology include the following:

- What motivates us to be moral? Are most people motivated to be moral simply to avoid punishment? To attain happiness? To conform to and "fit in" with others in society?
- Is it possible to be motivated by something other than self-interest? Is altruistic behavior possible? Is the appearance of altruism merely a disguised form of self-interest?
- Do people *develop* morally? Because we develop on a psychological level, are there important moral changes, progressions, or milestones that occur alongside our increasing psychological maturity?

The above questions reflect three fundamental controversies examined within the realm of moral psychology. These controversies entail: (1) moral motivation (why we are or should be moral), including an assessment of the kinds of motives that should induce moral agents;[2] (2) psychological egoism (the assumption that it is possible to act from something other than self-interest); and (3) moral development (how psychological maturation is related to the progression of or changes in moral motivation). Each of these controversies or debates is interrelated. In short, they collectively seek to understand the fundamental psychological conditions or mental states that incline people to act morally and whether (and how) these particular inducements develop over the course of our lives.

This chapter examines the role of self-interest (psychological egoism) in relation to our motivations to be moral. Moreover, the role of rewards and punishments as incentives—whether from the law, God, or our conscience—are reviewed. Here the issue is whether these motivators make us moral for the right reasons. In the next chapter, we will consider the various sources of morality other than reward and punishment, and in Chapter 7 the issue of moral development specifically is addressed. In each of these three chapters, however, the overriding purpose is to explore the timeless ethical question: *Why be moral?* Additionally, the goal is to demonstrate how an understanding of moral psychology and moral development can impact decision-making practices in criminal justice, as well as how we make sense of behavior defined as delinquent or criminal.

Morality and the Challenge of Self-Interest

All of us have been faced with situations where we want to do something that we probably should not do, or do not want to do something that we probably should do. In these instances, we are confronted by circumstances in which our *wants* and *shoulds* are in conflict. In other words, we are torn between our happiness, desires, and needs on the one hand, and the demands made of us by moral principles, duties, and obligations on the other hand. However, should moral concerns take precedence over those of desire, pleasure, comfort, the avoidance of pain, and other so-called self-interested motivations? If so, *why* should moral factors have such power of constraint over our choices and our actions?[3]

This conflict between self-interest and morality is one of the most basic and ever-present challenges facing both the theory and practice of ethical decision-making.[4] On a practical level, self-interest poses a formidable challenge to everyday behavior in that it can pull us toward the pursuit of our own personal inclinations at the expense of other, more lofty or noble considerations. It is the tension that often exists between acting to satisfy one's own wants and needs and, conversely, doing the "right" thing.[5]

Similar to determinism and relativism, self-interest also represents a metaethical concern—a challenge that must be confronted before proceeding to speculate as to how we should be with others and what we should do in specific situations or encounters. You may recall that determinism makes ethics a futile endeavor by removing our capacity for choice (see Chapter 3). Likewise, self-interest seeks to weaken the value of ethical inquiry by questioning the possibility of acting for *any* reason other than to satisfy one's own wants or interests. This line of thinking begs the question: Is it *possible* to make choices and undertake actions that are not purely, or at least not primarily, motivated by self-interest? Before we begin to talk about why we *should* be moral, we need first to consider whether we *can* be moral in the conventional sense of the term.

CAN WE BE MORAL?

Within moral philosophy, self-interest is often discussed in the context of *egoism* (ego = self or "I").[6] **Egoism** describes a form of human motivation whereby our decisions and actions are motivated primarily, if not exclusively, by our own interests. When we use the word "egoism" or one of its variations in everyday language, we are most often employing the term in a negative sense. For example, if we refer to someone as an "egoist," as "egotistical," or, perhaps, as an "egomaniac," we are offering a condemnation of that person's excessive—if not exclusive—focus on their self. These common usages suggest that we associate "egoism" with being unfeeling, inconsiderate, and concerned only with one's own happiness without any concern for the wants, needs, or interests of others.[7] In the extreme, the "egoist" perhaps even *uses* others as a means to attain her or his own happiness. In these respects, then, egoism carries undertones of amorality (i.e., being void of moral content altogether) or, perhaps, immorality (i.e., moral wrongfulness).[8]

Within conventional morality, egoism seems to be regarded as a moral flaw—an undesirable pattern of thought, feeling, and behavior whereby one promotes self-interest *beyond* that which is morally permissible.[9] Most of us would agree that it is often acceptable and even expected that we pursue our own interests. However, conventional moral sensibilities seem to entail a requirement that, at least on some occasions, we restrain our pursuit of self-interest in light of the wants or needs of others. Convention seems to carry a certain moral expectation that we regard the interests of others as equal to, if not more important than, our own interests, especially when the welfare or happiness of self and others are in conflict.

Consider the following two illustrations. If we smoke cigarettes, we are expected not to do so in the presence of young children; if we have neighbors who are trying to sleep, we are expected to keep the volume of our television, of our music, and/or our partying at minimal (indeed, acceptable) levels. In both cases, we are expected to sacrifice our own desires out of respect for other people's interests. The question that *psychological egoism* asks is whether we do so truly out of concern for others, or whether there is some other motivating factor at work such that what appears to be respect for the well-being of others is merely a concealed form of self-interest.[10]

Psychological egoism suggests that we are always, by nature of human psychology, motivated by self-interest; that all people, all of the time, act so as to promote (what they think are) their own interests.[11] This variation of egoism does not concern itself with what we *should* do. The degree to which we should act out of self-interest, or the degree to which it is acceptable to act out of self-interest, is a normative question. While there seems to be a normative convention that we remain considerate of the interests of others—even, on some occasions, sacrificing our own wants and desires for those of others—there is an important assumption underlying this point of view. In short, this convention rests upon the assumption that we *can* have motivations that run contrary to self-interest, or that it is (psychologically) possible to set aside concern for ourselves in the interest of the wants or needs of others. The question that psychological egoism poses can be stated as follows: Is it *possible* to be motivated by something other than self-interest and, consequently, to act such that our self-regarding inclinations are not given priority over other motivating considerations?

You might be surprised to learn that some variations of ethics do not necessarily regard egoism as immoral or undesirable. **Ethical egoism** is a normative variation of egoism. It holds that we *should* always act in such a way that we *rationally* maximize our self-interests.[12] We will look more closely at this normative argument in Chapter 8). Our concern here, however, is with the claim that egoism is an inevitable and inescapable product of human nature and that, consequently, everyone is an egoist all of the time. The psychological variety of egoism raises important questions about the very nature of human motivation.

Psychological Egoism

The claim being made by psychological egoism is a *factual* claim rather than a normative one.[13] That is to say, psychological egoism argues that all people, all of the time, *are* motivated to promote their own interests and, consequently, all human decision-making and behavior must be understood as self-interested in its underlying motivation. Because its claim is factual rather than normative, psychological egoism is not a theory that approves or disapproves of human actions or the motivations underlying human actions.[14] Unlike many of the ethical theories we will encounter beginning in Chapter 8 that make statements about how we *should* decide or act, psychological egoism simply makes a descriptive statement about the nature of human motivation.

There are several clarifications that are worth making at this point. First, to say that people are motivated by self-interest is not to say that people *actually* promote their own interests through those actions. Quite simply, we may be wrong about what actually serves our own interests.[15] As we saw in Chapter 2, Socrates had argued that all evil—including that which we do to ourselves—is a product of ignorance. People will always aim at some good, although they are not always—or even often—aware of what *is* good. The claim made by psychological egoism is simply that we are *motivated* by self-interest.[16]

There are countless examples of human behavior that would seem to contradict the principle of self-interest. The likely consequences of smoking, consuming too much liquor, dating the "wrong" person, or robbing a bank seem clearly to oppose what self-interest would dictate. However, this does not mean that the actor does not *believe*, at least on some level, that doing these things is in his or her best interest. Thus, the reality that people do things that fail to promote their best interests does not preclude the possibility that psychological egoism is at work.

Second, we might fail to act out of self-interest because we do not have the courage to do so. Suppose, for example, that Jane and Julie are both prosecutors slated for the same promotion at the district attorney's office. Jane is aware that she can secure the advancement over Julie by alerting her superior to several work-related violations in which Julie was involved. Clearly, Jane's best professional interest would be served by alerting her boss to Julie's improprieties and getting the promotion for herself. If she fails to do so, however, we cannot simply assume that Jane was motivated by something other than self-interest (e.g., some sense of concern for Julie's welfare). Rather, it might be the case that Jane simply could not find the courage to do what she knew would bring about the best employment outcome for her. Thus, while Jane might be *motivated* by self-interest, she might not possess the requisite personality trait (courage) enabling her to act accordingly. Again, this does not necessarily mean that we are not motivated to pursue our own interests—only that we do not always have the "will" to actually carry out the necessary actions.[17]

Third, psychological egoism does not necessarily imply that we always *intentionally* act in pursuit of self-interest. Self-interest can often work at a less-than-conscious level. For example, simply because we *feel* or *believe* that our actions are unselfish does not necessarily mean that they are. As Freud and others might argue, we are often not even consciously aware of why we do the things that we do (see Box 5.1).[18] Consequently, to argue that we are all "egoists" is not to suggest that we are consciously involved in furthering our own welfare or desires each time we make a decision or undertake an action. Psychological egoists would argue that while many actions may *seem* unselfish and, perhaps, even *feel* unselfish, they are nevertheless essentially self-directed acts.

Importantly, however, psychological egoism does not prevent acts of generosity, kindness, or those that benefit others in some way. We may even commit our lives to helping others, regularly acting to benefit or promote the interests of others. The claim being made by psychological egoism is simply that such acts are not purely "other-directed." While some decisions and actions may indeed benefit others, psychological egoism suggests that there is always some corresponding benefit in it for the individual engaged in the decision or act. Thus, psychological egoism eliminates the possibility of **altruism**.[19] Altruism is an unselfish behavior undertaken solely for the benefit of others. Consequently, given the logic of psychological egoism, what seem to be altruistic or other-directed acts can be *reinterpreted* in terms of one's own (unconscious) self-interest.[20]

The Reinterpretation of Motives

At least in some cases, psychological egoism seems contrary to our commonsense understanding of human behavior. What are we to make, you might ask, of cases that seem clearly to be motivated by concern for the welfare or interests of others? What are we to make of human behaviors that benefit others, yet are opposed to the actor's self-interest or well-being? What are we to make of persons who willingly risk their life, liberty, happiness, health, status, or wealth to achieve some end that benefits others but is potentially harmful to the actor in question?

Psychological egoism suggests that while such cases may appear to be selfless, they are not. Most often, we are merely furthering some interest of our own *through* benefiting others. What this means is that explanations of human behavior that appeal to altruistic motivations are mostly superficial or too simplistic. A deeper appreciation for human psychology reveals that seemingly other-directed behaviors are, at their core, self-regarding in nature. Consider the following possibilities:

- David routinely donates a substantial portion of his income to charity. He seems committed to helping those in need even when doing so is detrimental to his financial well-being. However, a more thorough analysis reveals that David is a deeply religious man whose faith teaches him that such charitable behavior will be rewarded in heaven.
- Tara works twenty hours per week as a volunteer at a chemical dependency clinic. Though she has a full-time job and two children to care for, she seems committed to helping others overcome their addictions. On a more probing level, however, Tara helps others in order to compensate for her own sense of guilt about the harm she caused to family and friends as a result of her own drug addiction at an earlier age.

BOX 5.1

The Case of Robert P. Hanssen

Understanding what motivates people to act morally or immorally is not easily accomplished. Psychological egoism draws our attention to the self-interests that underlie all of our decisions and actions, whether we are consciously aware of these wants, desires, and needs or not. One case in which the question of criminal justice ethics has been prominently featured comes from the true-life escapades of Robert Philip Hanssen. Mr. Hanssen was a loving husband and father of six; a well-respected member of his church and community; and a spy for the former Soviet Union (from 1985–1991) and Russia (from 1991–2001). Robert Philip Hanssen was also a twenty-five-year veteran of the Federal Bureau of Investigation and, during much of this time, the recipient of in excess of "one million U.S. dollars in cash and diamonds in return for leaking United States secrets to Moscow." Among the highly classified documents and information he exchanged were nuclear war plans, sophisticated intelligence and surveillance technology, and the identities of undercover operatives. In the latter instance, two U.S. spies were brutally tortured and executed by the Soviets as a result of Mr. Hanssen's disclosures. On May 10, 2002, after pleading guilty to fifteen counts of espionage and conspiracy, Robert P. Hanssen was sentenced to life in prison, without the possibility of parole.

Why would someone so seemingly accomplished and successful risk so much? Although on the surface the money and diamonds might appear to answer the question, other underlying forces were also at work. In part, a review of the emotional and physical abuse Hanssen suffered during his childhood (mostly by his father) offers some clues into this former F.B.I. agent's corrupt and self-interested behavior.

As a child and adolescent, Robert Hanssen was constantly reminded by his father (Howard) that he was "stupid" and "useless." The father subjected his son to public displays of criticism, withholding praise or affection of any sort toward the son. At the age of 6, Howard Hanssen spun his son around until he was dizzy and vomited. The father then pushed Robert's face into the vomit so that he would know the experience of defeat. On another occasion, Howard Hanssen grabbed his son's ankle pulling it in the air until Robert's hamstring was violently and agonizingly stretched beyond acceptable limits. This caused Robert to involuntarily urinate. He felt ashamed, helpless, and humiliated. According to some experts, the basis for Robert's adult conduct stemmed from these traumatizing and victimizing experiences. As one psychiatrist reported,

> "The person you are supposed to trust and identify with [the father] is doing everything from hurting you to humiliating you, and it is confusing. It creates the beginning of negative feelings about individuals who are supposed to be your protector and authority figures."

So, why did Robert Hanssen commit such devastating acts of espionage and conspiracy against the United States? The money and diamonds were only part of his motivation. Interestingly enough, another explanation dealt with the crippling fear he felt in trusting his country, the F.B.I., his work associates, and even his wife and children. Hanssen led a double life because he could not fathom the possibility that he was competent or even lovable. This was the legacy imparted to him by Howard, the father. Thus, in order not to relive his deep-seated feelings of betrayal, shame, humiliation, and disappointment, Robert Philip Hanssen risked everything: his family, his career, his country. His egoistic motivation to avoid the psychological pain he repeatedly encountered in childhood was Hanssen's underlying motivation.

Sources: Natalie Claussen-Rogers and Bruce A. Arrigo, *Police Corruption and Psychological Testing: A Strategy for Pre-Employment Screening* (Durham, NC: Carolina Academic Press, 2005); the quote is from D. A. Vise, *The Bureau and the Mole: The Unmasking of Robert Philip Hanssen, the Most Dangerous Double Agent in FBI History* (New York: Atlantic Monthly Press, 2002), p. 8.

■ Last week, Paul risked his own life when he jumped into a tumultuous river to save a drowning child. His apparent selfless act earned him considerable public attention. In fact, he is now regarded as a "hero" by many people across the country. However, a deeper inquiry into Paul's motivation indicates a profound wish to be recognized, perhaps even idolized, by others.

In each of these fictitious instances, what appears to be altruistic or other-regarding behavior can be *reinterpreted* in egoistic terms; that is, as self-serving. David desires his reward in heaven, Tara seeks atonement for past harms, and Paul craves public accolades. This strategy of **reinterpreting motives** is possible for any and all human choices and behaviors.[21] Indeed, following psychological egoism, if we look closely or deeply enough, we can always find self-serving interests underlying what seem to be altruistic behaviors.

A key proponent of this idea was utilitarian philosopher (and *ethical* egoist) Thomas Hobbes (1588–1679). Hobbes attempted to provide a general theory of human motivation whereby all individual actions could be understood in terms of egoistic motives.[22] Hobbes offered that, "of the voluntary acts of every man, the object is some good to himself."[23] Thus, for example, altruism and self-sacrificing behaviors are possible only if the actor perceives them to be in that person's best interest. However, don't people sometimes sacrifice their own well-being for the sake of the well-being of others? According to Hobbes, the answer is yes *provided* the self-sacrifice or the well-being of others is in some way in our own best interest. Hobbes employed the strategy of reinterpreting motives to show how a number of altruistic incentives could be understood as essentially self-regarding. Two such "other-focused" motives that, for Hobbes, can be reinterpreted as self-interest are *charity* and *pity*.[24]

CHARITY

Hobbes suggested that, "there can be no greater argument to a man, of his own power, than to find himself able not only to accomplish his own desires, but also to assist other men in theirs; and this is the conception wherein consisteth *charity*."[25] Charity seems to be a case of human benevolence—of kindness toward and concern for one's fellow human beings. However, rather than interpreting charity as benevolence, Hobbes argued that if we look more closely we find that it is better understood as *taking delight in demonstrating one's own power*.[26] The charitable person revels in her own superiority by showing both herself and the world that she is more capable than others. The pleasant sensation that most of us feel when giving to others comes from knowing that, "I not only have enough to take care of myself, but I have 'enough left over for others who are not so able.' "[27] Such a feeling is not one of kindness and concern, but one of power—the strength of one's own fortune, ability, status, and so forth in operation. This does not mean that we are *aware* of the deeper motive behind our selflessness. In fact, it is most likely that we will believe ourselves to be acting in a manner that is selfless, caring, kind, and giving rather than self-rewarding. However, as Hobbes explained, this is very much consistent with human psychology, especially since we typically interpret our own behavior in a way that is most flattering to ourselves.[28]

PITY

We often understand "pity" to entail some degree of sympathy or even empathy for some other person or persons experiencing misfortune. Decisions and actions motivated by pity might entail helping or assisting someone in need. In such cases, can we rightfully regard our motivation and subsequent actions to be a genuine regard for the well-being of others? Hobbes argued that we cannot and should not understand "pity" in this sense. Rather, our concern for others—the "feeling" we have for the misfortunate others—is nothing more than a *reminder* that we, too, could experience the same misfortune.[29] As Hobbes noted, "[p]ity is imagination or fiction of future calamity to ourselves, proceeding from the sense of another man's calamity."[30] In other words, what we are genuinely concerned for is our *own* well-being. Any expression of compassion merely reflects the reality that we, too, could face such circumstances in the future. Pity, then, is simply the experience of our own potential suffering through witnessing the present misfortune of others.

One logical consequence of Hobbes' position is that if I were to know that no such future calamity could come to me, I would be less moved by and less concerned for the pain and suffering of others. In fact, this reasoning seems perfectly consistent with our everyday experience. As a general rule, we tend to feel greater pity (or sympathy, empathy) for others who are *more like "us"* (see Box 5.2). If Hobbes is correct and we feel pity in proportion to the possibility that the same misfortune could befall us in the future, then we are more likely to have such feelings when adversity, trouble, or just plain bad luck strikes a person who is in some way similar to ourselves. At the same time, we would feel less pity for those individuals who are not "like us" or for persons experiencing misfortunes that are not likely to occur for us. Psychologically, compassion and empathy require *identification* with another person. To empathize, we must put ourselves "in another's shoes"—we must "imagine ourselves in the other's place." When the other person is like us in some way, we are more likely to identify with this other—the person's pain and suffering—and, consequently, are more likely to understand that the other party's misfortune could easily enough happen to us in the future[31] (see Box 5.3).

Problems with the Logic of Egoism

The difficulty for psychological egoism as an explanation for human motivation is that there is no empirical evidence that supports the existence of such "deeper" incentives. Freud, for example, theorized that much if not all human behavior is a product of underlying psychological conflicts of which the actor is unaware.[32] To illustrate, we might choose a marriage partner because that person shares qualities with our mother or father, although we are not consciously aware of those shared qualities. Moreover, criminal offenders may leave "clues" as to their identity because of a strong sense of moral guilt and a resulting unconscious desire to be punished. Surely, leaving clues is not in the best interest of the offender. What is important, however, is that the offender does not consciously or intentionally leave such evidence. The assailant's actions are theoretically motivated by latent or underlying forces of which the individual is not aware. It may be easy enough to argue that a given criminal offender unconsciously desires to be caught and punished, yet how are we to obtain evidence that this is, in fact, the case?

Psychological egoism argues that underlying self-interested motives compel us to act in such a way that our own interests are furthered and, in this regard, offers an *explanation* of motivated behavior. However, its explanation suffers from the same

BOX 5.2
On Pity, Egoism, and Criminal Justice

So how might the reinterpretation of pity in egoistic terms be relevant to criminology? Consider the following crime, law, and justice concerns. In each instance, ask yourself whether Hobbes' notion of pity explains the ethical stance in question.

- In support of the death penalty, many proponents argue something to the effect of, "you would want the offender to die too if it were your son or daughter that was murdered." In fact, as the argument is framed, advocates of capital punishment typically ask, "how would you feel if. . . ."
- Until the tragic events of 9/11, many (if not most) U.S. citizens were only marginally concerned with terrorist activities around the world. Although hundreds of innocent persons in other countries are victims of terrorism and violent militant extremism every year, we did not take notice of it until it happened to "us." In this instance, "us" did not require that we personally *knew* one or more actual victims, only that the 9/11 victims were U.S. citizens going about their daily lives in much the same way as the rest of us.
- The vast majority of the general public has little, if any, concern for the welfare of prisoners. "They" not only deserve whatever pain and deprivation to which they might be exposed, but many of "us" feel confident in our belief that such misery, anguish, and suffering will never come to us.

Although these cases do not entirely reflect what Hobbes meant by "pity," they each describe ways in which our feelings and our emotional identification with others can and do change in proportion to the degree that the person suffering a misfortune is similar to us. Moreover, they capture how our sentiments are impacted by the extent to which the misfortune in question is of a type that could potentially happen to us. Hobbes would argue that these psychological dynamics suggest that "pity" is not really experienced out of genuine concern for another human being, but out of our own self-motivated needs or desires. Do you agree or disagree?

Sources: Michael P. Arena and Bruce A. Arrigo, *Identity and Terrorism: Explaining the Terrorist Threat* (New York: NYU Press, 2006); Jeffrey I. Ross and Stephen R. Richards, *Convict Criminology* (Belmont, CA: West/Wadsworth, 2002).

sorts of criticisms as Freud's theory of human psychology. In short, it is **irrefutable.** In other words, it cannot be empirically tested and shown to be true or false.[33] To accept psychological egoism, we must agree with its premises employing merely faith and intuition for guidance.

What, then, do defenders of psychological egoism rely on to make their case? As discussed above, the strongest support for psychological egoism comes from the strategy of reinterpreting motives, which leads us to regard seemingly unselfish acts as

BOX 5.3

Identification, Pity, and Scientific Jury Selection

Research on jury decision-making suggests that jurors are more likely to favor defendants who are demographically or socially similar to themselves. This phenomenon is referred to as the **similarity-leniency hypothesis.** Jurors are more likely to favor those with whom they share characteristics, presumably because they can more easily identify with them. By this same logic, jurors will be less likely to favor defendants with whom they share few characteristics. This would be particularly true if they share more characteristics with the *victim* than with the defendant.

Given this phenomenon, attorneys might predict that jurors who are similar in one or more ways to the defendant will be more likely to favor the defense; conversely, jurors who are similar in one or more ways to the victim (or different in some ways from the defendant) would be likely to favor the prosecution. In theory, attorneys could utilize this social science knowledge to help select favorable juries during jury selection. Does this type of "scientific jury selection" have implications for fairness and justice in the legal system? Is it morally appropriate for attorneys to utilize such social science research to select favorable juries?

In Hobbes' language, we are more likely to experience "pity" when we can imagine ourselves being in similar circumstances—in this case, as either the defendant or the victim. If jurors are more or less likely to experience "pity"—or a lack of pity—toward one or the other side in a criminal or civil trial, how does this impact the struggle for a fair trial? Does this phenomenon lend greater support to the need for a "representative" jury of one's peers? In what ways might this phenomenon create *injustices*?

Source: M. Levine and L. Wallach, *Psychological Problems, Social Issues, and Law* (Boston: Allyn & Bacon, 2002).

producing some sense of self-satisfaction. When we act unselfishly, we feel good about ourselves. We feel as if we have done the "right" thing or the "moral" thing and are relieved because the sense of guilt that might otherwise accompany our failure to sufficiently consider the interests of others does not materialize. Whatever its origin, the "pleasant sensation" that follows from unselfish acts may be the underlying motivation behind the actions themselves. If this is true, then what seem to be moral acts are really nothing more than disguised forms of self-interested behavior. However, can we assume that simply because we "feel good" while engaged in doing good things for others that this feeling is the *reason* why we undertake these actions?

Perhaps the strongest attack that can be leveled against the logic of egoism is found in the simple idea that in order to feel satisfaction in something, we must first want that something in the first place.[34] If, on the one hand, we have a positive attitude toward say, helping others, we are likely to feel satisfied if and when we actually engage in this activity. If, on the other hand, we do not value helping others, we likely will not experience a pleasant sensation when engaged in this activity. We cannot say that people help others only for purposes of feeling good, as the feeling we get requires that we already attach *value* to that activity (i.e., that we previously determined that helping others was something good about which we *should* feel pleased). Under these circumstances, we could argue that our primary motivation is to help others, with the pleasant sensation simply being a consequence of achieving something that we find valuable or worthwhile. Our satisfaction comes from achieving interests or fulfilling desires that *already exist.* These interests and desires, in turn, exist only in relation to some object, goal, or experience. Consequently, it is the achievement of those goals or experiences that is the basis of the pleasant sensation.[35]

Critics of psychological egoism argue that in those cases where we "feel good" in helping other people, we derive that satisfaction only when we first desired the happiness and/or well-being of other people in the first place. A preexisting desire to help others, in turn, is a *moral* desire. Having such moral desires demonstrates that we *can* be moral people in the sense that we attach value to certain types of experiences and make determinations as to what is good, right, or just accordingly. Of course, achieving that which we identify as good, right, or just will make us feel satisfied. However, in this instance, it is the achievement, not the feeling, that is the basis of our choices and actions.

The possibility that psychological egoism is a fundamental component of human nature notwithstanding, we must at least assume that we *can* be moral. In other words, we must assume that moral considerations play an important role in the choices we make and the actions we undertake in our daily lives. The question, then, becomes *why* should we be moral and, further, what types of moral considerations are worthy of our attention? If we first attach value to certain types of goods, interests, or experiences, on what basis should we establish such attachments?

WHY BE MORAL?

The problem of self-interest is not simply a philosophical or theoretical dilemma. Self-serving behavior also has very real implications for our everyday lives. The simple reality is that people often do act out of concern for themselves, many times at the expense of the interests or welfare of others. Even if we are able to overcome the philosophical challenge posed by psychological egoism, demonstrating that people at least *can* be moral, we cannot so easily dispose of the greater challenge posed by self-interest in the context of everyday social life. In other words, just because we *can* be moral does not mean that we always *are* moral. The tension that we all feel between self-regarding actions and doing what is "right," "good," or "just" does not simply disappear if we can show that we are capable of moral behavior. Morality is not simply about having the capacity to act with integrity and virtue; it is about exercising that capacity for the right reasons.

The question then becomes, *What motivates us to exercise (or fail to exercise) that capacity?* Supposing that moral considerations other than self-interest do or should factor into our decisions and actions, we need to ask what these considerations are and/or should be. In relation to the challenge posed by self-interest, we need to ask ourselves why moral considerations should take precedence over our immediate needs, desires, and comfort. Assuming that at least some considerations should take precedence over self-interest, we then need to ask what they are and why they are important to us. These sorts of questions are often grouped under the more enduring ethical question, "Why *should* we be moral?"

The Ring of Gyges

In his *Republic*, Plato (427 B.C.E–347 B.C.E) tells the story of Gyges, a poor shepherd who lived in the service of the King of Lydia.[36] One day, a violent rainstorm and earthquake opened a hole in the ground. Coming upon this chasm, Gyges proceeded to explore it, finding a corpse wearing nothing but a gold ring. Gyges put on the ring, ascended from the hole in the ground, and continued about his normal business. Shortly thereafter, as he was sitting among several others at a monthly meeting, Gyges began playing with the ring. As he twisted the hoop of the ring toward himself, he became invisible. The others went on talking as if he had left. As he turned the hoop outward, he became visible again. Wanting to know whether the ring in fact held such power, Gyges continued to twist the ring, each time finding that he vanished as he twisted the hoop toward the inside of his hand, and visible again as he twisted it outward. The ring, it seemed, had the power to make the wearer disappear. Recognizing the opportunities the ring presented to him, Gyges began to make use of his newfound power. He immediately became one of the king's messengers. From within his new position, he proceeded to seduce the queen, plot with her to murder the king, and to take over the kingdom. By way of his power of invisibility, Gyges went from poor shepherd to powerful and wealthy ruler of Lydia.[37]

Plato's narrative of course has an underlying purpose. The fate of Gyges is one that is steeped in moral tension. The ethical question that arises from it is as follows, why should we (or Gyges) be moral when we know that we can reap tremendous benefit from acting immorally? Why *should* we do the "right" thing if we can do the "wrong" thing and get away with it? None of us will have the opportunity to become invisible, of course (at least not by wearing a ring!), but we all certainly have had and will be faced with situations in which we stand to benefit personally and/or professionally from immoral actions that can easily go undetected. In our personal lives, for example, we might have had or will have opportunities to commit adultery, to lie (or avoid telling the whole truth), or to appropriate that which does not rightfully belong to us. In our professional lives, we might have had or will have opportunities to personally benefit from bending the truth or taking "shortcuts" that allow us to bypass laws, rules, or policies. Thus, why, in any of these or similar instances, would we be motivated to avoid immoral conduct if we can remove the possibility of "getting caught?"

In the context of criminal justice, Gyges' plight might be likened to any of a number of typical scenarios. Consider, for instance, the "real-life" story of Officer John. John was a local law enforcement officer who had responded to a burglary call. Upon arriving at the scene of the burglary, he asked the victim to identify all the items that had been taken from her residence. After describing these household effects to the officer, the victim continued to tell the officer that she also had a significant amount of cash stowed away in the closet, but had not checked to see if the burglars had found and taken it. Officer John then checked the closet for the cash, found that it was still there, and proceeded to pocket the money for himself. He then told the victim that he was sorry, but unfortunately the burglars must have found and taken the cash. The victim, of course, did not question whether Officer John was being truthful. She simply assumed that, because he was an officer of the law, he was honest and looking out for *her* interests. She never even considered alternative possibilities. John, in turn, *knew* that he could get away with his unethical actions, and so proceeded to benefit himself at her expense. After all, why shouldn't he?

The one thing that both the story of Gyges and that of the corrupt officer seem to have in common is that the *fear of being caught and punished was removed*. Gyges was invisible and, consequently, could do and get away with anything he chose. The officer, by virtue of his status, power, and position, would likely never be suspected of wrongdoing, enabling him to capitalize on various opportunities for self-gain much like the case of the woman whose home had been burglarized. Thus, in some meaningful way, the officer was "invisible" as well.

The ethical concern embedded in these stories, however, is not one that requires us to have the opportunity to vanish or even to be granted opportunities for personal gain by virtue of our status, power, and/or position. Rather, for our purposes, the issue is what motivates us to be moral and, more specifically, how is motivation linked to the fear of punishment. In other words, why should we be moral when the motivation to be good that comes from the fear of punishment is removed? Is fear of punishment the only reason we behave morally? If so, does doing the "right" thing out of fear make us genuinely moral people?

In the story of Gyges, Plato implies a human nature that is motivated by self-interest. We do the right thing, Plato assumes, only because if we do the wrong thing we will be caught and punished. If, like Gyges, we could do whatever we wanted—knowing we would never be caught—we would all act out of self-interest, with little or no concern for the welfare of others. It might be helpful to reflect upon what *you* would do differently if you had the opportunity to be "invisible" (i.e., had greater power, influence, position than you presently do). When this question is posed, most people note at least several "small" immoralities they would consider. Perhaps we would not plot to have someone killed; perhaps we would not steal; perhaps we would not engage in infidelities. However, for many of us, the opportunity to advance our own interests, needs, or desires would be too great and too difficult to resist entirely. Regrettable though it may be, the reality is that if we remove the possibility of being caught and punished for our actions, at least some of our behaviors would be qualitatively different—not to mention less "moral." Thus, it seems that at least some of our motivation to be moral stems from the fear of punishment.

But does doing the "right" thing because we fear being caught and punished make us "moral" people? The short answer is, "no." We cannot make any claims to genuine morality if the only thing motivating us to be "good" is the fear of being caught and punished (whatever that may entail). This is not necessarily to imply that fear has no place in morality. It is simply to suggest that *fear is not sufficient for morality*. In the context of moral psychology, genuine morality is better regarded as stemming from motivations above and beyond something as inconsistent as fear. We know as a matter of fact that immoral behavior often—if not most of the time—goes undetected or, at least, unpunished. Consequently, fear of punishment is not only ineffective as a motivation for morality, but for other reasons is also undesirable as the sole source of motivation.

An important implication of this reasoning is that, while many of us *believe* ourselves to be moral because we avoid unethical or vice-ridden behavior in most areas of our lives, our belief may be misguided. Simply avoiding wrongdoing does not make us moral—particularly if our motivation for that avoidance is one of fear. In the next section, several sources of fear and punishment are more closely considered. These sources also represent some of the most common answers to the question, "Why be moral?" Importantly, each of these explanations still entails the possibility of suffering negative consequences (or being rewarded) in some fashion. Consequently, each account is, by itself, insufficient for genuine morality.

Sources of Fear and Sanction

Like Plato, many philosophers throughout history have maintained a very bleak and pessimistic view of human nature. It has often been assumed that we are driven to act immorally and selfishly *unless* there are restraints in place that motivate or compel us to behave morally. Many of these philosophers have argued that the only thing keeping us from acting immorally is the possibility of sanction. Sanctions keep our egoistic tendencies "in check" and motivate us to balance our own interests against those of others. British utilitarian philosopher Jeremy Bentham (1748–1832), for example, proposed that human conduct is governed primarily by four negative forces: (1) physical sensations of pain; (2) political or legal forces; (3) moral forces such as disapproval from family, friends, community; and (4) religious sanctions or condemnations from God.[38] What Bentham suggested, in effect, is that our behavior is largely a product of fear; that is, fear stemming from the pain, deprivation, and reprisal we would otherwise confront unless we acted morally. If no such sanctions were in place, our everyday lives would likely consist of the unrestrained pursuit of (our own) pleasure.

In this respect, then, sanctions (i.e., fear of punishment) are necessary for keeping our selfish motivations in check. A basic premise underlying this idea is that if we knew or were relatively certain that we could get away with immoral behavior, we would. Following Bentham, human beings cannot be trusted to behave virtuously without proper incentive to do so. These incentives, in turn, rest on the fear of being punished in some fashion. Many would argue, however, that genuine morality must consist of something other than—or at least in addition to—fear of sanctions or consequences. While sanctions can and often do function as *effective* motivators, leading people to recognize and respond to the possibility of negative consequences rationally, this is not necessarily the same as being a moral person. Before discussing this point more fully, it may be helpful to consider several common forms of potential sanctions that are often offered as motivations for moral behavior.

EXTERNAL SANCTIONS: FROM THE LAW AND GOD

The legal system was constructed as a source of formal social control. Its intent is to ensure behavioral conformity and social order by threatening citizens with various forms of sanction. We are taught very early in our lives that if we violate the law, we may be caught and subjected to unwanted consequences. Again, however, we must recognize that violations of the law *usually* go unpunished. Most of us *do* violate the law on a regular basis. Why, for example, do we regularly exceed the speed limit when driving on the interstate? Most people, perhaps, would note that: (1) they *want* to drive faster than the law allows; and (2) that either the *chances* of being caught are not high enough, or the *consequences* of being caught are not significant enough, to be of concern. In other words, we are not *afraid* to exceed the speed limit because we feel fairly certain that, most of the time, we can get away with it or that our suffering will be minimal.

Violating the speed limit exemplifies the fact that many of us are not deterred by the threat of legal punishment in many situations. Yet there are many more serious infractions of the law that routinely go unsanctioned as well. Some might argue that this is a function of the effectiveness of the criminal justice system. Perhaps if we made punishments more certain or even more severe, we would see a marked decrease in immoral behavior. A one thousand dollar fine for speeding as opposed to one hundred dollars might incline fewer people to violate the speed limit. The problem is that this brings us no closer to genuine morality. Our reason or motivation for not speeding, not stealing, and not lying must be something other than or at least in addition to simply attempting to avoid negative consequences. While institutions of formal social control such as the legal system may play an important role in controlling immoral behavior once it comes into existence, the "system" does little in the way of providing us with good reasons for not engaging in these behaviors at the outset. In other words, increasing *fear* may increase conformity, but it does not serve to develop our moral sensibilities. If speeding fines were increased enough to frighten us into conformity, we would not be abiding by the speed limit because we felt it was the "right" thing to do. Rather, we would conform because we feared the consequences of failing to obey the law. Indeed, most of us would still *want* to drive faster than the law allows.

Though we rarely think of the speed at which we choose to drive our automobiles as a moral concern, this same sort of reasoning can be applied to other issues that are clearly ethical in nature. Perhaps we have had the opportunity to take something that does not belong to us, to "cheat" on a spouse or lover, to break a promise to a friend, or to lie for personal gain. Perhaps in such cases we knew we *could* get away with such a wrongdoing, yet chose not to do so. Why? Most likely, we were motivated by something other than the simple fear of being caught. What this suggests is that morality is not as simple as following rules whose violations carry negative consequences. Moreover, most of us would probably agree that we would not *want* to live in such a world. For example, would we feel comfortable with a spouse or lover who was faithful only because she or he was afraid of being caught? Additionally, would we want to share a residence with a roommate who did not engage in stealing our belongings simply because the roommate feared the possibility of detection?

The same logic applies, although in slightly modified form, to sanctions issued by God or other higher powers. Within moral philosophy, religion has been employed as both *justification* for moral values and principles and as a *source of motivation* for moral behavior.[39] When used as a justification for moral principles, it is generally argued that God or some other higher being represents the basis for moral knowledge and, consequently, knowledge of such a being is necessary for knowledge of right and wrong.[40] The idea of religion as a source of moral values and principles will be taken up at the beginning of the next chapter. For now, however, what is important is that even if we believe that religion is necessary or beneficial for knowing about right and wrong, to suggest that it also represents a motivation for moral behavior is a different matter. When used in this latter context, it is usually argued that religion provides a *reason* for behaving morally and avoiding immorality. The reason most often employed is that those of us who behave morally will be rewarded, while the immoral among us will be punished. God rewards the good and punishes the evil—in this world or any other. The religiously inspired answer to the question, "Why be moral?" relies on the promise of divine reward and the avoidance of divine punishment.

Similar to the case of the law as a motivator for moral behavior, the idea of divine punishment as incentive forces us to confront the possibility that we behave morally simply because we fear the consequences of not doing so. Even if we know we can get away with wrongdoings in the face of human authorities, we might feel that we can never get away with them in the eyes of God. The only difference between this sort of reasoning and what was presented in relation to the law is that the chances of being caught increase, as does the severity of punishment. The suggestion here is not that religious motivations should assume no role in our beliefs, choices, or behaviors; rather, the suggestion is that we cannot and should not regard these incentives as the (sole) basis of or sufficient motivation for genuine morality.

INTERNAL SANCTIONS: CONSCIENCE AND GUILT

Punishment for immoral behavior need not come from only external sources such as the legal system or God. An equally important type of sanction emerges from our own conscience when our choices and behaviors contradict moral values and principles.[41] **Conscience** typically refers to our awareness that certain actions are morally right or wrong. To "have a conscience" implies that we are aware that the actions we undertake or those that we intend to undertake have a *moral quality*.[42] Such an awareness may include several interrelated components: (1) a self-examination of the morality of our desires, actions, etc.; (2) a set of internally felt standards by which we judge ourselves; and (3) a tendency to experience guilt or to suffer from a "bad conscience" when we examine the morality of our actions and judge them to be wrong by our internal moral standards.[43] Each of these components need not operate purely on a conscious level. In other words, our moral standards, our self-examinations, and our self-punishment through guilt can be largely unconscious or unreflective processes. We simply may have a "bad feeling" about something we have done. If our conscience functions as it should, it is simply part of who we are—not something we have to "use."

The phenomenon of the conscience is not well understood. It has been described in various ways and attributed to various sources.[44] In the Christian tradition, the notion of conscience has been understood as the "voice of God" within us.[45] Within the psychoanalytic (Freudian) tradition of psychology, conscience is understood as the voice of our parents and, to some extent, society, teachers, friends, and other important influences as well.[46] Through socialization, it is argued, we come to internalize certain values and standards of conduct through which we judge our own actions and desires. The construct termed "conscience" is most often referred to in the psychoanalytic tradition as the **superego.** Most importantly for our purposes, the existence of a conscience or superego creates a basis for feelings of **guilt**—the anxiety or discomfort felt when we deviate from those internalized values and standards of conduct.[47] Usually when we speak of "guilt," we are referring to legal guilt or responsibility for criminal wrongdoing that is judged by others as reprehensible and deserving of punishment. Far more often, however, guilt is something personal that results from a psychological process rather than something formal that results from a legal process.

In this way, guilt differs from religious or legal punishment in that it is a *self-imposed punishment* or sanction. *Moral* guilt is the experience of anxiety or emotional discomfort. It is what we ought to feel following behavior we should not have committed, or it is the emotional result of having neglected to do something that we should have completed. Guilt, then, can be understood as *emotional self-punishment.*[48] The distinguishing characteristic of guilt in relation to other forms of sanction is its tendency to continue *even after* other forms of sanction disappear. We may, for example, be punished by the law for some criminal behavior. Yet once we have "done our time," the legal sanctions are removed. Guilt, on the other hand, can be a continual self-punishment that extends far beyond any formal punishment. In this sense, it may be the strongest of all sanctions. In another sense, it may be the weakest and *least reliable* of the sanctions.

The effectiveness of guilt as motivation for moral behavior is jeopardized in several ways. On the one hand, guilt is a discomfort felt when we *believe* we have harmed someone or violated some moral standard. The necessity of this pre-existing belief gives guilt a cognitive dimension. For guilt to be an effective motivator, we must first believe we have committed, in some fashion, a wrong. Absent this belief (or following an attempt to *rationalize* our conduct), guilt fails to function as a sanction (see Box 5.4). Guilt or conscience presumes, then, that we have developed moral sensibilities—that we have some existing commitment to certain moral values and principles, the violation of which will result in some form of emotional self-punishment.

However, consider the case of the psychopath who experiences little, if any, guilt or remorse. If we do not *feel* or *experience* guilt or remorse, how is it to serve as a motivating factor in our choices and actions? Moreover, even if we believe we have committed some moral wrong and our conscience "kicks in," a second problem with conscience and guilt is that they do not seem to have the strength that we may sometimes presume. Most of us have at some point in our lives done something or some things for which we harbor no pride. Perhaps we hurt a close friend, either intentionally or through neglect. Perhaps we even "felt bad" or guilty about our actions. Nevertheless, we *learned to live with it.* More than likely, our guilt was short-lived and we were soon able to resume our normal lives without the burden of feeling at fault. The simple fact about guilt is that we "get over it."[49]

For several reasons, then, guilt and conscience seem to have limited power in our everyday moral lives. Some people simply do not feel guilt as a consequence of their personality structure; others rationalize individual instances of immoral behavior to avoid feeling guilt in that situation; and still others feel some sense of *temporary* guilt, but soon get over it. Our wrongful actions either do not bother us, or we learn to live with them. Because guilt and conscience are *internal,* we can confront and deal with them internally as well (see Box 5.5). Consequently, while conscience may play a role—and perhaps an important one—in morality, it is not sufficient in itself as a motivation for ethical conduct.

Reward and Punishment

What each of the above discussions—guilt, God, and the law—have in common is the idea that we are or at least can be motivated to be moral by either expectation of reward or, more commonly, fear of punishment or other negative consequences. Consequences—both positive and negative—can, in some cases, be *useful.* Yet the

BOX 5.4

Rationalizing Police Deviance

In their theory of delinquent behavior, Sykes and Matza proposed that lawbreakers are able to protect themselves from feelings of guilt and negative self-image by rationalizing or justifying their conduct. What they referred to as "techniques of neutralization" are of five basic types: denial of responsibility, denial of injury, denial of victim, condemnation of condemners, and appeal to higher loyalties. As Kappeler et al. suggest, these methods of rationalization or justification may also be useful in helping us understand forms of police deviance:

- *Denial of responsibility* ("they made me do it"). The injury caused (or that could have been caused) by an officer's actions was due to forces beyond her or his control. In the context of police work, *violence* may be regarded as an appropriate and necessary reaction to defiant citizens/suspects. Where force or excessive force is used, the officer's belief that she or he was provoked by the citizen may allow the officer to rationalize her or his behavior. Doing so shifts responsibility for the use of force away from the officer and onto the citizen.

- *Denial of injury* ("no innocent got hurt"). Wrongfulness depends upon whether anyone—or anyone innocent—was hurt by the action. Stealing from suspects (e.g., drugs, money) for personal gain, violating constitutional rights of suspects to make an arrest or secure a conviction, and abusing authority to maintain order are each excusable as no real injury was caused.

- *Denial of victim* ("they deserved it"). The injury or harm caused was not wrong given the circumstances under which they occurred. In many cases, this involves rationalizing the harm as a form of punishment or as justice. The use of force, for instance, can be rationalized as justifiable punishment in certain situations or with respect to certain types of people. Those who run from police, use illegal drugs, or defy authority are "threats"—predetermined as dangerous by virtue of who they are and in need of "punishment."

- *Condemnation of condemners* ("they don't know anything"). Attention is shifted away from the wrongdoing and the wrongdoer and toward those who disapprove of the action(s): the exclusionary rule is simply a "loophole" for criminals which makes police work more difficult; judges are "soft on crime"; citizens who bring lawsuits or complaints against officers are "hostile" or resentful toward the police; those who would pass judgment on the behavior of officers do not understand the realities of the job. In each case, the problem lies not with the officer's motives or behaviors, but with the rules, motives, perception of those who would control and judge them.

- *Appeal to higher loyalties* ("protect your own"). The most powerful of techniques of neutralization, appeal to higher loyalties involves perceiving certain (informal) norms as more important or as involving a higher loyalty than abidance by formal laws, rules, or norms. Larger societal norms or the formal norms of the organization can and should be sacrificed in the interest of abiding by norms of the smaller group to which the officer belongs (i.e., those of police subculture). The informal norm of secrecy and loyalty to other officers overrides the formal norm of not lying, giving rise to perjury or false testimony. Protecting another officer—even when this involves unethical and/or illegal conduct—is expected and regarded as noble as it demonstrates loyalty and solidarity.

Source: Victor Kappeler, Richard Sluder, and Geoffrey Alpert, *Forces of Deviance: Understanding the Dark Side of Policing,* 2nd ed. (Prospect Heights, IL: Waveland Press, 1998), pp. 113–125. Gresham Sykes and David Matza, "Techniques of Neutralization: A Theory of Delinquency," *American Sociological Review,* 22, (1957).

BOX 5.5

Rationalization and Cheating Among College Students

As we saw in Box 5.4, oftentimes we can avoid the feeling of guilt if we - *rationalize* or in some way justify our behaviors to ourselves. Another example might be the various justifications that college students sometimes use to excuse cheating or plagiarism. Research indicates that as many as two-thirds of college students have cheated on a major exam/assignment at some point in their college career. While rationalizing our immoral conduct may not allow us to escape punishment from authorities (e.g., professors, university officials), it often protects us from self-punishment. Consider how the following types of thinking allow students to avoid the feeling of guilt that would otherwise be attached to academic dishonesty.

- "Here at the University of _____, you must cheat to stay alive. There's so much work and the quality of materials from which to learn, books, professors, is so bad that there's no other choice."
- "Everyone has test files in fraternities . . . If you don't [cheat], you're at a great disadvantage."
- "If our leaders can commit heinous acts and then lie before Senate committees about their total ignorance and innocence, *then why can't I cheat at least a little?*"

In each of these cases, students are justifying their behavior. In other words, they are identifying what they believe to be reasons that defensibly excuse their immoral conduct. Rationalization prevents the psychological mechanism of guilt from working as it should. If we can convince ourselves that we were justified in behaving immorally, we will not "feel bad" about acting immorally.

Source: Donald McCabe, "The Influence of Situational Ethics on Cheating Among College Students," *Sociological Inquiry*, 62, 365–374 (1992).

utility of consequences is limited to instances where there is a *need to compensate* for a lack of morality. To illustrate, consider the situation of young children. Most parenting practices rely on the imposition of punishment or the granting of rewards for right and wrong actions. However, parents rely on reward and punishment only because they know (or, at least, believe) that children have yet to develop morally (see Chapter 7 on Moral Development for more details). Because children have yet to acquire a sufficient understanding of right and wrong—other than having linked certain behaviors to rewards and others to punishments—these sorts of incentives become necessary to some extent. However, as this chapter has indicated, expectations of reward and/or fear of negative consequences are insufficient for genuine morality. Even well-behaved children are not regarded as genuinely moral people.[50] Thus, what is it, we might ask, that makes adults different from children in this sense?

This topic will receive more attention in Chapter 7. For now, though, we need to recognize that whether alone or in conjunction with one another, God, guilt, and the law suffer from several problems that make them insufficient and/or undesirable motivators for instilling morality or ethical conduct in people. Instead, the fear of punishment that arises from the law, the expectation of reward or the fear of punishment from God, and the fear of emotional self-punishment stemming from guilt, are not always *effective* motivators. The administration of sanctions, too, is not necessarily a *desirable* incentive for promoting morality (consider the case of disciplining children). Thus, to revisit a question posed earlier, would you be comfortable with a spouse who was faithful only because she or he was afraid of legal, divine, or emotional punishment? Most likely, you would hope your partner remained faithful for reasons other than these. What are these other reasons for moral conduct? Several possibilities are explored in the next chapter. For now, what we need to keep in mind is that being a good person or doing the right thing requires something more than or something in addition to reward and punishment. Several reasons for this are worth considering.

REWARD AND PUNISHMENT ARE SELF-INTEREST

We have already discussed that, for most moral philosophers and the general public alike, morality does not consist simply of doing what is in one's own best interest. Although concern for one's self is inevitable to some degree, this does not make self-interest identical to morality. In fact, self-serving conduct may very well be opposed to morality in many instances. Yet if our most frequent response to the question, "Why be moral?," principally focuses on the possibility of suffering negative consequences, then we are indirectly citing self-interest as a reason for morality. In each case of punishment-as-motivation, our answer *still relies on self-interest*. If our motivation stems from a desire to avoid criminal sanction, to secure divine reward or to avoid divine punishment, or simply because we fear the inner-workings of our mind (i.e., conscience and guilt), we are still acting to further our self-interest. Although our specific actions might appear to be motivated by a concern for others, we would instead be placing the interests of other people as equal to or below ourselves in order to secure a better existence for ourselves, either through freedom in this life or happiness in the next. In short, the seeking of reward and the avoidance of punishment—in any form—remain self-interested pursuits.

THE NEED FOR REWARD/PUNISHMENT REFLECTS AN ABSENCE OF MORALITY

Prussian philosopher Immanuel Kant (1724–1804) argued that neither reward nor punishment should ever be regarded as incentives to action. That is, we should not do good deeds because of the expectation of some reward; and we should not avoid evil deeds because of the expectation of punishment. Kant makes a provocative argument that motivations involving reward and punishment in fact demonstrate a *lack of morality*.[51] If, for example, we refrain from being unfaithful to our spouse because we fear being caught, we have failed to recognize either the wrongfulness inherent in the act of unfaithfulness, or the harm we might cause others (especially our marriage partner and family) as a result of our actions. Arguably, concern for the wrongfulness of our actions and for the welfare of others is considerably more important than that for consequences that may come to ourselves. As Kant suggested, if we *rely* on reward and/or punishment to motivate us to be good or to do the right thing, this may reflect an absence of genuine morality. If we are honest only because we fear the consequences of not being so, we cannot say that we embody honesty in the first place. One who embodies the virtue of honesty will be so inclined even in the absence of rewards, punishments, and other nonmoral incentives.

As was discussed in Chapter 1, morality is not merely a matter of doing the right thing, but also of having the right reasons for doing those things. And while right reasons have been the subject of much debate within moral philosophy (we will look at some in the next chapter), all but a few moral philosophers would agree that reward and punishment are insufficient and, perhaps, irrelevant to this debate. The point is that while many of us may believe that we are moral because we refrain from acting immorally, Kant reminds us that the *absence of immorality does not equal morality.*[52] It may be unsettling to consider that, simply because we have abided by the law, been faithful to our lovers, and displayed honesty, trustworthiness, responsibility, and so on throughout the majority of our lives, we are not necessarily "moral" people. In short, being good is as much—if not more—about character, intention, values, virtues, and principles as it is about the "rightness" of our actions.

REWARD AND PUNISHMENT
ARE IMPEDIMENTS TO MORALITY

Might it be that rewards and punishments are not only insufficient for morality, but also serve to *prevent* the development and sustenance of morality? As Kant suggests, "a man [sic] who is rewarded for good conduct will repeat that conduct *because it is rewarded.*"[53] Similarly, "one who is punished for evil conduct *will hate not the conduct, but the punishment.*"[54] Rewards and punishments do tend to shape our decisions and actions, but their ultimate purpose is simply to encourage us to repeat the good and refrain from the bad. In other words, reward and punishment are not intended to encourage us to reflect on the morality of those decisions and actions. This principle is commonly applied in the approach to psychotherapy known as *behaviorism.* The behavioral model of therapy suggests that we can encourage people to refrain from doing unhealthy things by putting rewards and sanctions in place to mold behavior.[55] For instance, a person with a handwashing compulsion can receive an electric shock every time she or he turns on the faucet. While this method may be effective in curbing the person's compulsive behavior, it does nothing to treat the psychological dynamics that cause the compulsion in the first place. If our goal is simply to shape behavior, these techniques can be successful. If, however, our goal is to modify the unhealthy thoughts and feelings underlying the behavior, we must assume a very different approach.

The same can be said about reward and punishment in the context of morality. If our goal is simply to encourage certain forms of conduct and to discourage other forms of conduct, sanctions of various sorts can be effective. On the other hand, if our goal is to encourage the development of thoughts and feelings conducive to morality, reward and punishment will be of little value. Again, we should keep in mind that morality consists not only of "doing" the right thing, but also of understanding *why* it is right or, alternatively, why it is wrong. Instilling fear of consequences through the imposition of punishment is, as Kant noted, teaching a person to hate the consequences rather than the act itself. Rather than being or becoming moral people, we simply live in fear of being immoral *because of* the consequences we will suffer.

For this reason, Kant argued that "it is wrong for religion to preach that men [sic] should avoid doing evil in order to escape eternal punishment," because people will fear the punishment rather than recognize and accept the wrongfulness of the deed itself.[56] We could say the same about law, parenting, the system of education, health, criminal justice, and so forth. As indicated above, in young children at least, fear may be the *only* motivating factor that can be an effective deterrent to immoral or wrongful behavior. Many would argue, however, that genuine morality requires us to develop an appreciation for the wrongfulness of our actions rather than (or in addition to) the undesirability of negative consequences (see Box 5.6).

BOX 5.6
Desistance from Crime and Offender Rehabilitation

In Chapter 9, we will look more closely at the moral problem of criminal punishment and the purported goals of punishing offenders. For now, let's consider how the logic of reward and punishment might be applied in the context of desistance from crime and offender rehabilitation. It is often claimed that deterrence is an effective crime reduction strategy. Yet a person who is successfully deterred from committing criminal offenses is not likely to refrain from such behavior because she or he genuinely understands that these actions are wrong. Instead, the individual simply fears the consequences attached to the ongoing commission of these criminal acts. These consequences or penalties are likely to include additional if not increasing amounts of prison time, resulting in devastating outcomes for the individual's personal and professional life.

Offender recovery and reform, on the other hand, depend on meaningful forms of rehabilitation that teach ex-offenders to reconstruct various facets of their lives. This includes such things as their relationships, their outlook toward work, their commitment to change, their response to authority figures, etc. In short, the key is to identify the barriers that stand in the way of recovery (whether self-imposed or imposed by society), to work through them, and then to learn from these impediments. In contrast with deterred offenders, reformed or rehabilitated offenders come to appreciate the wrongfulness of their past criminal actions when experiencing a change in character and, thus, motivation. In other words, "making good" entails a form of "moral development," if you will (more on this in Chapter 7). In this context, rewards and/or punishments are simply inadequate when it comes to rebuilding one's life and doing things for the right reason. In fact, the problem with a system of rewards and punishments is that, in some ways, it can function to prevent or inhibit precisely the sort of moral character necessary to desist from crime, and to experience personal insight.

Sources: David Garland, *Punishment and Modern Society* (Chicago: University of Chicago Press, 1990); Elliott Currie, *Confronting Crime: An American Challenge* (New York: Pantheon, 1985); for an interesting study of crime desistance, see Shadd Maruna, *Making Good: How Ex-Convicts Reform and Rebuild Their Lives* (Washington, DC: American Psychological Association, 2002).

EGOISM AND THE CRIMINAL JUSTICE SYSTEM: CORRUPTION IN POLICING AND CORRECTIONS

As we have seen, egoism amounts to moral sensibilities that, either consciously or unconsciously, revolve around self-interest. Egoism is evident wherever persons or groups are motivated primarily or exclusively by personal advantage or a desire for selfish gain over and above other moral concerns. Similarly, egoism is evident in criminal justice wherever practitioners place personal gain above morality and legality, acting so as to further self-interest at the expense of ethical considerations. As we saw in Chapter 1, formal codes of criminal justice ethics, such as those that apply to police, court, and correctional professionals, explicitly prohibit decisions and actions that are motivated by personal gain. These formal prohibitions notwithstanding, instances of egoistic behavior in all fields of criminal justice are not uncommon. In fact, many forms of unethical conduct in criminal justice ultimately stem from egoistic motivations. Although there are other forms of professional deviance that are egoistically motivated, in this section we highlight several examples of *corruption* in both police and correctional contexts that illustrate the ways in which egoism can and sometimes does interfere with ethical responsibilities of criminal justice practitioners.

Police Corruption

Michael Johnston defines **police corruption** as actions that "exploit the powers of law enforcement in return for considerations of private-regarding benefit and that violate formal standards governing his or her conduct."[57] Corrupt acts, John Kleinig writes elsewhere, occur wherever officers "act with the primary intention of furthering private or departmental/divisional advantage."[58] What makes corrupt acts egoistic is that their underlying motivation is personal gain. By virtue of their authority, discretion, and the nature of their everyday work, police officers are routinely placed in situations where personal advantage can easily be furthered through unethical and even illegal means. As one might imagine, examples of acts motivated by personal gain are numerous. In his *Police Ethics: Crisis in Law Enforcement*, for instance, Tom Barker offers the following typology of police corruption:[59]

- *Corruption of Authority.* Accepting unearned rewards for doing one's regular duties, including free meals, liquor, sex, discounts of various sorts from businesses, payments from businesses to more closely monitor premises.
- *Kickbacks.* Receiving goods or services for referring business to attorneys or bondmen.
- *Opportunistic Theft.* Stealing money or property from suspects or victims, goods not taken by a burglar, evidence that has been confiscated (e.g., drugs or money from drug busts).
- *Shakedowns.* Accepting money or other forms of payment for not making an arrest.
- *Protection of Illegal Activities.* Accepting money from vice operators or companies operating illegally.

- *Fixes.* Accepting money or other rewards/favors for overlooking traffic violations, quashing prosecution proceedings by, for instance, tampering with evidence or committing perjury.
- *Direct Criminal Activities.* Engaging directly in various forms of criminal activity, such as selling drugs, robbing stores, or burglarizing homes or businesses.
- *Internal Payoffs.* Buying or selling employment-related benefits, such as off days, holidays, work assignment, evidence, or promotions.

Each of the above-listed activities is an unethical, and in many cases illegal, means of furthering one's own advantage. They illustrate some of the ways in which police authority and discretion can be used improperly and egoistically to advance personal gain.

Various attempts have been made to *explain* the persistence of police corruption. One popular set of explanations focuses on *predispositions* or characteristics of individual officers. The so-called **rotten-apple explanation** was widely accepted prior to the 1960s. It implies that the cause of corruption is to be found in the questionable moral character of a few individuals who, by virtue of their psychological makeup, were predisposed to engage in corrupt practices even before they joined the police force. More recent research on the "police personality" suggests that persons with certain personality traits such as *authoritarianism* that are linked to unethical conduct are more likely to be drawn to law enforcement. Corruption is thus the result of traits and values that a significant percentage of officers bring with them to the job or, in some cases, develop over the course of socialization and on-the-job experience.[60]

In effect, suggesting that corrupt practices are limited to a small number of "bad apples" or are otherwise the result of predispositions of individual officers diverts attention from departmental, institutional, and systemic factors. Explanations that involve the latter focus less on individual (psychological) characteristics of officers, and more on sociological variables. Implicated in departmental, institutional, and systemic explanations are factors such as ineffective anticorruption protocols, the wide discretion enjoyed by police officers, the difficulties of supervising officers, the lack of public visibility keeping officers "in check," and norms of secrecy and loyalty that pervade law enforcement.

Whatever its causes, corruption potentially brings a number of negative consequences for individual officers, departments, and the greater community. For instance, area residents may experience increased crime/victimization, offenders who cannot or do not pay may receive relatively harsher treatment, inner-city and other high-vice neighborhoods may experience stronger organized crime presence and increased deterioration, and the general public may lose trust and confidence in the police.[61] In light of these and other troubling effects of police corruption, a number of suggestions have been proposed as to how best to *combat* police corruption. Some have suggested that departments do more to detect corruption and increase accountability.[62] Others have suggested that reducing corruption begins with the recruitment, hiring, and training of ethical officers. Hiring officers with higher levels of moral character and placing greater emphasis on ethics in education and training will, in principle, reduce the likelihood that new officers will become involved in corrupt activities. Police training, as Alpert and Dunham suggest, "must help officers to *think* as well as to react and respond."[63] Officers "must not only be trained, they must be educated. . . . training must teach critical thinking and problem-solving techniques."[64] It is in part because of this need that more and more colleges and universities are requiring students to take ethics courses as one dimension of their criminal justice curriculum.

Prison Corruption

Prison corruption has been, in Bernard McCarthy's words, "a persistent and pervasive feature of corrections."[65] While patterns of corruption in prisons are in many respects similar to those in policing, there is at least one notable difference. Prisons are secluded, protected environments—existing and operating largely outside of the public's view. Because of this, corruption in prisons is often unpublicized, and small-scale unethical practices are often not even reported. Other than the relatively few instances where prison corruption erupts into a publicized scandal, very little is known about it. Although corruption exists at higher levels of prison operations (e.g., administration), in this subsection we focus on forms of and motivations for *staff corruption.*

Corruption in prisons exists in a variety of forms, from relatively minor instances of theft, to large-scale, organized drug-trafficking and counterfeit rings. What each has in common, however, is underlying egoistic motivation—whatever its form, corruption is fueled by the desire for personal gain and the willingness and opportunity to neglect moral and legal obligations in its favor. Through his examination of official records of an internal affairs unit, Bernard McCarthy identified several general categories of corrupt conduct in prisons:[66]

- *Theft.* Stealing valuables and other personal items from inmates during frisks and cell searches; stealing items from visitors during processing; and stealing items from other staff members.
- *Trafficking.* Conspiring with inmates and civilians to smuggle contraband into prisons in exchange for money, drugs, or other services. Common forms of contraband include much demanded and highly marketable items such as drugs, alcohol, and weapons. In some cases, guards act on their own, while others are of a much larger scale, involving street gangs and organized crime officials.
- *Embezzlement.* Appropriating goods belonging to the State for one's own use. Unlike petty acts of theft, embezzlement involves "employees, sometimes with the help of inmates, systematically stealing money or materials from state accounts (inmate canteens or employee credit unions) and from warehouses."
- *Misuse of authority.* Intentionally misusing one's discretion for personal gain. Misuse of authority involves three basic offenses: (1) "the acceptance of gratuities from inmates for special consideration in obtaining legitimate prison privileges (e.g., payoffs to receive choice cells or job assignments)," (2) "the acceptance of gratuities for special consideration in obtaining or protecting illicit prison activities (e.g., allowing illegal drugs sales or gambling)," and (3) "the mistreatment or extortion of inmates by staff for personal material gain (e.g., threatening to punish or otherwise harm an inmate if a payment is not forthcoming)."[67]

Corrupt acts in prisons can be further classified according to the traditional typology of misfeasance, malfeasance, and nonfeasance (a typology that is also sometimes used to categorize forms of police misconduct). Each involves the misuse of discretionary powers:

- **Misfeasance** is the "improper performance of some act that an official may lawfully do." Included herein are practices such as the accepting of gratuities in exchange for special privileges, selectively offering formal rewards and punishments for a fee, and the misuse of state resources for personal gain. The handing out of privileges (e.g., assignment to desirable cell block), rewards and punishment, and use of state resources are lawful acts falling within the authority of prison employees. Misfeasance occurs where this lawful authority is used in an unethical fashion for furtherance of self-interest.
- Whereas misfeasance involves the "improper use of legitimate power or authority," **malfeasance** is "direct misconduct or wrongful conduct by a public official or employee." Malfeasance includes such corrupt acts as theft, embezzlement, trafficking in contraband, extortion, assisting escapes, and conspiring with inmates in forgery, drug, or counterfeiting rings.
- In contrast to both mis- and malfeasance, nonfeasance does not involve the commission of unethical or unlawful acts. Instead, **nonfeasance** is the "failure to act according to one's responsibilities, or the omission of an act that an official ought to perform." Nonfeasance may include not reporting inmate violations (e.g., allowing inmates to have sex with visitors, looking the other way when drugs are smuggled into the prison), and may also include not reporting violations of other employees.

Efforts to explain correctional corruption have focused on both individual and institutional factors. Similar to individualistic explanations of police corruption, attention is sometimes drawn to characteristics and quality of prison personnel. Because correctional institutions typically offer low pay and provide poor working conditions, they often have difficulties hiring and retaining qualified, well-trained, and educated personnel. Less than half of the states in the United States, for instance, require even a high school diploma for correctional officer work. Coupled with authority, discretion, and a low-visibility environment, opportunities for and chances of corrupt behavior arguably increase. In this light, some have suggested that strategies such as increasing pay, improving working conditions, utilizing psychological testing or screening techniques at the hiring stage, and better emphasizing moral duties and ethical responsibilities may help to reduce corruption.[68]

On the other hand, structural and organizational characteristics of prisons must also be taken into consideration. The prison environment and the day-to-day realities of the prison experience, for instance, may provide incentives for corrupt behavior. As Cloward and others have noted, maintaining order and control in prisons may be perceived as *requiring* some level of corruption. In order to successfully maintain order and control—their primary objective—line staff may recognize that "coercive power must be supplemented with informal exchange relations with inmates."[69] In other words, correctional officers come to adopt a "you scratch my back and I'll scratch yours" attitude, tolerating violations of minor rules when doing so can assist in the performance of their job.

SUMMARY

When the question is posed, "Can we be moral?," for many of us the answer is clear. Morality is something that exists and it is something that we all embody; although, perhaps, to varying degrees. However, the purpose of this chapter was to challenge this notion. Both psychological egoism and the limits of rewards/punishments as motivators for morality—whether from the law, God, or our own conscience—raise significant doubts about this very prospect. Psychological egoism insists that we cannot be moral because of our fundamental self-interests. The use of sanctions or rewards suggests that we will be punished by law, God, or guilt for not being moral and/or we will be rewarded, in this life or another, for being moral. However, this concern for ourselves is not the same as authentic morality.

At the very least, then, it does not seem as if the existence of being or doing what is good for the right reasons is all that obvious or simple. In the realm of criminal justice ethics, this logic is problematic. What makes this logic so troubling is that *the basis for making any decision becomes suspect!* This position holds true for persons engaged in the everyday work of policing, law, and corrections, as well as the policies that govern the overall criminal justice system. Notwithstanding these concerns, most of us do believe we can be and often are moral. With this notion in mind, common sources of or motivations for morality other than reward and punishment are investigated in Chapter 6.

KEY TERMS AND CONCEPTS

altruism
conscience
egoism
ethical egoism
guilt
irrefutable
malfeasance
misfeasance
moral psychology

nonfeasance
police corruption
psychological egoism
reinterpreting motives
rotten-apple (explanation of police deviance)
similarity-leniency hypothesis
superego

DISCUSSION QUESTIONS

1. What is psychological egoism? How is it related to ethical egoism? Is self-interest at all necessary or desirable for practitioners within the criminal justice field? Discuss how egoism does or might appear in the following practices or for the following persons: (1) police officers, (2) district attorneys and prosecutors, (3) defense attorneys.

2. Thomas Hobbes offers some interesting observations on the reinterpretation of motives. What are they? How are his comments on this matter linked to charity and pity? Imagine that a parole officer during the course of his site visit work

confronts a client selling marijuana. The parolee, a mother of three preschool children, lives in poverty. She does not possess a high school diploma and professes to have no marketable skills. Your parolee explains that she sells the drug in order to feed her family and to pay her bills. Would you take "pity" on this parolee? If so, what are your motivations? Are they different from those articulated by Thomas Hobbes? Explain your response.

3. To what extent does the fear of punishment motivate you to act morally? To what extent are you motivated to obey the law because of the existence of punishments for violating the law? To what extent does divine sanction or the expectation of divine reward motivate your behavior?

4. How do conscience and/or guilt serve as motivators resulting in moral action? What are their limitations and in what ways can conscience/guilt "go wrong" as motivations? Do you believe that most people behave morally because they fear being guilt-ridden? Use an example from your own personal or professional life to illustrate the power—or lack of power—that conscience and guilt have over our behavior.

5. Psychopathic offenders are said to lack conscience. Examples of psychopathic offenders are individuals who demonstrate a callous disregard for the feelings or welfare of others; who are impulsive, manipulative, and deceitful; and who have a larger-than-life sense about themselves. One case of a (sexual) psychopathic offender was Jeffrey Dahmer. Dahmer tortured, mutilated, and killed a number of young men before having sexual intercourse with them. Eventually, he was caught by the police and sentenced to multiple life prison terms in Wisconsin. He was murdered by a fellow prisoner. Are persons like Dahmer capable of forming a conscience? If not, then how can we expect moral/ethical behavior from them?

SUGGESTED READINGS

Heil, John. (1993). *Rationality, Morality, and Self-Interest.* New York: Rowman and Littlefield.

Hobbes, Thomas. (1997). *Leviathan.* New York: Touchstone.

Kennett, Jeanette. (2003). *Agency and Responsibility: A Common-Sense Moral Psychology.* New York: Oxford University Press.

Rogers, Kelly. (1997). *Self-Interest: An Anthology of Philosophical Perspectives from Antiquity to the Present.* New York: Routledge.

Turiel, Elliott. (2002). *The Culture of Morality: Social Development, Context, and Conflict.* Cambridge: Cambridge University Press.

ENDNOTES

[1] Michael Slote, "Moral Psychology." In *The Concise Routledge Encyclopedia of Philosophy* (New York: Routledge, 2000), p. 596.

[2] Ibid.

[3] See, e.g., John Hospers, *Human Conduct: An Introduction to the Problems of Ethics* (New York: Harcourt, Brace & World, 1961), pp. 174–196; Christopher Falzon, *Philosophy Goes to the Movies: An Introduction to Philosophy* (New York: Routledge, 2002), pp. 81–114.

[4]John Heil, *Rationality, Morality, and Self-Interest* (New York: Rowman and Littlefield, 1993).

[5]But for an accessible analysis that bridges this divide, see Craig Biddle, *Loving Life: The Morality of Self-Interest and the Facts That Support It* (Glen Allen, VA: Glen Allen Press LLC, 2002).

[6]Donald Borchert and David Stewart, *Exploring Ethics* (New York: Macmillan, 1986); pp. 7–29; Johnathan Jacobs, *Dimensions of Moral Theory: An Introduction to Metaethics and Moral Psychology* (New York: Blackwell Publishers, 2002); Jeanette Kennett, *Agency and Responsibility: A Common-Sense Moral Psychology* (New York: Oxford University Press, 2003).

[7]Kurt Baier, "Egoism." In Peter Singer, *A Companion to Ethics* (Malden, MA: Blackwell, 1993), p. 197.

[8]See, e.g., Keith Ansell-Pearson and Carol Diethe (Eds.), *Nietzsche: On 'The Genealogy of Morality' and Other Writings* (Cambridge: Cambridge University Press, 1994), p. 132.

[9]Kurt Baier, "Egoism," p. 197.

[10]James Rachels, *The Elements of Moral Philosophy* (New York: McGraw-Hill, 1986), pp. 53–64.

[11]Borchert and Stewart, *Exploring Ethics*, p. 2; Kurt Baier, "Egoism," p. 197.

[12]Terrance C. McConnell, *The Argument from Psychological Egoism to Ethical Egoism* (Melbourne: Australasian Association of Philosophy, 1978).

[13]Borchert and Stewart, *Exploring Ethics*, p. 7.

[14]Elliott Sober and David Sloan Wilson, *Unto Others: The Evolution and Psychology of Unselfish Behavior* (Boston: Harvard University Press, 1998).

[15]Kurt Baier, "Egoism."

[16]Judith A. Boss, *Ethics for Life* (Mountain View, CA: Mayfield, 2001), p. 247.

[17]Kurt Baier, "Egoism."

[18]See, e.g., Jacques Lacan, *The Ethics of Psychoanalysis 1959–1960*, Dennis Porter (trans.) (New York: W. W. Norton & Company, 1999), p. 187.

[19]James Rachels, *The Elements of Moral Philosophy*, p. 53.

[20]Ibid., pp. 54–56.

[21]Ibid.

[22]Thomas Hobbes, *Human Nature and DeCorpore Politico* (New York: Oxford University Press, 1999); for a discussion of Hobbes on charity and pity, see James Rachels, *The Elements of Moral Philosophy*, pp. 55–56.

[23]Thomas Hobbes, *Leviathan* (New York: Touchstone, 1997).

[24]For a useful application of Hobbes' ideas on charity and pity in law and criminology, see Christopher R. Williams and Bruce A. Arrigo, "The Philosophy of the Gift and the Psychology of Advocacy: Critical Reflections on Forensic Mental Health Intervention," *International Journal for the Semiotics of Law*, 13, 219–222 (2000).

[25]Thomas Hobbes, *Human Nature and DeCorpore Politico*; quoted in James Rachels, *The Elements of Moral Philosophy*, p. 55.

[26]Ibid.

[27]James Rachels *The Elements, of Moral Philosophy*, p. 55.

[28]Ibid.

[29]Ibid., pp. 55–56.

[30]Thomas Hobbes, *Human Nature and DeCorpore Politico*; quoted in James Rachels, *The Elements of Moral Philosophy* (New York: McGraw-Hill, 1986), p. 56.

[31]For an application of the concepts of compassion and empathy in criminal justice, see Bruce A. Arrigo and Christopher R. Williams, "Victim Voices, Victim Vices and Restorative Justice: Rethinking the Use of Impact Evidence in Capital Sentencing," *Crime and Delinquency*, 49, 612–621 (2003).

[32]See, e.g., Sigmund Freud, *The Interpretation of Dreams* (New York: Avon Books, 1965/1900); Sigmund Freud, *The Ego and the Id* (London: Hogarth, 1927).

[33]James Rachels, *The Elements of Moral Philosophy* (New York: McGraw-Hill, 1986), pp. 62–63.

[34]Ibid., pp. 56–57.

[35]Ibid., pp. 58–60.

[36]Plato, *The Republic*. Translated by G. M. A. Grube (Indianapolis, IN: Hackett, 1974), pp. 31–33.

[37]See also, Christopher Falzon, *Philosophy Goes to the Movies*, p. 88.

[38]Jeremy Bentham, *The Principles of Morals and Legislation* (New York: Prometheus Books, 1988); see also, William Sahakian, *Ethics: An Introduction to Theories and Problems* (New York: Barnes and Noble, 1974), p. 30.

[39]For a biologically informed account of this notion, see Donald M. Broom, *The Evolution of Morality and Religion* (Cambridge: Cambridge University Press, 2004).

[40]Paul W. Diener, *Religion and Morality: An Introduction* (London: Westminster John Knox Press, 1997); Paul Tillich, *Morality and Beyond* (London: Westminster John Knox Press, 1995).

[41]Vincent Ruggiero, *Thinking Critically About Ethical Issues,* 5th ed. (New York: McGraw-Hill, 2001), pp. 32–40.

[42]Nicholas Dent, "Conscience." In *The Concise Routledge Encyclopedia of Philosophy* (New York: Routledge, 2000), p. 167.

[43]Ibid., p. 167; see also, Tom Kitwood, *Concern for Others: A New Psychology of Conscience and Morality* (New York: Routledge, 1990).

[44]Evelyn Shirk, *The Ethical Dimension* (New York: Appleton-Century-Crofts, 1965), pp. 194–197.

[45]Nicholas Dent, "Conscience," p. 167.

[46]Robert R. Holt, *Freud Reappraised: A Fresh Look at Psychoanalytic Theory* (New York: Guilford Press, 1989), p. 132.

[47]P. S. Greenspan, *Practical Guilt: Moral Dilemmas, Emotions, and Social Norms* (Oxford: Oxford University Press, 1995).

[48]Ibid.

[49]Christopher Falzon, *Philosophy Goes to the Movies: An Introduction to Philosophy* (New York: Routledge, 2002).

[50]See, e.g., Jerome Kagan and Sharon Lamb (Eds.), *The Emergence of Morality in Young People* (Chicago: University of Chicago Press, 1990).

[51]Immanuel Kant, *Lectures on Ethics*. Translated by Louis Infield (Indianapolis, IN: Hackett, 1963), pp. 52–57.

[52]Ibid.

[53]Ibid., p. 56 (authors' emphasis).

[54]Ibid., p. 56 (authors' emphasis).

[55]William M. Baum, *Understanding Behaviorism: Behavior, Culture, and Evolution,* 2nd ed. (New York: Blackwell Publishers, 2004).

[56]Immanuel Kant, *Lectures on Ethics*, p. 57.

[57]Michael Johnston, *Political Corruption and Public Policy in America* (Monterey, CA: Brooks/Cole, 1982), p. 287.

[58]J. Kleinig, *The Ethics of Policing* (New York: Cambridge University Press, 1996), p. 166.

[59]T. Barker, *Police Ethics: Crisis in Law Enforcement,* 2nd ed. (Springfield, IL: Charles C. Thomas, 2006).

[60]Michael Johnston, *Political Corruption and Public Policy in America* (Monterey, CA: Brooks/Cole, 1982).

[61]Ibid., p. 305.

[62]See, generally, Victor Kappeler, Richard Sluder, and Geoffrey Alpert, *Forces of Deviance: Understanding the Dark Side of Policing,* 2nd ed. (Prospect Heights, IL: Waveland Press, 1998), pp. 216–243.

[63]G. Alpert and R. Dunham, *Policing Multi-ethnic Neighborhoods* (Westport, CT: Greenwood, 1988). Quoted in Kappeler, Sluder, and Alpert, *Forces of Deviance,* p. 221.

[64]Victor Kappeler, Richard Sluder, and Geoffrey Alpert, *Forces of Deviance: Understanding the Dark Side of Policing,* 2nd ed. (Prospect Heights, IL: Waveland Press, 1998), p. 221.

[65]Bernard McCarthy, "Keeping an Eye on the Keeper: Prison Corruption and its Control." In Michael Braswell, Belinda McCarthy, and Bernard McCarthy, *Justice, Crime, and Ethics,* 3rd ed. (Cincinnati, OH: Anderson, 1998), p. 251.

[66]Bernard McCarthy, "Keeping an Eye on the Keeper: Prison Corruption and its Control," *The Prison Journal,* 64, (2), 113–125 (1984). Reprinted in Michael Braswell, Belinda McCarthy, and Bernard McCarthy, *Justice, Crime, and Ethics,* 3rd ed. (Cincinnati, OH: Anderson, 1998), pp. 251–262.

[67]Bernard McCarthy, "Keeping an Eye on the Keeper: Prison Corruption and its Control." In Michael Braswell, Belinda McCarthy, and Bernard McCarthy, *Justice, Crime, and Ethics,* 3rd ed. (Cincinnati, OH: Anderson, 1998), p. 254.

[68]Ibid.

[69]Ibid., p. 258. See also, R. Cloward, *Theoretical Studies in the Social Organization of the Prison* (Social Science Research Council, 1960); G. Sykes, *The Society of Captives: A Study of a Maximum Security Prison* (Princeton, NJ: Princeton University Press, 1958); and J. Irwin, *Prisons in Turmoil* (Boston: Little, Brown & Co., 1980).

Chapter 6

Why *Should* We Be Good? Sources of Morality

If reward and punishment—no matter their form—are insufficient motives for "genuine" morality, we are left still with the pressing question of why we should be moral. What reasons do we have for not acting solely out of self-interest? What are or would be sufficient motives for leading a "good life?" Setting aside answers that appeal to law, divine reward and punishment, or conscience/guilt, we need a convincing answer to the question of why we should be concerned about being good people and doing the right thing. What is it that motivates people to embody the principles of morality? What are the incentives that bring people to sacrifice their self-interests for those of others or for society as a whole? What reasons do we have for abiding by ethical principles even if we know we can get away with being unethical or immoral?

Over the course of the past two thousand years or so, philosophers have put forth a variety of answers to these questions. None, unfortunately, is widely regarded as *the* reason that we should be moral. Most, however, have something important to say along these lines. In the next few sections, several of these responses are considered.

Divine Command

Ethics and religion have become nearly synonymous for many people, with religion serving as both the theoretical foundation of ethics and as a point of moral reference (see Box 6.1).[1] This is true from a cross-cultural as well as a comparative perspective.[2] Thus, a second answer sometimes put forth in response to the question of why we should be moral (in addition to the fear of punishment or sanction as discussed in Chapter 5) brings us back to this intersection of religion and morality. The religious view of morality is sometimes described as *Divine Command Theory*.

BOX 6.1

Civil Religion and Flag Desecration

There are many controversies in criminology/criminal justice that have a religious or near-religious dimension to them. One such act that has brought decades of public concern, intense legal battles, and various forms of social control is that of desecrating the American flag. Throughout American history, repeated efforts have been made—sometimes successfully, other times less so—to criminalize what are thought to be improper and offensive uses of the Stars and Stripes. From politically charged acts such as flag burnings to controversial (and arguably distasteful) creative and artistic representations of Old Glory, destruction and desecration of the American flag has always elicited powerful emotional reactions from many among the American public. Yet why and how is it that a piece of cloth generates so much controversy?

In virtually all cultures, certain symbols are held to be "sacred" and expected to be cherished, honored, and revered. Because, as Michael Welch writes, it is "imbued with patriotic qualities of sacred proportion" and is characterized by "deep emotional—virtually religious—attachment," desecration of the flag often provokes particularly strong sentiments. The American flag is "emblematic of patriotism," represents freedom, opportunity, and all that is good and right about the United States—it is the foremost icon of America's history, power, and way of life. Should we be surprised that, in a 1992 Gallop poll, 77% of Americans indicated that the burning of the flag should *not* be protected by the First Amendment?

Michael Welch argues that the American flag embodies *civil religion*—a "nonsectarian faith in which secular objects are transformed into sacred icons." In part because it embodies civil religion, social movements intent on protecting the flag have arisen and persisted throughout much of recent American history. Welch describes "rallying around the flag" as "a ritual infused with patriotic fervor . . . resemble[ing] nondescript religion." Movements seeking to criminalize flag burning are one example of the interweaving of religion and the State. Though in principle they are to remain separate, church and state "frequently operate in concert to promote religion and patriotism, together becoming a potent unifying force in American culture." The influence of religious forces is evident even within the language of law, where the flag is a "venerated" object, its destruction a form of "desecration."

- What does the American flag symbolize to you and others around you (e.g., family, friends)?
- Do you consider the American flag to be a "sacred" object in the same way that religious symbols might be?
- How important is the American flag compared with other objects and symbols that you or others may hold to be "sacred"?
- Should desecration of the flag be protected under the First Amendment of the Constitution (freedom of speech)?
- If not, should burning of the flag be illegal? What about wearing a skirt made from the American flag? Wearing a T-shirt with a political message superimposed upon the flag? Flying the flag upside down? In what, if any, ways are these forms of flag "desecration" different?
- If illegal, what punishment should be proscribed for various forms of flag desecration?

Source: Michael Welch, *Flag Burning: Moral Panic and the Criminalization of Protest* (New York: Aldine de Gruyter 2001), quotes taken from pages 4, 5, 31, and 32.

Divine Command Theory argues that certain actions are good or bad, moral or immoral, because they are approved or disapproved of by God. Moral principles are God's rules and, while we do not *have* to follow them (we were created as free-willed individuals), we should make an effort to do so if we want to live morally good lives.[3] The advantage of such an outlook is that it seems to provide *certainty* about right and wrong, good and evil. Moreover, as we explained in the previous chapter, it also provides some *incentive* to be moral. Regrettably, as a matter of genuine integrity, the certainty and incentive offered by religion are largely inadequate. This is not to suggest that there is no room for religion in our everyday lives or even in our understanding of ethics and morality. However, it is to emphasize that relying on religion to define and motivate morality suffers from several important shortcomings.

Before considering these shortcomings, it is worth noting that Divine Command Theory comes in several variations. Most notably, there are both *absolutist* and *moderate* versions. **Absolute Divine Command Theory** holds that actions that are morally right are deemed so *because* God commands them (i.e., because God says so).[4] No other justification is needed or exists other than that it is God's directive. Thus, for instance, it is wrong to lie, cheat, or steal *because* God commands us not to do these things. Moreover, it is wrong to commit adultery *because* God asserts that this behavior is evil and wicked. There is no point in looking any further for a deeper justification or explanation.

Necessary Belief?

One of the biggest limitations stemming from the absolutist variety of Divine Command Theory is that it implies that *there is no morality unless one believes in God.* If what is right or wrong is purely and exclusively a function of God's command, then morality cannot exist unless one believes in such a deity and accepts this entity's authority. What makes this reasoning problematic is that while some religious fundamentalists would adopt the extreme position that all nonbelievers are immoral, the polarizing nature of this position makes it unattractive to most people and, thus, undesirable as a way of resolving ethical issues for them. By taking the absolutist stance, belief in God is essential in order to be a moral or ethical person. Belief, then, is argued to be a *necessary condition* for morality. As such, people who do not believe in a higher power or some other-worldly source that accounts for our very existences cannot hope to be moral unless they first convert to the particular faith in question. In the absence of such a conversion, there is no point in nonbelievers considering moral and ethical issues.

Most of us, however, would agree that it is at least possible for a person to be ethical without believing in God. In fact, many moral philosophers would argue that *belief in God is not necessary for morality.*[5] It is not only possible but common for people to embody integrity, to make morally-sound choices, and to act in virtuous ways out of concern for humanity, respect for other people, compassion, and other motives that are not necessarily linked with a belief in a higher power. It would make little sense to suggest that the time, energy, and/or money that a person donates to helping those in need or otherwise less fortunate is amoral or immoral unless it is motivated by a belief in God. It seems, then, that while religion may help some people to clarify their moral values and principles, it is not *necessary* as motivation for morality.

Common Ground

A second concern with Divine Command Theory (especially the absolutist version) is what is termed the **problem of common ground**.[6] It is important to note that religious motivations extend only to those people with similar beliefs. In other words, religion is limited as an ethical tool because it *only appeals to believers*. For example, if our principal motivation for moral behavior is a fear of punishment by God, what about the motivation of people who are not Christian or, perhaps, not religious at all? It is generally understood within ethics that for something to be a sufficient foundation for morality and/or a sufficient motivation for moral behavior, it should be acceptable and, thus, applicable to all people—regardless of religious beliefs, personal values, degree of education, and so forth. In this sense, it should be universally and objectively recognized as a reason for being or for doing what is good. Thus, all people of all faiths (and nonfaiths) must agree that we *should* be moral for certain reasons. Problematically, not only do ethical principles and arguments based in religion appeal only to believers, there are also significant differences in interpretation and application even for people within the same faith. In short, principles and arguments drawn from religious sources lack the *universalizability* (or *generality*) toward which ethics strives.[7]

Ethical discussions should occur on some ground that is common for *all* interested parties.[8] Thus, Christians, Buddhists, Moslems, Jews, agnostics, and atheists should all be able to affirm an ethical conclusion—if, that is, it is a good conclusion. Imagine, for example, that you must spend the rest of your life on an island with ten other people—none of whom are affiliated with any particular religious faith. Obviously, there will be a need for some common moral foundation to ensure that you all could lead safe, secure, and satisfying lives together. This morality would need to be built on *common ground*. Not only should you all be able to agree upon what values and principles are important, but you should all be able to agree on good reasons for pursuing those values and/or for following those principles. One value or virtue that might be desirable in this scenario would be compassion. Caring about the well-being of the other people on the island and assisting them in their pursuit to be safe and secure would undoubtedly create a climate beneficial to all. If, as a religiously inspired person, you tried to convince the others that they should all be compassionate in order to avoid divine punishment, you would likely not get very far. Instead, you would probably create more conflict than consensus and serve to diminish your prospects for living a good life. You would be much better off leaving religion aside and promoting compassion as a desirable means for making life better for everyone.

Independent Good

An alternative to absolutist versions of Divine Command Theory has its origins in Plato's *Euthyphro*. Though less popular than absolutist varieties, *moderate* versions of Divine Command Theory at least allow for the possibility that morality is possible without religion. Plato narrates a conversation that Socrates had with Euthyphro during which he posed the now famous question, "Why does God command something?" Certainly, what God directs is good and right, but what Socrates was asking is why are *these things* commanded? What is it about these things that make them worthy of being moral dictates?

Socrates proceeded to argue that God commands that which is good. Note the subtle but important difference between this statement and the position taken by the absolutist version of Divine Command Theory. The latter argues that something is good because God directs that it is; however, Socrates, in turn, suggests that God commands something because it is good. Thus, following Socrates, murder is not wrong because God commands that it is; rather, the wrongness of murder itself is what makes God command that it is so. In other words, murder is wrong because it *is* wrong. The absolutist position would hold that the reason we should be truthful is because God directs us to be so—not for any other reason(s) related to the intrinsic virtue of truthfulness. We are obligated simply to follow God's dictates, whatever those might be. Moreover, following the absolutist stance, notwithstanding the command to be truthful, telling the truth is neither inherently good nor bad. It is only good because it is directed by God.[9]

The problem with this logic is that God could just as easily have given different commands and those directives—whatever they might have been—would have to be considered good, right, and just. To illustrate, if God had commanded that we always lie, then lying would be good. If God had ordered that we murder our neighbors, be unfaithful to our spouses, and steal from our friends, then murder, infidelity, and stealing would be right. Many of us—even the most religious among us—would have considerable difficulties with this. You may respond, however, that God would never command such things. If so, the question is *why?* If God would never direct us to lie, cheat, and steal, then God must understand that these things are not good, right, and just. In other words, lying, cheating, and stealing must have been wrong *before* God commanded them to be so. If this is the case, then what is good, right, and just must exist independent of God's command.[10]

Plato's argument has come to be known as *moderate Divine Command Theory*. **Moderate Divine Command Theory** argues that what God commands is right and good, not simply because this deity directs it, but because it *is* right and good. In other words, God does not define what is good simply by commanding it; rather, God commands what is good because God *understands the good*. Thus, God has some conception of goodness and justice and, through this higher power's directives, shares and imparts this conception to us all. As such, God realizes that it is better to be truthful than to lie, better to preserve life than to take it, and so on and so forth. Following Plato, God's commands are a function of wisdom and of understanding what is good, right, and just.

For some, moderate Divine Command Theory raises a different problem. Namely, if God commands things because they are good, then there must be some standard of right and wrong that exists independent of God's will.[11] As Plato argued through Socrates, there must be some conception or realm of goodness that is set apart from God—some notion of the good that God recognizes and directs, but one that is not defined solely by way of this entity's dictates. If this is true, one implication is that determining what is good and right does not depend on a higher power. If God commands something, then this being, as a sacred source of authority, has good *reasons* for commanding it. Theoretically, then, anyone could reach the same conclusions about what is right and good without relying on God to tell them. Consequently, religion is not necessary for morality.

Commands, Duties, and Obligations

As the observations above clearly indicate, there are several problems with relying on religion as a source of and motivation for morality. However, one additional explanation is worth noting. In brief, being good or doing the right thing because we feel a duty or obligation to do so may not be sufficient for morality. Although the notion of ethical decision-making as linked to duty and obligation is the subject of review in Chapter 9, some brief commentary on this notion is warranted here.

Religious commands are only one source of such duties and obligations. Indeed, much like we would prefer it if our spouse chose fidelity based on values other than the fear of getting caught (see Chapter 5 for more on this), we would likely prefer it further if our partner chose faithfulness for reasons beyond mere duty or obligation. Similar to the threat of punishment, duties and commands can be effective ways of ensuring certain forms of behavior, and we certainly could not claim to be moral persons if we routinely failed to meet these ethical responsibilities. Yet being good and doing the right thing solely out of a sense of obligation or because we have been commanded to do so is hardly enough to make us genuinely moral people. Focusing on commands, duties, and obligations ignores the importance of sympathy, compassion, respect, care, and concern for the well-being of others and the communities to which self and others belong. These more life-affirming sources emerge from *within* people. Interestingly, legal punishment, divine punishment, divine commands, as well as duties and obligations are all things that shape our thoughts, feelings, and behaviors from without. However, as briefly noted in Chapter 1, morality is something that must be *authentic*—that is to say, our motivation to be moral must originate from *within us*.

COMMON INTEREST: MUTUAL ADVANTAGE AND MUTUAL AID

Thus far, Chapters 5 and 6 have illustrated that morality: (1) does not consist in pursuing our own interests exclusively; (2) does not consist of doing the right thing because we fear the (worldly or divine) consequences of not doing so; (3) does not consist of doing the right thing because we are commanded (by parents, law, religion) to do so; and (4) does not consist of doing the right thing simply because we feel a duty or obligation to do so. If not for self-interest, fear of punishment, following commands, or out of duty, *why, then, should we be moral?*

Another reason sometimes advanced for being moral is that it serves the *common interest*.[12] How it serves the common interest and why we are or should be invested in serving the collective good is a matter of some dispute. While a number of different arguments have been put forth along these lines, there are two key perspectives that are worth noting here: The first suggests that morality is to our mutual advantage; the second proposes that we are naturally concerned with the good of both ourselves and others and, consequently, morality is an expression of this innate inclination.

Mutual Advantage

To illustrate the mutual advantage perspective, think of any number of recreational games (e.g., checkers, poker, basketball). Why, for instance, is it considered wrong to cheat at poker? Why are there dozens of rules and regulations that govern the game of basketball? The answer, of course, is to ensure fairness and to promote the opportunity for everyone participating to play to the best of their ability and to enjoy themselves in the process. The rules and regulations that govern checkers, poker, and basketball are intended to prevent players from causing unnecessary and unjust harm or suffering to other participants, to resolve in an orderly and agreeable fashion any number of conflicts or disagreements that might arise during the course of the game, and to enhance the experience of the sport or the entertainment value for everyone involved.[13]

However, in some respects, recreational or athletic competitions are not the same as the game of life. Indeed, as Hospers explained, "[n]one of us is forced to play baseball or billiards, but the game of life is one which we all have to play in one way or another."[14] Each of us not only has to participate in the "sport" of living, but we have to play it together. Thus, the question becomes, what arrangements, values, principles, and rules create the most favorable conditions and relationships for everyone involved? Are there certain values and principles that create conditions within which each of us can pursue our own interests as much as possible, while allowing others to pursue theirs? Moreover, are there certain values and tendencies that *assist us* in pursuing our own interests and *also assist others* in their own quest for happiness?

By answering these questions we are putting forth certain moral values, principles, duties, and obligations that operate to the **mutual advantage** of everyone involved.[15] While we might derive personal benefit from cheating at poker, it is in the best interests of everyone concerned if we do not. By being honest poker players, we earn the trust and respect of others, we encourage all participants not to cheat, and we contribute to an overall climate of fairness and hospitableness that enables everyone to enjoy the experience. By the same token, if we are honest people in our personal and professional lives, our honesty not only benefits us personally, but positively enhances the well-being of the entire group to which we belong. As Kurt Baier notes,

> [t]he answer to the question "Why be moral?" is therefore ... [w]e should ... because being moral is following rules designed to overrule self-interest whenever it is in the interest of everyone alike that everyone should set aside his [or her] interest.[16]

Most of us would agree that we would not want to live in a community or a society (or to work in a professional setting for that matter) where people routinely lied, cheated, stole, harmed others, or put their own needs or wants above all other considerations. If this were the case, we would all be at a mutual *dis*advantage and life—especially life together—would be exceedingly difficult. This is the point that Thomas Hobbes attempted to make in writing his classic treatise, *Leviathan.*[17] We have already been briefly introduced to Hobbes by way of his strategic reinterpretation of motives (see Chapter 5 for more on this point). However, in the present context, what is important is Hobbes' contention that because we are all motivated by self-interest, it is in everyone's best interest to agree upon certain rules that will allow each of us to pursue those interests while not infringing upon the needs and wants that govern the choices and behaviors of others. Thus, while it may be in our personal best interest to be immoral, we must recognize that if everyone set aside their morality, we would all be left with an unpleasant social climate that would make it difficult for anyone to pursue their sense of happiness (see Box 6.2). Consequently, we all have a vested interest both in the existence of moral rules and in following those rules—even when we could selfishly benefit from doing otherwise.

BOX 6.2

Class, Race, Gender, and Mutual Advantage

The justification for laws and moral rules from a mutual advantage perspective is that they serve the best interests of everyone. Laws and rules ensure fairness and opportunity and thus promote favorable conditions for all parties who abide by them. Yet do rules, laws, and policies always work this way? Has our current system of social and economic "rules" been effective at ensuring fairness and opportunity for everyone? What about those of criminal justice?

Many have argued that women, racial and ethnic minorities, and persons of lower-class status are at a decided *disadvantage* when it comes to playing the "game of life"—a disadvantage that is amplified within the criminal justice system. Consider the following:

- Incarceration rates for poor and disadvantaged women of color around the world are increasing markedly. This not only includes women of color but immigrants and indigenous female citizens as well. For example, in the United States alone the incarceration rates for women witnessed a staggering 2,800 percent increase from 1970 to 2001! According to some experts, "tough on crime" policies and the international war on drugs have led to the criminalization of poor and disadvantaged women around the globe, making them one of the largest groups inside prisons despite being the clear minority outside of them.
- African Americans continue to represent nearly 50% of the prison population in the United States. Black males between the ages of 25 and 29 are nearly 10 times more likely to be incarcerated than White males of similar age. In fact, approximately 33% of young Black men are in prison or on probation/parole. As with poor women of color, some have suggested that the ongoing "war on drugs" has contributed to this disparity. African Americans represent nearly 60% of offenders convicted on drug charges, despite representing less than 13% of the U.S. population.
- A 1989 study by Albonetti, Hauser, Hagan, and Nagel revealed that class and race can be an important disadvantage in the context of bail decisions. Persons with less income and education generally, and Black defendants with the same income and education as White defendants, were less likely to be granted bail. Although other factors (e.g., perceived dangerousness and seriousness of the offense) seem to be more important considerations, class and race do appear to have a generalized effect on bail decisions that disadvantages minorities and persons of lower socioeconomic standing.
- In their 1987 analysis of over 30,000 cases in Los Angeles County, Spohn, Gruhl, and Welch found that African and Hispanic Americans were prosecuted at significantly higher rates than White Americans. In this same context, other studies have shown that Whites more often receive plea bargains than Blacks, and that terms of plea bargains comparatively advantage Whites.

■ Studies have repeatedly demonstrated that Black offenders are disproportionately sentenced to death when compared with White offenders. Black offenders who have murdered White victims stand the greatest likelihood of receiving the death penalty, while murders involving a Black victim—regardless of the race of the offender—are least likely to be met with death as a sanction.

While the degree to which racial discrimination exists in criminal justice remains a matter of some debate, it is evident that there are significant disparities that disadvantage minorities at various stages of the criminal justice process. In explaining these disparities, some have looked beyond discriminatory practices and toward broader social and economic factors. Notwithstanding laws and rules designed to ensure fairness and opportunity for all Americans, some have argued that there exists a demonstrable fairness and opportunity for minority citizens. Consider the following:

■ While the national unemployment rate is less than 5%, it is nearly 30% for young men in inner cities. Overall, the unemployment rate for African Americans is more than twice that of European Americans.

■ In 1996, the median income for White families was nearly $45,000, while for Black families it was less than $27,000. In 1991, the median *wealth* (the value of assets) of White families was nearly $45,000, while for Black families it was less than $5,000.

■ In 1995, the average salary of African American females with bachelor's degrees was approximately $30,000—only about $500 per year higher than White males with no college education.

■ The percentage of African American families living in poverty in 1996 (26.3%) was nearly 4 times that of Whites (7%). Approximately 16% of White children lived in poverty, while the percentage of Black children living in poverty was approximately 46%.

Even if the disparities within criminal justice listed above are not the result of discriminatory practices, we are still left to consider whether disadvantageous economic and social conditions might give rise to higher rates of criminality among minorities. Given the circumstances outlined above, do the rules of the game truly create a situation of mutual advantage? If not, in what ways might the "rules" (or laws, policies, etc.) be changed to better ensure mutual advantage?

Sources: Julia Sudbury, *Global Lockdown: Gender, Race, and the Rise of the Prison Industrial Complex* (New York: Routledge, 2005); Jeffrey Reiman, *The Rich Get Richer and the Poor Get Prison: Ideology, Class, and Criminal Justice*, 6th ed. (Boston: Allyn & Bacon, 2001); C. Albonetti, J. Hauser, J. Hagan, and I. Nagel, "Criminal Justice Decision Making as a Stratification Process: The Role of Race and Stratification Resources in Pretrial Release," *Journal of Quantitative Criminology*, 5, 57–82 (1989); C. Spohn, J. Gruhl, and S. Welch, "The Impact of Ethnicity and Gender of Defendants on the Decision to Reject or Dismiss Felony Charges," *Criminology*, 25, 175–192 (1987); D. Stanley Eitzen and Maxine Zinn, *Social Problems*, 8th ed. (Boston: Allyn & Bacon, 2000).

Mutual Aid

As you may have already gathered, the "mutual advantage" argument briefly outlined above still relies primarily on self-regard as a motivation for morality. However, by giving voice to the needs and wants of other people, it does move us (somewhat) beyond the more narrow positions that rely exclusively on personal reward and punishment as incentives. The logic of mutual advantage is that it is in our own best interest to consider the desires of others, and therefore we should abide by moral rules or guidelines in the interest of the common good (of which we, ourselves, are an important part). As we will see in Chapter 8, this argument is consistent with the *social contract* tradition of moral philosophy—a tradition that relies, in part, on the broader insights of *utilitarian* theory.

The mutual advantage argument holds that human beings are, by nature, competitive, self-interested, and engaged in a continual struggle for survival. When self-interested, competitive people are made to live together in communities, morality becomes necessary to ensure both their safety and their freedom. However, there is another "common interest" perspective that is clearly more optimistic in its view of human nature and the possibility of being moral. In short, this alternative argument suggests that we want others to be well not because it is in our own best interest, but because it is in our nature to want others to be well. This is the perspective of **mutual aid.**

Consider the fact that most of us are happy when others are happy. We smile and laugh when others are smiling and laughing. Similarly, we become upset when others are upset. We may cry when others cry, or, at the very least, we may feel something stirring deep within us that compels us to reach out and help or want to comfort them. None of us enjoys seeing pictures or video footage of people suffering from starvation, disease, homelessness, or other tribulations. For many of us, genuine concern emerges when someone is criminally victimized or when tragedy befalls another. All of these feelings come from within us. There are no laws or rules that force us to be happy when others are happy; there are no laws that require us to be sad when others are sad. These thoughts and feelings, as well as the behaviors that stem from them, are better understood as natural human tendencies.

As discussed earlier, Hobbes' strategy was to "reinterpret" these inclinations as fundamentally self-regarding. Thus, from his point of view, we feel sadness when witnessing starvation because it reminds us of our own vulnerability. Alternatively, however, we could just as easily argue that we feel sadness and sympathy in this same instance because we have genuine concern for the welfare of others. In this respect, then, if we provide aid to or otherwise assist those who are suffering or struggling in some capacity, our actions are not so much motivated by duty, obligation, or the promise of reward; instead, we are inclined to offer help because of our inherent sociality. When we lend money to a friend in need, take in a homeless animal, or volunteer at a local domestic violence shelter or rape crisis center, our actions can be defined as benevolent and arguably motivated by an inherent human tendency to be concerned with and invested in the welfare of others.

While Hobbes had painted a rather bleak portrait of human nature and social life without morality, several other social and moral philosophers have offered alternative portraits wherein human beings are intrinsically sociable, cooperative, and genuinely concerned about the welfare of others. For instance, social and political philosopher Jean-Jacques Rousseau (1712–1778) argued that it is "compassion that hurries us without reflection to the relief of those who are in distress . . ."[18] It is "natural compassion" that prevents us from harming others, while simultaneously inclining us to assist people in need. These tendencies toward nonharm and benevolence, as mutual aid anarchist Peter Kropotkin (1842–1921) offered, ". . . [do] not depend on presuppositions, concepts, religions, dogmas, myths, training, and education. On the contrary,

[they] reside in human nature itself . . ."[19] Rather than being competitive creatures involved in a continual struggle for individual survival (as Hobbes had implied), we are naturally sociable, cooperative beings involved in a continual struggle to be well as a human community—to secure health and happiness not only for ourselves, but for others. This struggle is best endured—and, in fact, *only* endured—through cooperative endeavors of mutual support.[20]

Morality, then, serves the common interest not by providing for mutual advantage, but by encouraging us to actualize our inherent pro-social nature. By being moral, we are connected to our fellow beings. By being moral, we recognize and participate in the interdependence that characterizes our existences. Because we are social beings, we cannot survive without the aid of and assistance from others. Morality serves to remind us of the importance of this life-affirming mutuality, as well as to remind us that we are all engaged members of a larger human (and moral) community.[21] Thus, when we act immorally, we "cut ourselves off" from our fellow beings. We make ourselves strangers not only to others, but to our true nature.

Consequently, following the logic of mutual aid, it is *shared support* rather than mutual advantage that does, or at least should, motivate us to be moral. Like many other species, humans naturally tend toward compassion, benevolence, and nonharm of their fellow beings. As some would argue, we do not need laws, rules, religions, and so forth to motivate us to be good and to do the right thing; instead, morality is something that is already within us.[22] Compassion, benevolence, kindness, and cooperation are natural dispositions. Our sociality, civility, virtue, and goodness are inherent human qualities that need only to be *allowed* to develop and flourish (see Box 6.3). The fact that many people fail to demonstrate these more organic capacities is not evidence that they do not exist. Instead, their absence invites us to ask, what *prevents* us from developing these capacities? There is ample research indicating that greed, envy, jealousy, and other so-called negative emotions are not universal. Instead, they are products of culture—ways of thinking and feeling that evolve within social and cultural contexts.[23] Thus, the question remains, what it is that encourages greed, envy, and possessiveness in us while, simultaneously, discouraging compassion, benevolence, and other pro-social thoughts, feelings, and behaviors.

CHARACTER: INNER BALANCE AND PSYCHOLOGICAL WELL-BEING

A final type of response to the question, "Why be moral?," involves some consideration of the importance of *character,* both for our own well-being and for that of society.[24] In Chapter 5, we considered Plato's tale of the ring of Gyges. This narrative was important for our overall assessment of morality and ethics for several reasons. Perhaps most noteworthy among these reasons is that Plato's tale forces us to consider why someone would do the right thing when that same person could just as easily do the wrong thing without getting caught. But how does Plato reconcile this moral dilemma? How does he address the fate of Gyges; a destiny that is most assuredly steeped in moral conflict?

BOX 6.3

Crime Prevention and Community Safety: An Ethic of Police–Citizen Trust

Neighborhoods riddled with crime impact not only the residents who inhabit them, but also the officers who patrol them. In recent years, criminal justice agencies are more carefully considering how they can prevent crime while simultaneously promoting harmony and well-being within communities. Some suggestions include community policing strategies, neighborhood block watch efforts, and the notion of collective efficacy. While there are important differences among these approaches, each intervention is based on the value of *trust*. *Community policing* strategies require that officers be a part of the communities they patrol, working to assist residents in various ways that might have little to do with crime and delinquency. *Neighborhood block watch* strategies invite residents to be active participants in preventing or controlling crime by forming citizen patrol groups that operate in conjunction with local law enforcement personnel. The goal of *collective efficacy* is the (re)formation of safe and secure communities built upon resident cooperation. Collective efficacy seeks, with the assistance of law enforcement officers, the reestablishment of agency and power among residents of drug and crime-infested neighborhoods through the collective—and peaceful—reclamation of the streets.

In each of these instances, an ethic of police–citizen trust accounts for the quality and type of crime prevention and community safety that will eventually emerge in a given neighborhood experiencing pervasive violence and criminality. Thus, much like the notion of mutual aid suggests, when the inherent human qualities of cooperativeness, kindness, civility, compassion, etc., are allowed to develop, morality (i.e., being good and doing the right thing) is no longer dependent on laws, religion, or rules. Instead, morality resides within people motivated to act accordingly, given their intrinsic pro-social inclinations to express these healing tendencies. These tendencies can represent a source of fellowship and collective good; an ethic of community, citizenship, and justice for all.

Source: Gordon Hughes (Ed.), *Crime Prevention and Community Safety: New Directions* (Thousand Oaks, CA: Sage, 2002).

Plato's purpose in reciting the story of Gyges was to dispute the notion that our fear of punishment is the only thing that keeps people from doing whatever they want to do. Plato's answer, outlined over the course of his work, *The Republic* (esp. Book IV), specifies that being moral *is* in our best interests—though we do not always or even often realize it.[25] What seems to be a struggle between self-interest and morality is only a tension because most of us have a false sense of self-regard. This bogus sense of self-interest, in turn, rests upon a counterfeit sense of the self whereby we tend to identify ourselves with our desires.[26]

For Plato, the "self" or "soul" is comprised of three "parts": an appetitive or desiring part, a rational part, and a spirited part. A "healthy" or well-functioning soul is *balanced:* each of the three parts performs its proper function, being kept "in check" by the others. An "unhealthy" soul, in turn, is characterized by imbalance: one or the other parts comes to dominate the entirety of the soul. The ideal balance is achieved when the soul is governed by the rational element (i.e., reason). The desirous or appetitive part of the soul is often what motivates us—it compels us to want certain things. What we want or desire, however, is not always in our best interest. It is up to reason (with support from the spirited part of the soul) to keep our desires in check and to ensure that we make good choices and act only on our healthy desires.[27]

To illustrate, many of us have at one point or another attempted to follow some form of diet. We know, however, that dieting can be extremely difficult. There are certain foods and drinks that we want—that we desire. Yet in the interest of our diet, we should not give in to our desires and consume what we want. What keeps us from doing this? For Plato, the answer is reason supported by spirit. We *know* that what we want is not in our best interests (assuming that dieting is), and thus reason tells us to avoid certain foods and/or drinks. However, reason alone typically is not strong enough to stave off desire. What helps reason in this struggle is the spirited part of the soul—experienced, perhaps, as the drive, commitment, sense of inner strength that motivates us to follow reason rather than desire. Reason tells us *what* to overcome, and spirit is what allows us *to* overcome the distractions and unhealthy desires that we routinely experience.

For Plato, then, our desires and appetites cannot be trusted. If we are driven by them alone, we will more often than not act contrary to our interests and welfare. Only reason is competent to determine what is good for us. Consequently, reason governs the healthy soul. We do, however, need desires. They help to ensure that all motivation is not lost, a condition that would otherwise lead us to spend the rest of our lives withering away without passion for anything. Appetite is what forces us to wake up in the morning and to pursue the things that are worthwhile in life; reason is that which determines what is worthwhile and how best to go about getting it.

Plato suggests, then, that morality is **inner balance**.[28] This sense of internal equilibrium is achieved when we are governed by reason or the rational part of ourselves. Thus, following Plato, why should we be moral? Rather than being contrary to our interests, being moral furthers our interests. Being moral is having a well-ordered, balanced, harmonious soul in which each of the three parts performs its appropriate function. When we are not moral (not well-balanced) we are unable to pursue our own best interests. In these moments, we are driven by the demands of desire, and pursue that which is often contrary to our well-being. Moreover, when we lack internal equilibrium, we harm other people as our desires interfere with our capacity to have genuine, meaningful relationships. We are not concerned with the needs, welfare, or happiness of others. We do not treat others with respect and, in fact, are likely to *use* or exploit people to further our own desires.[29]

Possessing the type of inner balance of which Plato spoke amounts to good mental health and/or to psychological well-being. This internal equilibrium is a condition in which we positively and meaningfully contribute to our interactions with others. Psychological well-being, in turn, is experienced as satisfying and provides a basis for leading a complete and fulfilled life. Thus, being moral *feels good*—the moral life is the *happy* life.

Although we do not need to accept Plato's "tripartite" or threefold model of the soul to answer the question about why we should be moral, there are several important points stemming from his position worth considering. While Plato felt that the well-balanced soul was the virtuous soul, he also believed that each of these parts had its own virtue: the virtue of reason is *wisdom;* the virtue of spirit is *courage;* and the virtue of appetite is *moderation.* When the parts of the soul are well-ordered, wisdom, courage, and moderation characterize the self.[30] Thus, the moral person is wise, courageous, and moderate. So, why should we care about wisdom, moderation, and other similar virtues that enable us to be moral? A better question might be to ask what would happen if we failed to embody these attributes. In other words, what would our lives be like if we embodied vice rather than virtue?

By being immoral and failing to demonstrate virtue, ourselves and our lives are characterized by varying types and degrees of decay, abuse, and wickedness. Greed, pride, intemperance, selfishness, callousness, and other desire-driven traits or feelings come to dictate our choices and actions. However, they are certainly not the kind of characteristics or sentiments that we hope others will possess. In fact, most of us would not want to be associated with family members, friends, or other so-called intimates who were greedy, selfish, and insensitive. Most likely, these are precisely the types of people we would (and do) seek to avoid. By exhibiting these traits or feelings ourselves, we become the type of individual that others do not respect—that others do not like and do not want to be around. If we embody these characteristics, we make things very difficult for ourselves both personally and professionally. Thus, we might ask if this is the sort of life that is worth living?[31]

On the other hand, if we are moral—if we embody wisdom, moderation, compassion, and other virtuous qualities—we not only earn the respect of others, but we earn our own respect as well. We are psychologically healthier, happier, and have more fulfilling relationships with others. By the same token, we are contributing to a better sense of community, civility, and humanity—not simply because we personify these qualities, but because we will tend to make choices and engage in behaviors that are motivated by these qualities. If we are compassionate, we will tend toward choices motivated by compassion, and actions stemming from compassion. We will take others' needs and interests into consideration before choosing and before acting. This creates, as some would argue, a social climate that is beneficial to all.[32] Thus, being virtuous—being moral—not only benefits the self, as Plato argued, but contributes to the welfare and happiness of everyone around us.

SOURCES OF MORALITY AND THE CRIMINAL JUSTICE SYSTEM: RELIGION, CRIME, AND JUSTICE

In the early part of this chapter, we were exposed to Divine Command Theory—the idea that morality is dependent upon or derived from the word of God. Although the theory of divine command may be unfamiliar to most, there are certainly a great many people whose conceptions of morality are intertwined with religious beliefs and teachings. Religious beliefs have been and are central to the lives of many people, in the United States and throughout the world. In the context of criminal justice, controversy surrounds the extent to which religious beliefs and values do and should infiltrate our understanding of crime, the making and enforcement of laws, and the ways in which we choose to treat (or punish) those who violate the law. To what extent do and should religious values influence the criminal justice system? We begin this section by looking briefly at the ways in which religion has shaped the history of criminal justice, and conclude by exploring a contemporary controversy which finds itself at the intersection of religion and criminal justice—that of capital punishment.

Religion and the History of Criminal Justice

The social history of criminal justice is one throughout which religion routinely emerges as in influence in nearly every sphere, from how crimes have been defined, to conceptions of justice, to the rationale for punishment and corrections. Throughout most of the Middle (or "Dark") Ages—spanning approximately one thousand years of Western history—religion was largely inseparable from conceptions and practices of law, crime, and punishment. As the dominant social force, the Roman Catholic Church was also the dominant legal force. Church leaders were often lawmakers and judges, many crimes were defined on the basis of Biblical prohibitions, and certain acts such as heresy and witchcraft were grounds for torturous trials and brutal and excessive punishments (imposed by the Church). As many crimes were also *sins*, lawbreakers were perceived to have offended both society and God. Consequently, the brutal and excessive nature of many punishments reflected an effort to impose both legal as well as divine justice.[33]

The crime of "heresy" is of particular historical significance. Broadly defined, "heresy" encompassed nearly any act that was contrary to the church doctrine. Of course, interpretation and application of heresy laws was left in the hands of church leaders, thereby allowing for nearly anyone to be judged a heretic, and nearly any act heretical. Facing the threat of heresy, the Church began to replace conventional trials with *ordeals* as a means of determining guilt and innocence. **Ordeals** (or *trials by ordeal*) subjected those accused of heresy to extremely painful and sometimes deadly "tests of faith." One of the better-known ordeals—sometimes called the "ducking" or "floating" ordeal—involved binding a "suspect" and throwing her or him into a river. The innocent would float, while the guilty would sink. It was believed that, for those who were truly innocent, God would intervene and assist the accused in passing the test. Of course, very few people passed such tests, and very few people were found innocent. Those who were found guilty, if they were still alive, would then be punished for their crimes and sins—oftentimes through an equally torturous and painful death sentence such as being burned alive.[34]

The interests of the Church in combating heresy eventually gave rise to a several-hundred-year law enforcement campaign known as the Holy Inquisition. Beginning in 1231, enforcers literally "hunted down" heretics and, at least for those who refused to confess, imposed punishments as severe as death. By its end, the Inquisition had claimed the lives of thousands—perhaps millions—of accused heretics (most of whom were women).

Although the history of the United States is comparably short, the influence of religious ideas concerning crime and punishment is equally evident. Many early settlers came to America in search of religious freedom and founded communities that were to be ruled by the word of God.[35] Well into eighteenth-century America, religion "entered into all discourse, marked all observations, and gave meaning to every private and public crisis—crime included."[36] Crimes were effects of demonic forces, offenses against God and were to be punished as such—"crime, sin, guilt, and punishment were understood as one."[37]

As it was closely tied to religion, the notion of crime and criminal definitions spanned a wide range of human behaviors in early America. Not only were obvious offenses such as theft and murder defined as crimes, so too did various other transgressions justify punishment. Profanity, drunkenness, flirting and gossiping, idolatry, blasphemy, and witchcraft were widely regarded as unlawful. As well, Puritan communities imposed punishments for various other religious violations, such as "failing to attend church or failing to pray on the Sabbath."[38] Crimes were met with punishments ranging from fines to "whippings, mutilation, shaming techniques, banishment, and death."[39]

By the early- to mid-1800s, conceptions of crime and punishment began to be divorced from their earlier religious foundations. As the principles of law and punishment outlined by Beccaria and Bentham (i.e., the classical school of criminology) gained increasing acceptance throughout the Western world, many American laws were rewritten in accordance with these principles. Religious notions such as guilt, sin, and repentance, however, remained evident in the correctional sphere. Around this same time, early prisons were developed, designed to facilitate reform by penance, isolating offenders from the outside world so that they could reflect upon and repent for their sins. The Pennsylvania and Auburn systems of prison discipline, for instance, reserved a central role for religious reform through penitence. Isolation, for example, was commonly employed as a means of maximizing time for reflection and repentance in the interest of reform.

The religious nature of colonial life in America has had a lasting impact on conceptions of law, crime, and justice. While law and religion are now understood as separate in principle, for many Americans they are or at least should be interrelated. Even today many of the fundamental ideas of the American criminal justice system are implicitly rooted in religious concepts such as sin and redemption.[40] As we have seen, the term "penitentiary" itself—still used today—derives from this religious concept of "penitence," and we are now beginning to see a reemergence of faith-based prison programs that include a spiritual/religious element to offender rehabilitation. As well, many current moral/legal controversies from abortion and euthanasia to prayer in public schools elicit strong religious sensibilities and are often argued on religious grounds. To illustrate the ways in which religious beliefs can and sometimes do impact arguments for and against criminal justice practices, we conclude this section by examining the role of religion in the ongoing debate surrounding capital punishment.

Religion and the Practice of Capital Punishment

Religious beliefs—in particular those stemming from variations of the Christian faith—unquestionably influence the opinions of a great many American citizens. In fact, when it comes to key social issues, religion is often a basis for divisiveness rather than consensus.[41] Notwithstanding the supposed need for separation of Church and State, some have argued that religious considerations *should* play an important role in the development and implementation of public policy. Many of these same people lament what they feel to be a decreasing role for religion in public life. America, it is argued, was founded upon Christian values and, consequently, those values should be an important part of how the country is run. One might expect, then, that Biblical teachings about various social issues would have a significant impact on public opinion concerning those issues.

Exactly *what* Biblical teachings say about these issues, however, is often a matter of interpretative conflict. One such issue over which much controversy exists and about which many Americans turn to religion for guidance and/or support for their position is that of the death penalty, or capital punishment for criminal offenders. As we have explored the ways in which religious beliefs have influenced crime and punishment throughout history, it may be interesting to briefly examine the contemporary issue of capital punishment through the lens of religion. As Christianity is by far the largest religious group in the United States, it is on Christian teachings that we focus.

RELIGIOUS SUPPORT FOR CAPITAL PUNISHMENT

Within the Christian faith groups, passages from the Old Testament (a.k.a. Hebrew Scriptures or Judaic Bible) are common reference points for the justification of capital punishment on retributive grounds. Retribution of the "eye for an eye" (i.e., *lex talionis*) variety is one of the most common reasons provided for supporting capital punishment, and for many people retributive sentiments are shaped by religious teachings:[42]

- Genesis 9:6—"Whoever sheds the blood of man, by man shall his blood be shed . . ."
- Exodus 21:23—"thou shalt give life for life, eye for eye, tooth for tooth . . ."

These passages, as well as several others, are sometimes interpreted as justifying—if not mandating—capital punishment for murderers. Problematically, however, a literal interpretation of the Old Testament would also have us support slavery and prescribe the death penalty for theft, blasphemy, laboring on the Sabbath, cursing one's parents, adultery, and a good number of other "crimes" that are no longer capital offenses and for which few—if any—people would continue to support death as a punishment.

The wide range of offenses (no less than 36) punishable by death in Biblical times notwithstanding, in practice the penalty was rarely used. Procedural rules made it difficult, if not impossible, to impose a sentence of death. Accused offenders enjoyed a variety of safeguards designed to protect against wrongful execution. The lack of such safeguards in today's criminal justice system (or, at least, the seeming ineffectiveness of those that do exist) is sometimes cited by contemporary religious authorities as grounds for supporting capital punishment in principle, yet opposing it in practice. For instance, the Reverend Whitney West, pastor of Lincoln Park Baptist Church in Ohio, argues that:

> The only way for life to have value is to follow the Scriptures: "A life for a life" . . .
> But under our current system, where it's not a matter of justice but a matter
> of money and lawyers, it's difficult to support it now . . . I think it should be
> done and done properly, but if it isn't done properly, fairly, and justly, then it
> shouldn't be done at all.[43]

The New Testament (a.k.a. Christian Bible) has fewer explicit references that allow for support to be drawn for capital punishment. Advocates sometimes cite

Romans 13:4, "if you do wrong, be afraid, for [the governing authority] does not near the sword in vain; for he is the servant of God to execute his wrath." As well, some have pointed out that when given the opportunity, Christ failed to explicitly renounce capital punishment. Where, in Matthew 5:17, an adulteress is nearing execution by stoning, Jesus is reputed to have saved her life, crying, "He that is without sin among you, let him cast the first stone. . . ." While this passage is sometimes used as evidence of Jesus' opposition to capital punishment, others interpret it as claiming that the death penalty might be called for in certain circumstances. While Jesus himself never resorted to violence, it is argued, he never specifically denies the governing authority that right.[44]

RELIGIOUS OPPOSITION TO CAPITAL PUNISHMENT

As is evident from Table 6.1, most Christian denominations and groups—both Eastern and Western—oppose capital punishment and support its abolition. In fact, since the 1950s and 1960s, the Catholic Church as well as all major denominations of Protestantism—save the Southern Baptists—have officially aligned themselves against the death penalty. Religious leaders who advocate the abolition of the death penalty have pointed generally to Jesus' advocacy of love (even for one's enemies), mercy, and forgiveness in the New Testament and to capital punishment's inconsistency with the effort "to promote respect for human life, to stem the tide of violence in our society and to embody the message of God's redemptive love."[45] As well, by executing a murderer, we are taking away her or his opportunity to repent. Finally, capital punishment is believed to "institutionalize retribution and revenge and to exacerbate violence by giving it official sanction."[46]

TABLE 6.1

Support for and Opposition to Capital Punishment among Major Religious Groups in the United States

Support/Retention	Mixed	Opposition/Abolition
Southern Baptist	Judaism*	Roman Catholic Church
Islam	Pentecostal	American Baptist
Latter-Day Saints (Mormons)	Atheists	United Methodist Church
	Agnostics	Evangelical Lutheran
		Eastern Orthodox
		Presbyterian
		Episcopal
		Reformed Church
		United Church of Christ
		Mennonites
		Amish
		Society of Friends (Quakers)
		Unitarian

*Although the American Jewish Committee officially opposes it, Judaism allows for capital punishment in a narrow range of circumstances.

Source: Ontario Consultants on Religious Tolerance. Available at religioustolerance.org.

While supporters of capital punishment often rely on passages from the Old Testament to support their views, opponents have referenced several sources that arguably denounce its practice. Even within the Old Testament's Book of Genesis, some argue, God prescribes the punishment of banishment and exile for the "first murder." Having murdered his brother Abel, Cain is sent by God to wander the earth and marked to indicate that no one else should kill him. Thus, while other passages in Genesis are often cited in support of capital punishment, some have pointed to the contradictory nature of even these messages.

Others have argued that killing—including state-sanctioned killing—directly conflicts with the principle of the sacredness of life espoused by the Christian faith. Franciscan Gino Concetti, for instance, wrote in *L'Osservatore Romano* that:

> In light of the word of God, and thus of faith, life—all human life—is sacred and untouchable. No matter how heinous the crimes ... [the criminal] does not lose his fundamental right to life, for it is primordial, inviolable, and inalienable, and thus comes under the power of no one whatsoever.[47]

Often cited in this light is the commandment—commonly listed as the Sixth—"Thou shalt not kill." This commandment would seem to prohibit killing and thus would disallow capital punishment. Some proponents of capital punishment, however, have argued that it better translates as "Thou shalt not commit murder," in which case the Sixth Commandment would prohibit *murderous killings* but not justified killings in times of war, self-defense, and the capital punishment of offenders.[48] For instance, the highly influential Christian philosopher Saint Augustine writes in his *The City of God*:

> The same divine law which forbids the killing of a human being allows certain exceptions, as when God authorizes killing by a general law or when He gives an explicit commission to an individual for a limited time. Since the agent of authority is but a sword in the hand, and is not responsible for the killing, it is in no way contrary to the commandment, "Thou shalt not kill" to wage war at God's bidding, or for the representatives of the State's authority to put criminals to death ...[49]

Most scriptural opposition to capital punishment draws from various passages in the New Testament. Jesus is argued to have advocated mercy for and forgiveness of all people, irrespective of their status or sins. In Matthew 5:44, for instance, he asks that people love their enemies ("You have heard that it was said, 'Love your neighbor and hate your enemy.' But I tell you: Love your enemies and pray for those who persecute you ...") and to forgive those who would trespass against them.[50] Jesus is said to have forgiven even his executioners while on the cross. Finally, Jesus seems to have advocated an alternative to violence where, in Matthew 5:38–40, he teaches, "You have heard the commandment, 'An eye for an eye, a tooth for a tooth,' but what I say to you is: Offer no resistance to injury. When a person strikes you on the right cheek, turn and offer him the other."

The ambiguous and sometimes contradictory nature of scriptural references has given rise to a storied history of disparate interpretations and a general lack of consensus within the Christian tradition concerning the morality of capital punishment. Interestingly, not all—or even most—members of Christian denominations share in the official position of their group. Notwithstanding the opposition to capital punishment by virtually all major Christian denominations, as many as 80% of Christians continue to support capital punishment—slightly higher than support within the American population at large. In other words, capital punishment seems to be an issue about which individual members hold opinions that are, on the whole, inconsistent with the official positions of their larger religious groups.

As Robert Bohm writes following Protestant scholar and journalist Reverend G. Aiken Taylor, much of the confusion may be a function of unanswered questions concerning the difference between the Christian personal ethic and Christian ethics as they apply to the maintenance of social order. Most Christians "tend to apply what the Bible teaches us about how we—personally—should behave toward our neighbors . . ."[51] However, it may be that this personal ethic should be understood differently from what the Bible teaches about ethics and the preservation of order within society. Perhaps the Bible encourages individual Christians to love, show mercy, and forgive, yet allows for governing bodies to impose capital punishment where it is in the interests of the common good. Indeed, as Bohm asks, does God have two different sets of rules—one ethic for individual Christians and a different ethic for governments and rulers?

We would seem to be without an authoritative answer to this and similar questions. Given the ambiguous nature of the Christian scriptures on the issue of capital punishment, the controversy over whether death is a morally acceptable sanction within the Christian paradigm will surely continue. In the meantime, as Bohm implies, the fact that such a lack of consensus is evident even within the Christian tradition should encourage us to question the value and desirability of religious influence on lawmaking and conceptions of justice—whether in the context of capital punishment or elsewhere.

SUMMARY

We have now considered several of the more common sources of morality. For purposes of review, we can summarize them as follows:

- *Divine Command:* Because God says so!
- *Mutual Advantage:* Because we are all self-interested and because interests will inevitably come into conflict, it is to the mutual advantage of everyone if we agree upon certain rules.
- *Mutual Aid:* We are naturally sociable and motivated to want others to be well.
- *Character:* We will be happier and psychologically healthier people if we are moral. At the same time, our morality will benefit the well-being of all humanity.

These answers are not necessarily mutually exclusive. While not to suggest that it *should*, our motivation to be moral probably derives from a combination of these things, and may well differ depending on the situation in which we find ourselves or the choices with which we are faced. Why *do* people choose to act morally? The reality is that in everyday encounters people behave morally for a variety of reasons: sometimes out of self-interest (e.g., hope of reward, fear of punishment as described in Chapter 5); sometimes from a genuine desire to want others to be well; sometimes from a sense of obligation or duty; and sometimes from religious or spiritual reasons. However, as we have seen, most moral philosophers would argue that some motivations are "better" or more desirable than others.

To more completely conclude our discussion of moral psychology, we need to examine what social science tells us about motivations or *reasons* for moral behavior, particularly with respect to their *development*. Simply put, the question is whether morality is something that does or can *develop*. If so, *how* or by what processes does it develop? Do or can we become "more moral" and, if yes, in what ways? If morality does indeed evolve, can some people then be said to be more "morally mature" than others? If so, does this in turn suggest that some motivations or reasons for moral behavior are somehow more advanced and desirable than others? Within philosophy and the social sciences (including criminology/criminal justice), these and similar questions are broadly understood as concerns for *moral development*. It is to this topic that we turn in the subsequent chapter.

KEY TERMS AND CONCEPTS

Absolute Divine Command Theory   mutual advantage
Divine Command Theory   mutual aid
inner balance   ordeals (trials by ordeal)
Moderate Divine Command Theory   problem of common ground

DISCUSSION QUESTIONS

1. What is the difference between Absolute Divine Command Theory and Moderate Divine Command Theory? What role should religion play in the making of law and policy in criminal justice? Is there a role for religion in settling disputes within criminal justice? In what ways might religion be used in rehabilitative practices? More generally, do you believe that religion can stand in the way of being moral? Explain your responses.

2. At a citizen review board charged with examining complaints regarding police misconduct, an officer describes the reasons why he "planted" evidence to convict a suspect. The officer points out that the suspect reportedly was responsible for the rapes of at least ten preadolescent girls. In fact, the suspect's alleged actions resulted in permanent physical and profound psychological injuries to at least three victims. Regrettably, despite the best efforts of the police, there remained insufficient evidence to arrest, prosecute, and convict the suspect. Everyone on the force knew who was responsible for the crimes and everyone wanted this particular suspect caught. So, in order to prevent future acts of sexual abuse, the officer under review planted blood samples at the latest crime scene. The officer concluded that he felt an obligation and a duty to act this way, given the serious harm the alleged offender had caused several innocent victims. In this case, to what extent could the officer be said to have a duty to the public? The victims and their families? To justice? Did the officer do the "right" thing?

3. Recently, the fledgling local newspaper in your community ran a story describing the release of a man convicted of murder. The man had served fifteen years in prison. Throughout this ordeal, he professed his innocence. Many residents in your hometown did not believe that the man was telling the truth; in fact, people recalled that the person was never particularly honest in anything he said or did. However, testing from new DNA technology revealed that the man was telling the truth all along. The newspaper saw the story as an opportunity to capture some public attention and bolster its circulation. It also felt that, given the lack of support the town displayed toward the convicted man over the years, it could help correct any injustice the town had committed against this person by not believing him. What motivation(s) informed the newspaper's decision? Given these motivations, was the action taken by the newspaper moral or not? Justify your response.

4. Following Hobbes, laws and moral rules create a social climate of mutual advantage in which our natural tendencies to be competitive, self-interested, and take advantage of others are held in check. But is this how things work in all facets of everyday life? Consider the world of business and corporate crime. Enron, for instance, grew to become America's seventh largest company in just fifteen short years. Its investments and holdings involved forty different countries; its workforce consisted of approximately twenty-one thousand employees. However, the success of Enron involved an elaborate hoax. In short, the firm lied about its profits to stockholders and to the government. This deception led investors and creditors to pull away from the company, believing that retreating sooner was far better than losing more money later. The company filed for bankruptcy and thousands of pensioners, stockholders, and other investors lost millions in revenue savings. Is Enron merely an exception to the rule, or are there other cases in which businesses and corporations lie, cheat, and exploit others for their own advantage? Do various types of corporate crime illustrate the ineffectiveness of the idea of mutual advantage? If some corporations are not motivated to "play by the rules," what might be done to reduce their harmful actions?

SUGGESTED READINGS

Fromm, Erich. (1947). *Man for Himself: An Inquiry into the Psychology of Ethics*. New York: Fawcett.

Fromm, Erich. (1966). *The Dogma of Christ and Other Essays on Religion, Psychology, and Culture*. Garden City, NY: Anchor Books.

Hospers, John. (1995). *Human Conduct: Problems of Ethics*. Belmont, CA: Wadsworth.

Ridley, Matt. (1996). *The Origins of Virtue: Human Instincts and the Evolution of Cooperation*. New York: Penguin.

Tifft, Larry. (1976). *The Struggle to Be Human: Crime, Criminology and Anarchism*. London, UK: Cienfuegos Press.

ENDNOTES

[1]See Berg, "How Could Ethics Depend on Religion?" In P. Singer (ed.), *A Companion to Ethics* (Malden, MA: Blackwell, 1993).

[2]Regina Wentzel Wolfe and Christine E. Gudorf, *Ethics and World Religions: Cross-Cultural Case Studies* (Maryknoll, NY: Orbis Books, 1999); see also, Judith Boss, *Ethics for Life* (Mountain View, CA: Mayfield, 2001), pp. 151–189.

[3]James Rachels, *The Elements of Moral Philosophy* (New York: McGraw-Hill, 1986), p. 41.

[4]S. Jack Odell, *On Consequentialist Ethics* (Toronto/Ontario, Canada: Wadsworth, 2004), pp. 24–25.

[5]Ibid.

[6]Vincent Ruggiero, *Thinking Critically About Ethical Issues,* 5th ed. (New York: McGraw-Hill, 2001), p. 7.

[7]Richard Brandt, *Ethical Theory* (Englewood Cliffs, NJ: Prentice Hall, 1959), p. 19.

[8]Vincent Ruggiero, *Thinking Critically About Ethical Issues,* p. 7.

[9]James Rachels, *The Elements of Moral Philosophy* (New York: McGraw-Hill, 1986) p. 42.

[10]Ibid.

[11]Ibid.

[12]John Hospers, *Human Conduct: An Introduction to the Problems of Ethics* (New York: Harcourt, Brace & World, 1961), pp. 189–191.

[13]Ibid.

[14]John Hospers, *Human Conduct: Problems of Ethics* (Belmont, CA: Wadsworth, 1995), p. 189.

[15]e.g., Will Kymlicka, "The Social Contract Tradition." In P. Singer (Ed.), *A Companion to Ethics* (Malden, MA: Blackwell, 1993).

[16]Kurt Baier, *The Moral Point of View* (Ithaca, NY: Cornell University Press, 1958), p. 314.

[17]Thomas Hobbes, *Leviathan* (New York: Touchstone Books, 1997).

[18]Jean-Jacques Rousseau, *Discourse on the Origins of Inequality* (Indianapolis, IN: Hackett Publishing, 1992), p. 76.

[19]Peter Kropotkin, *Mutual Aid: A Factor of Evolution* (Manchester, NH: Porter Sargent Publishers, 1976), pp. 148–149.

[20]For a recent application of Kropotkin's mutual aid ethic in crime and justice studies, see Christopher R. Williams and Bruce A. Arrigo, "Anarchaos and Order: On the Emergence of Social Justice," *Theoretical Criminology: An International Journal,* 5, 223–252 (2001).

[21]Ibid.

[22]Larry Tifft, *The Struggle to Be Human: Crime, Criminology, and Anarchism* (London: Cienfuegos Press, 1976).

[23]Zoltan Kovecses, *Metaphor and Emotion: Language, Culture, and Body in Human Feeling* (Cambridge: Cambridge University Press, 2003).

[24]Christopher Falzon, *Philosophy Goes to the Movies: An Introduction to Philosophy* (New York: Routledge, 2002), pp. 88–92.

[25]Plato, *The Republic.*

[26]Christopher Falzon, *Philosophy Goes to the Movies,* p. 88; see also, Kelly Rogers, *Self-Interest: An Anthology of Philosophical Perspectives from Antiquity to the Present* (New York: Routledge, 1997), p. 1.

[27]Plato, *The Republic;* Nickolas Pappas, *Plato and the Republic* (New York: Routledge, 1995).

[28]Christopher Falzon, *Philosophy Goes to the Movies,* p. 88.

[29]Ibid., p. 88; Nicholas P. White, *Companion to Plato's Republic* (Indianapolis, IN: Hacket Publishing, 1979), p. 44.

[30]Nickolas Pappas, *Plato and the Republic.*

[31]Christopher Falzon, *Philosophy Goes to the Movies*, pp. 88–89.

[32]Nickolas Pappas, *Plato and the Republic*, p. 69.

[33]See, e.g., Timothy Gorringe, *God's Just Vengeance* (New York: Cambridge University Press, 1996).

[34]See, e.g., Michael Welch, *Corrections: A Critical Approach* (New York: McGraw-Hill, 1996), esp. Chap. 3; Werner Einstadter and Stuart Henry, *Criminological Theory: An Analysis of Its Underlying Assumptions* (Fort Worth, TX: Harcourt Brace, 1995), esp. Chap. 2.

[35]Thomas Blomberg and Karol Lucken, *American Penology: A History* (New York: Aldine de Gruyter, 2000), p. 25.

[36]Ibid.

[37]Ibid., p. 26.

[38]Ibid.

[39]Ibid., p. 29.

[40]David Friedrichs, *Law in Our Lives: An Introduction* (Los Angeles: Roxbury, 2001), pp. 70–74.

[41]Ibid., p. 72.

[42]Robert Bohm, *Deathquest II: An Introduction to the Theory and Practice of Capital Punishment* (Cincinnati, OH: Anderson, 2003), pp. 242–243.

[43]*Akron Beacon Journal*, 4 March 1998.

[44]Avery Dulles, "Catholicism and Capital Punishment," *First Things*, 112, 30–35 (2001).

[45]Religious Leaders in Florida, "Religious Views Denounce the Death Penalty." In B. Szumski, L. Hall, and S. Bursell (Eds.), *The Death Penalty: Opposing Viewpoints* (St. Paul, MN: Greenhaven, 1986), pp. 86–91. Quoted in Robert Bohm, *Deathquest II: An Introduction to the Theory and Practice of Capital Punishment* (Cincinnati: Anderson, 2003), pp. 242–243.

[46]Robert Bohm, p. 243.

[47]Quoted in Avery Dulles, "Catholicism and Capital Punishment," *First Things*, 112, 30–35 (2001).

[48]Robert Bohm, p. 246.

[49]Quoted in Avery Dulles, "Catholicism and Capital Punishment," *First Things*, 112, 30–35 (2001).

[50]Robert Bohm, pp. 246–247.

[51]Quoted in Bohm, p. 248.

Chapter 7

BECOMING ETHICAL: THE DEVELOPMENT OF MORALITY

The notion of **moral development** implies that conceptions of morality and types of moral reasoning are not static across the lifespan. Instead, to suggest that morality is subject to development is to suggest that it changes and evolves over time. What this means is that some beliefs, values, and ways-of-thinking are, in a manner of speaking, "better" or more desirable than others because they reflect a higher level or more advanced form of ethical judgment. Thus, it is important to consider *how* moral development occurs and *how* different stages of moral development appear. In other words, the question becomes what modes of reasoning, expressions of motivation, and types of moral principles, values, and ideals are characteristic of people at more advanced stages of moral development? And, how is it that people do or can reach such evolved stages of ethical choice-making and action?

While philosophers have always been interested in moral development, most recently our comprehension of it has been furthered by researchers in the field of developmental psychology. Among the more influential works stemming from the psychological study of moral behavior are those of Lawrence Kohlberg (1927–1987).[1] Kohlberg's pioneering work during the 1960s, 1970s, and 1980s was responsible for tremendous growth and progress involving the theory of, research on, and knowledge about the evolution of morality and moral behavior. Kohlberg was particularly interested in the moral reasoning of children and adolescents; that is, the thought processes characteristic of young people in relation to moral dilemmas.

Through his research on moral development, Kohlberg suggested that morality and moral reasoning proceed through a series of "stages." More accurately, Kohlberg argued for an elaborate developmental sequence consisting of three levels, with each level involving two developmental periods. Kohlberg maintained that individuals progress through these six phases in a fixed order; that is, without skipping a stage. Following Kohlberg, what this suggests, then, is that there are (more or less) universal stages of moral growth linked to developments in human cognition. In other words, types of moral beliefs, motivations, choices, and actions will be characteristically different in relation to the stage of cognitive development or intellectual maturity individuals have attained.

For Kohlberg, motivations for moral choices and behaviors are based in thinking and reasoning rather than in affect or emotion. Consequently, good moral reasoning and good moral choices require us to be sound thinkers and to have refined *cognitive* (thinking as opposed to feeling) skills. Cognitive skills that are central to morality and moral development include such abilities as: imagination, conceptual thinking, the recognition of similarities and differences between (comparable) moral situations; and general reasoning ability that corresponds to the capacity for abstract and logical thought.

To illustrate, the capacity for imagination is essential to empathy (imagining oneself in another's position); and empathy, as many would argue, is central to moral reasoning and behavior. In order for any one of us "to put ourselves in another's shoes" we must utilize our powers of imagination. Theoretically, persons with more developed imaginative capacities are better able to empathize and, presumably, are more inclined to recognize the needs and feelings of others. When we recognize the needs and feelings of others, we are more likely to consider these interests in our moral reasoning, in the choices we make given that reasoning and, ultimately, in our actions toward others.

KOHLBERG'S MORAL STAGES

Before we explore Kohlberg's stages of moral development in greater detail, it should be noted that very few people are thought to ever reach the highest stages (5 and 6). This is not necessarily because they *can't*; rather, higher stages of moral development represent ideal phases that require more than simply the natural evolution of cognitive skills. As previously noted, Kohlberg proposed that moral development occurs in a series of stages that are linked with the more general development of cognitive skills or intellectual faculties. More specifically, Kohlberg's research led him to conclude that there exist three levels of moral growth, with each level having two stages. The levels and stages form a developmental sequence in which no one can "skip" a stage (see Table 7.1).

TABLE 7.1
Kohlberg's Stages of Moral Development

- *Level 1: Preconventional Morality*
  Stage 1: Punishment and Obedience
  Stage 2: Instrumental Purpose and Exchange
- *Level 2: Conventional Morality*
  Stage 3: Interpersonal Expectations and Conformity
  Stage 4: Law and Order/Social System Maintenance
- *Level 3: Postconventional Morality*
  Stage 5: Social Contract/Utility/Rights
  Stage 6: Universal Ethical Principles

Level 1: Preconventional Morality

At the preconventional level of morality, children (ages 1–10 years) approach moral issues purely from the perspective of *self-interest*. Preconventional morality is *self-focused* morality, prior to any conception of social convention or shared norms. Moral values are regarded as external to the self; that is, they do not reside in any internal processes, but exist "out there." The child experiences these values through the enforcement strategies or regulation efforts undertaken by authority figures. At this stage of development, the child abides by rules; however, they are understood only in terms of the consequences that attach when following or failing to follow them (e.g., punishment by parents, teachers, etc.). Thus, what matters most during this period of moral development are the *consequences* stemming from one's (potential) actions.

For example, during their early years of psychological growth, many children will share toys with other children while playing. However, when this activity occurs it is not because they recognize that sharing is the morally "right" thing to do or because they understand cognitively that sharing is ultimately in their own best interest. Rather, the motivation for sharing is better understood as *fearing the consequences* of not sharing. Thus, preconventional morality is a rule-following form of morality, but one in which the underlying function of those rules is not yet comprehended.

During Stage 1—the **punishment and obedience orientation**—moral thinking is characterized by *perceptions* of right and wrong that are based on obedience to authority and shaped by the *threat of punishment* or the *promise of reward*. Actions for which the child receives praise are understood as right; actions for which the youth is censored are understood as wrong. Within this phase, then, moral thinking does not extend beyond the association of certain behaviors with particular rewards and/or punishments. As such, the child fully submits to an authority figure's definition of right and wrong: The youth is concerned only with the consequences that attach to the behavior and *not the behavior itself*.

The child is motivated to do what is "right" in order to avoid punishment. This motivation stems from his or her cognitive inability to understand the reasons underlying (perhaps justifying) the rules that have been imposed on the youth. However, what the child does understand is that other people have the power to dispense negative consequences on those who fail to follow the rules defined by these authority figures. Moreover, the child recognizes that these rules must be followed in the interest of avoiding such consequences. Thus, at the punishment and obedience stage, the needs and interests of other people are largely irrelevant. For instance, stealing is not wrong or bad because of its victimizing effect on the person from whom one stole; rather, the child identifies the activity as wrongful because the youth understands that she or he will be punished for stealing.

During Stage 2—the **instrumental purpose and exchange orientation**—moral thinking is characterized by egoism or self-interest. The aim of persons at this phase is to advance their own desires; the pursuit of self-interest (for oneself and/or for others) is understood as "right." Thus, whatever is effective in satisfying the child's self-regarding needs or wants is defined as right or moral.

"Moral" actions are undertaken purposefully and instrumentally: They are *used* only to further one's self-interest. Additionally, at this stage, a greater degree of concern for other people is noted. However, the logic of this behavior is purely egoistic as well. Finally, children operating within this period come to understand the basic notion of reciprocity. Reciprocity entails an exchange of goods and services. For example, person "1" engages in activity "X" in return for person "2" engaging in activity "Y." During Stage 2 of preconventional morality, children do not agree to reciprocity based on some reasoned assessment regarding the idea of justice, fairness, gratitude, and so on. Rather, reciprocal activities are undertaken because children recognize the self-serving benefits of doing so (e.g., "I'll scratch your back if you scratch mine").

Level 2: Conventional Morality

The level of conventional morality implies a concern for social rules and shared norms. Beginning around the age of 10 years, children begin to recognize that right and wrong are in some ways tied to the interests of other people and to society as a whole. Persons at this level become invested in maintaining conventional order, meeting the expectations of others—be they a family, peer group, community, or country. In contrast to the preconventional focus on consequences and self-interest, the conventional level of morality is characterized by *conformity*.

At Stage 3—**interpersonal expectations and conformity**—the child's orientation turns toward approval from others or an interest in pleasing others. Sometimes called the "good boy/nice girl" orientation (approval from others is often attained by being "good" or "nice"), Stage 3 thinking defines morality in terms of what should be done to win the support of others. Children begin to understand what is expected of them by their parents, teachers, and friends, and morality is interpreted as doing what is necessary to achieve these expectations. As distinguished from Stage 4, the approval that is characteristically desired during the interpersonal expectations and conformity orientation period is limited in scope.

During Stage 4, the spectrum of concern begins to expand beyond the mere expectations of family, friends, and other close intimates. Termed the **law and order orientation,** this period of moral development is characterized by an interest in laws, codes, and commandments and a corresponding respect for authority. Unlike Stage 1 where fear of punishment or other sanctions is the primary motivating force, persons benefiting from Stage 4 growth exhibit some awareness about the need for laws. Moreover, at the same time, this recognition of law is tied to an understanding that social order must be maintained. Thus, persons within this phase of moral maturity display a respect for law and authority, recognized as legitimate and necessary tools that help further and maintain social order.

When people reach Kohlberg's Stage 4 development, then, their moral reasoning reflects an effort to abide by laws, codes, fixed rules, and social obligations. Additionally, by this stage, they have developed some understanding of the function of laws, codes, and other rules. Consequently, they possess some heightened sense of what is morally "right," that morality is related to their participation in the existing social order and that, through this participation, they help to ensure the system's stability and maintenance.

Stage 4 is an important milestone in Kohlberg's model of moral development for several reasons—particularly as it contrasts with higher (postconventional) phases of growth. Perhaps most significant among these reasons is that, for the majority of people, this is the highest stage of maturity they will experience in their lifetimes. Stages 1 through 4 reflect *natural* developmental processes. In other words, education, socialization, training, and other influences are thought by Kohlberg to have little, if anything, to do with the evolution of moral reasoning throughout the first four phases. Moreover, according to Kohlberg, the developmental process through Stage 4 represents a *universal* pattern of cognitive development (i.e., a process of growth that is the same for all people, everywhere). Consequently, almost everyone (regardless of class, race, religion, society, culture, etc.) should reach this stage. Interestingly, the *content* of morality may differ from culture to culture or from time period to time period (because laws and norms vary across societies). Moreover, the length of time it takes to reach certain stages may differ culturally and/or temporally. However, the *process* of moral reasoning exhibited through Stage 4 is presumed to be the same universally. In theory, while almost everyone advances to Stage 4, considerably fewer people ever advance past the law-and-order orientation into more progressive types of moral reasoning (perhaps 20–25% of adults in contemporary society).[2] (see Table 7.2).

There is a second characteristic of Stage 4 development that differentiates it from its Stage 5 and 6 counterparts. In brief, while persons in Stage 4 demonstrate a "law-and-order" orientation, they do not question the legitimacy of those laws (or codes, commandments, etc.). In other words, there is no critique regarding the *content* of those laws, only a concern for conformity to them. Having reached Stage 4 development, many people internalize societal and institutional (e.g., religious, legal) rules regarding moral behavior; however, their adoption of these rules occurs *without having considered the underlying principles involved*. For example, the law-and-order orientation is exemplified in such reasoning as, "it is wrong to kill *because it is against the law*"; or, "abortion is wrong *because the Bible says so*" (see Box 7.1). Interestingly, these cases fail to offer any thoughtful or sophisticated consideration of the fundamental values and principles from which the laws or rules themselves are formed. Instead, there is only a concern for their authority as laws and rules and a felt need to conform to them because they issue from established powers.

What this means, then, is that through Stage 4 moral development does not require any *independent* thought on the part of the subject. We come to embrace societal and institutional laws, norms, and values as part of a natural development of reasoning skills, not because we have carefully considered them and determined, for

TABLE 7.2
Summary of Kohlberg's Stages of Moral Development

Stage	Who Reaches It	When Reached
Punishment and Obedience	Everyone	1–5 yrs.
Instrumental Purpose and Exchange	Everyone	5–10 yrs.
Interpersonal Expectations and Conformity	Everyone	10–16 yrs.
Law and Order	Everyone	16 yrs.–mid-20s, for most the remainder of life
Social Contract/Rights	20–25%	Mid-20s, at least
Universal Ethical Principles	Very, very few	?? (Some suggest middle-age)

BOX 7.1

Moral Reasoning and the Ethics of Abortion

Abortion is and has always been a highly contentious issue in the United States. There are few moral (and political) issues that generate stronger emotional reactions for many people. Troublingly, much discourse on abortion consists of more name-calling (e.g., "baby killer," "Bible-banger") than reasoned argumentation. Positions on abortion range from radical pro-life advocates who argue that a moral "right to life" exists from the moment of conception, to radical pro-choice advocates who argue that a woman's "right to choose" and "right to privacy" are always primary.

Indeed, abortion was illegal in most states prior to the 1973 case of *Roe v. Wade* in which the Supreme Court concluded that laws prohibiting abortion are unconstitutional in that they violate the fundamental right to privacy. Even then, the Court did not find abortion to be an absolute right. Under some circumstances, the right may be overridden. The Court ruled that states may not interfere with a woman's choice during the first trimester of a pregnancy. During the second trimester, however, states may impose limitations in the interest of protecting the pregnant woman's health. Finally, during the third trimester, the state may justifiably interfere with a woman's decision for purposes of protecting potential human life (the beginning of the third trimester is the time of viability—that point at which the fetus is capable of surviving outside of the mother's womb).

We should keep in mind that the Supreme Court rules on the legality and constitutionality of issues, not their morality. The Court's decision in *Roe v. Wade* was not a ruling on the moral desirability or acceptability of abortion, but an effort to sort out a complex constitutional issue. Thus despite the Court's legal findings, the morality of abortion remains a pressing concern. The following is a list of questions that might be helpful when contemplating the abortion debate. Each of these is a difficult question that must be answered before reaching any reasoned conclusion about the morality of abortion:

- For moral and legal purposes, are unborn children *persons?* Most people will agree that fetuses are *human*, but some argue that being human is different from being a person. Mary Anne Warren, for instance, suggests that "personhood" requires the following characteristics: (1) consciousness, (2) reasoning, (3) self-motivated activity, (4) the capacity to communicate, and (5) self-awareness. Because a fetus's brain is not sufficiently developed for these characteristics, some have argued, it is not a person and therefore does not enjoy the same moral rights as people (e.g., the right to life).
- If unborn children are not persons, is the fact that they have the *potential* to become persons enough to justify a right to life? Even those who argue that fetuses are not persons will generally recognize that they are potentially persons. Nevertheless, some would argue that a potential person is still not a person and therefore does not enjoy moral and legal rights.
- Should women (or, for that matter, all persons) have absolute rights over their own bodies? In other words, on what—if any—grounds can we morally invade the most private possessions (i.e., mind and body) that people have?
- If abortion is killing, is killing always wrong? We saw in Chapter 1 that many forms of killing are considered justifiable (e.g., war, self-defense). Even if we admit that killing is generally wrong, is it necessarily always so?
- If abortion should be illegal, should we make exceptions for women who become impregnated through rape or incest? Some sexual relations are not voluntary.

Should a woman maintain the right to have an abortion in those cases where she is not in any way responsible for her own pregnancy?

■ How heavily should the health of the woman weigh in the morality of abortion? In extreme cases, if a woman faces a significant risk of death if she continues to carry a fetus, does her "right to life" trump that of the unborn child's? If so, how significant must that risk be to justify terminating the pregnancy?

Now consider the following reasons for *having* an abortion. As you read through them, ask yourself: (1) whether the reason is a morally good one; and (2) which of Kohlberg's stages of moral development is reflected in the reason provided:

■ The mother is a teenager
■ The sex of the child is undesirable
■ The mother is mentally ill or developmentally disabled
■ The mother is physically disabled and will be unable to care for the child
■ The mother is a 14-year-old who was coerced into having sex by a 25-year-old man
■ The child will be severely mentally retarded
■ The mother is poor and will not be able to provide well for the child
■ The mother is single, unemployed, and already has eight other children
■ The child will interfere with the mother's career plans

Sources: Emmett Barcalow, *Moral Philosophy: Theories and Issues*, 2nd ed. (Belmont, CA: Wadsworth, 1998), pp. 266–277; Mary Anne Warren, "On the Moral and Legal Status of Abortion." In T. Mappes and J. Zematy, *Social Ethics*, 3rd ed. (New York: McGraw-Hill, 1987); Wendy Simonds, *Abortion at Work: Ideology and Practice in a Feminist Clinic* (Piscataway, NJ: Rutgers University Press, 1996).

ourselves, that they are legitimate and necessary. For this reason, adopting societal and/or institutional norms and abiding by them (e.g., living ones' life as a law-abiding citizen) is regarded as but a natural and expected outcome of moral development and not a reflection of advanced moral sensibilities.

Level 3: Postconventional Morality

Postconventional morality is characterized by an understanding of mutuality, the common good, and a genuine concern for the interests and welfare of other people. At this point, morality is *post*conventional because individuals (now at least in the mid-20s) no longer rely exclusively on social conventions, norms, or laws as the basis for understanding. Instead, postconventional moral reasoning reflects some effort to determine desirable moral values and principles apart from everyday, shared understandings, and to live on the basis of those unique values and principles. This is not to suggest that these morals are necessarily different from customary interpretations; only that the process by which they come to be accepted is different. Postconventional morality is arrived at independently through critical reflection. Ultimately, it is *internalized*. In other words, concepts such as justice, fairness, civility, and community develop from *within us* rather than being derived from sources external to us (e.g., parents, law, religion, social norms).

Persons having reached Stage 5—**social contract/legalism**—demonstrate an understanding of morality that emphasizes the social good and the principles by which it is achieved. Values such as individual rights (e.g., freedom, citizenship, autonomy) are understood as those that a "healthy" civilization should uphold and those that make a society "good." At this stage, moral thinking becomes more abstract and conceptual, rather than a literal interpretation of laws, rules, and regulations. For the most part, right and wrong are still defined in terms of codes and other institutionalized rules and regulations; however, the individual acknowledges the under lying merits of these laws—that is to say, the individual comes to have some fundamental and critical understanding of *why* they are valuable to society.

In Stage 4, people are interested in an orderly society and in "playing their part" to maintain this order through obedience to rules, procedures, commandments, and so forth. However, during Stage 5, people recognize that following established laws or shared norms is not always good. Simply because certain rules promote social order does not mean that the form this order takes is good or healthy. For instance, a totalitarian society can be orderly and can function well. At the same time, though, it may also leave much to be desired in terms of promoting or securing moral ideals (e.g., justice, fairness, rights).[3] Kohlberg concluded that persons at Stage 5 generally believe that a good society is best conceptualized as a *social contract* in which everyone agrees on two basic principles: (1) that all people should have basic *rights* such as life and liberty; and (2) that there should exist *democratic* procedures for making and changing laws and for making society a better place.[4] While persons at Stage 5 may very well conform to established laws, principles, and commandments, adherence to them is based on the recognition that these rules are fairly and justly created, thereby fulfilling a greater ethical purpose. As we will see in the next chapter, the sort of morality Kohlberg has in mind during Stage 5 is consistent with *utilitarian* conceptions, while his position in Stage 6 is best represented by the moral philosophies of Kant and Rawls (see Chapter 9).[5]

What we have by Stage 5, then, is a developmental process in which a significant qualitative change in moral reasoning occurs. The social contract/rights orientation involves, for the first time, a *critical* dimension—that is, a willingness to evaluate and assess those with whom one identifies.[6] Conversely, Stages 1 through 4 largely are characterized by an unthinking association with the values and interests of those social groups to which one belongs (e.g., friends, community, political or religious affiliations, or society more generally). By contrast, Stage 5 persons are committed to certain moral values and principles and are willing to regard as wrong or unethical those behaviors that are inconsistent with these values and principles. They adopt this point of view no matter who thinks or how many people act otherwise. Thus, Stage 5 is the first time in one's moral progression that *moral courage* becomes important (recall the discussion in the previous chapter regarding Plato's threefold soul, the virtue of courage borne of the spirited part, and inner balance). As we will see, courage is more fully developed and becomes a defining feature of one's Stage 6 moral growth; however, by Stage 5, there is some willingness to maintain and defend moral beliefs that are at odds with larger social groups, as well as society as a whole.

Stage 6—**universal ethical principles**—is the most advanced period of moral development, theoretically representing the highest level of moral reasoning. Very, very few people are thought to ever reach this stage (attained, perhaps, during midlife). Kohlberg suggested that because Stage 5 moral reasoning can still produce injustices, there must be some point of development that stands above the social contract/legalism orientation. Laws, for instance, can be created and enforced democratically; however, they nonetheless can result in unjust outcomes. In a democracy, the influence of the majority can work to have legislation passed that is opposed to the interests of the minority. However, persons at Stage 6 recognize that while laws may be enacted fairly and democratically, this is not necessarily the same as doing what is, in fact, fair and just. Democratic procedures, the rule of law, religious principles, and codes of conduct (including criminal justice codes) are regarded as less authoritative than higher ethical values and principles. However, individuals at Stage 6 acknowledge that transcendent principles (e.g., multiculturalism, mutual respect, inclusiveness, dignity, autonomy, community) are the foundation of a just and good society (see Table 7.3).

One issue that exemplifies that distinction between Stages 5 and 6 moral reasoning is **civil disobedience.**[7] Civil disobedience involves a peaceful refusal to obey existing laws that are felt to be unjust—a conscientious disrespect for laws that conflict with one's commitment to higher ethical principles.[8] These principles include such things as humanism, justice, equality, and respect for the dignity of other persons. Once having acquired the insight of Stage 6 moral development, persons typically adopt the wisdom of these *universal* ethical principles as a basis for their reasoning, judgment, choices, and actions. For these "enlightened" individuals, this orientation to everyday life replaces what they believe to be the perpetuation of injustice built on a foundation of blind obedience to the authority of law. Because persons at Stage 5 demonstrate a commitment to changing unjust laws through democratic processes, they are less inclined to endorse civil disobedience. In other words, their criticism of the "system" is not an outright rejection of it. However, by Stage 6, commitments to higher ethical principles trump what are believed to be limited (and flawed) regulations, laws, and codes.

Civil disobedience toward or peaceful noncompliance of unjust laws exemplifies the *independent* and *self-chosen* nature of moral values, principles, and commitments characteristic of Stage 6 development. Thus, for example, respecting the dignity of all human beings (and all nonhuman living things) may be recognized as more important than the legal provisions that pertain to our treatment of them. Additionally, the law may allow for—even demand—slavery (consider cultures where slavery is still practiced); however, persons at this advanced period of ethical reasoning embody the principle of respect for the dignity of others and embrace the freedom to exceed the

TABLE 7.3
Motivations for Moral Behavior at Each Stage of Development

Stage 1:	avoiding punishment
Stage 2:	advancing one's own interests
Stage 3:	expectations of others
Stage 4:	what the law says is right and wrong
Stage 5:	greatest good for the greatest number of people
Stage 6:	reversibility; empathic understanding

demands of law or to otherwise renounce formal rules in forthright and virtuous ways. Consequently, such open-minded persons may refuse to keep slaves, perhaps even helping to liberate them despite potential adverse consequences. In this respect, then, moral reasoning at this point in an individual's life demonstrates the courage to adopt and live by one's own ethics, notwithstanding the harms that might result (e.g., ostracism, imprisonment, death). For instance, a person drafted during a time of war who refuses to fight for one's country could be subjected to imprisonment. However, at this stage of moral development, the person would likely accept these consequences because her or his opposition to a war deemed unjust is more important than any legal obligation or negative sanction.

What is the process of reasoning that underlies Stage 6 moral development? Kohlberg referred to it as *second-order Golden Rule role taking*.[9] Essentially, this process entails two steps: (1) making an effort to understand how each person involved in a given situation perceives it; and (2) imagining how every person participating in the situation would feel if they were placed in each other's position. In short, the reasoning process is imaginative, *empathic*, and aimed at finding a "reversible" solution. By "reversible" solution, Kohlberg is referring to *a remedy that would be equally fair and just from the perspective of everyone involved in the situation*. This requires that we treat the needs and interests of all parties impartially, respecting the dignity of each individual and attempting to come to a resolution that would be agreeable for all concerned.[10]

Implications of Kohlberg's Moral Psychology

Kohlberg's theory is grounded in human cognitive processes. Consequently, what is most important is not necessarily the beliefs, values, or even choices we ultimately subscribe to or make. Instead, what is of fundamental importance is the method of reasoning by which we come to adopt these values and beliefs. However, following Kohlberg's insights on moral development, are some principles "better" than others? (See Table 7.4.)

Upon closer inspection, the answer appears to be "maybe." While Kohlberg's model suggests that higher-order values including dignity, community, fellowship, and so on are more enlightened than several others (thus challenging relativist arguments as described in Chapter 4), what is more explicit is that some *reasons* for our choices and actions are, in fact, better than others. Thus, two people can have contradictory beliefs concerning capital punishment, racial profiling, internet pornography, and any number of criminal justice controversies. While Kohlberg's theory does not necessarily allow us to determine which view on any ethical controversy is correct (based on our values/principles), it does allow us to assess which perspective is more "moral" by determining which of them is grounded in "better" reasoning.

Let us consider the example of volunteering at a homeless shelter. Suppose that three different persons (John, Paul, and Laurel) each volunteer at the shelter twice a week—John to fulfill community service obligations that are a mandate of his probation; Paul because his girlfriend will act more positively toward him; and Laurel because she recognizes that impoverished persons have certain needs and interests they

TABLE 7.4
To Steal or Not to Steal?

Stage 1:	I should not steal because I will get in trouble (i.e., be punished).
Stage 2:	If I can get away with it, I should steal because it's an easy way to get something I want.
	I should not steal because I might bring great harm to myself if something goes wrong or if I get caught.
Stage 3:	I should steal because my friends will think I'm "cool."
	I should not steal because my parents, teachers, and friends will not think of me as a good person.
Stage 4:	I should not steal because it's against the law.
Stage 5:	I should not steal because it is in the best interest of my community and society. Not stealing from others is a basic principle that is necessary to allow people to live good lives in a just society.
Stage 6:	I should not steal because I know how I would feel if someone stole from me.
	I should steal if doing so rectifies a fundamental injustice—(e.g., I am fighting oppression, inequality, and helping to make the world a better place).

cannot address on their own. Each person is *doing* the same thing (i.e., volunteering). However, based on Kohlberg's model, each individual represents a different level of moral development. Laurel is clearly the "most moral" of the three: Her motivation for volunteer work reflects a commitment to higher level ethical principles. John is motivated by an effort to avoid undesirable consequences (punishment) that would result from his failing to fulfill the conditions of his probation. Paul is motivated by self-interest. Though all three are engaged in morally desirable behavior, they do not exhibit the same degree of ethical maturity. As noted in Chapter 1, morality is not simply about "doing the right thing." In the context of ethics, what is important are the reasons underlying one's choices and actions.

Perhaps the most important implication of Kohlberg's model is his insistence that being a morally good person—possessing ethical maturity—requires that an individual *develop* moral reasoning skills. As we have seen, through Stage 4 this progression is thought to occur naturally and in spite of social and cultural influences (e.g., parenting, education, class, ethnicity). However, development beyond this stage is not natural to the process of cognitive development. Instead, evolution or maturation to Stages 5 and 6 requires several things. Assuming that morality does develop, it becomes important to consider *how* it develops; that is, how do we *become* good moral thinkers and decision makers, exhibiting higher stage characteristics of virtue and integrity?

If postconventional morality represents a more advanced and, thus, desirable level of moral development, we should have an interest in pursuing such advances. However, we cannot simply "choose" to exhibit Stage 6 reasoning and ethics. We may admire the character, qualities, and achievements of a Gandhi or a Jesus of Nazareth. We may even make an effort to model our own lives after such exemplary historical figures. Still, our admiration for these "enlightened" individuals, particularly as symbols of morality, does not necessarily mean that we can so easily embody the level of moral development they exhibited. Following Kohlberg's model, this is because we must first acquire and then grow the sort of reasoning and other cognitive skills characteristic of great moral leaders. Consequently, it is not so much a matter of *imitating* the moral qualities or behaviors of Gandhi, but of understanding *why* Gandhi adopted the values and principles that he did; that is, of thinking and reasoning like Gandhi.

Most of us are by now familiar with popular slogans such as, "What would Jesus do?" or "What would Buddha do?" From a developmental perspective, the question, actually, is not what Jesus or the Buddha would do, but *how they would think about what to do*. We may acknowledge that several great moral figures throughout history engaged in forgiveness and that, as such, we should make an effort to forgive in similar situations. However, if we do not understand *why* mercy, compassion, and forgiveness are desirable traits, we are not embodying the same degree of moral wisdom and insight featured by past ethical leaders.

Thus, what is implied in Kohlberg's model is the notion that good moral behavior is not a matter of attempting to emulate persons of good moral fiber. Instead, it is a matter of *internalizing* the reasoning processes these persons employ. What this means is that ethical maturity is not so much about internalizing moral content (e.g., learning certain values and principles) as much as it is about developing cognitive skills and thinking about moral dilemmas in more advanced ways. Once we have developed the sort of advanced reasoning talents characteristic of great moral figures, we will not have to make a conscious effort to think about what they would do when faced with the moral problem confronting us. Instead, sound moral choices will emerge naturally for us by virtue of the ways in which we have come to think about complicated moral situations.

Kohlberg also recognized that sometimes there is a discrepancy between thinking and doing that characterizes our choices and behaviors in the face of moral concerns. In short, people do not always act as they think. While we may show evidence of advanced moral reasoning when asked about a moral predicament, in practice we may act in a way that reflects a lower level of moral development. For instance, we may agree that assisting the needy or the underprivileged is important, but choose not to make charitable contributions, fail to volunteer our time, or refuse to support tax increases even when earmarked for additional social programming (some of us may even go to great lengths to avoid paying taxes!).

How Does Morality Develop?

So, how do we acquire and nurture reasoning skills characteristic of higher stages of moral development? As previously indicated, according to Kohlberg, moral development through Stage 4 proceeds independently, absent any particular socialization or training. Fear of punishment (Stage 1), self-interest (Stage 2), concern for approval/disapproval from others (Stage 3), and the internalization of group and societal norms (Stage 4) are age-related occurrences that are thought to happen universally. We advance through these stages simply by being exposed to life experiences that encourage us to utilize and develop various cognitive skills. These experiences enable us to think about ourselves, other people, and various life situations.

In short, Kohlberg argued that children (and, at postconventional phases, adults) progress through different stages of moral development *from their own thinking about moral concerns.*[11] Various interactions we have over the course of the lifespan promote moral development by stimulating cognitive processes, thereby encouraging the refinement of reasoning skills essential to morality.[12] For example, becoming engaged in discussions or debates with others—especially those whose views differ from our own—can challenge us to reconsider our beliefs and encourage us to develop a more comprehensive position or to consider a variety of perspectives.[13]

Suppose that Marc (Stage 4) argues that we should obey the law under all circumstances because it is central to ensuring social order. In response to Marc's position, Sandra indicates that laws are not always moral, nor are they always in the best interest of the collective good. She uses the example of Nazi Germany, which was characterized by rules most people today would find morally objectionable, especially since these laws were opposed to the interests of a great number of people (e.g., the extermination of Jewish people, persons of color, gays, and various ethnic groups). Theoretically, Marc will recognize the inadequacy of his own view, experience some cognitive tension, and resolve this tension by modifying his own perspective to account for this inconsistency. In other words, Marc's debate with Sandra encourages him to move closer to Stage 5 development.[14]

Kohlberg suggested that when we are challenged to recognize the inadequacies of our existing reasoning, we are forced into a situation that motivates us to formulate better positions.[15] This sort of critical thinking about ethical issues is especially relevant at more advanced (postconventional) phases of moral development. Postconventional morality seems to depend upon the evolution of critical, independent thought and reasoning skills that require, for most people, considerable life experience, exposure to different cultural values and belief systems, emotional maturity, and/or education and training aimed at developing improved thinking skills. We will return to the importance of independent thought and critical thinking skills in significantly greater detail in the final chapter of this text.

Additionally, though, Kohlberg indicated that *role-taking opportunities* can provide worthwhile occasions for moral development by inviting us to reflect on the views of others.[16] Considering the perspective, needs, and interests of people is integral to Stage 6 moral development, and role-taking opportunities represent a context in which to increase these capacities. At the same time, however, a significant amount of research has been written in recent years questioning the ways in which our present system of education inhibits rather than promotes the development of empathy and role-taking.[17] As some have argued, the current educational system encourages social differentiation and competition more so than empathy, compassion, and cooperativeness.[18] Many educational theorists have called for a reconfiguration of the learning process built on alternative, pro-social values in which caring, interpersonal knowing, openness to different viewpoints, and a sense of community are emphasized.[19] In this replacement model of learning, the educational process would be restructured such that it sought to expose students to connections between learners rather than accept the barriers that follow from artificially constructed differences.[20] This is best achieved by providing opportunities for supportive participation, "community" problem solving, and role-taking interactions that promote a genuine receptiveness to the viewpoints and experiences of others. As we become more open to the views of people, not only do we develop our capacity for empathy, we also grow our connection to others, thereby establishing a corresponding sense of respect for and responsibility toward our fellow human beings (see Box 7.2).

BOX 7.2

Moral Development, Education, and the Criminal Justice Practitioner

Given the importance of moral decision-making in criminal justice, it could be argued that those invested with the discretion and authority to make and enforce laws and policies will, ideally, demonstrate advanced levels of moral reasoning. As we have seen, however, progression to higher stages of moral reasoning does not occur as part of a natural developmental process. Kohlberg emphasized that morality develops in large part from being exposed to challenging moral scenarios and being forced to think critically about those dilemmas. For the current or future criminal justice practitioner, this process of critical inquiry can encourage a more robust understanding of moral concerns and their application to professional situations.

Partly for this reason, college courses in ethics have become increasingly popular in criminal justice, business, and other disciplines for which developed moral sensibilities are an important prerequisite for entering the workplace. Ideally, these courses encourage students to critically reflect upon moral values, principles, and issues while giving special attention to those that are central to their respective discipline. As we have seen, Kohlberg suggested that advancement to higher stages of moral development occurs largely as a result of opportunities that expose us to moral controversies, allow us to analyze them from the perspective of all people involved, challenge our current thinking about those issues, and encourage us to understand and consider various alternative solutions to moral conflicts. While these opportunities can and often do emerge as we confront real-life situations, they also arise through exposure to issues and controversies and the more general atmosphere provided by *higher education*.

To illustrate the importance of higher education for criminal justice professionals and its potential link to moral development, we might consider the ways in which college education seems to impact *police attitudes*. Over the past several decades, the influence of college education on police attitudes and performance has become a developing area of research within criminal justice. As more and more law enforcement agencies are requiring at least some higher education, this research is not only timely, but also important. Though this area of research is still in the developmental stage, several themes have emerged. Compared with police officers who have no college education, research suggests that those who do generally:

■ Have more open belief systems
■ Are more flexible in their thinking
■ Are more aware of social problems
■ Are more aware of and sensitive to racial and ethnic tensions
■ Have greater acceptance of minorities
■ Better understand the psychological and sociological bases of human behavior
■ Are better able to empathize
■ Are better able to communicate
■ Are better able to adapt to complex situations
■ Demonstrate greater tolerance toward others
■ Are more ethical

Many of the characteristics highlighted above are arguably crucial to the law enforcement profession, particularly as practitioners carry discretionary powers into complex situations. Of course, the impact of college education on current and future law enforcement officers may vary depending upon the type and quality of that education. Based on Kohlberg's model of moral development, if courses—whether specifically on the topic of ethics or otherwise—are structured to expose students to controversy, to multiple points of view, and to encourage critical, independent thinking with regard to those issues, they would be more likely to have the desired effect. Even beyond specific courses, however, the college experience more generally would seem to expose students to diversity, conflict, and other situations that may benefit their moral development. As the research in this area continues to develop, we will no doubt attain a better understanding of the impact of education on law enforcement practitioners and other criminal justice professionals.

Gender Differences? Gilligan's Ethics of Care

A number of researchers have taken exception to Kohlberg's model of moral development. One of the more potent criticisms comes from Carol Gilligan (1936–), a former research assistant to Kohlberg and Harvard University Professor. Gilligan's work on moral development led her to conclude that there are significant *gender differences* in the ways men and women respond to moral dilemmas. Gilligan argued that Kohlberg's model was constructed almost exclusively from interviews with privileged white men and boys and, consequently, reflected a male-centered orientation that was biased against women.[21] Moreover, in Kohlberg's model, the higher stages of moral reasoning focus on justice, rights, rules, and other abstract principles. However, as Gilligan explained, these abstract notions are more characteristic of men and not women. Indeed, as she discovered, what distinguishes morality for women is a concern for human relatedness and caring.[22] Thus, rather than relying on formal rules and procedures, women tend to approach and resolve conflict through "a process of ongoing communication and involvement that considers the needs, interests, and motivations of all involved."[23]

Given these differences, women tend to score at Stage 3 when utilizing Kohlberg's model of moral development (emphasis on interpersonal relationships and helping/pleasing others). However, the implication is that they are somehow less moral than men because of their gendered focus on these, rather than other, male-centered values (e.g., rights and justice). While some researchers claim that Gilligan exaggerates the extent of these gender differences,[24] an interesting possibility nonetheless emerges.

Essentially, Gilligan suggests that morality may very well develop out of more than a single orientation: one focusing on justice, rights, and logic (for men)[25] and another on interpersonal relationships, compassion, and care (for women). Gilligan argues that each orientation should be valued equally. Moreover, if there are two different models of psychological and moral development, then, perhaps, these perspectives could become *integrated* such that each gender became more responsive to the other's viewpoint.[26] Ideally, men would become more attuned to the value of compassion, care, and responsiveness toward people; women would become more attentive to the principles of individual rights and rules. Imagine, for a moment, how the world might be quite different if legislators, judges, police officers, and military leaders were concerned about justice and fairness while, at the same time, were committed to caring for and responding to the welfare of others. We will have a bit more to say about Gilligan's work, the ethic of care, and its implications for criminal justice in Chapter 10.

MORAL DEVELOPMENT AND THE CRIMINAL JUSTICE SYSTEM: MAKING AND BREAKING LAWS

Moral development and its related concepts are pertinent in a variety of ways to the criminal justice system. As we saw in Chapter 1, individuals employed within criminal justice—whether as makers or enforcers of law, as attorneys or correctional officers—are expected to demonstrate a heightened degree of moral judgment. Decisions about when and how to exercise the authority and discretionary powers with which criminal justice practitioners are often invested are ideally informed by advanced moral reasoning skills. Beyond its application to criminal justice practice, the notion of moral development may also shed light on the processes of *lawmaking* and *lawbreaking*. Firstly, the notion of a "higher" morality and universal ethical principles may serve as a guide for lawmaking and as a means of judging the morality of existing laws. Secondly, differences in moral development may help us to understand motivations—good and bad—for violating criminal laws and, perhaps, to make distinctions on this basis. To illustrate the ways in which the concept of moral development can aid us in understanding these various facets of law, crime, and justice, we conclude this chapter by briefly exploring how it might further our regard for the making and breaking of laws. We begin by exploring the notion of natural law and its relation to justice and postconventional morality.

Justice, Natural Law, and Postconventional Morality

Natural law is an ethical theory, dating more than two thousand years to the ancient Greeks, that grounds morality in "nature" (or, more specifically, *human* nature). Its primary theme is that there exists a "higher" law or justice that transcends or stands above human-made law (i.e., *positive law*). It is through reference to this higher law that we are able to judge the morality and justice of human conventions—including those that have become part of written law. This higher, unwritten law has always existed, will always exist, and can never be superseded by human law. It consists of and promotes universal moral principles that protect and apply to all people, everywhere (e.g., those upholding basic human dignity and universal human rights—we will look more closely at natural or human rights in Chapter 9).

A widely discussed example of invoking natural law in the face of an unjust human law is one that we were briefly exposed to in Chapter 1. At the Nuremberg trials, judges appealed to natural law as a means of bringing Nazi leaders and war criminals to trial. The actions committed under the Nazi regime presented a challenging legal scenario, as they were not "crimes" under German law. Further, they did not occur within the legal jurisdiction of any other government. On what grounds, then, could Nazi leaders and war criminals be prosecuted and punished if they had violated no written law? Ultimately, the United Nations tribunal appealed to natural law in arguing that the Nazis had committed **crimes against humanity**—violations of universal moral standards. The tribunal generated a list of standards of justice that were held to transcend any human authority, thereby acknowledging that there are standards of justice that are more important than and supersede the authority of any nation or local government. By 1949, more than two hundred Nazi war criminals had been tried under these newly formed universal standards—with 131 found guilty and 37 sentenced to death.[27]

Natural law suggests that any human code of law must ultimately be consistent with this higher sense of justice. Justice and the universal moral principles it entails are the standard against which we measure human codes. In what ways can human laws be unjust? Judith Boss suggests that a law may be unjust if it has one of the following characteristics:

- *It is degrading to humans* (e.g., laws that permit slavery or torture)
- *It is discriminatory* (e.g., the Fourteenth Amendment gave men, but not women, the right to vote; laws that support apartheid in South Africa and the caste system in India)
- *It is enacted by an authority that is not truly representative*
- *It is unjustly applied* (e.g., search and seizure laws employed to harass political dissidents or other groups of people)

While there are certainly other ways in which human law can be unjust, the above examples illustrate that while human laws may be consistent with "natural" law, in some cases they contrast. Where there is a conflict between natural and human law, the former renders null and void all human laws that conflict with it. Because of this, natural law may justify knowing *violations of human authority* in the interest of justice. If human law is determined through natural law to be unjust and immoral, natural law may *demand* that we take illegal action—even if those actions bring negative consequences (e.g., prosecution and punishment). Natural law thus not only holds violations of human law to be morally justifiable in some cases, but may impose a *moral requirement* of noncompliance for the sake of justice.

As we saw earlier in this chapter, acts of *civil disobedience* characteristic of Kohlberg's universal ethical principles orientation are often justified by appealing to natural law or some higher sense of justice or morality. To exemplify the universal ethical principles orientation, Kohlberg referenced great moral leaders such as Gandhi and Martin Luther King Jr.—both of whom, not coincidentally, are recognized for employing strategies of civil disobedience as means of changing unjust laws, policies, and practices. Both Gandhi and Martin Luther King Jr. practiced peaceful noncompliance with existing power brokers because of their belief in and commitment to higher ethical principles. Gandhi did this during the British occupation and control of India, and King during the Civil Rights movement of the 1960s.

In his *Letter from a Birmingham Jail*, for instance, Martin Luther King Jr. argued that, ". . . there are two types of laws: just and unjust. I would be the first to advocate obeying just laws. One has not only a legal but a moral responsibility to obey just laws. Conversely, one has a moral responsibility to disobey unjust laws."[28] Practicing what he preached, King engaged in nonviolent acts of disobedience in Alabama, Mississippi, South Carolina, and Georgia to challenge the law's unmistakable denial of equal opportunity for persons of color in education, employment, and housing, as well as in general social life (e.g., separate bathrooms, separate seating in buses and restaurants). Although repeatedly imprisoned for his "criminal" behavior, for King (as well as for many others), the pursuit of a higher sense of justice and morality justified— even required—the intentional defiance of human law.

While critics have expressed concerns with the implications of Kohlberg's model, it does provoke more critical consideration of lawbreaking behaviors. While some have pointed to the dangers of people placing their own principles above respect for the law and the social order, we are at least encouraged to question the relationship between lawbreaking, motivation, and moral development.[29] Although the social desirability of postconventional morality remains open to debate, we cannot simply assume that morality and legality go hand-in-hand.

Lawbreaking and Moral Development

Gandhi, Martin Luther King Jr., Henry David Thoreau, and other nonviolent activists exemplify the ways in which violations of human law might be justified on moral grounds. In Kohlberg's model of moral development, they illustrate a recognition of and commitment to a "higher" or "natural" law, morality, and sense of justice consisting of universal ethical principles (e.g., equality) that serve as basic standards of moral behavior—whether for persons, organizations, institutions, or entire nations. Yet not all lawbreaking is motivated by a commitment to higher moral principles. How might Kohlberg's model of moral development help us make sense of motivations for lawbreaking?

Many people presume that criminality somehow reflects immorality or, at least, is an indication of lower levels of moral development. As we have seen, this is not always the case. That persons who have reached higher stages of moral development may violate human laws in light of a commitment to higher moral principles suggests that at least some instances of lawbreaking may reflect moral development that is more advanced than persons who abide by the law. Depending on the motivation and circumstances, obeying human laws may actually reflect a lower level of moral development. Because Kohlberg's model suggests that reasons or motivations for behavior are of more significance than the behavior itself, there are more and less advanced reasons for following the law, and more and less advanced reasons for violating the law. As we saw in Chapter 1, morality is not simply about doing the "right" thing or avoiding the "wrong" thing. Instead, what matters most is the reasoning that informs the choices we make and the actions we undertake.

To illustrate the ways in which different stages of moral development can provide different motivations for violating or respecting the law, consider the following motives for and examples of criminal behavior as they correspond to different stages of development:

Stage	Motive(s) and Possible Examples
Punishment and Obedience	fear of greater harm to oneself; obeying or respecting power and authority; obedience to leader/authority figure with power to impose sanctions for disobedience (e.g., organized crime, gangs, "pimps")
Instrumental Purpose and Exchange	pleasure, material gain, vengeance, drug use (e.g., joyriding, shoplifting, revenge or street justice for personal harm)
Interpersonal Expectations and Conformity	reputation, status, peer pressure or conformity to peer group (e.g., fights, fire-setting, thefts to look "cool" or "tough" within one's peer group; drug use within groups)
Law and Order	maintaining law and social order; punishing people who break laws or disrupt social order; while people at this stage generally respect and obey the law, some may take law into their own hands in an effort to maintain social order and punish lawbreakers (e.g., vigilantes)
Social Contract/Rights	protecting freedom and individual rights
Universal Ethical Principles	fighting injustices and advancing causes such as life and equality (e.g., environmental terrorism, Robin Hood-type thievery; draft-dodging)

Kohlberg's model suggests that, rather than criminality being directly equated with immorality, it may be better to understand the relationship between lawbreaking and morality as a continuum. Toward one end of the continuum are behaviors that violate the law and represent lower levels of moral motivation; toward the other end are behaviors that violate the law but are motivated by higher levels of moral reasoning. A provocative question is whether the system of law and law enforcement should, on any level, make distinctions between crimes motivated by more or less moral interests. For instance, should we consider persons who violate the law for moral reasons less reprehensible and thus less legally blameworthy than others? Should motivation and moral reasoning be considered in the sentencing process such that crimes motivated by higher-level moral interests are subject to lesser types or degrees of punishment? If so, who determines what moral interests justify more lenient treatment?

As a concluding exercise, consider the following hypothetical cases involving lawbreaking behaviors. Which, if any, of these behaviors are immoral? Based on Kohlberg's model, at what level and stage of moral development would you place the persons in the following scenarios?

- A recently laid-off husband and father of five steals several food items from a local grocery store to feed his hungry children.

- A concerned mother drives 80 miles-per-hour in a 55-mile-per-hour zone to get her child to the hospital. The child has a 104-degree fever.
- A new law is passed that requires all citizens in a community to keep a firearm in their house. A couple who has recently moved into the community refuses to do so, citing their moral opposition to firearm possession.
- A research laboratory is conducting biomedical experiments on small animals. A group of animal rights activists breaks into the laboratory, releasing the animals back into nature.

Now consider the following *legal* behaviors. Which, if any, would you consider to be immoral? Given Kohlberg's model of moral development, at what level and stage would you place the actor in question?

- Passing by a dark alley late at night, a young man witnesses what appears to be a rape in progress. As he is unsure what is happening and somewhat afraid to get involved, he chooses to simply continue on his way.
- A young couple has managed to accumulate $50 worth of late charges at a local video store. Upon their next visit, the store manager informs them that there has been a computer malfunction, resulting in the store losing track of all late charges on customer accounts. The manager asks them if they had any outstanding charges, to which the couple replies, "no."
- A large corporation, though acquiring $400 million in profits last year, manages to avoid paying *any* taxes through a variety of legal loopholes.

Of the seven scenarios described above, which are the most morally-reprehensible (if possible, rank-order them from most to least reprehensible)? Which, if any, of the seven people described should be convicted of criminal wrongdoing? Of those, which should be subjected to the harshest punishment? As a final consideration, ask yourself whether your responses are similar to or different from a purely legal approach to these questions.

SUMMARY

Over the course of the last several chapters, we explored a number of concerns pertinent to moral psychology. These included the following: can we be moral? (Chapter 5); the sources of morality (Chapter 6); and the issue of moral development (Chapter 7). Whether human nature is inherently egoistic, most of us assume that we have some capacity to act in a moral fashion (i.e., not exclusively out of concern for ourselves). To the degree that we *can* act morally, we are left to consider *why* we are inclined to act morally, noting especially the pro-social benefits that follow from engaging in such behavior (e.g., inner balance, mutual aid).

However, the issue of moral development as presented in this chapter considered *how* morality progresses, given the status of our cognitive skills. For example, we saw that the expectation of reward and the fear of reprisal leave much to be desired as motivations for moral behavior (Stage 1). In fact, Kohlberg identified obedience and punishment as reflecting the lowest level of cognitive development. Conversely, one's appeal to universal and transcendent ethical principles indicates more advanced moral reasoning capabilities (Stage 6). Additionally, however, this chapter noted that the acquisition of these more advanced skills was not necessarily the same as being moral. Ethics is about "doing" what is right for the "right" reasons. Consistent with this logic, Kohlberg explained that postconventional moral reasoning entails thinking critically and independently, questioning or, at least, seeking to understand the underlying reasons for laws, codes, and other formal ethical guidelines, and then moving to reasoned, empathic, justice-based action.

Interestingly, support for Kohlberg's perspective on moral development is not universal. For example, Carol Gilligan indicates that women's morality is based on an ethic of care, compassion, and intimacy rather than the logic of rights, judgments, and rules. Given these gendered-based psychological differences, Gilligan recommends that both models be valued—particularly when it comes to understanding the development and use of moral reasoning.

In Part III of this book (Chapters 8, 9, and 10), normative ethics is featured. Normative ethics formulates standards or guidelines for ethical behavior. In short, normative ethics addresses such questions as, "What should I do?" or "How should I be?" As we will quickly discover, the answers to these concerns are not so easily arrived at, especially within the realm of criminology/criminal justice. However, depending on the type of normative ethics in use (i.e., consequentialist, deontological, or virtue-based), a blueprint for moral reasoning, decision-making, and action is supplied. Normative ethics provides "tools" for ethical analysis—tools that can be employed when responding to moral dilemmas that most assuredly emerge for the criminal justice practitioner.

KEY TERMS AND CONCEPTS

civil disobedience
crimes against humanity
instrumental purpose and exchange
   orientation
interpersonal expectations and
   conformity orientation

law and order orientation
moral development
natural law
punishment and obedience orientation
social contract/legalism
universal ethical principles

DISCUSSION QUESTIONS

1. Stage 6 moral development requires looking at ethical problems empathically; that is, impartially and from the perspective of all parties concerned. In the following situation, consider what the relevant needs and interests are of the participants, giving equal attention to their various perspectives.

   ■ A second-time convicted pedophile has just completed a mandatory fifteen-year term in prison. The ex-offender is now living in your local community. Some residents are outraged that this man resides in this family-oriented neighborhood. The leadership of your home owner's association calls for a "special" meeting. The purpose of the meeting is to discuss how the community should respond to the presence of a "pedophile roaming their streets." At the meeting, some insist that the police should be contacted and that they should handle the situation; others suggest that any pedophile—even if "reformed"—is mentally unbalanced and, consequently, should be involuntarily hospitalized for psychiatric care; still others believe that the man should be completely shunned by all those who reside in the neighborhood because this will protect their children from the man.

■ How do you interpret this moral dilemma? What is the ethical thing to do here? Given Kohlberg's levels and stages of moral development, how would you interpret the respective positions taken by your neighbors?

2. To the best of your ability, indicate which of Kohlberg's stages of moral development might best explain the moral reasoning involved in the following:

   a. Waging war to protect or further economic interests.
   b. Engaging in a self-defensive war, having been attacked by another country.
   c. Waging war to retaliate against another country.
   d. Executing convicted murderers to serve vengeance.
   e. Executing convicted murderers to protect the public from further harm.
   f. Avoiding paying taxes to further one's profits.
   g. Refusing to pay taxes as a means of protest against injustice.

3. To the best of your ability, indicate how the following ethical dilemmas might be resolved based on *each stage of Kohlberg's model of moral development*: use Table 7.4 as a guide.

   a. Speeding versus not speeding
   b. Lying versus telling the truth
   c. Cheating on an exam versus doing honest work

SUGGESTED READINGS

Gilligan, Carol. (1982). *In a Different Voice: Psychological Theory and Women's Development.* Cambridge, MA: Harvard University Press.

Gilligan, Carol, Ward, Janie Victoria, and Taylor, Jill. (1990). *Mapping the Moral Domain: A Contribution of Women's Thinking to Psychology Theory and Education.* Cambridge, MA: Harvard University Press.

Hoff Sommers, Christina. (2001). *The War Against Boys: How Misguided Feminism Is Harming Our Young Men.* New York: Simon and Schuster.

Kohlberg, Lawrence. (1981). *The Philosophy of Moral Development: Moral Stages and the Idea of Justice.* New York: HarperCollins.

Kohlberg, Lawrence. (1984). *The Psychology of Moral Development: The Nature and Validity of Moral Stages.* New York: HarperCollins.

ENDNOTES

[1]Lawrence Kohlberg, *The Philosophy of Moral Development: Moral Stages and the Idea of Justice* (New York: HarperCollins, 1981); Lawrence Kohlberg, *The Psychology of Moral Development: The Nature and Validity of Moral Stages* (New York: HarperCollins, 1984).

[2]Anne Colby and Lawrence Kohlberg, *The Measurement of Moral Judgment: Volumes 1 and 2* (Cambridge, MA: Cambridge University Press, 1987).

[3]W. C. Crain, *Theories of Development* (Upper Saddle River, NJ: Prentice Hall, 1985), p. 21.

[4]Ibid.

[5]Among other things, Kohlberg has been criticized for his assumption that utilitarian conceptions are somehow less advanced. See, e.g., Edmund V. Sullivan, "A Study of Kohlberg's Structural Theory of Moral Development: A Critique of Liberal Social Science Ideology." In Bill Puka (Ed.), *The Great Justice Debate: Kohlberg Criticism* (New York: Garland, 1994), p. 46.

[6]Ibid.

[7]See, e.g., Hugo Bedau, *Civil Disobedience: Theory and Practice* (New York: Pegasus, 1969).

[8]The classic work on civil disobedience and an ethic of moral dissent is, Henry David Thoreau, *Civil Disobedience* (Bedford, MA: Applewood, 2000).

[9]Lawrence Kohlberg, *The Philosophy of Moral Development*, 1984.

[10]William Crain, *Theories of Development,* 5th ed. (Upper Saddle River, NJ: Prentice Hall, 2005), p.122.

[11]Ibid., p.124.

[12]Ibid., p.124.

[13]Ibid.

[14]Ibid.

[15]Ibid., p. 125.

[16]Ibid.; Lawrence Kohlberg, *The Philosophy of Moral Development, Vol. 1–2,* 1981.

[17]See, e.g., Carol Gilligan, Janie Victoria Ward, and Jill McLean Taylor, *Mapping the Moral Domain: A Contribution of Women's Thinking to Psychological Theory and Education* (Cambridge, MA: Harvard University Press, 1990); Martin L. Hoffman, *Empathy and Moral Development: Implications for Caring and Justice* (Cambridge, MA: Cambridge University Press, 2002), p. 21.

[18]Carol Gilligan, Nona P. Lyons, and Trudy J. Hanmer, *Making Connections: The Relational Worlds of Girls at Emma Willard School* (Cambridge, MA: Harvard University Press, 1990).

[19]Carol Gilligan, *In a Different Voice: Psychological Theory and Women's Development* (Cambridge, MA: Harvard University Press, 1982).

[20]Carol Gilligan, Nona P. Lyons, and Trudy J. Hanmer, *Making Connections: The Relational Worlds of Girls at Emma Willard School.*

[21]Carol Gilligan, *In a Different Voice: Psychological Theory and Women's Development.*

[22]Ibid.

[23]See, e.g., Carol Gilligan, "In a Different Voice: Women's Conceptions of Self and of Morality." In Bill Puka (Ed.), *Caring Voices and Women's Moral Frames: Gilligan's View* (New York: Garland, 1994), p. 1.

[24]Christina Hoff Sommers, *The War Against Boys: How Misguided Feminism Is Harming Our Young Men* (New York: Simon and Schuster, 2001).

[25]William Crain, *Theories of Development,* p. 136; see Carol Gilligan, *In a Different Voice,* chap. 6.

[26]William Crain, *Theories of Development,* p. 136.

[27]Judith Boss, *Ethics for Life,* 2nd ed. (Mountain View, CA: Mayfield Publishing 2001), p. 134.

[28]See, e.g., Martin Luther King, Jr., *The Martin Luther King, Jr. Companion: Quotations from the Speeches, Essays, and Books of Martin Luther King, Jr.* (New York: St. Martin's Press, 1998).

[29]William Crain, *Theories of Development,* 5th ed., p. 135.

Part III

NORMATIVE ETHICS: THEORY AND APPLICATION

Chapter

MEANS AND ENDS: THE IMPORTANCE OF CONSEQUENCES

Normative ethics attempts to formulate norms, guidelines, standards, and/or principles of right and wrong, and to propose answers to such questions as, "What should I do?" and "How should I be?" These responses (or "theories," "perspectives" or "frameworks") function as ethical "tools" for the analysis of various types of practice-based concerns found within criminal justice. Thus, normative ethics offers us a conceptual foundation to guide our assessment of applied ethical problems and practical ethical questions.

As was described in Chapter 2, normative theories can be broken down into three broad categories, with a number of variations located within each: (1) consequentialist ethics, (2) deontological or duty-based ethics, and (3) virtue ethics. These categories differ in terms of the relative weight they place on one or more of the following domains: acts or actions, consequences of actions, character, and motives or intentions. Generally speaking, *consequentialist* theories consider the effects of a choice or of conduct, *deontological* (duty-based) and rights-based moral theories attach the greatest significance to our actions themselves; and *virtue* ethics insists that we *be* good (i.e., virtuous) people, concentrating on developing our moral character and sense of integrity. The latter two ethical frameworks are the subject of Chapters 9 and 10. In the present chapter, our concern is with exploring those ethical perspectives that are *consequentialist* in nature.

All consequentialist perspectives on ethics argue that actions are "right" so far as they have beneficial *consequences*. Thus, the moral rightness or value of an action (or nonaction) depends on whether, and to what extent, it produces some good or some useful outcome.[1] Moreover, for a particular action to be morally appropriate, it must, on balance, yield better consequences than all other available courses of action. If all available options produce both good and bad consequences, then the morally preferred one is the action that yields more good than harm.[2] However, what constitutes a "good" or desirable consequence and *for whom* it should be beneficial is a matter of debate. Different variations of consequentialism propose distinct responses to these questions.[3]

The two most common forms of consequentialism are *ethical egoism* and *utilitarianism*. The difference between them lies in their answer to the question, "for whom should a consequence be beneficial?" The positions on this question (ethical egoism and utilitarianism) correspond to two basic types of consequentialism: those that are *agent-centered* and those that are *other-person-centered*. Agent-centered consequentialism is more commonly known as **(ethical) egoism.** It argues that our concern should be for good outcomes that attach *to the acting agent*. Egoism places little value in the interests, needs, or welfare of other people.[4] Nonegoistic forms of consequentialism such as utilitarianism tend to be *other-person-centered* or **altruistic.** They maintain that our concern should be for good outcomes or effects that benefit others. Altruistically motivated perspectives place a premium on the welfare, interests, or good of groups and collectives when it comes to ethical decision-making.[5]

In this chapter, our focus will be on three variations of consequentialism:

- *Ethical egoism*—what matters morally are consequences to *ourselves*
- *Contractualism*—what matters morally are consequences to ourselves, though our own interests are furthered by recognizing and agreeing to abide by certain rules of social living that are in the best interests of everyone
- *Utilitarianism*—what matters morally are the consequences of our actions for *everyone affected* by them

> **Point of departure for consequentialism:** each of us should act so as to produce consequences that are more favorable than unfavorable.

ETHICAL EGOISM

In Chapter 5, we confronted the challenge of *psychological egoism,* or the idea that all people, all of the time, act to promote their own interests. Psychological egoism is a metaethical concern—it is a theory of human nature that makes claims about our motivation and behavior *as human beings.* As a metaethical concern, psychological egoism says nothing about how we *should* be. It is not a normative theory and, therefore, does not provide us with principles or guidelines for moral choice and conduct. However, if we extend the basic idea of egoism or self-interest to the realm of normative ethics, what emerges is ethical egoism, or the theory that we *should* always act so as to promote our own interests.[6] Of course, we could accept *both* psychological and ethical egoism. In other words, we could argue that, by nature, we are motivated to pursue our own wants and desires (psychological egoism) and, therefore, *should* act in accordance with our nature by following them (ethical egoism). However, ethical egoism is not dependent upon psychological egoism. One could assert that psychological egoism is false, while still recommending that we live by the normative philosophy of ethical egoism. Notwithstanding this distinction, our focus in the following subsection addresses the normative claim that we should choose (and act on) what is in our own best interests.

> **Point of departure for ethical egoism:** each of us should act so as to satisfy our own best interests or maximize our personal welfare.[7]

The Principle of Self-Interest

It is important to keep in mind that the normative assertion being made by ethical egoism is different from the more basic claim that we *have* our own interests. That we possess wants and needs almost goes without saying; however, the morally relevant question to consider is when, where, and to what extent we are justified in *pursuing* them? Simply because all of us have interests and, further, that most of us chase those interests to some greater or lesser extent, does not mean that we should uphold self-interest as a desirable moral principle. The claim being made by ethical egoism is not simply that we have wants and needs; rather, it is that we are *morally obligated to pursue them on all occasions*.

The recommendation that each of us should exclusively follow our own interests seems contrary to what we typically contemplate in our everyday worlds, especially in our relationships with others. For instance, most of us believe that we should be considerate of the wants and needs of other people as often as humanly possible. Indeed, as the argument goes, we should at the very least avoid harming others and, where appropriate, even try to be helpful. Moreover, we often have obligations to others (e.g., parents, spouses, friends, and work associates). These obligations are moral responsibilities that, some would argue, must be fulfilled even when doing so is not necessarily in our own best interest. However, ethical egoism argues that each of us should pursue our own interests resolutely, endeavoring to maximize our own welfare purposefully.

In this way, ethical egoism seems to suggest that we ignore the needs and interests of others in favor of whatever our own desires might entail. Ethical egoists do not speak of duties, obligations, and virtues, other than those we have to ourselves. Our only moral *duty* is to act in such a way that we promote self-regarding outcomes. Following this line of analysis, we have no duties to anyone but ourselves! Thus, self-interest, for the ethical egoist, is not a psychological motivation but a *moral principle*.[8] Acting solely on the basis of the principle of self-interest is not immoral or morally questionable but, in fact, morally desirable.[9] Consistent with this theory, *not* acting in pursuit of one's own interests or welfare is immoral. According to ethical egoism, we act wrongly whenever we do not satisfy our own interests through our choices and actions.[10]

To be clear, ethical egoism does not require us to avoid helping others.[11] In fact, a key principle of ethical egoism is that, in many cases, we *are* helping others by helping ourselves. Ethical egoists point out that aiding others often produces some benefit to ourselves such that, while we *seem* to be acting altruistically or out of concern for the welfare or good of others, we are really deriving some benefit for ourselves from our actions.[12] It may be that, in at least some situations, the most effective way to bring some advantage to ourselves is to assist others or behave so as to further the interests or welfare of others. However, the principle of self-interest espoused by ethical egoism must always prevail. When conflict emerges between our interests and those of others, it is the former that should always take precedence. If we fail in some way to bring benefit to ourselves, we fail to act morally. Consequently, the only circumstance in which it is morally right to act out of concern for the needs and interests of others is when there will be some corresponding benefit to ourselves. Thus, for example, while it may be that loaning money to a friend in need would be widely hailed as a moral action, the perspective of ethical egoism interprets this situation differently. The behavior's morality consists not in altruistic intentions but in whatever benefit comes to me as a result of assisting my friend (e.g., praise, reward, reputation, future payback with interest). Ethical egoism should not be confused with the idea that we should never act out of regard for others; rather, the theory holds that the *reason* we should do things for others is to gain some benefit for ourselves.

Self-Interest versus Pursuit of Pleasure

Ethical egoism is a theory of *self-interest* and *personal welfare*. As such, it is important to point out that ethical egoism does *not* imply that we should always do what we want to do—for example, that we should always act to satisfy our desires. In many instances, there is a considerable difference between what we *want* and doing what is in our *best interest*. Therefore, we must distinguish between our best interests or welfare and what we may want, need, or desire. Pursuing what we want or desire is the basis of **hedonistic egoism.**[13] Hedonistic egoism is a normative theory with limited appeal. It argues that we should always pursue pleasure (i.e., what we subjectively feel to be satisfying or desirable). Most varieties of ethical egoism make no such claim. The reason for this is that, perhaps more often than not, what we want to do may not be what is good for us from the vantage point of our personal welfare. In cases where what we want or desire is in conflict with our best interests, actions in pursuit of what we want would not pass the test of self-interest as outlined by ethical egoism. To illustrate, in principle ethical egoism condemns smoking, excessive drinking, and other behaviors that are ultimately harmful to ourselves. Although such activities may bring us pleasure in the short term, ethical egoists would be quick to point out that they do not serve our long-term interests or maximize our overall welfare. Therefore, ethical egoism is *not* about the pursuit of pleasure—or even the pursuit of what we *want*. Rather, ethical egoism takes as its moral point of departure the best *interests* and the overall *welfare* of the acting individual.

The Rationale for Ethical Egoism

If ethical egoism argues that our primary concern should always be ourselves—an argument that, on its face, seems objectionable—we need to ask on what basis or by what reasons we can legitimately make such a claim. Perhaps the most common defense of ethical egoism consists of an appeal to psychological egoism. If, as is claimed by psychological egoism, we are inclined by nature to be self-interested, then it would be a mistake for us to attempt to act outside the boundaries of this more natural, organic tendency. Indeed, following this perspective, we not only *are* self-interested, but *should* be as a matter of moral principle. Of course, the flaw in this simple line of reasoning is that it rests upon the assumption set forth by psychological egoism. To the degree that the latter is false, the argument for ethical egoism falls apart. Consequently, proponents of ethical egoism sometimes appeal to other claims to support their position. Several of the more common arguments in favor of ethical egoism include: (1) knowledge of interests, (2) the issue of privacy, (3) concerns of dignity, and (4) the devaluation of the individual.[14]

KNOWLEDGE OF INTERESTS

Simply stated, *we know what is in our own interests.* Each of us knows what we need, want, and desire, and each of us is capable of determining how to pursue effectively these things. While we may not always make the right determinations, we are still in a better position than others to do so. After all, they are *our* needs, wants, and interests. At the same time, ethical egoists point out that we can know the needs and interests of other people but only imperfectly.[15] We may think we know what others want or need, but can never know this with certainty or complete understanding. The problem, then, is that if we attempt to look after the needs and interests of others, we are likely to do more harm than good. Therefore, ethical egoists would argue that pursuing our own interests is the most rational basis for action because we are more likely to "get it right."

THE ISSUE OF PRIVACY

Some ethical egoists have argued that looking out for other people's needs and interests is akin to invading their privacy.[16] In effect, moralities that encourage us to help, aid, or assist others are essentially asking that we mind other people's business—something that is offensive at the very least, and, perhaps, a violation of privacy rights that many people consider to be fundamentally unacceptable under all conditions.

CONCERNS OF DIGNITY

A third claim commonly made by ethical egoists is that aiding or assisting others is *degrading* to them. In short, it robs them of their dignity and self-respect.[17] In a way, offering aid to others assumes that they are sufficiently incapable or otherwise lacking competence to meet their own needs and to care for their own interests (see Box 8.1). This is why, for instance, some homeless persons refuse charity or why some poor persons decline welfare assistance (despite governmental eligibility). Moreover, even when people want our help, providing it can foster a cycle of passivity and dependence, diminishing their need to be self-reliant.[18]

DEVALUATION OF THE INDIVIDUAL

Another argument commonly offered in support of ethical egoism was popularized during the 1960s and 1970s by philosopher and social commentator, Ayn Rand.[19] Her position was that each of us has one—and as far as we know *only* one—life to live.[20] Thus, we have a single opportunity to find happiness, peace, prosperity, or whatever it is that we personally value. If we place any importance on our quest to be happy, we must first and foremost value the *individual.* Following altruistic ethical formulas, the individual is something to be sacrificed—if need be—for the common good. Indeed, within other person-centered models of ethics, the life of the individual and that person's pursuit of happiness are devalued; both are deemed less important than the welfare of others or of groups. However, as Rand explained, "If a man accepts the ethics

BOX 8.1

Egoism and the Ethics of Involuntary Mental Health Intervention

In Chapter 4, we were introduced to paternalistic justifications for law and policy. In short, *paternalistic* practices were described as involving an authority relating to persons in need as a father might to his dependent children. As we have seen, however, ethical egoism questions whether we can ever know the needs and interests of others. Consequently, not only might paternalistic practices be misguided and unfruitful, they may be construed as invasions of privacy and affronts to the dignity of those whom we are attempting to aid.

One current controversy that raises precisely these issues is that of involuntary intervention by mental health professionals into the lives of persons who are presumably in need of psychological or psychiatric care. Mental health treatment, whether in the form of therapy, chemical intervention, or otherwise, is premised upon the notion that educated and trained professionals are in a position to understand the interests of others and assist them in overcoming their maladies. Further, it assumes that those persons aided or "treated" want and need that assistance. Whereas this latter assumption may be true in the majority of voluntary cases, in others it is less so. Especially troubling are cases of civil commitment (again, see Chapter 4) in which persons are *involuntarily* hospitalized and subjected to various forms of mental health intervention. In such cases, ethical egoism might raise the following concerns:

- Mental health professionals presumably provide a service (i.e., treatment) to persons who are in want and need of that assistance. The direction and content of that service, however, is not based on the patient's expressed wants, needs, or desires, but on the professional's "expert" knowledge of what the patient needs. In effect, mental health professionals presume to know patients' needs and interests better than the patients themselves do. Ethical egoists, of course, would suggest that because we can only know other people's interests imperfectly—even with the expertise provided by advanced education, training, and professional experience—our assumptions may well do more harm than good.

- The assumption that treatment provided to mentally ill persons is not only needed, but also *wanted* is also problematic. Some have argued that patients who are treated against their will eventually come to appreciate the services they have received. Sometimes referred to as "thank you therapy," the argument is that persons who are mentally ill are not—because of their illness—in a position to know what is in their best interests. Because of this, they may initially resist treatment. Once they are "better," however, they come to realize that treatment was in their best interest and are grateful for the intervention. Others, however, point out that in many cases, quite the reverse is true. Some studies have suggested that a *majority* of civilly committed persons still objected to treatment even after they were "better." Involuntary mental health treatment thus also raises concerns about unjustified violations of privacy and lack of appreciation for human dignity in cases where professionals intervene following a wrongful presumption of knowledge about what patients want and need.

Sources: A. Stone, *Mental Health Law: A System in Transition* (Washington, DC: U.S. Government Printing Office, 1975); J. Beck, and E. Golowka, "A Study of Enforced Treatment in Relation to Stone's 'Thank You' Therapy," *Behavioral Sciences and the Law*, 6, 559 (1988).

of altruism, his first concern is not how to live his life, but how to sacrifice it."[21] When speaking of "sacrifice," it should be noted that Rand was not referring literally to dying for the sake of another.[22] Instead, what she meant was simply that each person's life consists of a variety of projects and goods—things we value, desire, and strive for. Altruism suggests that we abandon these projects and goods, to some considerable extent, for the sake of the projects and goods of others. In a very meaningful way, then, since these things make up our lives, we sacrifice ourselves when forfeiting what is important to us about them.[23]

In contrast, ethical egoism encourages each person to place primary emphasis on one's own life and happiness and, therefore, invites us to celebrate the individual. Ethical egoism makes sense as a moral philosophy because it permits us to value the individual as a heroic being whose only ethical purpose is happiness, productively achieved through work, struggle, and progress but guided always by the absolute of reason.[24] Altruism and many "other-directed" ethical theories do precisely the opposite. If individuals matter, there is no rational basis to require them to sacrifice their own aspirations or their happiness for the sake of other people or for the common good. Moreover, following the theory, ethical egoism *better serves* the good of society than even altruism. This is because altruism or other-person-centered theories inhibit the development of outstanding individuals when emphasizing the interests of the group over that of the person. Arguably, great societies are achieved through the work and insight of great individuals.[25] If we want society to grow and prosper, we need a morality in which outstanding individuals are allowed to flourish rather than hampered by requirements that force them to sacrifice their own pursuits.

The Problems with Ethical Egoism

Aside from being contrary to commonsense notions of what is right and good, ethical egoism suffers from a number of deficiencies. These flaws make ethical egoism morally contestable and less attractive than other normative theories. While these shortcomings are plentiful, several of the more noteworthy limitations include: (1) conflicts of interest, (2) partiality, and (3) self-defeat or the problem of the prisoner's dilemma.

CONFLICTS OF INTEREST

A powerful critique of ethical egoism is that it does not provide a solution for conflicts of interest that certainly arise between competing self-interested individuals.[26] Simply stated, this criticism suggests that our happiness and aspirations can and often do come into conflict with those of others. Because of the inevitability of conflict, an adequate system of morality must provide some way to solve these disputes when they arise. Moreover, this morality should establish rules of conduct that enable the peaceful and harmonious resolution of conflict. After all, creating such codes is one key function of morality.[27]

However, ethical egoism provides no such rules or principles. Instead, it understands life to consist of a never-ending series of conflicts in which each of us struggles to "come out on top."[28] As a moral philosophy, then, ethical egoism suggests that each of us should approach such disagreements by simply doing our best to "win." Thus, as James Rachels notes, the moral system offered by ethical egoism "is not like a courtroom judge, who resolves disputes. Instead, [it] is like the Commissioner of Boxing, who urges each fighter to do his best."[29] Following ethical egoism, conflicts of interest are not settled by applying moral rules or principles in the interest of reaching an agreeable solution; rather, they are resolved when one party or another "wins" the struggle.[30]

PARTIALITY

A second shortcoming of ethical egoism is that it violates our sense of impartiality. Essentially, ethical egoism encourages us to "divide the world into two categories of people—ourselves and all the rest."[31] However, in so doing, ethical egoism draws on the same human tendency to categorize and differentiate which results in racism, sexism, ageism, and other forms of social distinction and prejudice. In each case, we draw divisions between people and groups, attaching differential standing to those divisions and to those persons in those respective groups. Racism, ethnocentrism, and sexism are all founded upon an assumption that we can divide the world into groups with distinct characteristics and, further, that the characteristics of some groups are better than those of others. The only difference between ethical egoism and the attitudes and behaviors mentioned above is that egoism divides the world into "me" and "everybody else." Ethical egoism suggests that we should not only create such divisions, but that the interests of the first group (ourselves) should be regarded as more important than the interests of everyone else.[32]

However, following the criticism of partiality, the question is: *What is it that makes "me" so special?*[33] While many of us may *feel* that our needs, interests, and abilities are greater or more important than those of others, the more objective reality is that they are not. Notwithstanding minor differences, there are no significant variations between ourselves and other people justifying that our happiness be treated as more special and, therefore, more deserving than the happiness of others. The same can be said about creating a world filled with categories of people or groups: There is no valid basis for making claims that certain races, sexes, and so on are somehow better or more important than others. However, ethical egoism asks that we engage in this very practice.

SELF-DEFEAT: THE PRISONER'S DILEMMA

A third criticism leveled against ethical egoism is that it is self-defeating.[34] In other words, our *own* best interests are not served by "looking out for number one," but by embracing cooperation and trust. If everyone tried to live in accordance with the principle of self-interest, the results would be devastating rather than beneficial for all parties concerned (recall the discussion of Hobbes in Chapter 5 for more on this point).[35] Indeed, if everyone succeeded in following the view of ethical egoism, the theory's own goal (self-interest) would not be achieved but would be hindered.[36] This is what is meant by the claim that ethical egoism is *self-defeating*.

Perhaps the self-defeating nature of ethical egoism can best be exemplified by what is known as the *prisoner's dilemma*. The dilemma, in slightly embellished form, can be stated as follows: Suspect A and Suspect B have been arrested for armed robbery, transported to the police station, and placed in separate cells. Assuming that both suspects are rational and have not had an opportunity to speak with one another, both of them are aware of the following:

- If one confesses to the armed robbery and the other does not, the suspect who confesses will be released while the other will be convicted and sentenced to ten years.
- If *both* suspects confess to the armed robbery, each will be convicted and receive a sentence of seven years.
- If *neither* suspect confesses to the armed robbery, each will be convicted only on charges of possession of stolen property and each will receive a sentence of one year.

Now, assume that both suspects want to minimize their own sentence (i.e., they are both seeking to serve their own interest exclusively). Under these circumstances, Suspect A *should* confess because, in doing so, she or he could potentially be relieved of all charges and released (that is, if Suspect B chooses to remain silent). Moreover, if Suspect A does *not* confess and Suspect B does, Suspect A will be faced with the maximum punishment possible in this scenario (10 years for armed robbery). Therefore, if Suspect A desires to maximize his or her own interests by minimizing the pain and suffering, confessing seems to serve Suspect A's interests *no matter what* Suspect B does. If Suspect A *knows* that Suspect B will not confess, his or her interests will be served by *not* confessing. However, because Suspect A cannot know what Suspect B will do, confessing better serves his or her interests by protecting against the possibility of a ten-year sentence *and* creates the possibility of Suspect A being released altogether if Suspect B does not confess. Thus, it seems as though the rational action for Suspect A is to confess.

	Suspect A Confesses	**Suspect A Remains Silent**
Suspect B Confesses	7 years each for armed robbery for *both* suspects A *and* B **Third best scenario for both suspects*	0 years for Suspect B, 10 years for Suspect A **Best scenario for Suspect B, worst for Suspect A*
Suspect B Remains Silent	10 years for Suspect B, 0 years for Suspect A **Best scenario for Suspect A, worst for Suspect B*	1 year for possession of stolen property for *both* suspects A *and* B ** Second best scenario for both suspects*

On the other hand, Suspect B is faced with the same dilemma. Suspect B *should* also confess for the same reasons outlined for Suspect A. Given that each makes a rational, self-interested decision, both will confess and both will get seven years for armed robbery. Mutual confession, however, results in only the third most desirable scenario for both suspects. The circumstances are such that the best possible scenario for *both* parties is to remain silent.

Further, let us assume that both suspects are aware that if they both remain silent they will each get only a one-year sentence and, moreover, let us assume that each suspect does, in fact, *know* that the other will remain silent. Would both suspects then choose to remain silent? If motivated purely by self-interest, the answer must be, "no." If Suspect A knows that Suspect B will remain silent, Suspect A also knows that he or she can escape punishment altogether by confessing. The consequences, of course, are that Suspect A would cause significant pain and suffering to Suspect B. However, if Suspect A's interest are the only concern, he or she will confess.

What the prisoner's dilemma suggests is that the only way for both suspects to benefit from the situation is through *cooperation* and *trust*. For cooperation to be beneficial, both suspects must risk assuming that the other is not self-interested enough to choose confession over cooperative silence. Additionally, even if both suspects had *arranged* to remain silent, each would have to trust the other to act according to this promise.

CONTRACTUALISM

By now, you might be thinking that ethical egoism paints a mostly unattractive and undesirable normative portrait. Indeed, ethical egoism has not found much support among mainstream philosophers. Yet there are other reasons why the concerns of ethical egoism need to be given serious attention. Many, if not most, people, it would seem, *are* essentially egoistic. Problems such as that epitomized by the prisoner's dilemmas arise as soon as people have different goals.[37] Because goals differ, we inevitably experience conflicts of interest—conflicts for which, as we have seen, ethical egoism provides no viable solution. While on paper ethical egoism may fail to provide an adequate or desirable normative philosophy, in everyday life many people *do* accept and live by its key assumptions. Even if we are not purely egoistic, people often cannot help but to act somewhat egoistically. Whether because of who we are intrinsically or because of what we are exposed to environmentally (nature versus nurture), we routinely demonstrate a preference for pursuing our own interests. Of course, this tendency does not mean that we *should* make choices and engage in action consistent with this inclination. However, it does suggest that we need to consider this reality. Dismissing ethical egoism as a normative philosophy only gets us so far; we must contend with the reality that self-interest plays a key role in how many people think of themselves, how they examine their needs and interests, and how they evaluate their relationships with others.

Despite its problematic nature and general lack of appeal, egoism nonetheless permeates contemporary American culture. For instance, consider frequently watched television shows such as *Survivor* that promote and glorify self-regarding conduct. In popular culture, egoistic sensibilities are typically portrayed as necessary for survival or, at least, for "winning" or emerging victorious from situations of conflict or competition. And though participants on *Survivor* and similar game shows seem to have some sense that cooperation is minimally necessary, the motivation for doing so is limited to that which is required for defeating one's competitors. Indeed, competition is always primary and cooperation among persons is most often merely a tool of self-interest—a means of securing safety or power in numbers that, in turn, is necessary for individual victory.

The State of Nature

Television shows like *Survivor* make liberal use of what philosophers refer to as the "state of nature." Widely discussed in moral, social, and political philosophy, the **state of nature** is a hypothetical state of social existence where there is no government or law to direct or regulate people. Philosophers utilize the state of nature concept to hypothesize about what social life would be like if we removed controls, sanctions, and limits on what people could do. The state of nature debate is really a question about *human* nature—that is, about whether human nature is characterized by a tendency to cooperate and assist one another for the benefit of the group, or whether people are inherently egoistic, looking out only for themselves and pursuing their own good at the expense of others.

Several philosophers have offered different responses to this fundamental question. Among them, Thomas Hobbes (1588–1679) is perhaps best known for his pessimistic perspective on human nature and his bleak portrait of life without government (see Chapter 5 for additional commentary on Hobbes).[38] Hobbes' position can be summarized thusly: The natural state of existence for human beings is one of selfish desire and competitiveness coupled with a condition of scarcity (i.e., a limited supply of goods). We all want a variety of goods (e.g., basic necessities of life, money, power), but those goods exist only in restricted supply. What results is a constant *struggle* between persons for the possession of these various, though sparse, goods. For instance, if we are each driven to acquire wealth and there is only so much of it to go around, we naturally will compete with one another to secure that wealth. Moreover, without government (e.g., laws, police, courts), we would likely cheat, steal, and even murder to get what we wanted. In short, the "state of nature" is not one of peaceful and harmonious co-existence, but one of conflict and strife. In his classic work, *Leviathan*, Hobbes famously depicted the state of nature as follows:

> . . . every man is an enemy to every man . . . there is no place for industry . . . no culture . . . no navigation . . . no building . . . no knowledge . . . no arts; no letters; no society; and which is worst of all, continual fear and danger of violent death; and the life of man, solitary, poor, nasty, brutish, and short.[39]

Hobbes was a psychological and ethical egoist. His argument presumes that human beings are self-interested by nature, as well as competitive by design. Often, his portrait of the state of nature is described as a "war of each against all." Absent are considerations of cooperation, trust, altruism, compassion, and any other prosocial qualities and practices. For Hobbes, these things are only possible when we have some sense of security—some comfort in knowing that our lives and possessions are not continually in danger of being taken from us by other self-interested persons. How is this sort of comfort possible? If we are naturally competitive and self-interested, what must be present in order to avoid the conditions that would otherwise arise in a state of nature? Morality, we would assume, only emerges when self-interested people living together in groups come to accept some basic rules that are essential for social living.[40]

The Social Contract

Though Hobbes' contention that life in a state of nature would be "solitary, poor, nasty, brutish, and short" may sound a bit on the extreme side, his basic position is shared by a number of other philosophers. The elements of his position include the following points:

- Human beings are, by nature, social—compelled to live together in groups for purposes of survival, safety, and the simple companionship of other beings like ourselves.
- Each of us has needs—a desire for basic goods that allow us to survive and flourish.
- The goods that allow us to survive and flourish are scarce—they are in short supply.
- Each of us will want to get as much in the way of these goods as we can, but because we are all more or less equal in terms of power, we are all in a position to potentially lose our goods to others.
- Human beings are—either by nature or nurture—egoistic or at least mostly egoistic, caring much about themselves and displaying a limited willingness to set aside their wants and needs in the interest of other people.

In light of the above assumptions, Hobbes concluded that life in a state of nature would essentially be a continual "war" that no one could win. Each person would attempt to secure what that individual wanted or needed and then would prepare to defend these acquired goods from attack. Hobbes noted that every other person would do precisely the same thing.[41] However, as people increasingly became concerned only with seizing and protecting those goods necessary for survival—finding themselves amidst a continual state of fear—there would be no time, space, or even desire for industry, culture, knowledge, art, and as forth. Though the idea of a "state of nature" is widely criticized for being nothing more than philosophical fiction, Hobbes suggested that this is what actually happens when governments collapse. For instance, during civil insurrections history indicates that people begin to "hoard food, arm themselves, and lock out their neighbors."[42] What emerges is a primitive state of anarchy in which people detach themselves from their commitments to laws, rules, and people more generally.

But how can we escape such an undesirable state of affairs? Does the inevitability of egoism commit us to adopt it as the only viable moral system? Are we effectively fated to live in such a bleak state of human and social existence? Might there be some minimal level of cooperation agreed upon by people—notwithstanding their inclinations toward self-interests—that would ensure peace and harmony, foster a sense of personal safety, and promote security for our possessions?

According to Hobbes, two things must be in place to attain these goals: (1) some "guarantees that people will not harm one another, and (2) some pledge from people that they will "rely on one another to keep their agreements."[43] Once we realize that some degree of egoism is inescapable and, further, that Hobbes' state of nature is undesirable, we obviously look for a way to avoid these circumstances. For Hobbes, some form of political authority with the capacity to enforce cooperation among a society of rational egoists was absolutely necessary.[44] If, as we saw in the prisoner's dilemma, acting from the motive of self-interest turns out to be worse than acting cooperatively, how can we be certain that people will act cooperatively to ensure the best interests of everyone? The answer is what has come to be known as **contractualism,** or **social contract theory**. To make certain that the above-mentioned guarantees are in place, some form of *government* must be established. It is only through government—with its corresponding laws and regulations functioning to enforce cooperation—that citizens can live with minimal fear and can take comfort knowing that people will keep their agreements with one another.[45]

Contractualism as a *Moral* Theory

The social contract notion was developed as an attempt to justify the existence of the state, as well as various functions of the state such as law enforcement. So how is the social contract a theory of morality? Under contractualism, the purpose of the state is to enforce what we have determined to be the most important rules—those necessary for social living. Many of these—including those prohibiting murder, theft, cheating—are elemental and widely accepted moral rules. However, not all moral rules are enforced by the state. Morality consists not simply of the rules that have been codified and officially imposed, but the whole range of explicit and implicit rules that enhance social living.[46]

The social contract can be thought of as *making possible* the existence and embodiment of moral values and principles. Some philosophers, such as Jean-Jacques Rousseau (1712–1778), argued that the existence of the state allows us to become fundamentally different types of people. Once we no longer have to worry about our own safety and welfare, we can afford to be moral—we can afford to care about others.[47] Thus, altruistic behaviors, it could be argued, become possible only under the security offered by the state. We are able to enter civilized relations based upon mutual concern and trust only when we no longer fear one another. As Rachels suggests, we are able to:

> . . . set aside [our] private, self-centered "inclinations" in favor of rules that impartially promote the welfare of everyone alike. But [we] are able to do this only because others have agreed to do the same thing.[48]

Contractualism, then, understands morality to consist of:

> . . . *the set of rules, governing how people are to treat one another, that rational people will agree to accept, for their mutual benefit, on the condition that others follow those rules as well.*[49]

The Problems with Contractualism

Several key questions arise when we look more closely at contractualism. First, as we have seen, contractualism justifies the state and its laws (i.e., codified moral rules) by appealing to the necessity of such basic principles for civilized social living.

Consequently, the state and its mechanisms of social control (e.g., law, policing, courts, corrections) must exist to prevent society from regressing into a state of nature wherein theft, violence, and other social problems would rum rampant, thereby preventing us from living safe, secure, and satisfying lives. Clearly, this is true of many legal prohibitions that are currently in place. For example, most of us would agree that our best interests are served by having laws against murder, rape, theft, and actions that cause harm. However, it is less clear whether other forms of behavior are similarly harmful and similarly warrant state sponsored sanction.[50]

For instance, consider the prohibitions against or restrictions on prostitution, pornography, and gambling. These are behaviors that do not appear to pose a significant threat to social living and, according to some criminologists, amount to victimless crimes.[51] Recall that contractualism simply states that social rules should exist for purposes of allowing us to pursue our lives without fear of harm from others. As such, many people could reasonably question the extent of injury actually caused or potentially caused by the above-mentioned actions. Moreover, if we accept the fundamental ideas contained within contractualism, then any behavior that does not or cannot be shown to pose an objective threat to our well-being (however much it may offend us), is really none of our business and the imposition of moral rules against it therefore are not justified.[52]

A second concern for contractualism is as follows: As a variation of ethical egoism, contractualism argues that we should abide by moral rules because it is to our own advantage to do so. Moreover, it is better for all of us if we live in a society where everyone accepts certain basic rules and where state mechanisms are in place for dealing with those persons who break them. Interestingly, however, at least in some cases, it *is* in our best interest to deviate from the rules rather than abide by them—especially if we know we can get away with it. What, then, prevents us from doing so?[53]

According to contractualism, the answer is linked to the value we assign to the social contract. In short, the contract allows us to count on others to uphold their end of the bargain. Its rules represent provisions that all rational people can agree to accept. Because we do not want others to violate these rules, especially when doing so advances their best interests, it is equally rational for us to uphold our own end of the arrangement. We should do so because, despite the inconveniences it may bring, it is ultimately to our advantage. Theoretically, however, we would be allowed to break the rules in cases where others failed to live up to their end of the contract. So, how much value do we really assign to the contract? The answer, it seems, is somewhat unclear.

A third problem arises for contractualism in this context as well. If the basis of this doctrine is that it is in everyone's best interests to abide by the contract, how do we account for the significant numbers of people who do not benefit from existing rules and arrangements?[54] The social contract is, in effect, a means of maintaining the status quo—we each agree to abide by the rules of the contract (e.g., the law) and, in doing so, protect and reinforce the existing state of affairs (including prevailing social arrangements, institutions, rules, and conventions). However, not all people benefit equally from the status quo. In a society characterized by class, race, gender, and age inequalities, there will always be disadvantaged groups whose interests are not furthered by keeping things as they are. If existing arrangements are organized such that certain people or groups are not granted the same rights and liberties as others or do not benefit from the same safety and security others experience, how can the best interests of everyone be furthered when accepting, following, and reinforcing the rules of the social contract?

Some have argued that, to the degree that existing arrangements systematically disadvantage some citizens or groups, the terms of the social contract have been violated. In other words, the state has violated its end of the bargain. If we insist that such disadvantaged groups continue to abide by the terms of the contract nonetheless (e.g., obey the law, pay their taxes, uphold their social institutions) we are essentially "*demanding that they accept the burdens imposed by the social arrangement even though they are denied its benefits.*"[55] Failure to distribute benefits of social living to all segments of society equitably is, in effect, a violation of the terms of the contract. As such, it releases those on the other end of the agreement from their responsibilities. We are obligated to adhere to the contract only so long as others maintain their end of the bargain. When others—including the government—fail to do so, are we not released from our agreement? The egoistic incentive for endorsing the social contract seems to disappear if one's interests are hindered or harmed rather than supported and furthered by it. In such cases as these, it may be in the best interests of at least some people to violate the social contract, seeking instead to disrupt, perhaps change, the existing order of things. Under these circumstances, are we then justified in conscientiously violating laws, rules, and customs? Again, social contract theory provides an incomplete response to this sort of concern (see Box 8.2).

A fourth problem for contractualism relates to the form of morality the theory promotes. Overall, the social contract provides an easy solution to moral concerns. The basis of morality is simply a set of rules and conventions that "rational people . . . agree to accept for their mutual benefit."[56] This amounts to each individual willingly giving up certain freedoms in exchange for some guarantee of security and other benefits of social living. Each of us is harmed in the sense that the social contract places limitations on what we can do; however, the benefits we enjoy by avoiding a "state of nature" and by being ensured certain rights are said to significantly outweigh whatever freedoms and liberties we agree to give up. However, we should remember that under contractualism, morality consists of pursuing our own interests. Self-regarding inclinations are restrained by rules and laws that hold in check the unbridled pursuit of these ends. Yet, the theory holds self-interest to be morally acceptable and socially desirable. For many people, this is problematic. For example, while contractualism may be an effective means of ensuring that most people do not harm others, it does not necessarily provide us with any reason for being moral (other than simply following moral rules that we are obligated to follow). Additionally, it does not help us reach conclusions concerning the moral dilemmas we face in our everyday personal and professional lives.

UTILITARIANISM

The emergence of utilitarianism was nothing short of a revolution in the Western intellectual tradition—one whose effects have been felt not only in ethics, but also economics, law, social policy, and elsewhere.[57] Given full expression by Jeremy Bentham (1748–1832) and John Stuart Mill (1806–1873), **utilitarianism** is a moral and political philosophy whose influence pervades our everyday thinking perhaps more than any other—so much so, in fact, that its core ideas seem by now to be commonsense. As a consequentialist theory, utilitarianism holds that actions are morally right so far as they

BOX 8.2

Urban Crime and the Social Contract

Simply by virtue of where they live, work, and play, many urban residents are at a continual risk of victimization for both violent and property offenses. Inner cities have the highest victimization rates for many street crimes, including homicide, assault, and robbery. What is more, many residents of these areas feel that police efforts to protect them are ineffective. When crimes are reported, police show up hours later or sometimes not at all. In many urban areas, residents are left to live in continual fear, for themselves, their children, family, and friends. An interesting moral question from a contractualist perspective is, as Bill Lawson asks it, "If a segment of the population thinks that the state continually fails to protect them from crime, at what point are these individuals morally justified in taking on the responsibility of protecting themselves from crime?"

Note that in its basic form, contractualism suggests that in exchange for citizens willingly giving up certain liberties, the state assumes an obligation to protect them—including protection from criminal victimization. The state's end of the social contract obligates it to ensure that citizens—*all* citizens—are protected in their property (including life and physical well-being). Laws, law enforcement, courts, and the system of punishment and corrections are collectively part of the state's effort to uphold its end of the contract by enabling citizens to live in security and peace. Yet what if, as many urban residents would suggest, the state fails in its obligation to protect citizens or certain groups of citizens from crime? If certain groups of citizens, such as inner-city minorities, are forced to live in a perpetual state of fear, surely the state has not been effective in providing for their safety and security? With this basic reality in mind, consider the following:

- Would you agree that, in many urban areas at least, the state has in fact failed to meet its end of the social contract?
- If so, does the state's failure to live up to its end of the contract thereby release those citizens from their obligations?
- Do inner-city residents, at continual risk of criminal victimization, have a moral right to ensure their own protection by taking matters into their own hands?
- Social contract theorist John Locke argued that whenever the state cannot protect its citizens, those citizens have a right to take measures to protect themselves—including choosing the most effective means by which to do so. If the state has proven that it cannot protect certain groups of citizens, do these citizens have a right to resort to extreme—even violent—measures to ensure their own safety?
- What measures might be taken—either by the state, community members, or a combination of both—to make crime-ridden inner-city neighborhoods safer for residents?

Source: Bill Lawson, "Crime, Minorities, and the Social Contract," *Criminal Justice Ethics*, 9 (2), 16–24 (1990).

have beneficial consequences. For an action or type of action to be morally good or right, it must produce more desirable consequences than other possible courses of behavior. This basic idea is one that utilitarianism shares with ethical egoism. However, where utilitarianism differs from ethical egoism is in its contention that the consequences of our actions should be considered in light of everyone who is (or stands to be) affected by them. Whereas ethical egoism emphasizes consequences for the acting agent, utilitarianism stresses that the interests of everyone should be considered equally.

> **Point of departure for utilitarianism:** always act so as to maximize the sum total of welfare among everyone affected by what we do.[58]

The Principle of Utility (or the Greatest Happiness Principle)

For Bentham, "utility" is the fundamental normative principle by which we should determine which choices to make and which actions to take. In more specific terms, Bentham defined **utility** as "that property in any object whereby it tends to produce benefit, advantage, pleasure, good or happiness . . . or . . . to prevent the happening of mischief, pain, evil or unhappiness . . ."[59] The basis of utilitarianism is a simple idea the Bentham called the "Principle of Utility." Plainly stated, the **Principle of Utility** holds that "whenever we have a choice between alternative actions or social policies, we must choose the one which has the best overall consequences for everyone concerned."[60] In his, *The Principles of Morals and Legislation*, Bentham stated:

> By the principle of utility is meant that principle which approves or disapproves of every action . . . according to the tendency which it appears to have to augment or diminish the happiness of the party whose interest is in question.[61]

Because more than one "party" will be affected by an action, the action which is "right" in a given situation is the one that produces the "greatest happiness for the greatest number of people" or, conversely, "eliminates pain for the greatest number of people." For this reason, the principle of utility is often referred to as the **Greatest Happiness Principle.** Actions are morally justifiable only if they have a tendency to produce happiness or eliminate pain for the greater number of people relative to other courses of action. In 1861, John Stuart Mill restated this basic idea in his short classic, *Utilitarianism.*[62] We can best understand the Greatest Happiness Principle with reference to a state of being—an ultimate end or ideal state of affairs—that is as far removed from pain as possible, and as rich in enjoyments as possible. Morally, we should imagine what this state of affairs would be like—a state in which all people are as happy as possible and/or as free from pain as possible—and act in the interest of bringing about that state of affairs.[63] This, then, is the primary principle of morality. Simply stated, we should act so as to bring about the greatest amount of happiness for all those affected by our decisions and actions or, on a more social level, all those citizens impacted by our laws and policies.[64]

Though utilitarianism has undergone some revisions since its inception, we can summarize *classic utilitarianism* (i.e., that of Bentham and Mill) by stating its three basic propositions:[65]

- Actions are judged right or wrong only with reference to their consequences
- In determining consequences, what is important is the amount of happiness or unhappiness that is brought about
- No one's happiness is more important than anyone else's

This third proposition is especially important. Within it lies the principle difference between utilitarian and egoistic consequentialism. In short, while ethical egoism holds that what matters is bringing about happiness for the acting agent, utilitarianism suggests that *each person's welfare is equally important*. As John Stuart Mill wrote,

> the happiness which forms the utilitarian standard of what is right . . . is not the agent's own happiness, but that of all concerned. As between his own happiness and that of others, utilitarianism requires him to be as strictly impartial as a disinterested and benevolent spectator.[66]

Thus, utilitarianism requires that we weigh equally the happiness of everyone affected by our actions, without placing more or less importance on that of anyone (including ourselves). In fact, in some cases, the morally right action may be one in which *we* endure harm or pain in the interest of bringing about happiness for a greater number of people. We cannot, then, consider our own happiness to be more important than anyone else's—much like we cannot (or should not) make distinctions on the basis of personal relationships, wealth, status, race, gender, age, or any other potential source of bias. Utilitarianism demands that we become "disinterested spectators" in making a rational assessment of what consequences will result from our actions and in determining which course of action will have the most beneficial consequences for everyone (see Box 8.3).[67]

"Good" Consequences?

Consequentialism, including both egoistic and altruistic varieties, understands morality or morally good actions as those that bring about good or beneficial outcomes or effects. A crucial consideration, then, is what things are *good*? If our concern should be for bringing about these results, we should first know what kinds of effects are considered "good" ones. Classic utilitarianism understood only one thing to be good—*happiness*. In John Stuart Mill's words, "The utilitarian doctrine is that happiness is desirable, and the only thing desirable, as an end; all other things being desirable as means to that end."[68] In other words, anything other than happiness that we might consider to be good is only good because it serves to bring about or help us attain happiness. Wealth, status, food, love, knowledge, and many other things commonly understood as "goods" can only be understood as such because they are means by which we attain the more primary end of happiness.

In Chapter 2, we explained how values and goods are often categorized as *intrinsic* or *instrumental*. Intrinsic goods are those things that are good in and of themselves or for their own sake; instrumental goods are those things that help us attain intrinsic goods. Thus, money is generally understood to be an instrumental good because its value lies in its ability to help us attain other things that are intrinsically good—by itself, money is of limited worth or utility. Happiness, however, is not a means to anything—we do not *use* it to get other things that are desirable. Instead, we desire happiness because the state of being happy is, by itself, something we consider to be good. Thus, happiness is an intrinsic good, valuable on its own, and, arguably, a legitimate basis for determining what constitutes good consequences.

BOX 8.3

Plea Bargaining and the Greatest Happiness Principle

The practice of plea bargaining is one that is widely employed in criminal justice, yet has been attacked from a variety of perspectives. In effect, a **plea bargain** is an agreement between a defendant and the prosecution whereby the latter reduces charges or recommends a reduced sentence in exchange for the defendant pleading guilty before (or, on occasion, during) trial. Plea bargaining became a popular means of resolving criminal cases in the early decades of the twentieth century and, today, over 90% of criminal cases are disposed of through plea bargains.

Utilitarianism would have us consider the consequences of plea bargaining for everyone affected by its practice. Morally "good" practices are those that produce the greatest happiness (or eliminate the greatest pain) for the greatest number of people. In the case of plea bargaining, we would need to consider the ways in which it affects the defendant, prosecution, victim(s), and the greater community. Because each of these parties will be affected, the morality of plea bargaining becomes a matter of whether it tends to produce the "greatest happiness for the greatest number of people" when compared with alternative responses (in this case, a criminal trial). What consequences—good and bad—are produced by the practice of plea bargaining? Do the "good" consequences sufficiently outweigh the "bad" such that plea bargaining can be morally justified on utilitarian grounds?

Following is a list of possible effects, both beneficial and detrimental, to each of the major parties affected. As you read through them, weigh the costs and benefits and ask yourself whether the practice of plea bargaining on the whole passes the test of greatest happiness. If so, are there other reasons that plea bargaining might not be morally desirable?

- *Prosecution.* By most accounts, the party most positively affected by the practice of plea bargaining is the prosecution. Reaching a compromise with the defendant saves the prosecution countless hours of preparation, the time and monetary costs of trial, and ensures a conviction. This latter point is significant, as prosecutors often face strong administrative and political pressures to maintain a high conviction rate. This tension only increases where district attorneys are elected and must appease the public to secure reelection. Particularly in cases where the prosecution's case is weak, plea bargaining can serve a variety of interests with relatively few negative consequences.
- *Victim(s).* Critics have argued that plea bargaining often leaves victims feeling as though justice has not been done. Defendants often receive more lenient sentences than would have been imposed by a judge following a conviction. We might imagine how a rape victim would feel upon learning that the offender had pled guilty to a lesser sexual assault charge and will only serve a minimal amount of time in prison. On the other hand, victims are spared the pain of enduring—and perhaps participating in—a criminal trial. As well, even though a lesser sentence may be imposed, victims are not exposed to the uncertainty that comes with not knowing whether a jury will reach a guilty verdict. In other words, the victim is assured that the offender will be punished in some fashion and to some extent.
- *Defendant.* Although on the surface it may seem as if the defendant has the most to gain from plea bargaining (e.g., a lesser charge, reduced sentence), the alleged

(Continued)

offender may also be most negatively affected by the process. Defendants find themselves in the unattractive predicament of having to choose between pleading guilty and thus ensuring their own punishment, or braving the uncertainty of a criminal trial that may or may not bring a conviction on a more serious charge and/or a harsher punishment. This dilemma is especially troubling in cases involving *innocent* defendants who may fear being found guilty by a jury following an unsuccessful defense. Those defendants who are poor, represented by public defenders, and/or do not understand the legal process may be especially at risk. Critics have argued that plea bargaining exploits the fear and uncertainty that defendants feel, thereby *coercing* them into surrendering their constitutional (Sixth Amendment) right to a trial by jury.

- *Community.* In some ways, plea bargaining serves the interests of the community. Firstly, the costs associated with criminal trials are shouldered by taxpayers. If most criminal cases went to trial, the financial burden on taxpayers would increase substantially. As well, in those cases involving defendants who present a continued danger to the community (e.g., violent offenders, drug dealers), plea bargaining offers a more certain means of ensuring public protection—even if for a shorter period of time. On the other hand, if the public feels that criminals are "getting off easy" and/or that innocent persons are being coerced into pleading guilty to crimes they did not commit, pubic confidence in and respect for the legal system may be undermined.

Sources: Jeff Palmer, "Abolishing Plea Bargaining: An End to the Same Old Song and Dance," *American Journal of Criminal Law,* 26, 3(1999); Michael Gorr, "The Morality of Plea Bargaining," *Social Theory and Practice,* 26, 1 (2000); Kenneth Kipnis, "Criminal Justice and the Negotiated Plea," *Ethics,* 86 (1976).

HEDONISTIC GOOD

Bentham defined good not simply as happiness, but more specifically as *pleasure.* What is good—what constitutes happiness and unhappiness—is a matter of pleasure and pain. In so doing, Bentham followed a philosophical tradition dating as far back as the ancient Greeks known as hedonism (*hedone* = a state in which pleasure is present or a quality that produces pleasure). **Hedonism** is a simple and popular theory which suggests that pleasure and pain are the only things we can say are intrinsically good or intrinsically bad.[69] Everything that we normally consider good is good only because it produces pleasure; while anything bad is bad because it produces pain. Thus, pleasure is considered central to human motivation, choice, and action—including moral considerations. While there has been long-standing disagreement about what kinds of things are pleasurable, all hedonists favor the basic idea that pleasure—whether linked to good food, wine, sex, as well as to tranquility, friendship or peacefulness—is the "ultimate good" in life and the only thing worth pursuing.

Bentham's utilitarianism fits squarely within this broader tradition of hedonism. More fundamentally, Bentham's moral philosophy assumes that human beings are *by nature* hedonistic or pleasure-seeking. Indeed, all human behavior ultimately is motivated by pleasure and/or pain alone. Thus, we naturally seek to maximize pleasure while avoiding pain. This is the principle of **psychological hedonism**: the claim that the pursuit of pleasure is a fact of human nature. As Bentham famously wrote, "Nature has placed mankind under the governance of two sovereign masters, pain and pleasure. It is for them alone to point out what we ought to do. . . " In terms of normative implications, psychological hedonism suggests that we can determine what we *should* do by appealing to what we naturally seek—happiness in the form of pleasure (see Box 8.4).

THE FELICITY CALCULUS

How do notions of happiness and pleasure assist us in making moral decisions? Bentham argued that we can make moral decisions by considering the amount of pleasure or pain that our actions bring. More specifically, he believed that we can *quantify* such pleasures and pains along a number of dimensions. Bentham described this process of categorizing and measuring pleasures as the **felicity** (i.e., - happiness, pleasure) **calculus.** The seven dimensions of pleasure are as follows:

- **Intensity** of pleasure—how strong is it?
- **Duration** of pleasure—how long does it last?
- **Certainty** of pleasure—how sure are we that it will be experienced?
- **Proximity** of pleasure—how soon will it be experienced?
- **Fecundity**—will the pleasure lead to or produce other pleasures as well?
- **Purity**—how free will the pleasure be from pain?
- **Extent**—how many people are affected?

Bentham suggested that whenever we are contemplating an action, we should analyze its consequences in terms of these seven dimensions of pleasure, contrasting it with alternative courses of action.[70] For instance, suppose you are trying to decide whether to stay home and study for a midterm exam tonight or go out with friends. In making your decision, you should consider how intense the pleasures of studying versus going out with friends are, how long those pleasures will last, how certain you are that these respective pleasures will occur, how soon you will experience them, whether they will lead to further instances of happiness, how free from pain either or both will be, and whether they each will bring pleasure to other people as well. Your felicity calculus might look something like Table 8.1 (numbers in parentheses are "*hedons*" or "happiness units" along a ten-point scale with the score of "1" representing very low happiness and the score of "10" representing very high happiness).

Admittedly, the above example is drawn from decision-making in everyday life rather than from moral choice-making; however, the same "calculus" applies to the decisions we make that have ethical implications. To illustrate, if you were considering whether to lie to a friend in order to protect that person's feelings, to have an abortion in order to not be subjected to parenting as a teenager, or to take sick leave from work when not sick (a type of "stealing") in order to have some time off from a stress-filled period in your life, you could apply the same formula. To be clear, however, there are some obvious problems with this approach. One of these problems is that Bentham focused on the *quantity* of pleasure as opposed to its *quality*. In the above example, the felicity calculus would have you go out with friends rather than study for your exam. For at least some people, this would seem unsettling. So, what is missing from the formula?

BOX 8.4

Hedonism, the "War on Drugs" and "Noble-Cause" Corruption

Though remaining within the tradition of hedonism, Bentham made some important modifications. In particular, his utilitarianism represents a variation of *social hedonism* (as distinguished from egoistic hedonism). **Social hedonism** regards pleasure as the ultimate good, but demands that we consider the pleasures and pains of *others* in our moral contemplations. In fact, utilitarianism demands that, at times, we place the interests of others *above* our own if in so doing the result is happiness to a greater number of people. Indeed, the Greatest Happiness Principle demands that our actions bring the greatest amount of pleasure to the *greatest number of people*. This is the social and altruistic element of utilitarianism, and this is what distinguishes it from the tradition of *egoistic hedonism* in moral philosophy.

One prominent issue in criminal justice ethics that is an interesting illustration of this difference is police corruption—particularly as it intersects with the "war on drugs." Indeed, drugs are a significant force in police deviance, with as many as half of all convictions in police corruption cases involving drug-related crimes. As we saw in Chapter 5, much corruption in law enforcement, courts, and corrections can be explained through egoism—selfish desires for personal gain. In other cases, however, corruption might be better understood as stemming from *socially hedonistic* incentives; that is, a desire to produce good consequences for others. In their discussion of drug-related police corruption, for instance, Kappeler, Sluder, and Alpert describe four types of corruption that can be linked with drugs:

- **Use corruption** occurs where police officers *use* illegal drugs. In one study, as many as 20% of officers admitted to smoking marijuana.
- **Economic corruption** occurs where officers use their power and discretion for personal monetary gain, such as by keeping drug money confiscated from offenders.
- **Police violence** may occur in the context of extracting confessions or information from drug suspects.
- **Subjugation of a defendant's rights** occurs where police commit perjury or plant drugs on a suspect in the interest of obtaining a confession or getting a conviction.

While the first two of these forms of corruption would seem to be explicable in terms of egoistic hedonism (i.e., self-interested pursuit of pleasure or personal gain), the latter two (use of violence and subjugation of rights) might be linked to what is sometimes called **noble-cause corruption.** Rather than a purely egoistic form of corruption, noble-cause corruption occurs when police officers violate ethical and legal obligations in the interest of achieving the "good" ends of police work. Getting the "bad guys" and protecting communities and potential victims are seen as more important than ethical and procedural restrictions on police conduct. Planting evidence at a crime scene, for instance, may result in the apprehension and conviction of a notorious offender who has avoided criminal prosecution and continues to present a significant danger to the community. While "noble-cause" corruption is by all accounts still unethical and often illegal, would you consider the latter two types of drug-related corruption to be less morally reprehensible than the first two?

Sources: Roy Roberg, Kenneth Novak, and Gary Cordner, *Police and Society*, 3rd ed. (Los Angeles: Roxbury, 2005), pp. 304–305; Victor Kappeler, Richard Sluder, and Geoffrey Alpert, *Forces of Deviance: Understanding the Dark Side of Policing*, 2nd ed. (Prospect Heights, IL: Waveland, 1998), pp. 166–173.

TABLE 8-1
Bentham and Measuring Pleasure

	Studying for the Exam	**Going Out with Friends**
Intensity	Not intensely pleasurable; perhaps even more painful than pleasurable (2)	Moderately to very intense, depending upon the specifics of the evening (7)
Duration	Potentially long-lasting; though studying is short-lived, the knowledge you gain will last indefinitely (9)	Short-lived; likely lasts only a few hours (2)
Certainty	Not very certain that it will be pleasurable; in fact, more certain that it will be painful (3)	Fairly certain that you'll have a good time (7)
Proximity	More than likely, you won't experience the pleasure until later in life, although doing on the exam could be pleasurable in the near future (4)	Pleasure will be experienced in the very near future (9)
Fecundity	There are many additional benefits that come from studying: knowledge, wisdom, better career prospects, income, etc. (9)	Probably will not lead to other pleasures, although you could meet new friends, contacts, learn new things, etc. (2)
Purity	Probably not free from pain, unless you really enjoy the subject (2)	Could lead to some pain (e.g., arguments with friends, hangover), but overall probably more pure than not (7)
Extent	In the near future, studying probably only benefits you; but it is possible that your knowledge could benefit many other people in the future (4)	May bring pleasure to your friends as well, but mostly affects your happiness (5)
Score	33	39

Quality of Pleasure: Quantitative versus Qualitative Hedonism

Bentham's utilitarianism describes "good" in terms of *pleasure* and, more specifically, the quantity of pleasure that results from our actions. As we have seen, this is consistent with the doctrine of hedonism—that pleasure and pain are the only things that we can say are intrinsically good and bad, with everything else being in some way dependent on or secondary to pleasure and pain. However, even within the tradition of hedonism, there has been some debate regarding the interpretation of happiness and pleasure for purposes of moral decision-making.[71] Perhaps the most notable detractor from Bentham's original formulation of utilitarianism was his disciple, John Stuart Mill (Mill's father was a friend of Bentham's and a key figure within his intellectual circle). Though working within the utilitarian tradition established by Bentham, Mill sought to rework what he understood as several problematic dimensions of Bentham's original formulation. In particular, while Bentham saw pleasure as good and pain as bad, John Stuart Mill argued that there are *degrees of goodness* associated with different types of pleasures. In other words, we should understand some pleasures as *better* than others.

Given the formulation of the felicity calculus put forth by Bentham, we could easily conclude that we should go out with friends rather than study for our examination, or that watching reality television is better than pursuing knowledge in the arts and sciences. These sorts of prospects were especially troubling to Mill. In fact, he believed that utilitarianism needed to be reworked in order to demonstrate that certain pleasures (e.g., reading Shakespeare) were more important than, better than, or of a *higher quality* than other pleasures. As Mill saw it, the problem was that the felicity calculus was purely quantitative in nature, with no regard for qualitative differences in types of pleasures. In turn, Mill claimed that our concern should not be with the quantity of pleasure, but with its *quality*.[72]

Mill argued that some kinds of pleasures are of higher quality than other kinds. Thus, "lower" pleasures such as eating, drinking, and sexual activity are qualitatively different from the "higher" pleasures of intellectual, creative, and spiritual activity.[73] The pleasure of studying for and doing well on an exam is of a higher quality than that of going out with friends and having a few drinks; the pleasure of reading classic literature is greater than that of reading a sports magazine; and the pleasure of doing volunteer work to help persons in need is of a higher quality than that of going fishing. In cases such as these, Mill argued that there are important differences between types of pleasures, and that these differences are a function of the quality of enjoyment being experienced: "It is quite compatible with the principle of utility to recognize the fact that some kinds of pleasures are more desirable and more valuable than others."[74]

As an example, Mill suggested that, "anyone who has experienced the pleasure of solving a mathematical equation will attest to the fact that it is indeed superior in kind to the pleasure of eating an exquisite meal." Even though the "lower" pleasure of eating an exquisite meal may be more *intensely* gratifying, the "higher" pleasures tend to be of more benefit in the long run. As most of us have experienced, the pleasure associated with eating a good meal comes and goes in a matter of hours. Even though it may be intensely pleasurable during the time we consume the food, it does not offer any long-term pleasure—and may even produce long-term pain (e.g., overeating, weight gain). "Higher" pleasures—though not always immediately and intensely experienced—are capable of contributing to our *continued* happiness.

Although Mill accepted the basic principle of hedonism (i.e., that pleasure is the basis of determining what is good), he clearly believed some pleasures were *better* than others.[75] The question then becomes, *"By what or whose criteria are we to make such determinations?"* For Bentham, pleasure is "measured" in terms of duration, certainty, fecundity, and as forth. However, for Mill "better" pleasures are those that possess a higher quality.[76] With quality of pleasure in mind, Mill essentially reformulated the Greatest Happiness Principle from "greatest happiness for the greatest number of people," to the greatest quantity *and quality* of happiness for the greatest number of people. The problem with this reformulation is that many people do not know which qualities are desirable and valuable and, thus, are unaware of those qualities that should be taken into consideration in the Greatest Happiness Principle. So, how should qualities of pleasure be judged?

Determining Quality of Pleasure

How are we to figure out those kinds of pleasure that are "more desirable and more valuable than others?" Mill claimed that, "Of two pleasures, if there be one to which all or almost all who have an experience of both give a decided preference . . . that is the more desirable pleasure."[77] In determining which types of pleasures are of higher quality, we must rely on the opinions of those who have experienced various types. In other words, establishing the quality of a pleasure requires a judge or an "expert" on the subject. This person can distinguish between them. Thus, for example, we cannot expect a person who has never solved a complex mathematical equation to be able to distinguish the happiness derived from it versus the pleasure experienced while watching football. Following Mill's utilitarian theory, anyone who has experienced both of these types of pleasure clearly should recognize that solving a difficult arithmetic problem produces happiness that exceeds the pleasure experienced from watching football. Of course, many people have no point of reference when it comes to deciphering complicated mathematical equations. As such, they are not in a position to make a distinction between the quality of happiness that follows from doing this successfully versus enjoying an athletic event on television. In fact, given the choice, we might suspect that most people would choose the pleasure of watching football. For Mill, this possibility was the source of considerable concern. The "uncultivated cannot be competent judges of cultivation," he argued, as their preference for "lower" desires and pleasures may lead to the eventual degeneration of entire cultures.

The Problems with Utilitarianism

Bentham's utilitarianism is intuitively and practically appealing: there is one—and only one—principle to apply in all situations. This simple rule pertains equally to personal and professional scenarios; to love, friendship, and acquaintance relationships; to law, crime, and justice decision-making; and to environmental, economic, and health care policy. In all cases, we are to maximize happiness or pleasure, and/or minimize suffering or pain. What is more, Bentham offered a means of quantifying pleasure and pain such that in any given instance we can calculate and impartially apply our measurements to the issue or situation in question in order to determine what we should do. Additionally, some have argued that utilitarianism is valuable in that it "seems to get at the substance of morality."[78] Following utilitarianism, morality is not simply a formal system of rules and principles, but has a function or end to which it should aim. Ultimately, this end is about promoting happiness and alleviating suffering. Morality, then, is not so much about following rules as it is about helping people and doing what we can to alleviate the misery in the world. Utilitarianism seems to recognize this feature of morality. It asks us to consider the happiness we can cause and the suffering we can reduce by way of our (quantitatively and qualitatively calculated) choices and actions.

However, despite its appeal, utilitarianism is certainly not without its shortcomings. The three most significant criticisms leveled against utilitarianism include: (1) its requirement that we predict the future; (2) its focus on happiness as the only consequence of importance; and (3) its exclusive regard for the consequences of our actions.[79]

THE PROBLEM OF PREDICTION

Utilitarianism has been accused of asking—or requiring—us to do that which we cannot possibly do: *know* what the consequences of our actions will be.[80] Bentham's felicity calculus requires us to make a *prediction* about the intensity, duration, extent, and so on of pleasure brought about by certain courses of action. Yet, none of us can ever know the consequences of our actions—especially including the more long-term effects.

Recall the decision to stay at home and study for an exam or go out with friends. Now suppose that in choosing to go out you run into an ex-lover, have a heated argument, go home upset, stay up all night thinking about the encounter, and miss your exam. Conversely, suppose you choose to stay home and study when, had you gone out, you would have met your future husband/wife or would have made an important contact resulting in your career being launched upon your graduation. The point is that there are an infinite number of possible events that could follow whatever choice you make. And while each of these events represents a possibility, none can be predicted with any degree of success. Given all of these possibilities, how can we possibly be expected to make an informed decision?

In response to this difficulty, supporters of utilitarianism distinguish between *real* consequences, *expected* consequences, and *intended* consequences.[81] Since it is impossible to determine what the actual or real consequences of our actions will be, the moral "rightness" of our choices must be based on what we *reasonably expect* the consequences to be. The best we can do—and that which we should do in any situation—is to use whatever information we have at our disposal to make a choice that any reasonable person would, anticipating that it will result in the best possible (most pleasurable) outcome.[82] If our actions fail to produce the expected consequences, perhaps even causing more pain than happiness, we cannot be said to have made a poor choice. So long as we do what a reasonable person would do in light of the expected consequences, we are fulfilling utilitarian requirements. Since we cannot predict the future, we simply need to do what "reason judges to be the best act based on likely consequences."[83]

ONLY HAPPINESS?

Utilitarianism simplifies morality in that it reduces "good" to happiness or pleasure. However, in doing so, arguably it *oversimplifies* morality. While most of us would not deny that happiness is intrinsically good and that it is worth pursuing, the more important question is whether happiness is the *only* thing that is good in itself, worthy of consideration in our moral decision-making. The notion that happiness is the one ultimate good and the only thing worth considering when faced with ethical choices is problematic on a number of grounds.

Consider the following illustration from James Rachels. Your neighbor insists that he is your friend and so you believe him. However, in actuality he ridicules you behind your back. Not one of the other neighbors discusses this with you, so you believe the person who professes to be your friend.[84] By hedonistic standards, this situation is *not* a concern because you were never caused any unhappiness. However, in evaluating this situation, most of us know or at least feel that something *is* wrong here. You are led to believe that someone is your friend when, in fact, that person is just using you as a source of humor for himself and others. On utilitarian grounds, the problem is that, because you do not know this, you are not caused any unhappiness and, consequently, do not suffer in any way. At the same time, as a good source of humor you unknowingly bring happiness to a group of people. Clearly, because no harm is being caused and a good amount of happiness is taking place, the situation is not a moral predicament, according to utilitarianism. In fact, happiness is produced for everyone involved, and, moreover, "the truth would hurt."

However, for many people there is something deeply disturbing about the situation as it exists, despite the happiness it brings. What seems to make it disturbing is that we value other things in addition to happiness. We value truth, honesty, and fairness. Moreover, we are generally upset by people who use or exploit others for their own benefit, despite the considerable pleasure that materializes because of it. Thus, in cases like this, many of us would likely determine that ridiculing a person for the sake of so many people's happiness is not the morally right decision to make.

ONLY CONSEQUENCES?

The most fundamental principle of utilitarianism is that, in making moral decisions, we should attend to what will happen as a result of our doing one thing or the other. While being considerate of the consequences of our actions seems like a good rule of thumb, utilitarianism's *exclusive* focus on consequences carries with it several limitations. Suppose, for instance, that we are troubled by overpopulation. We might then define beneficial consequences as those that reduce overpopulation in the world. Any number of questionable actions (e.g., suicide, abortion, euthanasia, murder) might have to be defined as "good" because they bring about the beneficial consequence of reducing the world's population. Of course, undertaking these sorts of actions would be a problem for most people. However, if we focus *only* on the consequences of our actions—to the exclusion of other considerations—they must be regarded as good in that they bring about desired consequences.

Utilitarianism has been criticized for precisely this reason. In addition to utility, what other considerations should be important when determining what actions are morally right? Critics have pointed to several. For example, *justice* requires that people be treated fairly, according to what they need or deserve.[85] If consequences are the only consideration deemed important when making moral decisions, then injustices might be warranted by appealing to their beneficial effects. Additionally, critics of utilitarianism's consequences-only approach object that it can lead to *violations of rights*.[86] According to utilitarianism, these infractions may be morally permissible if they serve the greater good. Again, the example of the neighbor who professes to be your friend when, in fact, he privately ridicules you, undermines your "right" be treated decently and honestly. Finally, a third objection to the idea that only consequences are of moral importance is that the theory does not allow for "*backward-looking reasons*."[87] Utilitarianism is future directed. It demands that we consider what *will* happen as opposed to what *has* happened. The problem with this reasoning is that most of us believe that the *past* is important, or at least certain types of past actions (e.g., promises we have made) should be regarded as important for purposes of determining what we should do in the present.

CONSEQUENTIALISM AND THE CRIMINAL JUSTICE SYSTEM: MEANS AND ENDS IN POLICING

All varieties of consequentialist ethics ultimately raise questions about the relationship between *ends* and the *means* used to achieve those ends. As we have seen, consequentialism holds ends to be more important than means, such that actions that might otherwise be considered immoral (e.g., lying) become moral so long as they serve to bring about good ends. In the next chapter, we will see that varieties of deontological ethics generally hold means to be the more important moral consideration, such that immoral or illegal means are never justifiable—even if they lead to morally good or desirable outcomes.

This tension between means and ends is one that criminal justice practitioners are forced to confront and work within on an everyday basis. In the context of criminal justice practice, this tension is perhaps best summarized by Carl Klockars' question, "When and to what extent does the morally good end warrant or justify an ethically, politically, or legally dangerous means for its achievement?"[88] In other words, can the "good" ends of police work ever justify the use of morally questionable means to achieve them? If so, when and under what circumstances are we willing to accept or at least overlook immoral or illegal law enforcement practices? To illustrate this tension as it applies to criminal justice work, we focus on two important—and interrelated—ethical controversies in policing, linking them to ethical utilitarianism as discussed earlier in the chapter.

The Dirty Harry Problem

The "Dirty Harry" problem is titled after a series of films in which the protagonist "Dirty" Harry Callahan (played by Clint Eastwood) employs a variety of questionable and sometimes outright objectionable means to "get the bad guy." Callahan's techniques involve everything from illegal stops and searches, to intimidation and coercion, to the use of torture to obtain the whereabouts of a kidnapped girl. As the hero, Callahan's methods are presented as justifiable—"dirty" but necessary methods of getting the job done in a society plagued by dangerous criminals who prey on innocent victims.

Outside of popular film, "dirty" methods are regularly practiced and assume a number of forms in everyday police interactions. Nearly any legally or morally questionable police practice undertaken to achieve the "good" end of preventing or controlling crime can be made to fit the moral dilemma raised by the Dirty Harry Problem. For our purposes, the **Dirty Harry Problem** can be outlined as follows:

- A police officer is in a situation in which a morally good or desirable outcome may be accomplished.
- The officer believes that the only way (or, at least, the most certain way) to accomplish this end is through the use of techniques that would otherwise

be considered morally questionable or even illegal (e.g., falsifying probable cause to make a stop, manufacturing a false arrest to justify an illegal search, using deceptive interviewing and interrogation techniques).

- The officer believes that the good brought about by accomplishing the desirable outcome outweighs the evil done through the use of immoral or illegal techniques.

The moral dilemma of this scenario is contained in the third statement above; namely, can good ends ever justify immoral or illegal means? According to utilitarian varieties of ethics, the answer to this question may be affirmative. Of course, as Carl Klockars points out, there are other considerations:

- How certain is the good outcome? As critics of consequentialism suggest, we cannot predict the future and thus can never be certain of any outcome. When a police officer is in a situation in which she or he believes that a desirable outcome may be accomplished, the officer is necessarily dealing only with probabilities. With this in mind, how certain must one be that the outcome will be accomplished in order to justify the use of dirty means? If an officer believes that there is a 10% chance that a suspect knows the whereabouts of a kidnapped victim, does this justify the use of intimidation, coercion, force, and even torture to try to extract that information? What if the officer is 50% certain? 99% certain?

- Are dirty means necessary? How certain are we that dirty means are the only—or only reasonable—method of achieving the good end? If dirty means are simply the easiest or most convenient means of accomplishing the end, this may dramatically change the extent to which they are justifiable. How certain is the officer that she or he has considered all alternatives and all possible nondirty means?

- Because the consequences of our actions are unpredictable, the question is not only whether a given action will bring about the desired end, but also whether that action might bring about other, unintended or undesirable outcomes. In other words, what if the use of dirty means accomplishes the good end, but at the same time has the effect of causing other harms that were not predicted? While the good of the end might outweigh the evil of the means, can the good of the end outweigh the evil of the means *and* the additional evil consequences that are brought about by the means?

Deceptive Interrogation

Deceptive interrogation strategies present intriguing ethical questions. While brutal or otherwise physically coercive means are no longer commonly used by police officers to obtain confessions, officers regularly use deception as an interrogation strategy. Jerome Skolnick and Richard Leo suggest that "psychological persuasion and manipulation" are "the most salient and defining features of contemporary police interrogation," as officers are "instructed to, are authorized to—and do—trick, lie, and cajole to elicit so-called 'voluntary' confessions."[89] The ethical question is on what, if any, moral grounds the use of deception as an interrogation strategy is justifiable.

Skolnick and Leo offer a typology of interrogatory deception which is worth briefly reviewing as we consider the ethics of ends and means. As you read through each type of deception, consider whether it is a justifiable means of reaching the desired end.

- *"Interview" versus "interrogate."* By telling a suspect that she or he is free to leave at any time and having her or him acknowledge the voluntariness of the encounter, police can sidestep *Miranda* requirements that would apply to a suspect taken into custody. An interrogation becomes, for legal purposes, a noncustodial interview.

- *Miranda warnings.* Police cannot deceive a suspect into waiving her or his *Miranda* rights, although some officers consciously recite the warnings in such as way (e.g., as if they are merely a bureaucratic ritual) as to increase the likelihood of obtaining a waiver.

- *Misrepresenting the nature or seriousness of the offense.* This particular strategy comes in several varieties. For instance, police may tell a suspect that a murder victim is still alive, hoping she or he will then openly talk about her or his role in the lesser offense (e.g., assault); exaggerate the seriousness of the offense, hoping the suspect will then admit to a lesser role in the offense to "save" herself or himself; or suggest to a suspect that they are interested in her or his role in one crime, when they are in fact investigating another (e.g., suggest that they are interrogating a suspect for possession of stolen property when, in fact, they are hoping the suspect will admit to participating in a robbery which involved a homicide).

- *Role-playing: Manipulative appeals to conscience.* Interrogators may project sympathy, compassion, and understanding to "play the role" of the suspect's friend, brother or father figure, or therapeutic/religious counselor to elicit a confession. Doing so may produce an "illusion of intimacy between the suspect and the officer while downplaying the adversarial aspects of interrogation."

- *Misrepresenting the moral seriousness of the offense.* This common strategy involves an officer offering excuses or justifications for the offender's conduct by providing an "external attribution of blame that will allow [the suspect] to save face while confessing." The officer may, for instance, suggest to a rape suspect that the victim was "asking for it" or is somehow responsible for the incident. Doing so displaces moral guilt, encouraging the suspect to think of herself or himself as justified or less morally responsible for the offense.

- *The use of promises.* While officers cannot legally make direct and specific promises of leniency, they can make vague and indefinite promises. Officers may suggest to a suspect that they will "inform the court of [her or his] cooperation," that showing remorse will be a mitigating factor, or that they will do whatever they can to aid the suspect if she or he confesses. In each case, officers are creating implicit expectations of leniency that will not be met.

- *Fabricated evidence.* This strategy involves confronting a suspect with false evidence of guilt through one of several deceptive techniques: (1) falsely informing a suspect that an accomplice has identified her or him; (2) falsely state that physical evidence (e.g., blood, fingerprints) exists that confirms her or his guilt; (3) falsely suggest that a victim or eyewitness has identified the suspect; (4) staging a lineup in which a false witness identifies the suspect; or (5) have the suspect take a lie detector test and suggest that its results confirm her or his guilt.

The various types of deceptive interrogation outlined by Skolnick and Leo are morally problematic in that they involve the intentional use of deception or dishonesty to accomplish the aim of a confession (or the revealing of other desired information). As you may have realized, many—if not all—of these strategies *could* be legitimized or justified on utilitarian grounds. In each case, the use of deceptive means may allow law enforcement officers to accomplish the "good" end of a confession or the obtaining of information that may lead to solving a crime. The larger question, however, is whether deception, deceit, and dishonesty are ever justifiable on moral grounds—despite the "goodness" of the outcome they may produce. As you read through the next chapter on deontological ethics, consider how the moral legitimacy of these practices might be more questionable when approached from an alternative ethical perspective.

Summary

This chapter examined the normative theory of consequentialism, especially as a basis or a set of "tools" for engaging in ethical choices and moral actions. In this chapter, we presented the following three variations of consequentialist ethics: (1) ethical egoism, which argues that what matters morally are consequences to *ourselves*; (2) contractualism, which relies on self-interested motivation to justify basic rules for living that benefit everyone; and (3) utilitarianism, which suggests that what matters morally are the consequences for *everyone affected* by our actions. Although the theory's respective forms offer considerable insight into how to make choices and undertake actions that are ethical—including decisions within criminal justice—this moral system is not without its significant and varied limitations. In part because of this, examining other normative approaches is worthwhile. Along these lines, Chapter 9 explores how duties, rights, and obligations represent another normative basis for ethical reasoning, decision-making, and behavior, mindful of several ethical problems posed in the realm of crime, law, and justice.

Key Terms and Concepts

altruism	noble-cause corruption
contractualism (social contact theory)	plea bargain
deceptive interrogation	Principle of Utility
Dirty Harry Problem	psychological hedonism
ethical egoism	social hedonism
felicity calculus	state of nature
Greatest Happiness Principle	utilitarianism
hedonism	utility
hedonistic egoism	

DISCUSSION QUESTIONS

1. Suppose that John regularly watches Jane undress by peeping through a small hole that he has managed to drill through her wall. Suppose further that John has planted a small camera in a second hole, which allows him to take photographs of Jane undressing. Using each consequentialist approach to moral decision-making (i.e., ethical egoism, contractualism, and utilitarianism), explain the context in which John's behavior is ethical or not.

2. A police officer close to retirement is training a rookie cop. Their shift is over and they are returning to the precinct. Suddenly, they spot several teenagers smoking marijuana. Relying on each approach to consequentialist decision-making, explain how the officers' choice *not* to pursue the matter is (or is not) consistent with ethical behavior.

3. An overworked and underpaid public defender represents a woman accused of prostitution. Her conduct supports her drug use habit. The woman has no prior convictions or arrests. What arguments from consequentialism might the attorney utilize when discussing this case with the assistant district attorney prosecuting the matter? Would these arguments change if the woman had been previously arrested and/or convicted? Explain your response.

4. A successful *Fortune* 500 company manufactures tires. In an effort to make the tires more affordable for and more readily available to the general public, several modifications to the tires are proposed by the marketing division of the company. The automotive engineering division objects, arguing that the changes will likely produce an increase in accidents and fatalities. The proposed changes are approved by the company's corporate board of directors. An increase in accidents and fatalities occurs. Explain how this decision *is* ethical based on insights from consequentialism.

5. To illustrate Mill's concern with the uncultivated making poor decisions, consider the following example. Your state government determines that it has a budget surplus of $5 billion that it must spend before the end of the fiscal year. So, the legislature puts the following to a popular vote: *ALL* citizens currently residing in the state are entitled to *either* (1) a free college education; *or* (2) a free lifetime supply of beer. Because the "uncultivated" among you may not be able to distinguish between the "lower" good of free beer and the "higher" good of free education, do you believe that the majority of citizens would choose the beer? In what, if any, ways might decisions such as this lead to the eventual decline of the cultural and intellectual life of your state? Mill argued that we should implement a requirement that people be "competent" judges, familiar with differences, before they could vote. Do you agree? If so, how should we determine who is competent or who is not?

SUGGESTED READINGS

Bentham, Jeremy. (1988). *The Principles of Morals and Legislation.* New York: Prometheus.

Hobbes, Thomas. (1982). *Leviathan.* New York: Penguin Classics.

Mill, John Stuart. (2002). *Utilitarianism.* Indianapolis, IN: Hackett.

Odel, Jack S. (2003). *On Consequentialist Ethics.* Belmont, CA: Wadsworth.
Rand, Ayn. (1964). *The Virtue of Selfishness.* New York: Signet.

ENDNOTES

[1] S. Jack Odell, *On Consequentialist Ethics* (Belmont, CA: Wadsworth, 2003).

[2] Ibid., p. 1.

[3] David S. Oderberg, *Applied Ethics: A Non-Consequentialist Approach* (New York: Blackwell, 2000).

[4] Terrence C. McConnell, *The Argument from Psychological Egoism to Ethical Egoism* (Sidney, Australia: Australasian Association of Philosophy, 1978).

[5] Thomas Nagel, *The Possibility of Altruism* (Princeton, NJ: Princeton University Press, 1979).

[6] Terrence C. McConnell, *The Argument from Psychological Egoism to Ethical Egoism,* p. 3.

[7] Torbjorn Tannsjo, *Understanding Ethics* (Edinburgh: Edinburgh University Press, 2003), p. 41.

[8] Ellen Frankel Paul, Fred D. Miller, Jr., and Jeffrey Paul (Eds.), *Self-Interest* (Cambridge, MA: Cambridge University Press, 1997).

[9] David Schmidtz, "Self Interest: What's in It for Me?" In E. F. Paul, F. D. Miller, and J. Paul (Eds.), *Self-Interest* (Cambridge, MA: Cambridge University Press, 1997), pp. 107–122.

[10] Torbjorn Tannsjo, *Understanding Ethics,* p. 42.

[11] Michael Slote, "The Virtue in Self-Interest." In E. F. Paul, F. D. Miller, and J. Paul (Eds.), *Self-Interest* (Cambridge, MA: Cambridge University Press, 1997), pp. 264–285.

[12] Thomas Hurka, "Self-Interest, Altruism, and Virtue." In E. F. Paul, F. D. Miller, and J. Paul (eds.), *Self-Interest* (Cambridge, MA: Cambridge University Press, 1997), pp. 286–308.

[13] Torbjorn Tannsjo, *Understanding Ethics* p.41.

[14] James Rachels, *The Elements of Moral Philosophy* (New York: McGraw-Hill, 2002), p. 73.

[15] Ibid., p. 68.

[16] Ibid.

[17] Ibid.

[18] Ibid.

[19] Ayn Rand, *The Virtue of Selfishness* (New York: Signet, 1964).

[20] James Rachels, *The Elements of Moral Philosophy,* p. 70.

[21] Quoted in Ibid., p. 69.

[22] Ibid.

[23] See, e.g., Ayn Rand, *Atlas Shrugged* (New York: Signet Books, 1996); Ayn Rand, *The Fountainhead* (New York: Signet, 1996).

[24] Ayn Rand, *The Virtue of Selfishness,* 1964.

[25] Ayn Rand, *The Fountainhead,* 1996.

[26] Kurt Baier, *The Moral Point of View* (Ithaca, NY: Cornell University Press, 1958).

[27] James Rachels, *The Elements of Moral Philosophy,* p. 74.

[28] Ibid.

[29] Ibid., pp. 74–75.

[30]Ibid., p. 75.

[31]Ibid., p. 77.

[32]Ibid.

[33]Ibid.

[34]Torbjorn Tannsjo, *Understanding Ethics*, pp. 45–47.

[35]Ibid., p. 45.

[36]Ibid.

[37]Ibid., p. 48.

[38]Thomas Hobbes, *Leviathan* (New York: Penguin Classics, 1982).

[39]Quoted in James Rachels, *The Elements of Moral Philosophy*, pp. 125–126.

[40]James Rachels, *The Elements of Moral Philosophy*, p. 125.

[41]Ibid., p. 127.

[42]Ibid.

[43]Ibid.

[44]Torbjorn Tannsjo, *Understanding Ethics*, p. 49.

[45]James Rachels, *The Elements of Moral Philosophy*, pp. 127–128.

[46]Ibid., p.128.

[47]Ibid.

[48]Ibid., 129.

[49]Ibid. (emphasis in original).

[50]Ibid.

[51]Justin Fernandez, *Victimless Crimes: Crime, Justice, and Punishment* (New York: Chelsea House Publishing); Robert F. Meier and Gilbert Geis, *Victimless Crime?: Prostitution, Drugs, Homosexuality, and Abortion* (Los Angeles, CA: Roxbury Press, 1997).

[52]James Rachels, *The Elements of Moral Philosophy*, p. 134 (emphasis in original).

[53]Ibid., p. 129.

[54]Ibid., p. 134.

[55]Ibid. (emphasis in original).

[56]Ibid., p.131.

[57]William H. Shaw, *Contemporary Ethics: Taking Account of Utilitarianism* (New York: Blackwell, 1999).

[58]Torbjorn Tannsjo, *Understanding Ethics*, p. 17.

[59]Jeremy Bentham, *An Introduction to the Principles of Morals and Legislation*. In Joram Haber, *Doing and Being: Selected Readings in Moral Philosophy* (New York: Macmillan, 1993), p. 31.

[60]James Rachels, *The Elements of Moral Philosophy*, p. 80.

[61]Jeremy Bentham, *An Introduction to the Principles of Morals and Legislation*. In Joram Haber, *Doing and Being: Selected Readings in Moral Philosophy* (New York: Macmillan, 1993), p. 31.

[62]John Stuart Mill, *Utilitarianism*, 2nd ed. (Indianapolis, IN: Hackett Publishing, 2002).

[63]James Rachels, *The Elements of Moral Philosophy*, p. 80.

[64]Ibid., pp. 80–81.

[65]Ibid., p. 90.

[66]John Stuart Mill, *Utilitarianism*, quoted in James Rachels, *The Elements of Moral Philosophy*, p. 90.

[67]Ibid.

[68]Ibid., p. 91.

[69]Ibid.

[70]Donald Palmer, *Does the Center Hold? An Introduction to Western Philosophy*, 2nd ed. (Mountain View, CA: Mayfield, 1996), p. 256.

[71]Michael Flocker, *The Hedonism Handbook: Mastering the Lost Arts of Leisure and Pleasure* (Cambridge, MA: De Capo Press, 2005).

[72]Donald Palmer, *Does the Center Hold? An Introduction to Western Philosophy*, pp. 257–258.

[73]Ibid., pp. 258–261.

[74]Quoted in Ibid., p. 259.

[75]Ibid., p. 261.

[76]Ibid.

[77]Ibid.

[78]Louis Pojman, *Life and Death: Grappling with the Moral Dilemmas of Our Time*, 2nd ed. (Belmont, CA: Wadsworth, 2000).

[79]James Rachels, *The Elements of Moral Philosophy*, pp. 91–97.

[80]Louis Pojman, *Life and Death*, pp. 40–41.

[81]Ibid., p. 40.

[82]Ibid., p. 41.

[83]Ibid.

[84]James Rachels, *The Elements of Moral Philosophy*, p. 92.

[85]Ibid., 94.

[86]Ibid.

[87]Ibid.

[88]Carl Klockars, "The Dirty Harry Problem," *The Annals of the American Academy of Political and Social Science*, 452, 33–47 (1980).

[89]Jerome Skolnick and Richard Leo, "The Ethics of Deceptive Interrogation," *Criminal Justice Ethics*, 11 (1), 3–12 (1992).

Chapter 9

RESPECTING PERSONS, RESPECTING RIGHTS: THE ETHICS OF DUTY

In the last chapter, we looked at several approaches to ethics that emphasize the consequences of our actions—either for ourselves, others, or both. However, as we have seen, focusing exclusively on consequences tends to devalue, if not altogether ignore, other key features of morality and ethical behavior. Several of these other features include a concern for duties, rights, and obligations. Indeed, by appealing exclusively to beneficial effects, consequentialist variations of ethics justify violating these matters and, by extension, other general moral principles that, on occasion, exceed our concern for the pursuit of self-interests, social welfare, or happiness. This is true even when such outcomes quantitatively and qualitatively serve the needs of the greater good.

The theories under review in this chapter all de-emphasize the importance of consequences as a basis for determining what choices we should make and what actions we should undertake. Moreover, each of the theories examined places considerable weight on making decisions and engaging in behavior that is bound by moral duties. Ethical theories of this sort are called *deontological*. **Deontological** approaches place primary importance on duties or rules (Greek *deon* = "duty"). They are sometimes referred to as nonconsequentialist. This is because they not only stress the value of obligations over consequences, but argue that pleasurable outcomes for the greatest number of individuals are largely irrelevant when it comes to moral considerations.

In this way, deontological ethics shifts attention away from the effects of our actions, placing the focus squarely on the *actions themselves*. As such, the question to examine is not what consequences might result from those actions, but whether a given action conforms to relevant moral duties, such as rules prohibiting lying, killing, and dishonesty. Over the course of this chapter, three schools of thought consistent with the deontological tradition will be featured. These include the following:

- **Kantian Ethics**—what matters morally is whether our actions conform to relevant duties and absolute moral laws (i.e., those that cannot be violated).
- **Prima Facie Duties**—what matters morally is whether our actions conform to relevant duties and moral laws, though these duties can sometimes be overridden by other duties that are more significant in a given situation.
- **Rights-Based Ethics**—there exist certain basic moral guarantees that all ethical subjects enjoy and which should not, under any circumstances, be violated.

KANTIAN ETHICS

Suppose that you are sitting on your front porch one afternoon when a woman suddenly runs past you, dives behind some bushes, and quietly hides herself from view. After a moment, you approach the woman and ask her what she is doing. She proceeds to tell you that someone is trying to kill her and asks if you would please leave so she can remain hidden. After a moment, you return to the front porch and make yourself comfortable again. A couple of minutes later, a man approaches with a knife in his hand and asks if you have seen a young woman run by this way. Assuming that the man probably intends to kill the young woman, should you lie to him or tell him the truth?[1]

Of course, most of us would be quick to say that we clearly should lie. If we were to tell the truth, informing the man as to the whereabouts of the woman, he would probably take her life. If we lie, he will likely proceed searching unsuccessfully and the woman will live. And while the answer to this dilemma may seem obvious, there is at least one highly influential philosopher who would likely claim otherwise. What James Rachels refers to as the "Case of the Inquiring Murderer" is a classic example of the difference between consequentialist and Kantian moral philosophies.

Immanuel Kant (1724–1804) is one of the most important philosophers in the history of Western civilization. The moral consideration raised by the Case of the Inquiring Murderer, and one which marks the foundation of Kant's moral philosophy, is whether there are *absolute moral rules.* In other words, the question is whether there are moral obligations that we must adhere to under *all* circumstances, regardless of the consequences that may or may not result. Kant's philosophy is one in which absolute principles, duties, or rules of this sort are notably showcased. To be clear, Kant's position is that there are certain rules that *must be followed* no matter what consequences may befall an individual, a group, a social institution, and/or society more generally. One such moral rule is the prohibition against lying. For Kant, lying to our hypothetical murderer would be immoral because this action is absolutely unacceptable under any and all circumstances, including those from which "good" consequences might result. For instance, even if lying to the inquiring murderer leads to the death of the young woman, we can still be said to have done the ethically "right" thing. Kant rejected outright the notion that consequences should be an appropriate measure of right and wrong. As the section on Kantian ethics explains, acts are only considered right when they are performed in accordance with *duty* (e.g., the moral duty not to lie).

> **Point of departure for Kantian ethics:** Morality amounts to doing our moral duties, which means abiding by universal moral laws without exception

Hypothetical and Categorical Imperatives

To get a better sense of Kant's moral philosophy, we can begin by distinguishing between what he termed, "hypothetical imperatives," and what he termed, "categorical imperatives."[2] An *imperative* is a command. More specifically, it is a command that we perform or not perform some action. Various forms of "oughts" or imperatives govern much of what we do in all areas of our daily lives. For instance, if we claim that we ought to study or that we ought not to lie, we are making use of imperatives. However, Kant argued that with examples of the sort just specified, we are making use of two fundamentally different types of imperatives. That we "ought to study" is, at least in the sense that we would normally make such a claim, very different from the contention that we "ought not to lie." Let us examine the difference.

In the first instance, by stating that we ought to study we are really saying that we ought to study *if* we wish to bring about some desired consequence. In other words, *if* Joe wishes to receive an "A" in geometry, he "ought" to study. Similarly, *if* Jane wishes to make the basketball team, she "ought" to practice this summer. In both illustrations, we are claiming that we ought to do this or that *if* (and only if) we wish to achieve some end.[3]

Much of our everyday conduct is governed by precisely these ways of thinking, whether explicitly or implicitly. We wish or desire to bring about certain states of affairs, particular outcomes that matter to us. We realize that in order to get what we want there are certain courses of action we should follow. Consequently, we conclude that we ought to follow that course of action in order to reach one or another desired state of affairs. The types of imperatives at issue here are what Kant called *hypothetical* or *conditional* imperatives.

A **hypothetical imperative** is a command that we ought to follow *if we have certain desires* that we wish to achieve or realize.[4] If Joe did not care about getting an "A" in geometry or if Jane did not care about making the basketball team, they would have no reason to abide by those respective commands or imperatives. Hypothetical imperatives, then, have no binding moral force. To avoid adhering to them, all we need to do is renounce the wish or desire that they are intended to produce.[5] Thus, escaping the force of hypothetical imperatives—"getting out of" the obligations they entail—is as simple as foregoing our desire for certain consequences. In short, hypothetical imperatives are "if-then" (i.e., conditional) statements of fact that address the relationship between goals and means.

Moral obligations, however, are not conditioned by or dependent on any particular desire or the realization of any particular outcome. For Kant, moral obligations are *categorical*. **Categorical imperatives** are absolute commands that we ought to follow, *period!*[6] A conditional imperative might consist of the moral principle that we ought to respect others if we want them to respect us. However, a categorical imperative would indicate that we ought to respect others regardless of what we want or desire from them, including their respect. For Kant, then, categorical imperatives are the basis of morality. We have certain moral duties and obligations that we cannot avoid or escape even when abandoning our wants or desires. In other words, in some instances moral duties and obligations must be followed irrespective of our wants or the consequences they bring about for us or for others.

Living our lives on the basis of hypothetical imperatives would be as simple as adopting the means necessary to attain the various ends we seek to realize. In other words, we ought to do that—and only that—which is necessary to secure the respect from a friend or work associate, to get an "A" on an exam, or to ensure that no harm comes to our family and loved ones. In contrast, though, categorical imperatives are much more difficult for and demanding of us. But how can there be moral rules that we are obligated to follow under *all* circumstances? How can certain moral duties exist that are independent of our desires and equally independent of their consequences? These are complicated matters, and ones that Kant spent considerable time answering.

Maxims and Universal Laws

Kant suggested that categorical "oughts" are a product of human reason alone. As he argued, they are derived from a single principle that *every rational human being must accept.*[7] Once we understand this basic principle, we have a formula or procedure by which we can infer a number of more specific moral oughts. Since all categorical oughts are derived from this one basic principle, our obligation to abide by them should be clear to any sensible person. While there are several variations to or formulations of this principle, Kant suggested that they are all similar in nature. He termed this principle the *Categorical Imperative.* In its first formulation, the Categorical Imperative can be stated as follows:

> *Act only according to that maxim by which you can at the same time will that it should become a universal law.*[8]

Through the Categorical Imperative, Kant effectively proposed a procedure that we should use when determining whether any given act is morally permissible or morally right. When contemplating a given action, we should first ask ourselves what *maxim* we would be following in so doing. By **maxim,** Kant simply was referring to a moral rule—whatever rule we would be adhering to is the *maxim* of the act.[9] For instance, if we determine that we should lie to our best friend in order to avoid hurting that person's feelings, the maxim we would be following is: "We should lie to our friends whenever telling the truth stands to hurt another's feelings." Once we figure out the rule or maxim we are adopting, the next step is to ask ourselves whether we would be willing to make it a *universal law.* By **universal law,** Kant meant a rule that would be followed by everyone, all of the time. Thus, in the above example, we would need to ask ourselves whether we would want all people, all of the time, to lie to their friends whenever telling the truth would hurt their feelings. If we answer "yes" to this question, then the act is morally right or permissible. If we answer "no"—that we would *not* be willing to have everyone follow this principle on all occasions—we must conclude that the maxim is not a universal law and, as such, is not morally permissible.

All moral principles that we could wish to become universal laws are categorically imperative—they are principles that we must, in all situations, follow irrespective of our desires or the consequences that may issue forth from them. At the same time, all such principles that we could not wish to become universal laws are those that we ought not to adopt. Again, this logic follows, regardless of our desires or the potential consequences. Kant's most notable examples on this subject include borrowing money and charity.

BORROWING MONEY

Suppose you need to borrow money. Further, suppose you know that no one will lend it to you unless you promise to repay it. Finally, assume that you know that there is no way you will ever be able to repay the loan. Given this, the question becomes whether you should promise to repay the money, knowing full well that you will never be able to do so, in order to persuade someone to financially assist you. The maxim of the act would be as follows: When a person needs a loan, one should promise to repay that loan even though the person knows he or she will not be able to do so. Can we say that this maxim becomes a universal law? Kant indicates that the answer is no. His reasoning is as follows: If everyone who needed a loan promised to repay it, despite knowing that they could not, then no lenders would believe any such promises and no borrowers would ever be granted the money.[10] Obviously, this would be self-defeating—the entire practice of loan making would be jeopardized if not altogether undone.[11] Consequently, we cannot will that this maxim should become a universal law and, moreover, we are categorically bound to abide by the moral principle that we should not make promises that we know we can never keep.

CHARITY

Suppose that Scott refuses to help people who are in need, claiming that its not any concern of his. In Kant's words, "What concern is it of mine? Let each one be as happy as heaven wills, or as he can make himself . . . to his welfare or to his assistance in time of need I have no desire to contribute."[12] Can Scott will that this maxim—that we should not concern ourselves with others who are in need—become a universal law? Again, Kant says no. Such a maxim would contradict itself because there may be future cases in which one "would need the love and sympathy of others, and in which he would have robbed himself . . . of all hope of the aid he desires."[13] In other words, because we, at some point in the future, may ourselves be in need, we clearly cannot will a maxim by which we do not assist others in distress to become a universal law.

Moral Duties and Absolute Rules

According to Kant, then, ethics is about following absolute moral rules, derived from the Categorical Imperative. These imperatives are universal in that they must be followed by all persons, all of the time. Strictly adhering to these rules—applying them without exception in all situations—is our *duty* as rational, moral human beings. **Duties** are things we *must* do—or must *not* do—no matter how we feel about engaging in this behavior, no matter how undertaking this behavior might affect us or other people, or no matter the peculiarities of the situation in which we find ourselves. In short, duties are obligations that *must* be fulfilled.

For Kant, our various moral duties can be derived from the general moral principle of the Categorical Imperative. Of course, we have many moral duties because there are many absolute rules or universal laws. All of them, however, are derived from the Categorical Imperative. One of Kant's most notable examples is our duty not to lie. As he suggested, lying could not be a universal law and, thus, would not pass the test of the Categorical Imperative. Lying would be self-defeating in that, if we fail to tell the truth, we must be willing to wish that all other people do so as well. If this were the case, we would all soon enough stop believing what other people said. If none of us could trust what others said, then lying would be ineffective (and social living would be exceedingly difficult).[14]

Recall the "Case of the Inquiring Murderer" discussed at the beginning of this section. Kant held that even in a situation where undesirable consequences plainly might result (e.g., the death of another person), we were morally bound to uphold our duty—we were still obligated to abide by the universal law not to lie. The problem for Kant is that he supposed that by telling the inquiring murderer the truth, we endorsed a universal law that prohibits lying. However, there are other potential interpretations or formulations of this general law that might be applicable in this case.

For instance, suppose that by lying the moral rule we followed was not that it is permissible to do so but, rather, that it is acceptable only when doing so saves someone's life.[15] Many of us probably *would* be willing to have this latter formulation become a universal law. Thus, when put to the test of the Categorical Imperative, the potential universal law that "it is permissible to lie when doing so saves the life of another" seems defensible and justifiable. This action would rescue or salvage lives and, more than likely, would not result in a situation in which none of us believed anything anyone else said. Because circumstances in which people lie in order to save another person's life would be extremely rare, especially in the context of our everyday realities, we would have no reason to cease trusting the word of other people.

Changing the maxim on lying as delineated above represents a basic problem with Kant's ethical approach on the whole. Namely, "for any action a person might contemplate, it is possible to specify more than one rule that he or she would be following."[16] Anytime we posit certain moral rules or laws as absolutes, we can "get around any such rule by describing our action in such a way that it does not fall under that rule but instead comes under a different one."[17]

Exceptions and Consequences

In his own analysis of the Case of the Inquiring Murderer, Kant suggests that:

> ...whoever tells a lie, however well intentioned he might be, must answer for the consequences, however unforeseeable they were, and pay the penalty for them.[18]

Suppose that you lied to the inquiring murderer, believing that doing so would save the woman's life. Not knowing that the woman is hiding in the bushes, the would-be murderer proceeds to continue about his search, leaving your porch step and making his way around the back of your house. In the meantime, however, the woman has decided to find a more secure place in which to hide. She has quietly removed herself from the bushes, called the police, and sought shelter in a storage shed in your backyard. Unfortunately, the storage shed is the next place the inquiring murderer looks. He finds her in hiding and, before the police can arrive to apprehend him, kills her. At least to some degree, Kant would argue, you were responsible for the woman's death. In lying to the potential murderer, you encouraged him to search elsewhere, which eventually led him to locate her and, in so doing, to take her life. Of course, you could not have known that this would happen, but this is precisely Kant's point. Had you told the truth, it is possible that the man would have wasted time searching in the bushes, thus giving the police time to get to the scene and thereby preventing the woman from being murdered. On the other hand, she might still have been hiding in the bushes and your honesty would have led him directly to her, resulting in the woman's untimely death.

But these various conditions help to make Kant's argument even simpler: "*We can never be certain what the consequences of our actions will be.*"[19] Though we may often consider lying, cheating, stealing, and so forth in order to prevent evil or bring about good consequences, we can *never* know exactly what the results of our actions will be. This is a considerable problem for all approaches to morality that emphasize consequences—consequences require us to *predict the future*, something which cannot always be done by any of us with a sufficient degree of accuracy (recall the limitation of utilitarianism on this point as discussed in Chapter 8). Even if we are motivated to lie (or to tell the truth) in order to bring about good (e.g., preventing a murder), we can never be certain that our actions will, in fact, bring about that good. It is at least possible that the results of our action would be much worse than those that would have resulted had we told the truth.

In the Case of the Inquiring Murderer, there are several important considerations that might factor into our decision about whether we should lie:

- In telling the truth, we are *avoiding* a *known evil* (lying), which might:
  1. bring about good consequences (preventing a murder), or
  2. bring about evil consequences (causing a murder by leading the assailant to his victim)
- In lying, we are *committing* a *known evil* (lying), which might:
  1. bring about good consequences (preventing a murder), or
  2. bring about evil consequences (accidentally causing a murder)

For Kant and his deontological moral system, these considerations should lead us to tell the truth. Again, we can never be certain what the consequences of our actions will be. However, we *can* be certain that lying would be committing an evil, and that telling the truth would be avoiding an evil. Whether good or bad consequences follow is largely beyond our control. What *is* in our control is whether we intentionally commit an act that we know to be an evil. Kant argues that in every situation, the best policy is to "avoid the known evil . . . and let the consequences come as they will."[20] On the chance that bad consequences arise from our telling the truth, they are not our fault. We have abided by the moral law not to lie, and this is as much as we can do.[21] Again, following Kantian ethics, so long as we have done our duty we cannot control the consequences nor should we be held accountable for them (see Box 9.1).

Respect for Persons

Kant also offered us a second variation of the Categorical Imperative. This alternative formulation has slightly different but equally important implications:

> Act so as to treat humanity, whether in your own person or that of any other, as an end and never as a means only.[22]

BOX 9.1
Policing and the Duty to Tell the Truth

You are a police officer called to testify at a murder trial. Through your investigation of the case, you and your partner collected enough physical evidence to ensure a conviction, including the murder weapon with the defendant's fingerprints, an audiotape of the defendant confessing the crime to a cellmate, and a videotape showing the defendant entering the victim's apartment building shortly before the time of the offense. However, you also know that the murder weapon was obtained through an unconstitutional search of the defendant's place of residence, and that the audiotape was acquired in such a way that, if truth be told, it would likely not be admitted at trial as legally obtained evidence. Upon taking the stand, you are directly questioned concerning the constitutionality of the search and the acquisition of the tape.

Kantian ethics would ask that you consider the following: (1) if you lie, this will likely (but not certainly) result in the conviction of a known killer; (2) if you tell the truth, this will likely (but not certainly) result in the case against a known killer being dismissed for lack of evidence. Importantly, Kant's deontology would remind you that there are other potential consequences that you cannot possibly predict as well. Suppose that having lied, the truth comes out through some other means—either during the trial or sometime thereafter. If this happens, not only will a known killer be found not guilty (or released on appeal), but you and your partner will likely be brought up for disciplinary action and reprimand, face criminal prosecution, and/or lose your jobs. Moreover, the case would bring national media attention, making you, your partner, your department, the chief of police, and your entire city look bad in the eyes of the public. Though it is likely that the criminal trial will be dismissed for lack of evidence if you tell the truth, it is also possible that the defendant may be found guilty anyway—perhaps he unwittingly confesses at trial, or there is additional testimony from witnesses, friends of the defendant, etc., of which you are unaware. Even if the case were to be dismissed, perhaps new evidence would emerge sometime in the near future and the defendant would then be convicted legitimately.

Whatever the consequences of lying or telling the truth might be, Kant reminds us that we cannot ever know for sure. The best we can do is to pursue our moral duty and let the consequences come as they may. In this instance, our moral duty is to tell the truth. If the criminal case against the murderer is dismissed because evidence is lacking, this is certainly not your fault—no one can blame you for abiding by your moral duty to tell the truth.

This version of the Categorical Imperative entails a key component of Kant's moral philosophy—and arguably a key feature of any moral philosophy. In brief, Kant argued that *all* human beings have *intrinsic worth* or *dignity*.[23] Because of this, we have a moral imperative to treat all human beings with respect—to affirm, through the way we treat others, the inherent dignity of every person. This imperative or absolute exceeds any self-interested gain or loss we might experience as a consequence of so doing. Moreover, it transcends any personal feelings we might have or might not have for individuals. The very basis of morality, then, is to demonstrate—through our intentions and actions—a respect for the inherent value or worth of others.

More specifically, Kant presented this ultimate law of morality as an imperative to never treat others "as a means only." In other words, we should never "use" others purely as a means to some end—whatever the end is or its importance might be.[24] For instance, some of us may have friends who we do not truly respect as human beings; however, we are willing to spend time with them in order to benefit from something they possess or could get for us. Maybe we date someone because the person has money; maybe we invite someone out with a group of our friends because the individual has physical qualities that attract members of the opposite (or same) sex; maybe we associate with a co-worker because the person's parents are season ticket holders to the football games played by our city's professional team.

In each hypothetical case, we are using someone because of what that person can do for us. Missing in these interactions is any genuine regard for the individual's inherent worth as a human being. Kant reminds us that in none of these cases would we be acting morally. Of course, this does not mean that we can never benefit in various ways from others. Instead, it is simply to say that our treatment of others— whether they are friends, stockbrokers, convicted criminals, or the clerk at the checkout counter from the local convenience store—should reflect a genuine respect for that person's inherent and *ever-present* importance as a human being. By "ever-present," we mean that dignity is not something that people must earn or that people will lose through their actions; rather, it is something that each of us possesses *by virtue of being human*. This sense of worth and respect endures so long as we are alive. In many cases, it remains long past our time on this earth.

What, more specifically, does this innate respect for and call to value others mean, especially in terms of our treatment of them? According to James Rachels,

> we have a strict duty of beneficence toward other persons: we must strive to promote their welfare; we must respect their rights, avoid harming them, and generally "endeavor, so far as we can, to further the ends of others."[25]

Given the above observations, there is yet another implication embedded in the second formulation of the Categorical Imperative. Kant believed that the inherent worth of human beings stems from their nature as *rational* creatures—as "free agents capable of making their own decisions, setting their own goals, and guiding their conduct by reason."[26] As such, treating people as "ends" requires that we *respect their rationality*. In part, this clearly entails assigning value to the capacity of others to make free, autonomous choices about their own welfare through the exercise of their reason. As Kant insisted, we should never select courses of action *for* others or influence their choices through manipulation, deceit, or trickery. Manipulating people or otherwise using people to satisfy our own needs or to achieve our own goals—no matter how significant or valuable those needs and goals might be—fails to respect the rationality of others and, consequently, fails to conform with the moral imperative to always treat others as ends. By treating people as "things," we are regarding them as beings without the capacity for reason and autonomy. Reason is what differentiates human beings from other "things" in the world. Thus, following Kant, our moral duty is to respect that difference.[27]

Returning to the example of pursuing a loan, Kant asks us to consider the following: If we were to ask for the money, promising to repay it even though we knew we could not, we would be manipulating someone for purposes of getting financial assistance (i.e., using the lender as a means or as a way to achieve our own ends). On the other hand, if we told the truth—that we needed money but would not be in a position to repay it—the lender would be in a better position to assess whether to grant the loan or not. In short, by being truthful we allow the lender to utilize his or her own capacity for reasoning and autonomous decision-making as this person endeavors to determine whether financial assistance in our case is warranted. In doing so, even though we would still be relying on that individual as a means to get money, we would be respecting that person's rationality and, thus, dignity in the process.[28]

To be clear, Kant did *not* claim that we could never use people as a means; instead, he argued that we should not use them this way exclusively. To illustrate, we cannot avoid "using" our stockbroker as a means to purchase stock (or to make money); we cannot avoid "using" the waitress at our favorite local restaurant as a means to obtain food and drink; and we cannot avoid "using" our teachers as a means to gain knowledge or a degree. However, in doing so, we can still treat these persons as human beings with intrinsic value and dignity. In all such situations, then, Kant reminds us that in order to be ethical we should recognize and respect people's capacity for reason and autonomous choice, fully acknowledging them as unique and valuable individuals with their own needs, wants, and goals (see Box 9.2).

PRIMA FACIE DUTIES

One of the key concerns with Kantian ethics—as with absolute moral rules more generally—is that it provides no resolution for or guidance in the face of *conflicting duties*. Most of us have confronted or will face situations in which we are forced to choose between doing "A" and doing "B," where both "A" *and* "B" are governed by moral imperatives. Returning again to Kant's Case of the Inquiring Murderer, suppose there are two absolute moral rules at issue: (1) it is wrong to lie; and (2) it is wrong to permit the murder of an innocent person.[29] If both of these as maxims are absolute, then each of us is morally obligated to follow them in all situations. However, the inquiring murderer presents a dilemma: we cannot *both* not lie *and* not permit the murder of an innocent person. The co-existence of two equally weighty imperatives seems to have created an irreconcilable ethical quandary.

While the Case of the Inquiring Murderer is not likely to occur in "real life," there are certainly other situations in which conflicts between absolute moral duties can and do arise. For instance, think of prisoners of war who are forced to choose between revealing government secrets and watching an innocent person be executed as a consequence of their refusal to cooperate with the enemy. Assuming that there is an absolute moral duty to be loyal to one's country *and* an absolute moral duty not to permit the murder of innocent people, a moral dilemma arises that seemingly cannot be reconciled simply by appealing to absolute moral rules. Whatever choice is made,

BOX 9.2

Means, Ends, and Intimate Relationships: The Case of Mary Jo Laterneau

Consider the following: Is there a difference between "using" one's spouse or someone with whom one is involved in an intimate, caring relationship to meet one's sexual needs versus "using" a person one has just met at a night-club for purposes of satisfying one's own sexual desires? The answer, of course, is that there most often *is* a significant difference.

Intimate, caring relationships are (hopefully) founded upon a genuine respect and concern for the other person and recognition of that person's value as a unique human being. As spouses, girlfriends, boyfriends, etc., we not only respect the other person as a human being, but value the fact that the individual has unique wants and interests. Moreover, we should do whatever we legitimately can to help that person satisfy those needs and interests.

Conversely, "one-night stands" and other short-term sexual relationships are often characterized by one or both parties using the other purely to fulfill selfish desires. As Kant would remind us, this is especially the case—and especially morally problematic—when manipulation or deceit is involved. Making false promises or implicit false promises (e.g., the pledge of a long-term relationship when this is not intended) or offering false compliments (e.g., "you have the most beautiful eyes I have ever seen") are ways of manipulating the other person for one's own ends. In doing so, Kant would argue that we fail to allow that other person to make a free and rational choice about whether to engage in the relationship. Instead, that person's decision is—at least in part—influenced by the promises, compliments, or other falsehoods we have offered. Kant would suggest that we should always be completely honest and up-front with the other person, allowing the consequences to come as they may.

Now consider the case of Mary Jo Laterneau. Mary Jo was a school teacher. She found her "Romeo" in a 12-year-old boy whom she had initially met and taught while he was in second grade. At the age of 35, Mary Jo entered into a "consenting" and ongoing sexual relationship with the boy when he was 14 years of age. She had a child with him and the case erupted into a national debate about responsibility and intimacy. To make matters more complicated, Ms. Laterneau's affair occurred while she was married with children of her own. Although eventually resigning from her place of employment; separated and divorced from her husband (losing custody of her children); and prosecuted, convicted, and sentenced to a prison term, Mary Jo professed deep and abiding true love for the boy. After serving a term in prison, Ms. Laterneau defied a court order upon her release requiring her to terminate all contact with the boy. Ms. Laterneau resumed the relationship with her "Romeo" and had a second child with her lover. The boy, now an adult, and Ms. Laterneau recently were married. Following the ethical insights of Kant, the only obligation in life one has is to be true to oneself and those others with whom one interacts. Despite our likely repulsion concerning this story, it would appear as if this is precisely what happened in the case of Mary Jo Laterneau, especially given the nature and quality of the intimate relationship she established.

one or the other moral rule will be violated. Thus, it appears as if Kantian ethics and the notion of absolute moral duties is seriously flawed. Or is it?

In situations where we are forced to choose between multiple moral duties (i.e., imperatives), we have no ethical basis for making such a choice. W. D. Ross (1877–1971) recognized this problem with traditional Kantian ethics. In response, he argued for an ethics of **prima facie duties**.[30] "Prima facie" duties—also called *conditional* duties—are different from those of the absolute variety that are central to Kantian ethics. While prima facie duties should be followed in most circumstances, they can be *overridden* by other duties that are more imperative in a given instance. In situations where more than one prima facie duty is at issue, we should "study the situation as fully as [we] can until [we] form the considered opinion . . . that in the circumstances one of them is more incumbent then any other . . . ."[31] In other words, certain duties can and should be violated if, given the situational factors in play, we determine that other duties override them.

This is the key difference between prima facie duties and absolute moral duties—the former are not absolute in the sense that they must always be followed. So, how would conflicting prima facie duties function in an everyday context? Let us return to the inquiring murderer, supposing that we have both a duty not to lie *and* a duty not to permit the death of an innocent person. If our duty not to permit the death of an innocent person outweighs (or is more important than) our duty not to lie, then we may—with good conscience—violate our moral duty not to lie in favor of saving someone's life. If the duty not to lie is a prima facie duty—one that is not absolute but can be overridden—we are allowed the possibility of violating it if the circumstances demand that we do so.

The Role of Prima Facie Duties

While Ross offers a tentative list of prima facie duties (see Box 9.3), we are still faced with the question of how to determine which prima facie duties override others. This question is not easily addressed. In part, Ross attempts to respond by focusing on those concerns that emerge from Kant's emphasis on absolute moral duties. Again, these are imperatives that we all must adhere to no matter what the situation is or the "good" consequences that follow. We can use prima facie duties to determine what we should do in any given situation. Remember, these types of imperatives *are* binding or obligatory *unless* they are superseded by other duties. For example, we have a prima facie duty of fidelity that includes keeping the promises that we make. Thus, we are morally obligated to keep our promises *unless* there are other, stronger moral considerations that override or "trump" that duty in a particular situation.

However, we should keep in mind that by "other, stronger moral considerations," we are not referring to consequences. Similar to Kant, Ross provides us with a deontological variation of morality. Our ethical choices should be based on whatever prima facie duties apply to the situation at hand. Unlike Kant, Ross recommends using conditional duties to address moral dilemmas involving more than one imperative. In other words, if the application of duty "A" conflicts with the application of duty "B" in the *same* situation, we are not obligated to follow both unconditionally or absolutely. Rather, we can violate one in favor of the other, *provided* the one we select to follow is more imperative.

So, which conditional duties are more imperative than others? Regrettably, Ross's theory does not offer a precise way for us to determine which ones take precedence

BOX 9.3

A Brief List of Prima Facie Duties

Exactly what are prima facie duties? In response to this question, W. D. Ross offers an "incomplete," though useful, list of major types:

Duties arising from our own previous acts:

- *Duties of Fidelity* —These include duties that stem from our own previous promises, contracts, or other agreements. Prima facie duties of fidelity can be explicit or implicit. The duty not to tell a lie is a prima facie duty arising from an implicit promise that we make to others upon entering a conversation, writing a book, etc. The duty not to lie can also be an explicit prima facie duty of fidelity arising from the oath we take as a witness in a criminal trial or the pledge of faithfulness that we make when getting married.
- *Duties of Reparation* —These are duties that issue forth from our own previous wrongful acts. We have prima facie duties to make reparations for harms or damages that we have caused previously. Examples include criminal conduct, school bullying, gossiping.

Duties issuing from the previous acts of others:

- *Duties of Gratitude* —These are duties that surface, given the previous acts of others. Prima facie duties of gratitude require that we be grateful for the assistance of others, returning that aid or kindness whenever possible. Examples include buying lunch for a friend who has done the same for you in the past; volunteering your time at a rape counseling or drug abuse center, given that others have done the same for you previously.

Duties that emerge from an imbalance between the distribution of happiness (or the means by which to attain happiness) and the merit of the people concerned:

- *Duties of Justice*—These duties require that we act so as to distribute benefits and burdens in a fair and equitable manner. We have a prima facie duty to prevent an unfair distribution of goods, or to disrupt an existing unfair pattern of distribution. Workplace inequities (e.g., salary discrimination, scheduling imbalances) based on race, gender, ethnicity, age, disability, etc., illustrate this principle.

Duties arising from the notion that there are other individuals in the world whose condition we can improve:

- *Duties of Beneficence*—Doing good deeds for others such as aiding their health, happiness, welfare, etc.

Duties stemming from the fact that we can improve our own condition:

- *Duty of Self-Improvement*—This entails the duty to promote our own good—our health, security, wisdom, happiness, virtue, etc.

Duties that can be summarized as not injuring others:

- *Duty of Nonharm or Nonmalfeasance*—This duty entails not harming others—physically, emotionally, or otherwise. Examples include avoid causing harm to the health, safety, character, happiness, etc. of others. The duty of nonharm has also been interpreted to include the duty to prevent harm to others.

Source: W. D. Ross, *The Right and the Good* (Oxford: Clarendon Press, 1993).

over others or which ones serve as "trump cards" in particular situations. In short, he does not offer a ranking of prima facie duties nor does he suggest that one exists. Each situation must be judged uniquely.

RIGHTS: THE "OTHER SIDE OF DUTY"[32]

In contemporary American culture and society, the idea of "rights" plays a crucial role in the consideration of moral behavior, as well as in our response to contentious social, political, and legal issues. Examples such as the "right" to have an abortion, the "right" to bear arms, the "right" to punish criminal offenders or to utilize animals and the natural environment as we see fit, all convey this point.[33] Similarly, discussions surrounding rights *violations* inform our views on such matters as torture, poverty, and slavery.[34] What this suggests, then, is that the idea of rights is especially important when addressing various topics in law, crime, and the justice system.

For instance, the significance of procedural rights tends to be one of the first topics to which students and practitioners of criminal justice are exposed in their educational and professional careers.[35] Along these lines, we commonly hear stories of the rights of criminal suspects, defendants, or prisoners being in some respect violated by persons working within the criminal justice system.[36] The appellate court system operates for precisely this purpose—it hears arguments and makes rulings on these sorts of infractions. What all of this suggests, then, is that irrespective of how we might feel about rights or certain types of rights (e.g., for defendants, for victims, for those criminally confined, for women, for minorities), the reality is that we cannot easily escape their consideration.[37] This is as true in ethics as much as it is in criminology and criminal justice.

Typically, when we talk about rights in the context of crime and justice, we are referring more specifically to constitutional or legal rights.[38] However, as we will see, formal rights that stem from the U.S. Constitution or from various levels of law are but one kind. Moreover, the formal, legal rights of criminal justice are less significant (not as fundamental) than a different sort; namely, *moral* rights.

For purposes of this section, then, we will not outline various specific rights that persons enjoy or fail to enjoy. Moreover, the role that rights play in the system of justice will not be introduced. Although both are worthwhile endeavors, neither of them enables us to appreciate the relationship between rights and morality. For instance, how does the existence of rights place constraints on our ethical behavior in both professional and everyday contexts? How, if at all, does the presence of rights *justify* or fail to justify certain decisions and forms of behavior in these same situations? What implications does the existence of rights have for the ways in which we treat ourselves and others? These and similar questions address the relationship between rights and morality, and this concern is exactly what will be reviewed in the pages that follow.

When rights are invoked in moral contexts, they frequently are employed either to *justify* certain behavior or to *place limitations* on conduct. In both instances, a claim is made about how we should act toward others or about how others should treat us. For example, we might assert that an act of self-defense was warranted, given our right to protect self and/or property against harm from others. In this case, we are relying on the idea that rights function as moral justification for our—perhaps violent—actions toward fellow citizens. Moreover, we might appeal to a right to privacy when claiming that we should be able to engage in whatever forms of sexual behavior we choose within our own homes. Still further, in everyday encounters, we might—explicitly or otherwise—profess a right to be respected, to be told the truth, to be free from abuse, and so forth. Given all of these observations, the remainder of this section discusses more specifically what "rights" are as well as how they can, do, and/or should inform moral behavior.

Rights and Duties

In the last section, we were introduced to Kant's deontological or duty-based claim that there exist absolute moral imperatives that each of us is obligated to follow, irrespective of consequences, contexts, and desires. In this approach, our moral duties spring forth from universal maxims or laws. Similarly, the tradition of rights also can be regarded as deontological in the sense that it argues for moral duties. However, the duties that stem from moral rights do not emerge from universal moral laws but, instead, they arise from the moral rights themselves.[39] How so?

First, consistent with deontology, the notion of rights implies that consequences are irrelevant moral considerations. If you have a "right" to own a handgun, then your possession of it has nothing to do with the consequences that might arise from your doing so. If a criminal defendant has a "right" to an attorney, there is no suggestion that having counsel should depend, in any way, on what the consequences will be for the defendant, the prosecution, the victim, or the criminal justice process overall. Thus, the various rights that we enjoy are not contingent upon whatever effects may or may not result. The same can be said for the sorts of absolute moral rights that underlie other duties. Your right to be treated with respect and dignity stems alone from your status as a human being. Each of us can be said to have a moral duty to respect your status as a person and, therefore, to revere your moral right to be treated as such.

Second, rights are often said to be *correlative* with duties. The **correlativity of rights and duties** means that the rights of people imply duties that others must acknowledge and value.[40] To illustrate, if you have a right to privacy, then people (including the government) have a duty to respect what you define as intimate or confidential. If you possess a right to refuse unwanted and invasive medical treatment, this right implies that others have a duty not to interfere by imposing or forcing it on you, even if it is deemed therapeutic (see Box 9.4). If you have a right to worship as you see fit, this means that others have a moral duty to respect your right by not interfering in any way with your religious preferences or practices.

Natural Rights Ethics

Rights are generally understood as either natural or derived from duties.[41] The idea of *natural rights* has its conceptual basis in a type of moral universalism. Recall from Chapter 4 that ethical universalism refers to the notion that there exist moral principles or standards that can and should be relevant to everyone, everywhere, in all situations. To say that such principles or standards are universal is to suggest that they are true of and applicable to all people in all cultures and all time periods. Thus, we are obligated to recognize and utilize them in all cases in which those principles or standards are

BOX 9.4

The Right to Refuse Treatment and Competency to Be Executed

Just because rights and duties are correlative does not mean that this relationship is supported in all situations or with all ethical dilemmas. One such example is the problem of treatment refusal invoked by mentally ill persons on death row. Complicating this matter is the process of competency restoration. Typically under these conditions, returning one to a state of mental fitness involves the forced administration of drug treatment over the confined person's objection. The goal is to restore competency such that the individual is cognizant of his or her imminent execution. Clearly, there are ethical concerns about physicians forcibly administering mind altering drugs to psychiatrically ill death row offenders who object to them, particularly when the expressed purpose is execution and nothing more. To some extent, the court has addressed this matter. However, the issue at hand is one of respecting the rights of individuals as a moral duty, notwithstanding the individual's psychiatric condition.

In the instance of treatment refusal for persons on death row, this is difficult to assess. Part of this difficulty relates to whether a person can exercise a right to refuse treatment knowingly and voluntarily. After all, if someone does not know what she or he is requesting and/or does not make such a decision freely, it remains to be seen whether the exercise of this right should be respected and honored at all. Ethically speaking, the absence of both (awareness and volition) may very well erode one's duty to adhere to the request.

Perhaps one way to gauge whether one's treatment refusal is undertaken freely and knowingly is to consider whether the mentally ill death row inmate's position changes after competency is restored. Some have suggested that if a person's competency is restored and the individual still insists that the forced medication remains objectionable, that the person was, at the least, *competent enough* prior to the restoration to have had their right respected in the first place. Unfortunately, this "after the fact" sort of proof does not value the person's deontological right and the corresponding duty that should have been adhered to initially. At best, the right to refuse treatment and competency to be executed demonstrate how the politics of mental illness and fitness for death can trump the fundamental rights of citizens, despite disability.

Sources: Bruce J. Winick, *The Right to Refuse Treatment* (Washington, DC: American Psychological Association, 1997); Bruce A. Arrigo and Christopher R. Williams, "Law, Ideology, and Critical Inquiry: The Case of Treatment Refusal for Incompetent Persons Awaiting Execution," *New England Journal on Criminal and Civil Confinement*, 25 (1999); Kursten Hensly, "Restored to Health to Be Put to Death," *Villanova Law Review*, 49, 225–251 (2004).

pertinent. Moreover, that which is identified as universal supersedes all other considerations (e.g., cultural, historical, situational contexts).

The doctrine of natural rights suggests that all human beings enjoy certain basic rights irrespective of their membership in a particular political society.[42] In this sense, then, rights are enjoyed universally and apply globally. The natural rights that all people benefit from are not derived from laws or granted by governments; rather, they stem from human nature. That these rights stem from human nature means that: (1) they do not need to be earned; and (2) they cannot be taken away. Thus, natural rights function as universal moral laws or principles that must be respected regardless of circumstances. What are these principles and what implications do they hold for morality?

In short, the tradition of moral rights maintains that each "moral subject" has a right to "a kind of integrity."[43] This "kind of integrity" implies that each individual has moral worth wherein the individual is endowed with certain rights that cannot be taken away and which must be respected in all instances. These rights are said to be shared by all citizens, irrespective of who, where, what, or when they are, and irrespective of consequences, motivations, situational factors, and so forth.

The universality or absoluteness of moral rights has its roots in the tradition of *natural law* (see Chapter 4 for more on natural law). This tradition emerged in antiquity and, more specifically, in the writings of ancient Greek philosophers such as Aristotle and the Stoic philosopher, Chrysippus.[44] The Greeks routinely distinguished between *nomos*, or human law, and *phusis*, or laws of nature. Human laws included established practices such as customs, and "positive" or human-constructed written laws that varied by time and place. Consequently, they were subject to change. Because they were variable and changeable, human laws were understood to be fallible; that is, they could be unjust or misguided. In contrast, *phusis* represented a general term referring to what was unchangeable, such as the laws of physics. Thus, as philosophers reasoned, there must be some moral equivalent to the laws of nature—an unchanging moral order that was, like the laws of physics and biology, part of the natural world. This natural law was thought to exist independently of human laws and codes, applicable to everyone, everywhere.

The *ethics of human rights* begins with the natural law assumption that there is a certain universal moral order that exists apart from social, cultural, and historical conditions—a moral order which supersedes or "trumps" the "man-made" laws and socially constructed moral principles that are particular to civilizations and time periods.[45] Within this all encompassing order exists a universal moral community that includes all human beings (and, by some accounts, all living things). By virtue of being connected to this global community, all human beings enjoy equal moral worth and status. This standing cannot be removed by others, and we are all morally obligated to honor it. In some important respects, the tradition of natural law is not unlike the laws of God or the sorts of universal laws that are found in many religions. However, the difference is that the natural law tradition does not depend on any conception of a supernatural being; instead, the source of its laws are derived from the natural order of the universe and apply to all human beings who are a part of that order.

While the concept of "rights" was not specifically discussed by Aristotle, the Stoics, and other early Western philosophers, the notion of natural law that emerged from Greek antiquity would later generate the idea of **natural rights**. Natural rights refer to the notion that basic guarantees exist and that all people possess them simply by virtue of being human.[46] For example, the eighteenth-century philosophers argued for the

BOX 9.5
Ethics and the United Nations Declaration of Human Rights

The *United Nations Declaration of Human Rights* makes the following claims in support of natural rights:

- All human beings are born free and equal in dignity and rights
- Everyone has a right to life, liberty, and security of person
- No one shall be subjected to slavery or servitude
- No one shall be subjected to torture or to inhuman or degrading treatment or punishment
- Everyone is equal before the law
- Everyone has a right to freedom of thought, conscience, and religion

With these universal human rights in mind, identify three controversial issues in criminal justice that seem to challenge or question the legitimacy, universality, or applicability of natural rights. In other words, try to identify at least three issues in which the natural rights listed above are ignored or set aside for the sake of other interests. Given our discussion of natural rights in this chapter, do the issues you have identified seem more morally problematic than you may have thought? If not, are there legitimate moral grounds for ignoring or violating human rights? If so, what are they?

existence of a number of **negative rights** that were understood as *limitations* impacting the treatment of citizens by governments or political authorities.[47] More recently, the idea of rights has come to include a **positive** element as well—rights *to* various things as well as rights against unjust interference by lawmakers. Unlike earlier conceptions that worked to restrict government, subsequent variations justified the expansion of the State. Rights to education, health care, housing, and so forth, all justify increased government involvement in the lives of its citizens. Examples of natural rights include those of life, liberty, and property, as well as the right to be treated fairly and equally no matter one's class, race, gender, political or religious affiliation, and the like (see Box 9.5).

Legal and Moral Rights

In many cases—including several of those noted above—discussions of rights revolve more specifically around various **legal rights**. This is especially true in criminal justice where the notion of rights typically refers to legal protections that people enjoy when interacting with representatives of the justice system. For instance, the right to the presence of an attorney in a criminal trial and the right to humane treatment are specific legal protections. Moreover, as an indication of the importance that legal rights assume in criminal justice, consider the decision in *Miranda v. Arizona* (1966). In this case, the United States Supreme Court guaranteed criminal suspects a right to *be informed of* their protections under the law. The aim was to ensure that such citizens, although thought to be responsible for criminal wrongdoing, were not treated unfairly. However, the legal rights that are so crucial to criminal justice are different in an important sense from the broader notion of **moral rights.** To be clear, moral rights are of greater concern when it comes to ethics.

When Thomas Jefferson (1732–1799)—writing under the influence of British philosopher John Locke (1632–1704)—authored the United States Declaration of Independence, he claimed a "right" to life, liberty, and the pursuit of happiness for all citizens. Clearly, the Declaration of Independence is not concerned with outlining legal rights that U.S. citizens have or should have in relation to these basic goods. This was the function of the Bill of Rights. However, what Thomas Jefferson and others did have in mind with the Declaration was basic, fundamental guarantees that each of us should enjoy irrespective of our backgrounds, statuses, or positions within society. In this respect, then, this document is similar to a variety of more recent provisions on rights, including the Universal Declaration of Human Rights (1948), the European Convention on Human Rights (1954), and the International Covenant on Civil and Economic Rights (1966).[48] What each of them has in common is a profound conception of rights in which certain "inalienable" liberties and protections possess deeper and more enduring significance than any formal rights that might or might not be created by government. In other words, the *moral rights* enumerated or implied in these declarations attach to people simply by virtue of their being human and this is why they are considerably more fundamental than the articulated legal protections.

It is worth noting that there is often an overlap between moral and legal rights. For example, many legal rights—such as those derived from the U.S. Constitution—are themselves traceable to some more elemental conception of human and moral rights. To illustrate, the notion of a right to life gives rise to a number of more specific legal guarantees including those pertaining to self-defense; the right to liberty gives rise to a variety of specific legal protections against unjustified interference with our pursuit of happiness. In many cases, then, human or moral rights (to life, to liberty) ground the drafting of legal rights.

However, what is more important in the context of ethics are the ways in which legal and moral rights differ. Notwithstanding the overlap, not all legal guarantees originate from moral rights, and many moral rights exist apart from an appeal to legal assurances. To be clear, *moral* rights exist *prior to* and *independent of* any legal considerations. And, as we have seen, some interpret moral rights as being derived from a universal moral order that precedes social and historical conditions—a moral order that applies to all human beings, everywhere, in every time period. Whether the legal system recognizes them, all human beings are said to have certain needs and interests, and corresponding moral rights that exist to protect and further these needs and interests. For instance, governments that deny political participation to ethnic or racial groups (whether the groups represent majority or minority constituencies) may do so legally; however, the moral "rightness" of political participation cannot be denied to people because of one's heritage or skin color. Similarly, slavery in the United States was deemed objectionable because its practice violated certain moral rights pertaining to humanness and personhood, even though existing laws made slavery entirely permissible.

What the above observations make evident is that moral rights possess binding force, irrespective of whether they are translated into law. Under these circumstances, even if laws exist requiring us to violate a particular moral right, it is unethical to do so. This is because in those situations where the law and moral rights come into conflict, our ethical duty is to obey the moral order rather than the formal law. Thus, moral rights transcend and "trump" human law. After all, human law can be, and some times is, constructed in error. Perhaps most importantly, the presence of moral rights suggests that laws made by people are subject to *limits* that emerge because of moral rights. In other words, precisely because moral rights are not derived from legal guarantees or from a Constitution, it is possible for existing laws and constitutional protections to be in violation of moral rights (see Box 9.6).[49]

BOX 9.6
The Scope of Moral Rights and International Criminal Justice

As we have seen, moral rights are said to be possessed by all people, everywhere, and in equal degree. Thus, irrespective of class, race, religion, nationality, or any other social distinction, each person enjoys the same basic moral rights simply because he or she is a human being. At the same time, though, this implies that all persons have a duty to protect and promote the moral rights of everyone else, regardless of whom these individuals are or where they might live.

Notwithstanding our personal moral responsibility to protect and promote the moral rights of others, in practice this duty often falls upon nations and international governments. According to some, government is best situated to effectively undertake these actions. Indeed, we need such institutions to protect rights for two reasons: (1) as individuals we tend to place higher moral priority on persons close to us (e.g., family, friends, community); and (2) our ability to exercise our duties with regard to the protection and promotion of moral rights is often limited by our personal circumstances (e.g., financial, geographical). To illustrate, it might be difficult for individuals in the United States to intervene in rights violations taking place in countries on the other side of the globe. If we consider various claims to rights that we are said to possess (e.g., the right to an adequate education; protection against cruel and unusual punishment), it seems necessary to have some form of governmental body to ensure that these rights are promoted. But how do these rights translate into actions that countries and political authorities can and must ensure ethically?

- Generate a list of rights that you believe to be fundamentally important in the context of crime and justice.
- With the rights you have identified, ask yourself whether they should also be protected in foreign lands, or if there is room for cultural variability.
- Moreover, ask yourself whether and to what extent the United States has a duty to ensure that these crime and justice rights be enjoyed by all citizens in other countries. Would you argue that the United States has an affirmative obligation to ensure these rights exist in other countries even if the result is war? In what ways are these rights moral imperatives?

Source: Philippe Sands (Ed.), *From Nuremburg to the Hague: The Future of International Criminal Justice* (New York: Cambridge University Press, 2005).

DEONTOLOGY AND THE CRIMINAL JUSTICE SYSTEM: THE MORALITY OF LEGAL PUNISHMENT

To illustrate the significance of deontological ethics for criminal justice issues, as well as to demonstrate how it differs from consequentialist perspectives, we turn in the remainder of this chapter to a common but morally-controversial criminal justice practice—that of punishing lawbreakers. In Chapter 1 (Box 1.1), we were exposed to the *moral problem of punishment*. In short, the problem is one of *justifying* punishment. In other words, because punishing people involves inflicting pain and suffering—things we typically should not do—we must have some ground upon which we can claim that it is morally appropriate to impose punishments upon criminal offenders.[50] To find this ground, we must turn to normative ethical theories. Although many justifications for punishment have been proposed, most of them can be classified as either utilitarian or deontological. As normative moral frameworks, both utilitarianism and deontology offer ethical recommendations for how we *should* or *ought* to treat people who violate criminal laws. As we will see, however, utilitarian and deontological justifications for punishment are largely incompatible; that is, we cannot have both. Importantly, the ethical perspective we employ to justify punishing criminals will have important implications for why, how, and when we punish.

Utilitarianism and Criminal Punishment

As we saw in the previous chapter, utilitarian ethics holds the morality of actions to be a function of whether they bring about good consequences to all affected parties. As you might imagine, whether punishment of any sort is justifiable from a utilitarian perspective depends upon whether it brings about good or desirable consequences for the people who are affected by it. While the offender herself or himself is most directly affected by punishment, the positive (or negative) effects of punishment also indirectly impact the larger community and society. Because punishment typically causes pain and suffering to those individual offenders who are subjected to it, utilitarianism would have us look to its beneficial impact on the greater community to find moral justification.

What are the "good" consequences of criminal punishment for the community? In what ways can these benefits be said to outweigh the pain caused to those who are punished? While we will shortly see that there are several ways in which punishing criminals arguably benefits the greater good, all of them are said to have the same basic positive effect—*preventing* future crime. From a utilitarian standpoint, we punish lawbreakers *so that* future crime is prevented (and *only* for this purpose). As you may anticipate, if punishment practices fail to achieve the intended effect of preventing future crime, then they cannot be morally justified on utilitarian grounds.[51]

From a utilitarian standpoint, then, the negative consequences for the punished lawbreaker are "smaller evils" that may be outweighed by the greater moral good that is the prevention of future harm to others. In other words, *if* punishment can prevent many future victims from suffering the effects of crime, the gain in public safety is enough to justify the harm caused to individual offenders. It is important to keep in mind, however, that there are a variety of types of punishment available in any given case (e.g., fines in various amounts, probation, imprisonment). As a general rule, utilitarianism holds that punishment should entail as little harm as is necessary to achieve the desired goal of prevention. If, for instance, a sentence of probation can effectively prevent an individual from committing future crimes, then any more severe punishment would cause harm above and beyond what is necessary and therefore morally justifiable. It is in part for this reason that utilitarians often *oppose* the practice of capital punishment. If an offender can be prevented from committing further crimes by imposing a life sentence, then capital punishment causes harm above and beyond what is necessary to achieve the goal of crime prevention.[52]

While crime prevention is the overriding utilitarian goal of punishment, there are several ways in which this goal can be accomplished. Each of the following is a purported beneficial effect of punishment that, from a utilitarian standpoint, serves to justify its practice:[53]

1. *Disablement.* Commonly referred to as *incapacitation,* **disablement** prevents future crime by *physically disabling* the offender. The most common form of punishment that serves the goal of disablement is *incarceration.* The imposition of a jail or prison term makes it physically impossible for the offender to victimize persons outside of that immediate environment. *Mutilation,* or physically dismembering or disfiguring an offender (e.g., removing the hand of a thief or the penis of a rapist), may also prevent certain offenders from repeating certain types of offenses (see Box 9.7). Finally, disablement can occur where a person (e.g., public official, medical or mental health professional, accountant) is simply removed from her or his position. In these instances, eliminating access to resources needed to commit future crimes can physically prevent the offender from repeating her or his offense.

2. *Specific Deterrence.* The aim of **specific deterrence** is to prevent an *individual offender* from committing future wrongdoings by instilling in her or him *fear* of punitive consequences. To "deter" is to "discourage" or even "scare away." Recall that utilitarianism views humans as free-willed, rational beings, motivated to pursue pleasure and avoid pain. In the context of criminal motivation, lawbreakers will choose the pleasures of crime when they outweigh its associated pains. Contrarily, potential lawbreakers will choose law-abiding behaviors if the painful consequences of crime outweigh its pleasures. One such painful consequence is that of legal punishment, whether it be in the form of a fine, community service, probation, incarceration, etc. As we have discussed on several occasions throughout this text, many persons choose to follow the law because they fear such consequences. It is this fear by which deterrence operates and through which future crime is arguably prevented. Punishment in all forms, then, serves as an example or reminder *to the individual offender* of the "evil" that will be inflicted if she or he should choose to violate the law again in the future.

3. *Reform.* Importantly, deterrence does not eliminate the *desire* to engage in wrongdoings; rather, it simply makes a potential offender afraid to commit them for fear of consequences. The goal of **reform** or *rehabilitation,* on the other hand, is to *change the inclinations, motives, habits, and character of the offender* so that the offender no longer desires to engage in criminal activities. For example, a prisoner who is released back into the community after serving a five-year term may refrain from committing future crimes because she or he

BOX 9.7

Chemical Castration as Disablement

A contemporary controversy involving mutilation is that surrounding the practice of *chemical castration* for sex offenders. While surgical castration has never found popularity in the United States, beginning in the late 1990s many states proposed laws that would require qualified convicted sex offenders to submit to chemical castration. In 1997, for instance, the state of Florida enacted a law mandating weekly injections of Medroxyprogesterone acetate (commonly known as female contraceptive Depo-Provera) for sex offenders who met certain qualifications. In principle, Depo-Provera reduces testosterone production, thereby reducing sexual desire in males. Metaphorically "cutting off" an offender's sex drive will thus disable him from committing future sex crimes.

While the use of Medroxyprogesterone acetate (MPA) has been successful with certain types of sex offenders, it is much less effective with others. Problematically, the logic behind both surgical and chemical castration entails the errant belief that most sex crimes are sexually motivated. Indeed, MPA has proven successful with many offenders whose crimes stem from sexual desire. Most sex offenders, however, tend to be motivated by nonsexual factors such as anger, power, and a desire to dominate other human beings. Disabling an offender's sex drive will have little—if any—effect on these underlying nonsexual motivations.

The reasoning behind chemical castration laws is clearly utilitarian in nature. Castration of sex offenders is performed in the interest of rehabilitation and protection of the public from dangerous criminals. The advancement of these utilitarian goals is held to justify the practice of chemical castration on moral grounds. If, however, castration fails to work—as is often the case with offenders who are not motivated by sexual desire—then there is no corresponding gain in public safety. For those offenders for whom chemical castration is ineffective, the practice becomes unjustifiable on utilitarian grounds. In addition, critics have raised a number of other moral concerns about the practice of castration:

- The U.S. Supreme Court has held that competent adults—including prisoners and the civilly committed mentally ill—maintain a constitutional *right to refuse medical treatment*. This right may be subject to limitation, however, where there is a compelling government interest at stake (e.g., preserving prison safety). Where chemical castration is *required* as a condition of release for convicted sex offenders, the right to refuse medical treatment has in effect been taken away. Does the State's interest in protecting the public from known sex offenders outweigh an offender's constitutional right to refuse treatment? If so, does it matter that some drugs—including MPA—have known side effects?
- An implied *right to privacy* under the Fourteenth Amendment has been acknowledged by the Supreme Court. The Constitution thus generally protects autonomy and bodily integrity with regard to decisions concerning childbearing and contraception. Forced castration could be interpreted as a violation of an offender's reproductive autonomy—the fundamental civil right to procreation that we all enjoy. Again, does the State's interest in protecting the public morally justify infringing upon an offender's autonomy and bodily integrity with regard to reproductive decisions?

fears going back to prison. While it would be accurate to suggest that the offender has been effectively deterred by her or his previous punishment, she or he cannot be said to have been rehabilitated. In principle, reform efforts should be tailored to fit the individual offender's needs and therefore may occur in a variety of settings and may include treatment for drug and alcohol problems, education and job training, psychological or spiritual counseling, and participation in other programs designed to aid in the offender's rehabilitation.

4. *General deterrence.* Whereas disablement, specific deterrence, and reform all seek to prevent crime by modifying the behavior of *specific offenders* who have already violated the law, **general deterrence** seeks to prevent crime by deterring people "in general." The underlying principle of general deterrence is the same as that of specific deterrence; namely, people will choose law-abiding behavior where the negative consequences of crime outweigh any pleasure it might bring. The key difference between specific and general deterrence is that, in the latter, punishing criminals serves as an example *to others* of the negative consequences of lawbreaking.

Deontology and Criminal Punishment

From a deontological ethical perspective, a number of objections to utilitarian justifications for punishment can be raised. One such objection was noted above; namely, because utilitarianism justifies punishment by appealing to the beneficial end of preventing crime, it fails to justify punishment if *the means don't achieve the end.* If it can be shown that punishment fails to prevent crime (e.g., incapacitate, deter, and/or rehabilitate criminals), then by utilitarian standards we have no grounds on which to punish. In short, it could be argued that punishment *does not work* and we are therefore inflicting harm on persons without any corresponding "greater good." If punishment fails to achieve its utilitarian objectives, then it becomes an exercise in increasing the amount of suffering in the world without the increase in happiness that would be necessary to justify it.[54] As support for this claim, many have pointed to high rates of *recidivism* as evidence that deterrence and reform efforts are ineffective. For the utilitarian, however, this is merely a practical problem. It is not, for instance, that criminals cannot be rehabilitated, but that the system has been ineffective in doing the job of rehabilitating criminals.[55]

A second deontological objection to utilitarian grounds for punishment is one that Kant alluded to on a number of occasions. Recall that Kantian ethics holds *human dignity* to be of fundamental moral importance. With this in mind, Kant claimed that utilitarianism ignores human dignity. More specifically, justifications for punishment that appeal to beneficial consequences—incapacitation, deterrence, and rehabilitation—violate Kant's second variation of the categorical imperative ("treat others as an end and never as a means only"). When punishment practices are grounded in a concern for the incapacitation, deterrence, or reform of offenders, we are *using* offenders as a means to an end. While the objective of preventing crime may be worthy, using people—treating them as a means rather than an end—is fundamentally incompatible with the deontological commitment to and respect for human dignity:[56]

■ *Incapacitation.* If we imprison an individual to secure the well-being of the community, we are *using* that offender to benefit others.

- *Deterrence.* Philosopher Georg Wilhelm Friedrich Hegel once wrote, "to base a justification of punishment on threat is to liken it to the act of a man who lifts his stick to a dog. It is to treat a man like a dog instead of with freedom and respect due to him as a man."[57]
- *Rehabilitation.* Reform or rehabilitation would have us treat others as "unfree, immature being[s], whose behavior may legitimately be reshaped by others in accordance with their notions of what is good, desirable, and socially acceptable."[58] Rehabilitation can thus be criticized as an attempt to mold people into what *we* think they should be. For Kant, this violates respect for *autonomy*—if we are to treat others as free, rational beings, then we must recognize that they are entitled to decide for themselves what sort of people they wish to be.

If incapacitation, deterrence, and reform are not moral grounds for punishing law-breakers, how are we to justify punitive practices? Rather than justifying punishment by appealing to *future* consequences, deontology looks *backward*. The moral basis for punishment is not in future consequences, but is the offense which has been committed and for which justice must be done. Offenders should be punished because—and only because—they have committed a crime.[59] Further, where an offense has been committed, punishment of the offender *must* occur—irrespective of consequences. We punish the guilty because that is what is demanded of us by justice. If it so happens that good consequences result, then so much the better. Yet consequences, whether positive or negative, should have no bearing on our decision to dispense justice.

The principle of justice found in the practice of punishment is that of **desert**—giving people what they *deserve*. Punishment is "just" because it entails treating offenders the way they deserve to be treated in light of their offenses. The justification for punishment is thus **retribution**, or the principle that the State should "pay back" the offender for her or his offense.[60] Importantly, the notion of desert implies that punishments must be *proportionate* to the seriousness of the offense. **Proportionality**—the principle that the "punishment should fit the crime"—is crucial to deontological justifications for punishment. If an offender has been convicted of rape, for instance, he deserves to be punished for his crime. He does not, however, deserve to be punished with death. In this case, the severity of the punishment would unjustly outweigh the seriousness of the crime. On the other hand, while utilitarianism does not generally allow for the imposition of capital punishment, deontology can justify the punishment of death where—and only where—it is proportionate to the offense (e.g., murder).

Deontologists would argue that utilitarianism potentially violates both of these key principles (that punishment *must* be administered following a conviction, and that the punishment *must* be proportionate to the offense). In this respect, they argue, utilitarianism fails to account for justice and, in fact, would have us commit injustices if doing so would bring beneficial consequences. The focus of utilitarianism is on preventing crime, not ensuring that offenders get what they deserve. Consequently, there are several scenarios in which utilitarianism might allow for persons to receive something less, more, or other than what is deserved in relation to their actions.[61]

There is nothing, for instance, in utilitarianism that limits the amount of punishment that can be imposed. Utilitarianism could allow for *disproportionately harsh or disproportionately lenient penalties* if their imposition would achieve the desired end of crime prevention. A ten-year prison sentence for speeding may be effective in deterring crime, but would be arguably unjust in that the severity of the penalty would be undeserved in relation to the severity of the crime. Conversely, the experience of killing an innocent pedestrian while driving intoxicated and having to apologize to the victim's family may be enough to deter an offender from ever again driving drunk, yet without further punishment many would argue that the offender received less than was deserved and, thus, that justice had not been done (see Box 9.8).

BOX 9.8

Mandatory Sentencing Laws: The Case of California

On June 30, 1992, Douglas David Walker and friend Joe Davis attempted to rob 18-year-old Kimber Reynolds of her purse in the Tower District of Fresno, California. Kimber resisted and, during the ensuing struggle, was shot and killed by Davis—who himself was later killed in a shootout with police. Subsequent investigation revealed both Walker and Davis to have long histories of criminal conduct. Davis had two prior felony convictions and Walker—who entered a plea agreement to avoid murder charges—had a criminal record dating to age 13.

On October 1, 1993, 12-year-old Polly Klaas was kidnapped from her home just a few hours from Fresno in Petaluma, California. The perpetrator crept into the Klaas household and abducted Polly at knifepoint as her family slept not far away. In late November, after a troubling investigation, police arrested Richard Allen Davis for the murder of Polly Klaas. Davis's criminal record revealed that he had twice been convicted and sentenced to prison for prior attempted kidnappings.

The tragedies of Kimber Reynolds and Polly Klaas generated public outcry and political pressure to "crack down" on habitual criminal offenders. In November of 2004, California voters passed Proposition 184—California's "Three-Strikes Law"—by an overwhelming 72% majority vote. Under California's new legislation, offenders who were convicted of three serious crimes would, following their third "strike," receive a lengthy mandatory prison sentence (often life in prison). California allows for a variety of offenses to count as strikes, and for *any* felony to count as the third strike. Since its enactment, nearly 50,000 people have been incarcerated under California's law—most *nonviolent* offenders, and most African American males.

By 1997, over half of the states in the United States (as well as the federal government) had passed similar legislation. Proponents of three-strikes laws and other habitual felony statutes appeal to their purported *deterrent* effect for justification. The threat of severe punishment is, in theory, enough to convince those with felony records to refrain from committing any additional offenses. The morality of mandatory sentencing laws is thus justified on utilitarian grounds—harsh penalties pass the test of utility if they bring about good consequences (i.e., reduction in crime). On the other hand, critics have argued that the severity of punishments handed out under mandatory sentencing laws are *disproportionate* to the severity of the offenses for which they are imposed. From a deontological perspective, sentences of up to life imprisonment for crimes as minor as shoplifting violate the imperative that the punishment must fit the crime.

Sources: Peter W. Greenwood, *Three Strikes and You're Out: Estimated Benefits and Costs of California's New Mandatory Sentencing Law* (Santa Monica, CA: Rand Corporation, 1994); Paul G. Cassell, "Too Severe: A Defense of the Federal Sentencing Guidelines (and a Critique of Federal Mandatory Minimums)," *Stanford Law Review,* 56, 1017–1032 (2004); Shamica Gaskins, "Women of Circumstance: The Effects of Mandatory Minimum Sentencing on Women Minimally Involved in Drug Crimes," *American Criminal Law Review,* 41, 1533–1554 (2003).

As well, there is nothing in utilitarianism that prevents innocent persons from being punished, or guilty persons going unpunished. In all of those cases where punishing an offender would do more harm than good, utilitarianism commits us to refrain from punishment. On this note, Kant once asked, "What then are we to think of the proposal that the life of a condemned criminal should be spared if he agrees to let dangerous experiments be carried out on him in order that the doctors may gain new information of value. . . ?" Justice, Kant notes in response to this question, "ceases to be justice if it can be bought at a price."[62] Similarly, in those cases where punishing the innocent may bring about good overall consequences, utilitarianism may allow for it to be introduced. In both cases, although the punishment (or nonpunishment) has passed the test of utility, many would argue that justice has been compromised.

How is it that retribution, unlike incapacitation, deterrence, and reform, *respects human dignity*? Kant tells us that to treat others as ends involves treating them as rational beings, responsible beings. In punishing offenders, we are respecting their freedom and rationality, holding them responsible for what they have done, and treating them as they deserve to be treated. In other words, we are allowing *their conduct*—rather than the system's objectives—to determine how they will be treated.

In sum, the deontological justification of criminal punishment suggests that: (1) the State has a moral *right* to punish offenders on the basis of what they have done; (2) the State has a moral *duty* to punish offenders in the interest of justice; (3) that punishments must be proportionate to the offense committed; (4) that punishment serves to rectify or "even out" the harm of the offense; and (5) offenders have a moral right to be treated by respect and, therefore, punishment is a moral *right of the offender.*[63]

SUMMARY

This chapter examined the deontological approach to the choices we should make and the actions we should undertake. Central to this approach are a focus on duties, rights, and obligations. As we have seen, deontological ethics binds us in ways that transcend laws, rules, codes, and procedures. Although this brand of ethics is difficult to uphold in our daily lives, it attempts to establish universal principles of doing what is good for others, for ourselves, and for society more generally. Deontological ethics commits us to concerns for personhood, fairness, dignity, and worth for all people everywhere, regardless of timeframe or historical period. Whether in the context of personal responsibility or international accountability, these types of concerns are woven into the operation of criminal justice practices and are crucial to decision-making in criminal justice contexts. While the deontological approaches entertained in this chapter offer several strategies for advancing ethical conduct, there remains one further normative approach warranting consideration. Unlike consequentialist or deontological ethics that emphasize what it means to *do* good, *virtue ethics* stresses what it means to *be* good. This topic is the focus of review in the subsequent chapter.

KEY TERMS AND CONCEPTS

categorical imperative
correlativity of rights and duties
deontology
desert
deterrence (specific and general)
disablement (or incapacitation)
duties
hypothetical (or conditional) imperative
legal rights
maxim

moral rights
natural rights
negative rights
positive rights
prima facie duties
proportionality
reform (or rehabilitation)
retribution
universal law

DISCUSSION QUESTIONS

1. Explain the difference between hypothetical and categorical imperatives. Provide three examples of each, taken from the field of criminal justice. How might this distinction be used to explore the practice of correctional facilities placing violent prisoners in solitary confinement?

2. A citizen is held up at gunpoint. A second person is a witness to this crime. The second person has a permit to carry a weapon and is in possession of this handgun. The second person reasonably believes that the attacker is likely to shoot and kill the citizen. Given these circumstances, the second person is trying to determine what course of action is ethically justified. Following the observations on prima facie duties, how would you reconcile this dilemma? Are there any conditional duties in operation here? Explain your response.

3. Explain the relationship between rights and duties. Identify three rights that help to understand a particular problem in crime and justice. Identify what corresponding duties attach to these rights and who is responsible for these corresponding duties.

4. Explain the concept of natural rights. Apply your definition to the following situation. A suspect is seen fleeing the scene of a crime. The suspect, brandishing a handgun, allegedly shot a police officer. A second police officer is in pursuit. The second officer firmly instructs the suspect to stop. The fleeing suspect does not adhere to the officer's command. The officer repeats the instruction a second time, but the suspect does not yield. The officer fires at the suspect, killing him instantly.

5. What is the difference between human rights, legal rights, and moral rights? Rely on a criminal justice ethical dilemma to substantiate your perspective.

SUGGESTED READINGS

Finnis, John. (1980). *Natural Law and Natural Rights*. New York: Oxford University Press.

Finnis, John. (1983). *Fundamentals of Ethics*. New York: Oxford University Press.

Kant, Immanuel. (1998). *Groundwork of the Metaphysics of Morals*. New York: Cambridge University Press.

Paul, Ellen Frankel, Miller, Fred D., and Paul, Jeffrey (Eds.). (2001). *Natural Law and Modern Moral Philosophy*. New York: Cambridge University Press.

Rawls, John. (1971). *A Theory of Justice*. Cambridge, MA: Harvard University Press.

Ross, W. E. (1993). *The Right and the Good*. Oxford: Clarendon Press.

ENDNOTES

[1]James Rachels, *Elements of Moral Philosophy* (New York: McGraw-Hill, 2002).

[2]Immanuel Kant, *Foundations of the Metaphysics of Morals* (Indianapolis, IN: Bobbs-Merrill, 1959), pp. 30–31.

[3]Ibid., pp. 31–33; James Rachels, *Elements of Moral Philosophy*, p. 105.

[4]James Rachels, *Elements of Moral Philosophy*, p. 105.

[5]Ibid.

[6]Ibid.

[7]Ibid., p. 106.

[8]Immanuel Kant, *Foundations of the Metaphysics of Morals*, p. 39.

[9]Rachels, *Elements of Moral Philosophy*, p. 106.

[10]Immanuel Kant, *Foundations of the Metaphysics of Morals*, p. 40.

[11]Rachels, *Elements of Moral Philosophy*, p. 106.

[12]Immanuel Kant, *Foundations of the Metaphysics of Morals*, p. 41.

[13]Ibid.

[14]Rachels, *Elements of Moral Philosophy*, p. 107.

[15]Ibid., p. 108.

[16]Ibid., p. 108.

[17]Ibid., p. 109.

[18]Quoted Ibid., p. 109.

[19]Ibid., p. 109 (authors' emphasis).

[20]Ibid.

[21]Ibid.

[22]Immanuel Kant, *Foundations of the Metaphysics of Morals*, p. 47.

[23]Rachels, *Elements of Moral Philosophy*, p. 114.

[24]Ibid., p. 116.

[25]Ibid., p. 116.

[26]Ibid., pp. 115–116.

[27]Ibid., pp. 116–117.

[28]Ibid.

[29]Ibid., pp. 110–111.

[30]W. D. Ross, *The Right and the Good* (Oxford: Clarendon Press, 1993).

[31]Ibid., p. 216.

[32]Judith Boss, *Ethics for Life* (Mountain View, CA: Mayfield, 2001), p. 355.

[33]John Finnis, *Natural Law and Natural Rights* (New York: Oxford University Press, 1980).

[34]Lee Epstein, *Constitutional Law for a Changing America: Rights, Liberties, and Justice* (Washington, DC: CQ Press, 2004).

[35]Ronald J. Allen, *Criminal Procedure: Investigation and Right to Counsel* (New York: Kluwer Law International, 2005), p. 33.

[36]Ibid.

[37]See, e.g., Barbara Rafel Price and Natalie J. Sokoloff (Eds.), *The Criminal Justice System and Women: Offenders, Prisoners, Victims, and Workers* (New York: McGraw-Hill, 2004).

[38]Lee Epstein, *Constitutional Law for a Changing America: Rights, Liberties, and Justice.*

[39]Judith Boss, *Ethics for Life* (Mountain View, CA: Mayfield, 2001), pp. 372–374.

[40]Ibid.

[41]Ibid., p. 361.

[42]John Finnis, *Natural Law and Natural Rights.*

[43]Ibid., p. 17.

[44]See, e.g., Knudd Haakonssen, *Natural Law and Moral Philosophy: From Grotius to the Scottish Enlightenment* (New York: Cambridge University Press, 1997); Ellen Frankel Paul, Fred D. Miller, and Jeffrey Paul (Eds.), *Natural Law and Modern Moral Philosophy* (New York: Cambridge University Press, 2001).

[45]Knudd Haakonssen, *Natural Law and Moral Philosophy: From Grotius to the Scottish Enlightenment.*

[46]John Finnis, *Natural Law and Natural Rights.*

[47]Ellen Paul Frankel, Fred D. Miller, and Jeffrey Paul (Eds.), *Natural Law and Modern Moral Philosophy,* p. 9.

[48]Henry Steiner and Philip Alston, *International Human Rights in Context: Law, Politics, and Morals* (New York: Oxford University Press, 2001).

[49]Judith Boss, *Ethics for Life,* p. 359.

[50]Igor Primoratz, *Justifying Legal Punishment* (Atlantic Highlands, NJ: Humanities Press, 1989).

[51]Ibid.

[52]Jonathan Glover, *Causing Deaths and Taking Lives* (New York: Penguin Books, 1977); see, generally, Gertrude Ezorsky (Ed.), *Philosophical Perspectives on Punishment* (Albany, NY: SUNY Press, 1972), pp. 249–280.

[53]See Igor Primoratz, *Justifying Legal Punishment,* pp. 18–22.

[54]Ibid; see also, Ted Honderich, *Punishment: The Supposed Justifications* (New York: Penguin, 1984).

[55]Ibid., pp. 33–35.

[56]Ibid.

[57]Quoted in Igor Primoratz, *Justifying Legal Punishment,* p. 35.

[58]Ibid.

[59]Immanuel Kant, "The Right of Punishing." In Gertrude Ezorsky (Ed.), *Philosophical Perspectives on Punishment,* pp. 103–104.

[60]Edmund Pincoffs, *The Rationale of Legal Punishment* (New York: Humanities Press, 1966), pp. 2–16.

[61]See Igor Primoratz, *Justifying Legal Punishment,* pp. 35–61.

[62]Immanuel Kant, "The Right of Punishing." In Gertrude Ezorsky, *Philosophical Perspectives on Punishment,* p. 104.

[63]Igor Primoratz, *Justifying Legal Punishment,* p. 12.

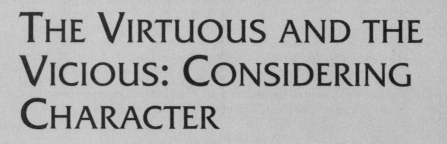

Chapter **10**

THE VIRTUOUS AND THE VICIOUS: CONSIDERING CHARACTER

In the previous two chapters, we explored normative ethical theories that concentrate on the consequences of our actions and on our actions themselves. Consequentialist ethics asks that we consider the results of our actions, with those that produce the greatest benefit (i.e., good consequences)—for oneself and/or others—being the "right" ethical choice in a given situation or with regard to a particular issue. Deontological ethics, in turn, asks that we consider relevant duties and principles, making choices and engaging in actions that are consistent with those duties and principles. What each has in common is an emphasis on *doing*. The overriding question of both types of theories is that of, "What should I do?" The importance of actions and consequences notwithstanding, what each of these types of theories fails to consider is the types of people we should *be*. When we shift moral focus from our actions and their consequences toward the notion of good moral *character,* we begin asking questions common to the third major tradition of normative ethics—that of *virtue ethics.*

Virtue ethics is the eldest of all ethical traditions, having its roots in the ancient Greek and Roman moral philosophies of Plato, Aristotle, the Stoics, and Epicureans, as well as a storied history in Eastern philosophical traditions such as Buddhism, Taoism, and Confucianism. Each of these philosophers and philosophical traditions shares an interest in examining what it means to lead a "good" life, with the "goodness" of our lives having much to do with the kinds of people that we are. In short, they are each concerned with our being *virtuous* people. The principal question asked and contemplated by the virtue tradition is, "What kind of person should I be?" Consequently, our goal or task as moral people is to develop into and continue to be that type of person; that is, to develop certain types of character traits (i.e., virtues), while seeking to "avoid or extinguish" others (i.e., vices).[1] In this third and final chapter on normative ethics, we explore this eldest of all ethical traditions and the crucial questions it poses about what it means to *be* a moral person.

> **Point of departure for virtue ethics:** Morality Amounts To Being A Certain Type Of Person, Embodying Certain Types Of Character Traits (Virtues) While Avoiding Or Eliminating Others (Vices)

VIRTUE AND VICE

Think of the people that you most admire ethically—people that can and do commonly serve as ethical role models or after whom you pattern (or try to pattern) your own moral behavior. Now, consider if you will what all of those people have in common. Most likely, it is not that they were all skilled at considering the consequences of their actions. It is also probably not that they were steadfastly committed to certain ethical imperatives and always placed their duty to abide by certain moral laws above all else. While they may have demonstrated one or both of these qualities, it is more likely that what they all have in common is that they are all certain *types of people.* Perhaps the people that came to mind are historical figures such as Jesus, the Buddha, Mother Teresa, or Martin Luther King Jr.; perhaps they are parents, family, friends, or teachers. In any case, what the people we most admire as exemplars of moral goodness seem to share is usually not so much about what they *do,* but the types of people they *are.* They tend to be caring people, compassionate, forgiving, merciful, respectful, and considerate of the needs and interests of others. In short, when we think of ethical or moral people, we probably think of what moral philosophers would call *virtuous* people.

Virtue and Character

When we talk about the types of people that we or others are, we usually do so in terms of character traits. A **character trait** is "a tendency to behave in certain ways in certain circumstances."[2] Character traits can dispose us toward moral or immoral behaviors; they can encourage us to be considerate of the needs and interests of others, or incline us to be indifferent to or harmful toward others. Selfishness, for instance, is a character trait that, when embodied, disposes us to act in selfish ways. Likewise, honesty is a character trait that disposes us to be truthful and to avoid dishonesty, deception, and fraudulent behaviors. In any case, what is important about character traits is not only that they define us as people, but that they dispose us to act in certain ways when we encounter certain types of situations.

When taken together, character traits define a person's character. By **character,** we mean a collection—a "cluster, or perhaps system"—of character traits as they appear in a given person.[3] Thus, a person who possesses the individual traits of honesty, integrity, humility, and self-respect possesses an overall character that is constituted by these dispositions. Ultimately, as we will see, being a "good" or virtuous person

BOX 10.1
Virtue and Leadership

As Judith Boss points out, people tend to emulate those who are at a higher stage of moral development. Because of this tendency, placing virtuous persons in *leadership roles* can have a positive moral impact on an entire organization, community, or society. Think of persons you know who are in leadership roles—presidents, legislators, judges, police chiefs—and discuss whether those people serve as good moral role models by exhibiting virtue. What virtues *should* persons in such positions embody? What, if any, *vices* should they embody? What are the dangers of embodying different virtues and vices for each of the following positions?

- The President of the United States
- Legislators in your state
- Judges and Supreme Court Justices
- Chiefs of Police

requires more than simply possessing a few individual character traits; rather, it is about possessing a collection of traits that work together to generate a moral character that is typified by its collective "goodness." (see Box 10.1).

While it is common in everyday language to refer to "character traits," moral philosophers have historically used the more specific terms *virtue* and *vice* to refer to traits of character that are regarded as "good" or "bad" in moral contexts. Good character traits such as honesty and integrity are considered *moral virtues,* while traits such as selfishness and arrogance are regarded as *moral vices*. Most generally, then, **moral virtues** are traits of character that dispose a person to act in a moral fashion, while **moral vices** are traits of character that dispose a person to act in an indifferent or harmful fashion. In the remainder of our discussion of moral character, we will typically use the terms "moral virtues" and "moral vices" rather than the more generic term "character traits." Here are but a few character traits that are widely regarded as virtues:[4]

Benevolence	Compassion	Courage
Faithfulness	Generosity	Gratitude
Honesty	Humility	Integrity
Justice	Kindness	Loyalty
Mercifulness	Modesty	Nonharm
Open-mindedness	Patience	Politeness
Prudence	Reliability	Responsibility
Self-control	Self-respect	Sincerity
Tactfulness	Tolerance	Trustworthiness
Unselfishness	Wisdom	

VIRTUE, CHARACTER, AND BEHAVIOR

Moral virtues are thus dispositions to act, out of habit, in ways that benefit self and others.[5] Compassion, generosity, and tolerance, for instance, are most always cited as examples of virtue—as character traits that, when motivating action, stand to benefit all those affected by the action. Persons of virtuous character are those who are disposed to act in ways compassionate, generous, and tolerant in situations that demand such actions. Importantly, to say that we act *out of habit* or in light of virtue is different from saying that we act on principle or in consideration of consequences. Instead, dispositions and habits are part of who we are as people. As we will see, however, this does not mean that we somehow either have these virtues or do not (e.g., as a function of personality); rather, virtue is something that, through regular *practice,* one *comes to* and continues to embody.

The exercise of virtue, then, does not follow from rational reflection or a desire to conform to duty; rather, it simply emanates from the person herself or himself. In other words, persons who demonstrate prudence through their choices and actions tend to *be* prudent people. This does not, however, mean that we should regard virtue as independent of actions and consequences. Rather, it is important to realize that there is a strong *correlation between character and behavior.* Though admittedly oversimplified, on the whole we can think of the relationship as follows:

> *VIRTUOUS CHARACTER* gives rise to **GOOD INTENTIONS** which lead to **RIGHT ACTIONS** which produce **GOOD CONSEQUENCES**

Part of the reason that right actions and good consequences are less significant in the virtue tradition than character is that the former tend to follow automatically from the latter. In other words, if we are virtuous people, we will almost invariably engage in right actions and right actions, in turn, often lead to good consequences. It would be difficult, for instance, for the kind person *not* to act kindly; it would be difficult for she or he who is compassionate to act other than compassionately. Virtue ethics recognizes that if we focus on character, ethically-sound choices and behaviors will often follow (see Box 10.2).

Virtue and Negative Emotions

In our discussion of metaethics earlier in the text, we explored the notion of "moral psychology," examining psychological motivations for moral and immoral actions and the kinds of emotions, feelings, and desires that are common incentives for human action. Importantly, virtues are not only tendencies to act in certain ways in certain situations, they are also tendencies to *think, feel, believe,* and *desire* in certain ways.[6] Humility, for instance, has much to do with how we think about ourselves, our accomplishments and importance, while tolerance has much to do with how we think and feel about others. Having moral character is not simply a matter of being disposed to have good intentions and engage in right actions, but also concerns the psychological states that give rise to intentions and that inform our choices and behaviors.

Especially problematic within the virtue tradition are incentives for human action that stem from "negative emotions"—often referred to as *vices.* Whereas virtues are dispositions to act in ways that benefit self and others, *vices* are traits of character

BOX 10.2

Actions and Intentions

Consider the following two scenarios:

> *Ralph is independently wealthy. Several years ago, he sold a company that he owned for a hefty $400 million. As part of that deal, he continues to receive an annual "payment" of $4 million per year. Yesterday, Ralph donated $1 million to Cure for Cancer—a charitable organization. His donation, of course, is tax deductible. In addition, Cure for Cancer has decided to use the money to open the "Ralph Research Center."*

> *Louisa is a seventy-two-year-old widow who is currently unemployed and lost her entire retirement savings in an investment scandal. She has no savings, no checking account, no investments, and about $20 in her purse to last her until next week. While walking downtown yesterday, she came upon a homeless person who seemed tired, hungry, and suffering a good deal. After talking with him for several minutes, Louisa took her last $20 to the grocer on the corner and bought the homeless person food and a warm jacket.*

Looking at the stories of both Ralph and Louisa, who would you consider to be the most virtuous? Why? The difference between the two is not the *action*, nor is it the *consequences* of those actions. Ralph's donation might be regarded as a right action with overall good consequences—particularly for himself. Louisa also performed what would likely be considered a moral action. The consequences of her charity, however, will not have the large-scale impact that Ralph's did.

This, however, is where virtue ethics differs somewhat from Kant's ethics and from utilitarian ethics in particular. Virtuous persons act on the basis of an "underlying disposition of concern for the well-being of others and themselves." Louisa's actions, it would appear at least, were motivated by just such a concern—she acted, in short, out of compassion. One might have difficulty, however, saying the same of Ralph's actions. More likely, Ralph donated to the Cure for Cancer Foundation not out of compassion for persons with cancer, but largely from self-interest. While Ralph's actions have further-reaching consequences, most of us would likely consider Louisa to be the more virtuous (and, therefore, *moral*) of the two. If we were interested only in consequences, we would be logically forced to regard Ralph's actions as of higher moral quality. This is a function of something to which utilitarian moral philosophers do not attend; namely, the role of *intention*.

Source: Jupith Boss, *Ethics for Life* (Mountain View: CA. Mayfield, 2001). Quote is from p. 405.

or dispositions to act in ways that are *indifferent toward* or that *harm* oneself and/or others. In other words, vices are those characteristics that interfere with our capacity to be moral and that dispose us toward indifference or harm rather than morally desirable behavior. Below is a list of *some* character traits that are widely regarded as vices or "ways-of-being" that are in some ways harmful to oneself and/or others:[7]

Arrogance	Callousness	Cowardice
Cruelty	Dishonesty	Disloyalty
Envy	Faithlessness	Greed
Ignorance	Impatience	Imprudence
Ingratitude	Insincerity	Intolerance
Irascibility	Irresponsibility	Jealousy
Laziness	Manipulativeness	Mercilessness
Prejudice	Promiscuity	Rudeness
Selfishness	Servility	Shamelessness
Tactlessness	Unreliability	Untrustworthiness

Part of the importance or value of virtue is that it enables us to *overcome* these sorts of negative emotions, desires, and tendencies. Contemporary virtue ethicist Philippa Foot suggested that virtues are *corrective*—they "correct" our tendencies toward indifference or harm.[8] The virtues of compassion and forgiveness, for instance, help us to overcome tendencies toward anger, hatred, and the desire for revenge; open-mindedness can help us overcome tendencies toward prejudice; and humility and modesty can help us overcome arrogance and excessive pride. Virtues not only have the positive function of disposing us to do good, but have the negative function of aiding us in overcoming tendencies to think, feel, and act in ways that are immoral or otherwise demonstrate a lack of moral goodness (see Box 10.3).

VIRTUE AND THE GOOD LIFE

Ancient Greek philosopher Aristotle (384–322 B.C.E.) is perhaps the most widely recognized and widely discussed of virtue ethicists. Some would argue, in fact, that his *Nichomachean Ethics* (titled in reference to his son, Nichomachus) is the most important book ever written on ethics and morality. In any case, it is a text of crucial significance in philosophy, ethics, and virtue ethics more specifically. While some of Aristotle's conclusions have since been the subject of controversy, his general theses about morality, virtue, and the "good life" are mainstays in discussions of ethics. In what follows, we outline several ideas that play a central role in the *Nichomachean Ethics* and that are vital to our discussion of virtue and its importance.[9]

The Purpose of Human Life

Aristotle begins the *Nicomachean Ethics* by offering a simple but significant point— every action and every pursuit aim at some end or good.[10] In other words, all actions are done for a reason or purpose. Why do we wake up in the morning? Eat breakfast? Brush

BOX 10.3

Crime, Anger, and Forgiveness

In a recent essay on the role of virtue in criminal justice, Williams argues that the vice of *resentment* has come to define the American public's attitude toward criminal offenders and, consequently, has come to play an important role in many criminal justice practices (e.g., determinate sentencing, capital punishment). Problematically, he argues, the embodiment and expression of resentment and related desires for vengeance, retribution, and punishment more often lead only to further harm. Virtues such as forgiveness and mercy are crucial in helping us to overcome the negative emotions of resentment and the passion for revenge and punishment.

The emotional experience of anger, Williams suggests following Aristotle, is not one and the same with the belief that the offender should endure harm as a consequence of her or his offense. The experience of anger is justified; in fact, ignoring, overlooking, or forgetting about harms caused would be equally *vicious* (a deficiency indicative of an absence of proper anger). Yet the desire to *express* anger through harming the offending party is a *learned* response to those initial feelings. Alternatively, the virtue of forgiveness asks not that we cease to feel anger, but that we overcome the desire to cause further harm that often issues from our emotional experience of anger. In this case, forgiveness "checks" anger, encouraging us to feel it with proper intensity and for the right length of time. Excessive anger can easily lead to hatred and the desire to respond excessively to an offense, causing more harm that what is called for.

Do you feel that the American criminal justice system is built upon resentment or the desire for vengeance and retribution? What practices demonstrate this? What practices are at odds with this claim? What role do you feel forgiveness plays in our current system of criminal justice? What role can or should forgiveness play?

Source: Christopher Williams, "Toward a Transvaluation of criminal 'Justice:' On Vengeance, Peacemaking, and Punishment," *Humanity and Society*, 26 (2), 100–116 (2002); reprinted in J. Victor (ed.), *Annual Editions: Criminal Justice 05/06*. (Dubuque, IA: McGraw-Hill).

our teeth? Go to school or work? To each of these questions we could no doubt offer one or more reasons (e.g., because we want to be healthy, because we want to make money or earn college credit). For Aristotle, however, each of these reasons has a further aim or purpose—we want to earn college credit so that we can get a job, we want a job so that we can earn money, we want to earn money so that we can . . . and so on. Ultimately, Aristotle tells us, all of these aims are motivated by one overriding aim or purpose. What is this ultimate aim or "highest good" toward which all of our actions in some way lead?

ARISTOTLE'S TELEOLOGY

In asking what we *aim at* in life, Aristotle was ultimately concerned with what makes a life worthwhile or "good." Answering this question, however, requires some understanding of the ultimate *purpose* of human life. It is only once we know the purpose of human life that we can begin to talk about what a "good" human life would be. This notion of "purpose" is fundamental to Aristotle's ethics and his philosophy more generally. Aristotle has a **teleological** (*end, purpose, goal*) view of the world, meaning that he understands behavior to be goal-directed or aimed at achieving some purpose or end. Everything in the world—from inanimate objects such as knives, to plants and animals, to human beings has some "inborn" purpose. Knives cut, flowers blossom, caterpillars turn into butterflies, and so forth. If we know that the purpose of knives is to cut, then we can deduce that a "good" knife is one that cuts well; if we know that the purpose of a flower is to blossom, we might say that a flower which has blossomed has in some sense lived a good, meaningful life in that it has fulfilled its purpose.

INTRINSIC GOODNESS

Aristotle applies this same logic to human purpose and existence. What is the highest human good or ultimate purpose of human existence? Before looking more closely at this idea of "purpose" as it relates to human life, we need to revisit an idea we were exposed to in Chapter 2 and again in Chapter 8. In our discussion of values, we briefly discussed the distinction between *intrinsic* and *instrumental* goods and values—the former being those things that are good in themselves, and the latter being those things that are good only because they allow us to get some higher or more important good. Money, status, and power, for instance, are instrumental goods in that they are valuable only to the extent that they allow us to achieve or maintain other things that are more intrinsically valuable or desirable. Other things such as health and knowledge are regarded by many to have intrinsic value. Even if health and knowledge may help us to achieve or maintain other goods (in fact, they may even be necessary to achieve or maintain certain other goods), they are valuable in and of themselves. The purpose of health, for instance, is simply to be healthy. The value or "goodness" of health and knowledge do not disappear even if they are not used for anything in particular.

THE HIGHEST GOOD

You may recall that we mentioned in this same context that, for many of the ancient Greeks, the *only* thing that was intrinsically good was *happiness*. Happiness was the "highest good" and, ultimately, all other goods, values, and human pursuits could be reduced to means or efforts to attain or maintain a "happy" existence. Indeed, Aristotle makes precisely this claim in the *Nichomachean Ethics*. His answer to the question of what we aim at in life is that we aim at *happiness*. This, for Aristotle, is the "highest good"—the good toward which all other goods lead. Leading a "happy" existence, in fact, is the very purpose of human life—it is what we aim for in life, what we naturally strive to achieve, and what all of our other pursuits are ultimately about. If we think about why we do anything at all, our answers will eventually lead us to realize that everything we do is done to further our pursuit of happiness. Consider the following example:

Why do I wake up in the morning?
I wake up in order to go to school.

Why do I go to school?
I go to school in order to get a degree.

Why do I want a degree?
I want a degree in order to get a job.

Why do I want a job?
I want a job in order to make money.

Why do I want money?
I want money in order to buy a house, food, etc.

Why do I want these things?
I want these things so that I can have shelter, nourishment, etc.

Why do I want these things?
Ultimately, I want these things because they allow me to pursue a "happy" existence.

Although your answers to the above questions may vary, Aristotle would argue that eventually we are led to conclude that everything we do is ultimately done as a means for achieving the highest human good—*a happy existence*. All other goods are good only in that they allow us to pursue or maintain happiness, and all other values are valuable only in this same sense. Yet what exactly is "happiness"? How are we to achieve it? We will return to these concerns shortly. Before we judge Aristotle on this claim, however, we should understand that what Aristotle means by "happiness" and "happy existence" is a bit different from how we might use these terms in everyday conversation.

The Fulfilled Life

"Happiness" has a particular meaning for Aristotle (and the ancient Greeks more generally), and one that is central to understanding his ethics. The term Aristotle uses to describe the "good life" is **eudaimonia**—a Greek term that is often translated as "happiness" or "well-being" but, for Aristotle, means something closer to "*flourishing.*" To be "happy" or to "flourish" is to live a *fulfilled life*. When flowers blossom and caterpillars become butterflies, they are flourishing in that they are fulfilling their ultimate purposes. In an important way, they are living "good" or "happy" lives. To know the "good life," we must know in what the fulfilled life would consist; and to know the fulfilled life, we need to know something about the function or ultimate purpose of that life.

BEING EXCELLENT

So far, we know that the highest good for human beings is happiness, that happiness consists in flourishing, that flourishing has to do with living a fulfilled life, and that fulfillment has something to do with our ultimate purpose as human beings. What is a realized or fulfilled life for human beings? To answer this, we need to consider Aristotle's conception of human *function*. Before doing so, however, we need to consider one more concept that appears prominently in Aristotle's ethics—that of "*excellence.*"

For Aristotle, "function" is closely linked with the notion of "excellence" or "virtue." The "good" or "fulfilled" life requires the embodiment and exercise of excellence (or virtue) in relation to function (i.e., performing one's function with excellence). Thus, a knife is good to the degree that it excels at the function of cutting, while a medicine is good to the degree that it excels at its intended function of healing or alleviating symptoms of illness. By knowing the function of something, we can know what it means to be an "excellent" or virtuous thing of that sort. Generally, to exercise excellence or virtue is to do something "in such a way that one's skill, or virtue, is expressed in the way it is done."[11] The degree to which someone or something acts or performs its function with excellence or virtue, in turn, is the degree to which we can attribute "goodness" and "fulfillment" to that person or thing.

The excellences or virtues that are of primary concern for Aristotle are those that belong to one's *moral character.* Courage, for instance, might be regarded as a moral excellence, and the exercise of moral excellence or virtue would entail doing something in such a way that one's courageousness is expressed in how it is done. Again, moral excellences or virtues are traits that would allow for human beings to flourish in pursuing their ultimate function or purpose as human beings. To talk about moral virtues, then, we need to ask questions about the function of human beings, the purpose of human existence, and the qualities and characteristics that allow for human beings to fulfill those functions and flourish with respect to those purposes.

HUMAN FUNCTION AND PURPOSE

Aristotle would thus suggest that when we talk about the virtue, excellence, or goodness of a thing, we should understand it in relation to the function of that thing (i.e., what the thing is *for*). "Excellences" or virtues are traits that enable things to flourish in performing their intended functions or in fulfilling their purposes (e.g., a knife is *for* cutting and the sharpness of a knife is an excellence or virtue that assists in the performance of that function). If we know that the function of ears is to hear and the function of teachers is to impart knowledge, then we can deduce whether someone's ears are excellent and whether a given teacher is excellent. Both ears and teachers are excellent or virtuous to the extent that they fulfill their function. Logically, if we can know the function of human beings, we can know what it means to be an excellent or virtuous human being. What does Aristotle suggest is the function of human beings?

If we are looking for an answer that is provocative, controversial, or entertaining, we are not going to find it in Aristotle. However unsatisfying it may be to some, Aristotle's answer to this question is nevertheless an important one. Specifically, he claims that the function and purpose of human being, and thus the characteristic feature of human excellence, is *rational activity.* Our capacity to reason is what distinguishes us from all other living (and nonliving) things. Unlike pleasure and procreation (other common answers to the question of human purpose), higher-level reasoning is a characteristic that human beings do not share with other animals. Thus, the good or excellent human life must have something to do with making use of this distinctive capacity. Being excellent or virtuous is thus about utilizing and expressing our rational potential in our choices and actions.

For Aristotle, then, virtue is a kind of *practical use of reason,* whereby we utilize our specifically human capacity for reason and rational reflection to determine what choices to make and what actions to undertake. We will see shortly that the exercise of virtue is not as simple as being a certain way in a certain situation. For Aristotle, there are no easy answers to what types of choices or actions are virtuous in a given context. Instead, we have to "figure it out"—we must use *judgment*. In so doing, we are employing **practical wisdom** or *moral rationality*. When we lead our lives in such a way that we exercise practical wisdom or moral rationality, we are acting with virtue and we are living a fulfilled or "happy" human life.

THE ACTIVITY OF VIRTUE

In other words, for Aristotle, the fulfilled life is a life in which our specifically human capacity for rational activity is put to good use. We are well, happy, and flourish when we exercise virtue. Importantly, happiness and flourishing are *ways of doing things*. They are *activities*. Excellence or virtue, well-being and happiness are not about possessing something or attaining a certain condition or state of affairs; rather, they are about living our lives a certain way. A flourishing life is a life of *virtuous activity*. More specifically, flourishing involves the exercise of reason or practical wisdom as we make the choices that we do and engage in the actions we undertake while experiencing our lives. Before we turn to a closer examination of virtue and practical wisdom, let us conclude here with several summary points about Aristotle's conception of the "good life".

- The good life involves the possession of *good character*
- More specifically, the good life further involves living in such a way that one *expresses one's good character in one's choices and actions*
- Expressing virtue (moral character) in our choices and actions is the *foundation of well-being, happiness, and flourishing* (i.e., *eudaimonia*)
- Well-being, happiness, or flourishing is ultimately *what we aim at in life* (i.e., the highest good)
- In living a life according to virtue, we are flourishing and, in so doing, we are *fulfilling our very function or purpose as human beings*

VIRTUE AND HUMAN FLOURISHING

We have seen that, for Aristotle, everything in the world has some "inborn" purpose. Just as flowers blossom and caterpillars turn into butterflies, all things strive to fulfill their purpose—including human beings. Once we have identified these purposes, we can then talk about *what traits enable them to flourish* in fulfilling that purpose. Once we recognize that the purpose of a knife is to cut, for instance, we can ascertain that the trait of "sharpness" is that which allows it to excel at that purpose. In the context of human life, once we understand human purpose and what we aim for in life (i.e., the highest good), we can begin to talk about what *traits of character* and what types of behaviors are necessary for helping us live purposively. Virtues become moral excellences that enable humans to function well, and vices become precisely the opposite. In other words, we can redefine *virtue* and *vice* respectively as traits of character that promote human flourishing, and those that hinder it.

Consider, for instance, how embodying the virtue of courage might assist a person in living a good life (earning respect from peers, doing well in academic and athletic pursuits, interviewing for and getting a job); alternatively, consider how lacking the virtue of courage might inhibit a person in these same pursuits. Some traits of character clearly aid us in living a good life, while others such as envy and jealousy clearly interfere with this purpose.

Human Flourishing

Aristotle was interested in offering a generalized portrait of human well-being, happiness, and flourishing that applies to *all* people *everywhere*. In other words, Aristotle believed that, despite individual differences, all human beings are similar in certain respects. It is not differences between people that tell us something about human happiness and flourishing; rather, it is the similarities that we share as human beings that can help us to understand what it means to be well, flourish, and be happy. Though we depart somewhat from Aristotle's conception of human flourishing here, we might consider more recent philosophical and psychological insights into human well-being. Our interest in this section is in outlining what we can call "universal conditions of well-being, happiness, and flourishing"—those elements of being well, happy, and flourishing that are characteristic of and sought after by all people and, consequently, represent a foundation for thinking about virtues and vices, good and evil in relation to human life.

Biogenic Needs

At a most fundamental level, all human beings have basic biological needs that must be met as a *precondition* for the possibility of further well-being, happiness, and flourishing. How, for instance, can we expect the homeless person who struggles for food and warmth to spend time developing traits of character that will enable him to flourish? What we might call **biogenic needs** are those linked with the maintenance of life.[12] These include such universally-necessary and desired goods as food, housing, clothing, clean air, adequate medical care, exercise and physical recreation. To this we might also add goods such as safety and security that are necessary for biological survival (animals will go days without even food and water if they feel their physical safety is at risk). Each of these goods must necessarily be met *before* one can pursue higher goods. It will do little good, for instance, to encourage the homeless, starving, and physically ill person to pursue a life of compassion, justice, and generosity.

Cooperation

Fulfillment of biogenic needs is, however, not sufficient for well-being, happiness, and flourishing. As psychologist Erich Fromm (1900–1980) reminds us, "man does not live by bread alone."[13] Indeed, simply having one's basic biological needs fulfilled does not make for the "good life" in the sense in which Aristotle discussed it. In large part, this is because human beings also share another universal feature—in addition to being biological entities, we are also *social beings*. Our nature as human beings demands that we live in communities, cooperating with and depending upon one another—not merely for survival, but also to be well, happy, and flourish.

Aristotle recognized that human beings, like many other species of beings, are **social animals**. In other words, we are not best suited for solitary lives independent of other human beings. We live in *groups* because we must live in groups to survive and to have better opportunities for being well and flourishing. As *interdependent* creatures, our needs and desires are best met or satisfied by *cooperating* with others. If John is a good farmer yet knows nothing about managing finances or building houses, Liz has exceptional money-management skills yet knows little about farming and building houses, and Jane is adept at building houses but not so good with farming or money, then each stands to benefit from the others. Liz's financial talents do little for her flourishing if she has no house in which to live and no food to eat. The same logic applies to John and Jane. Although this is obviously an oversimplified example, it demonstrates Aristotle's point that human beings must live in groups if we are, collectively, to survive and flourish.

CONNECTEDNESS

Because we are social animals, destined to live interdependently and cooperatively in groups, we have other types of social needs that emerge from these living circumstances. We seem, for instance, to have needs for affection, love, friendship, and family, as well as those for belonging and to be "connected" in meaningful ways with other people. We thus depend on other people not only for survival and for purposes of meeting basic biological needs, but also to meet social and psychological needs.

The necessity that human beings live in groups to flourish creates consequent needs. While French existentialist philosopher Jean-Paul Sartre once suggested that "hell is—other people!,"[14] there is a sense in which life without other people would be equally hellish. Imagine, for instance, having to live the rest of your life on a deserted island or in solitary confinement in a prison.[15] Even if your basic needs were met, chances are you would not consider it a life of well-being, happiness, and flourishing. Humanistic philosopher Carliss Lamont once suggested that, ". . . people experience their deepest and most enduring joys, not as solitary hermits on some mountain top or desert isle, but in association with their peers, their friends, or their family."[16]

The Value of Virtue

Healthy, cooperative, and caring relationships with other people thus become necessary elements of the "good life." Much as life as social animals provides us with opportunities to flourish that we would not otherwise enjoy, it also creates difficulties that we would not experience in solitary circumstances. In short, group life means that we must be able to "get along" with one another. We must cooperate with one another, respect one another, care for one another and be considerate of one another's interests; we must reach compromises with others, be willing to sacrifice our own wants and desires for the sake of the needs of others; we must be able to resolve conflicts—ideally in constructive, nonviolent ways—when they arise; on the whole, we should be able to be well, happy, and flourish ourselves while contributing to the well-being, happiness, and flourishing of others. This, we might suggest, is precisely where the value of virtue is to be found.

Imagine, for instance, the difficulties that might arise in a family, organization, community, or society in which members are disposed toward selfishness, prejudice, envy, and intolerance. Not only will such persons be unhappy themselves, as Aristotle suggested, but their dispositions will give rise to a host of interpersonal conflicts and problems. In such a situation, we would no doubt find a family, organization, community, or society in which the possibility of well-being, happiness, and flourishing for *all* people would be substantially diminished—in fact, nearly impossible. Part of the value of the virtues is that they can assist us in overcoming these vices, thus allowing for meaningful, productive human relationships that benefit the well-being of all involved. Dispositions toward compassion, care, and concern for others, for instance, not only give rise to positive relationships (thus augmenting our own pursuit of happiness), but create a foundation for group life wherein all people have a better opportunity to realize their own potential and thus flourish as human beings.

Virtues, then, are not valuable in that they can get us money, status, power, or other instrumental goods; rather, virtues are good in that they allow us to pursue the ultimate or highest "good" of human existence—happiness or flourishing. The embodying and practice of virtue (and the avoidance or elimination of vice) will, in turn, provide the greatest opportunity to live a life of wellness, flourishing, and happiness and, simultaneously, provide the same sorts of opportunities for others. Thus virtues can be understood as all of those traits that in some way contribute to human well-being and flourishing, while vices are those traits that interfere with human well-being and flourishing or make them less likely.[17] With this in mind, let us look more specifically at the types of character traits that are typically regarded as virtues.

VIRTUE, WISDOM, AND THE "GOLDEN MEAN"

Of moral virtue, Aristotle suggested that it, "is concerned with feelings and actions, and these involve excess, deficiency, and a mean."[18] One of Aristotle's most widely discussed ideas on virtue is this notion of the **golden mean** (sometimes called the "doctrine of the mean"). Aristotle suggested that all virtues are *means between two extremes of deficiency and excess.* More specifically, he suggests of virtue that it is, "a mean between two kinds of vice, one of excess and the other of deficiency."[19] In any given situation and with regard to any given feeling or action, it is possible to have too much or too little of something. In both instances, what amounts is vice. On the other hand, we can find virtue by identifying these vices of deficiency and excess and finding the "middle road" between the two. It is possible, for instance, to feel too much anger, pity, or pleasure. It is equally possible to feel too little of these things. Virtue requires that we have such feelings, "at the right times on the right grounds towards the right people for the right motive and in the right way."[20] This "middle way" of feeling, he tells us, "is the mark of virtue."

For every type of feeling, Aristotle is suggesting, there is some form of it that would be considered excessive and some form of it that would be regarded as deficient. The same applies for every type of action:

- "For both excessive and insufficient exercise destroy one's strength, and both eating and drinking too much or too little destroy health, whereas the right quantity produces, increases and preserves it."[21]
- In cases where we face danger, being "cowardly" would constitute a moral deficiency, whereas being "foolhardy" would constitute a moral excess. The mean lying between the vicious extremes of cowardliness and foolhardiness is the virtue of *courage.*
- With regard to how we should feel about ourselves and our own accomplishments, we might recognize as vices the excessive trait of arrogance (thinking *too much* of oneself) and the deficient trait of servility (thinking *too little* of oneself). Somewhere between these vices of deficiency and excess lies a middle ground that entails "self-respect" and "self-esteem," or what Aristotle called "proper pride." Self-respect and self-esteem can benefit one's well-being,

happiness, and flourishing, while traits such as servility and arrogance will have a detrimental impact on this pursuit.

The Golden Mean and Practical Wisdom

Recall that Aristotle suggested that virtue had to do with practical wisdom. This link with human reason and rationality is most evident in his conception of virtue as a mean. Supposing we know that courage is a virtue, what exactly is a courageous act? Aristotle in no way meant for his doctrine of the mean to serve as a "science" of ethical decision-making and behavior. In fact, he tells us that virtue and morality are in no way exact. Instead, they are *situational*—what may be courageous for one person may be cowardly for another, and what may be courageous in one situation may be cowardly in another.[22] The exercise of virtue demands that we exercise practical wisdom in any given situation.[23]

In other words, virtue requires *experimentation*. It requires that we *engage in life*. Persons of practical wisdom "have developed skills to make the right decision at the right moment and to act efficiently on those decisions."[24] A courageous act is one that a person of practical wisdom deems to be courageous at a given moment in a given situation. As there is no "quick and easy" definition of virtue and virtuous behavior that can apply to all persons in all situations, the exercise of virtue requires that we practice, learn from our experiences, and make an effort to continually develop our moral character. While some traits are inborn, the moral virtues must be developed. They are *habits* of character, and habits are developed through *practice*. We learn the virtues by exercising them regularly. In Aristotle's terms:

> Anything that we have to learn to do we learn by the actual doing of it. People become builders by building and instrumentalists by playing instruments. Similarly we become just by performing just acts, temperate by performing temperate ones, brave by performing brave ones.[25]

Aristotle's Virtues

Aristotle named only a handful of virtues, including the "intellectual" virtues of wisdom and prudence, and the "moral" virtues of courage, temperance, liberality (i.e., generosity), magnificence, proper pride, gentleness, truthfulness, justice, patience, friendliness, modesty, and wittiness. In relation to these named virtues, his "golden mean" looks something like this:

Deficiency (Vice)	Mean (Virtue)	Excess (Vice)
Cowardice	*Courage*	Foolhardiness
Inhibition	*Temperance*	Overindulgence/intemperance
Miserliness	*Liberality*	Prodigality/extravagance
Shabbiness	*Magnificence*	Bad taste/vulgarity
Lack of ambition	*Proper pride*	Ambitiousness
Poor-spiritedness	*Gentleness*	Irascibility
Peevishness	*Friendliness*	Obsequiousness/flattery

Deficiency (Vice)	Mean (Virtue)	Excess (Vice)
Maliciousness	*Righteous indignation*	Envy
Sarcasm	*Truthfulness*	Boastfulness
Boorishness	*Wittiness*	Buffoonery
Shamelessness	*Modesty*	Shamefacedness

We can also think of vices of excess and deficiency as they appear in our attitudes toward ourselves and our attitudes toward others. Contemporary moral philosopher Lawrence Hinman gives us the following list:[26]

Attitude Toward Self

	Vices of Deficiency	Virtues	Vices of Excess
Attitude Toward Self	Self-deprivation; Servility	Proper self-love; Proper pride; Self-respect	Arrogance; Egoism; Narcissism; Vanity
Attitude Toward our Own Offenses	Indifference; Remorselessness; Downplaying	Agent regret; Remorse; Making amends; Learning from them; Self-forgiveness	Toxic guilt; Scrupulosity; Shame
Attitude Toward our Own Good Deeds	Belittling; Disappointment	Sense of accomplishment; Humility	Self-righteousness
Attitude Toward our Own Desires	Adhedonia	Temperance; Moderation	Lust; Gluttony

Attitude Toward Others

	Vices of Deficiency	Virtues	Vices of Excess
Attitude Toward Other People	Exploitation	Respect	Deference
Attitude Toward Offenses of Others	Ignoring them; Being a doormat	Anger; Forgiveness; Understanding	Revenge; Grudge; Resentment
Attitude Toward Good Deeds of Others indebtedness	Suspicion; Envy; Ignoring them	Gratitude; Admiration	Over-
Attitude Toward Suffering of Others	Callousness	Compassion	Pity; "Bleeding heart"

The Unity of Virtue

Finally, we should point out that, even though it is common to discuss the virtues as though they were individual traits, Aristotle reminds us that virtue is better regarded as an "overarching quality of goodness or excellence that gives unity and integrity to a person's character."[27] On this note, we can think of virtuous people not only as those who exhibit virtuous traits, but as those who serve as examples to follow—as *role models for moral behavior*. They are people who can be "counted on to act in a manner that benefits others" and who show a "willingness to perform supererogatory actions—going beyond what is required by everyday morality."[28] Rather than a collection of personality traits, then, virtue is best thought of as a unifying concept.[29] A "good person" is virtuous in the sense of having a more global disposition to act in ways that benefit herself or himself and others.

VIRTUE AND THE CRIMINAL JUSTICE SYSTEM: THE ETHIC OF CARE AND PEACEMAKING CRIMINOLOGY

As we have seen, virtue ethics emphasizes moral character, the embodiment of virtue in one's decisions and actions, and the avoidance of vice. By conventional conceptions, however, some virtues seem largely incompatible with criminal justice. While it is customary (perhaps expected!) to extol bravery and honesty as admirable qualities among criminal justice professionals, it is less customary (and less expected!) to consider compassion, mercy, and love as necessary (or even desirable) qualities among police officers, judges, prosecutors, prison guards, and others in the practice community. However, some critics of the status quo would argue that conventional conceptions and methods are not the most effective or morally-desirable means of pursuing justice. As John Fuller reminds us about the future of criminal justice, "The next generation of criminal justice practitioners . . . will be responsible for determining the nature, tone, and philosophy of how we deal with those who break the law."[30] What follows is a discussion of two alternative approaches that may seem quite different from traditional conceptions of criminal justice and which, in many ways, fit within the broader tradition of virtue. As you read through the remainder of this section, consider whether these alternative philosophies might be a meaningful part of the future of criminal justice.

Justice and the Ethic of Care

In Chapter 7 we were briefly introduced to Carol Gilligan's research on gender differences in moral development and moral reasoning. Gilligan's insights, along with those of Nel Noddings and others, are sometimes referenced as grounds for an alternative moral framework that emphasizes *care* and related virtues such as compassion, tolerance, and benevolence. The **ethic of care** stresses relationships, situational and contextual factors, and the unique needs and interests of affected parties as key considerations in the face of conflicts and dilemmas. Although the implications of caring as an ethic have not been fully developed within criminal justice studies, it raises some important questions about (and criticisms of) many current criminal justice policies and practices. In this section, we briefly review the fundamentals of care ethics, contrasting it with conventional models of morality and justice, and conclude by suggesting several possible implications for criminal justice.

THE ETHIC OF CARE

Based on her research, Gilligan suggests that there are two fundamentally different orientations toward moral scenarios—one more characteristic of, but not limited to, males, the other more characteristic of, but not limited to, females. The "male" orientation (termed the *rights/justice orientation*) is more consistent with the dominant mode of Western moral reasoning that perceives the world as comprised of isolated, independent, rights-bearing individuals. Through this lens, justice is a matter of impartially and universally applying laws, rules, procedures, and principles to the case at hand.[31]

The alternative mode of moral reasoning—that which is more "feminine" in nature and presumed to reflect a lower level of moral development than the rights/justice orientation—is that of "care/response." The *care/response orientation* conceives morality "contextually and in terms of interpersonal relationships and connections."[32] Rather than isolated, independent individuals, we are each fundamentally interdependent and connected to one another; rather than justice being linked with impartiality and universally-applicable rules, it is best understood in relation to the situation and the particular or unique needs and interests of all parties involved.[33]

In contrast with those models of morality that emphasize individual rights, moral duties, and impersonal and abstract principles, care ethics can be thought of as a form of virtue ethics. Specifically, it places focus on attitudes and dispositions such as empathy, compassion, love, benevolence, generosity, and tolerance. "Care" is thus not a principle that should or must be followed, but a way-of-being or way of perceiving, experiencing, and responding to the world.

Especially important to a caring disposition is that we be *mindful*—seeking to understand and know the needs and interests of others and take these into consideration in our moral reasoning. We must "take on the standpoint or role of others . . . We must imaginatively project ourselves into the emerging dramas of *their* lives . . ." Consider the problem of homelessness. Being mindful, compassionate, and caring might entail imagining what it would be like to be homeless and thereby becoming connected to the nature of that form of suffering; ". . . being upset, distressed, regretting the different aspects of [the] plight" of the homeless, and wishing that such suffering did not exist; and "giving thought to what might be done to alleviate" that suffering.[34] It is not so much that we feel a moral duty or obligation to aid the homeless, but that we perceive ourselves as being connected to them through their suffering, and this connection inclines us to act in benevolent ways and to avoid causing further harm or exploitation (see Box 10.4).

CARE AND CRIMINAL JUSTICE

Seeking to know others and project ourselves into their situations is not only the basis of caring, but arguably is crucial to justice as well. It is this element of the ethic of care that is perhaps most relevant to the resolution of conflicts, cases, and issues in the realm of criminal justice. Those promoting an ethic of care would point out that the American criminal justice system leaves little—if any—room for the types of considerations that are central to caring. The American legal system, for instance, operates largely according to the "rights/justice" approach. Judges are expected to decide cases

BOX 10.4

Caring, Suffering, and the Perception of Desert

Especially important to an ethic of care is that we recognize that, despite our superficial differences, we are all similar in important respects. We are, for instance, "fellow sufferers"—we know, on some level, what it is like to suffer physically and emotionally. Whether we have limited food to eat, not enough money to pay bills, are victims of crime and abuse, grapple with a debilitating illness, or are shunned by friends, suffering is an experience to which all of us can relate. Because it is universal, suffering is perhaps the most fundamental way in which we are all connected to one another. Recognizing this connectedness allows us to increase our awareness of and sensitivity toward the pains and struggles of others.

Indeed, suffering is a fundamental human experience that cuts across social divisions such as race, class, gender, religion, and age. Moreover, it does not discriminate between those who deserve it and those who do not. However, we often perceive suffering as something experienced only by those who do not deserve to deal with the situation in which they find themselves—the undeserved suffering of innocent children, crime victims, persons afflicted with disease, and the like. In contrast, others are perceived as deserving of their condition and, consequently, may be considered less worthy of our care and sympathy. Aristotle made precisely this point in his discussion of the virtue, noting that our experience and exercise of compassion may be tied to our perception of whether a fellow sufferer *deserves* her or his suffering. In other words, our belief about whether suffering is justified may interfere with our capacity to relate to others in compassionate ways.

In a study of contemporary American attitudes, for example, Candice Clark found that sympathy is less forthcoming when we perceive suffering to result from malfeasance, negligence, risk-taking, or when it is perceived as in some way being brought on by the sufferer's own actions. Poverty may be regarded as a deserved form of suffering if perceived in terms of personal responsibility rather than economic forces or "bad luck," and even sexual assault victims are sometimes regarded as provoking or precipitating their own victimization. In the context of criminal offending, of course, we regularly regard the suffering of legal punishment as deserved—even as "justice."

Even in such cases where persons "deserve" to suffer by most accounts, the absence of compassion is not justifiable from a care or virtue perspective. How are we to have compassion for a convicted criminal offender? As moral philosopher Lawrence Blum suggests, we can ". . . have compassion for someone in a difficult or miserable situation without judging his overall condition to be difficult or miserable." In other words, it is possible to regard the condition of imprisonment as just and deserved without losing our compassionate awareness for the suffering an offender endures as a consequence of that imprisonment (e.g., isolation, separation from family, victimization by other offenders).

How might we "care" in such a situation? If compassion inclines us to refrain from adding more suffering to those who already suffer, what policies and practices might we support (or oppose) within jails and prisons? As is often argued with regard to imprisonment, offenders are sent to prison *as* punishment, not *for* it. Combined with compassionate awareness, what implications might this logic have for how we treat incarcerated criminals?

Source: Candice Clark, *Misery and Company: Sympathy and Everyday Life* (Chicago: University of Chicago Press, 1999); Lawrence Blum, "Compassion." In A. Rorty (ed.), *Explaining Emotions* (Berkeley: University of California Press, 1980).

with reference to the rule of law and legal precedent; to approach cases in an impartial, unbiased fashion and decide similar cases in a like-minded fashion. In other words, the same resolution (e.g., determination of guilt, sentencing decision) may be applicable in many different cases, so long as the *legal* facts of those cases are similar.

The ethic of care would seem to promote a radically different approach to the resolution of legal cases. Rule of law, legal precedent, and legal facts would be less important considerations than contextual or situational factors. As we have seen, the ethic of care centralizes contexts, situations, and relationships. Justice cannot follow from the application of universal rules and principles; rather, justice emerges when we attend to the uniqueness of human situations and of the people involved in those situations. Resolving conflicts in both criminal and civil spheres would require that judges come to know the details of a particular situation, the persons involved in and affected by that situation, and make a determination on the basis of those particulars—not, as traditional conceptions of law and justice would have it, on the basis of a law, rule, principle, or precedent that is meant to apply to all similar cases. In a criminal case, for instance, this may mean that judges would need to make an effort to "know" the defendant, consider her or his life circumstances and motives, and take these into consideration when making a ruling.

A contemporary criminal justice trend that would seem to be at odds with this type of approach is the movement toward **determinate sentencing** schemes. Many states have now implemented sentencing guidelines that severely restrict the amount of discretion judges have in deciding sentences in individual cases. Consequently, judges are unable (or less able) to take situational and circumstantial factors into consideration. Instead, judges are forced to impose sentences within a limited range that is defined by legislatures. For example, an offender convicted of a residential burglary might be sentenced to twenty-three months in prison, as mandated by sentencing guidelines, regardless of the circumstances of the crime or the offender. In theory, determinate sentencing produces uniformity, proportionality, and equity in sentencing decisions. On the other hand, it prevents judges from considering the types of situational factors that an ethic of care might otherwise showcase.

Beyond judicial decisions, the ethic of care would seem to have relevance for a range of decisions and decision-makers in criminal justice settings. In policing, for example, caring would entail officers seeking to know the people and circumstances involved in the situations they confront on a daily basis. Approaching law enforcement scenarios in this way would require individual officers to make liberal use of discretionary powers, considering the needs and interests of all parties involved in a conflict or situation before resolving it. To illustrate, not all persons who violate the law would require arrest. In at least some cases, the needs and interests of lawbreakers, victims, and the public may be better served by *not* making an arrest (or *not* ticketing traffic violators, etc.). This is commonly referred to as **selective enforcement** of the law. Because situations and the people involved in them are unique, the same approach may not be desirable in all factually similar cases. On the other hand, critics of selective enforcement have argued that allowing officers to rely on their own judgment (including moral sensibilities) in deciding when to make arrests markedly increases the likelihood of discrimination, favoritism, and other undesirable influences affecting decision-making. In other words, discretion *might not always be used in the interest of care* (see Box 10.5).

BOX 10.5
Domestic Violence and Mandatory Arrest Policies

A good example of a conflict situation involving relationships and unique needs and interests—yet for which the breadth of officer discretion has been criticized—is that of *domestic violence*. Historically, domestic violence offenders were not always—or even often—arrested. Decisions about whether to arrest, separate the parties for a temporary "cooling off" period, attempt to mediate the dispute, refer the couple to counseling, or employ some other means of resolving the conflict were largely in the hands of the officer(s). In part because of concerns raised by victim advocates, some police agencies have implemented **mandatory arrest policies** that *require* police officers to make an arrest wherever possible. Nonarrest often requires written justification, and failure to follow departmental policy may result in disciplinary action against the officer. Do such policies potentially undermine the possibility of exercising an ethic of care? Consider whether any or all of the following *should* influence how domestic violence scenarios are handled by law enforcement officers:

- Whether the couple is married, separated, divorced, etc.
- Whether the victim and offender are of the same sex
- The potential financial consequences of making an arrest (for one or both parties)
- Whether there is a history of prior incidents
- Whether alcohol or drugs are involved
- The emotional state of the victim
- The emotional state of the offender
- The extent of injuries
- The victim's expressed desires

Source: William Doerner and Steven Lab, *Victimology*, 2nd ed. (Cincinnati: Anderson, 1998), pp. 151–153.

Do the benefits of adopting a care orientation in judicial and law enforcement decision-making outweigh the potentially negative consequences of selective enforcement and individualized sentences? Should judges, juries, police and correctional officers, and others involved in the criminal justice system embody an ethic of care when deciding cases or making decisions? Do virtues such as compassion, mercy, tolerance, and benevolence have a place in criminal justice? From a care perspective, these are precisely the questions that we should be asking ourselves. Further, our answers to these and related questions might have a profound impact on the future of criminal justice practice.

Peacemaking Criminology

Peacemaking is a relatively recent perspective in criminology, though its core values and principles—like the tradition of virtue—have an historical basis dating back thousands of years. Peacemaking criminologists have borrowed heavily from Buddhist, Christian, and Islamic religious traditions, as well as from spiritual and humanist figures such as Jesus, Gandhi, and Martin Luther King Jr. As the name implies, **peacemaking criminology** suggests a need to centralize *peace*, encompassing virtues such as nonharm, care, compassion, and love, in our relationships with ourselves, others, and in the policies and practices of our institutions (e.g., education, politics, criminal justice).[35] In this respect, peacemaking shares much in common with and draws considerably from the broader moral tradition of virtue.

Although peacemaking has practical implications for criminal justice, it is perhaps best regarded as a global alternative to the "war" perspective which has come to dominate criminal justice thinking, policy, and practice and which arguably pervades our relationships and characterizes many of our institutional practices (e.g., punishment, death penalty, and war). Its overarching emphasis on peace and nonviolent problem-solving stands in sharp contrast to the largely ineffective and morally-undesirable "fight fire with fire" approach. Peacemaking emphasizes participation in meaningful communities and, in this respect, promises "long-lasting solutions not only to the problems of crime, but also for the issues and controversies that create crime."[36]

Why do we *need* an alternative to the "war" perspective? Peacemaking criminologists ask us to consider whether the wars on crime and drugs, for instance, have produced any real results? As John Fuller ponders, "Is the crime situation getting better? Are our communities safer? Are prisons doing their job [of rehabilitating criminals]?"[37] It would seem that the "tough on crime" approach and its corresponding policies and practices have not only failed to produce positive results, but may have actually *caused more harm than good*. Much of what has been carried out under the guidance of the war-making philosophy has quite possibly done little other than perpetuate existing cycles of violence and harm and reinforce existing social problems.

THE PRINCIPLES AND PRACTICE OF PEACEMAKING

A principle insight of peacemaking criminology is the extent to and ways in which we do violence to ourselves, others, our communities, societies, and the greater environment. Perhaps more importantly, peacemaking criminologists draw attention to the extent to and ways in which we often *use* violence as a response or reaction to the violence we encounter (e.g., capital punishment for murderers). Doing so, they argue, serves only to create more and greater violence—to amplify the cumulative extent of harm and suffering in the world. In place of policies and practices that counter violence with more violence, we should seek alternative responses that promote the greater goals of peace and healing for all parties affected.

Nonviolent problem-solving and the goals of peace and healing are not limited to the practices of our institutions. Peacemaking is an overarching philosophy which provides a means of addressing various problems on personal and social levels. More specifically, peacemaking criminologist John Fuller suggests four levels to which the basic principles and insights of peacemaking might be applicable:[38]

- *Intrapersonal*—encompassing the ways in which we think and feel about ourselves, as well as how we treat ourselves. Various prison programs, for instance, have encouraged personal growth and development. Religious services, meditation, weightlifting, and yoga are "ways for inmates to develop self-discipline and a healthy self-concept."[39]

- *Interpersonal*—encompassing the ways in which we think and feel about others, as well as how we treat others. Peacemaking promotes the Golden Rule—"Do unto others as you would have others do unto you." As well, interpersonal virtues such as compassion are especially relevant here.
- *Societal and institutional*—encompassing the policies and practices of our social institutions, including education, politics, media, and law/criminal justice. Our social institutions should strive to embody the values and virtues promoted by peacemaking more generally, and to model pro-social behavior and nonviolent problem-solving.
- *Global*—encompassing policies and practices that affect people of other nations, as well as the environment in which we exist. As relationships between nations are often characterized by war and conflict, peacemaking argues that we must strive toward cooperative and mutually-advantageous relationships.

As violence operates at each of these levels and as every level is interrelated, we should not be surprised to find "wars" existing between nations, on the streets of our communities, in our classrooms, in our bedrooms, and even within ourselves. Importantly, because of the interrelatedness between these levels, if we can begin to change one, we begin to change the others as well. How do we go about making such changes? In part, according to Fuller, by practicing a series of key principles at each of these levels:[40]

- *Non-violence.* As the goal of peacemaking is to stop the cycles of violence in all spheres, violence should be used only as a last resort. While never using violence may not be a feasible option—especially given the nature of criminal justice work—we should always be mindful of and seek to employ alternatives to violence in every situation.
- *Social justice.* As we saw in Chapter 1, criminal justice and social justice are always interrelated. As a society and within the criminal justice system we should seek to eliminate racism, sexism, and inequalities linked with race, class, gender, age, and sexual orientation. Promoting equal rights, equal opportunities, and cooperation can go a long way toward reducing violence, improving communities, and creating a social climate characterized by virtue and peace.
- *Inclusion.* Rather than justice simply being imposed upon the offender, we should seek the participation of all affected parties working toward a resolution to the justice process. The offender, victim, victim's family, offender's family, and representatives from law enforcement and the community should work cooperatively to resolve a dispute or create a sentence.
- *Correct means.* Derived from Gandhi, correct means requires us to pursue the good ends of peacemaking through morally good means. Correct means are nonviolent, compassionate, and cooperative. Within criminal justice, correct means requires us to recognize and respect the constitutional and civil rights of suspects and offenders, treating them "fairly, equitably, and without rancor or deception."[41]

- *Ascertainable criteria.* Everyone who participates in the criminal justice process should "have a clear understanding of the rules and procedures employed by the criminal justice system."[42] As an example, offenders should be fully aware of their options and the implications of pursuing those options before accepting a plea bargain.
- *Categorical imperative.* Borrowed from Kant, the categorical imperative requires us to make decisions that could be applied to all other similar cases and to avoid using people as a means to an end. While discretion is a desirable part of criminal justice, decisions based on racial prejudice and other forms of bias should be eliminated.

PEACEMAKING AND RESTORATIVE JUSTICE

Following the basic principles outlined above in all spheres of our lives can help to create and sustain the types of "meaningful communities characterized by harmony, mutual cooperation, and peace" that peacemaking envisions.[43] Yet how, more specifically, do these principles translate into practice in the realm of criminal justice? One way to apply peacemaking principles to the criminal justice system is through the emerging paradigm of restorative justice. **Restorative justice** focuses on repairing harms caused by criminal offending through programs that seek to involve the offender, the victim, and the community in the restorative process.[44] As traditional approaches to criminal justice focus almost exclusively on the offender, restorative justice is argued to provide an alternative that allows for the forgotten victim as well as representatives from the community to become involved in forging a solution that benefits all parties involved.[45]

One of the more popular and widely used restorative justice programs is Victim-Offender Reconciliation. **Victim-Offender Reconciliation Programs** (**VORP**) bring offenders and victims together in a setting that promotes a healthy interaction between them. Under the guidance of a trained mediator, victims have the opportunity to explain the harm that was caused by the offender and the ways in which the criminal event has affected their lives. The offender, in turn, has an opportunity to explain her or his motivations to the victim. As John Fuller writes,

> Sometimes all the victim wants is to tell his or her story to the offender and receive an apology. Sometimes the offender welcomes the opportunity to confess his or her transgression without fear that the court will use it to impose a harsh sentence.[46]

Overall, as "each side learns more about the humaneness and circumstances of the other, they are able to craft solutions" that identify the injustice, make things right, and establish mechanisms for future action.[47]

Victim-Offender Reconciliation Programs, as well as other restorative justice programs such as *family group conferencing* and *victim-offender panels* seek to reinvolve the victim and the community in a legal process that has lost sight of them. Justice, some have argued, requires that victims, offenders, and communities be healed, and that all involved parties are offered an opportunity to participate in the healing or restorative process.[48] Doing so not only repairs the harm caused, but arguably does much more for the prevention of future offending than traditional models of criminal justice.

SUMMARY

Virtue ethics differs from consequentialist and deontological ethics in the very question with which it begins. Rather than asking the question, "What should I *do*?" virtue ethics insists that we ask a different normative question—"What kind of person should I *be*?" In so doing, the virtue tradition displaces emphasis on duties and consequences and shifts it to considerations of moral character—on "being" a certain kind of person instead of "doing" certain kinds of actions or bringing about certain types of consequences. *Character* is thus emphasized more than duties, principles, rules, or consequences. This is not to say, however, that we should understand character as entirely independent of actions and consequences. Many would argue that "being" certain kinds of people means we are disposed toward "doing" certain kinds of actions, while those kinds of actions, in turn, have a tendency to produce certain types of consequences.

Historically, it is this emphasis on *being* as opposed to *doing* that distinguishes virtue ethics from other moral theories. Importantly, people who embody virtues—those disposed to *be* kind, caring, compassionate, forgiving, respectful, generous, and just—act out of a genuine respect and concern for the well-being of themselves and others. Compassion, for example, does not stem from a commitment to the principle of compassion, conformity to a duty to be compassionate, or a thoughtful and rational consideration of the consequences of being compassionate. Instead, people who act out of compassion tend to *be* compassionate people. Mother Teresa—perhaps the quintessential exemplar of the compassionate character—was not exercising compassion in the interest of acting morally; rather, her compassion was a function of her character as a compassionate person. It is for this reason that the virtue perspective regards right actions and good consequences as less morally significant than developing good habits of character that dispose us to do the right thing or incline us to act in a certain fashion. If we are disposed, by way of our character, to be compassionate, caring, forgiving, and so on, our actions will naturally follow from these dispositions or traits of character.

KEY TERMS AND CONCEPTS

biogenic needs

character

character trait

determinate sentencing

ethic of care

eudaimonia

golden mean

mandatory arrest policies

moral vices

moral virtues

peacemaking criminology

practical wisdom (moral rationality)

restorative justice

selective enforcement

social animals

teleological

Victim-Offender Reconciliation Programs (VORP)

DISCUSSION QUESTIONS

1. Describe in detail the difference between moral virtue and moral vice. As you think about criminal justice professionals (e.g., police officers, probation/parole officers, lawyers) list the five characteristics that you would argue are most typical of the character of these types of professionals. Are these characteristics virtues or vices? Finally, list five characteristics that you feel would be ideal or desirable for such professionals to embody.

2. Using an example from juvenile justice (e.g., teenage prostitution, underage drinking, waiver to the adult system, execution), explore how a virtuous or vicious character can give rise to "good" intentions, "right" actions, and "good" consequences.

3. Recalling the section of this chapter on virtue and the good life, what is the end to which criminal justice is directed? To what extent is this end consistent with the highest good as described by Aristotle? Use examples to explain and/or justify your response.

4. What is the function and purpose of the criminal justice system? To what extent are these functions and purposes consistent with Aristotle's notion of the "good life"? To what extent do these functions and purposes promote or fail to promote the good life for citizens? Be specific!

5. Explain the relationship between virtue and human flourishing. In what ways are biogenic needs, cooperation, and connectedness important to this relationship? Do you believe that the adult and juvenile justice systems are structured to support these values? If not, what does this tell you about virtue ethics and the overall criminal justice system?

6. As the ethic of care requires us to consider situational factors before making decisions, what types of situational factors might be important in determining whether an arrest needs to be made in the following cases: solicitation of prostitution, possession of small quantities of illicit substances, a simple assault stemming from a drunken verbal confrontation at a bar, public intoxication, loitering.

SUGGESTED READINGS

Aristotle. (1976). *Ethics.* J. A. K. Thomson (trans.). New York: Penguin.

Baumeister, Roy. (1997). *Evil: Inside Human Violence and Cruelty.* New York: W. H. Freeman.

Beck, Aaron. (1999). *Prisoners of Hate: The Cognitive Basis of Anger, Hostility, and Violence.* New York: HarperCollins.

Hamilton, Christopher. (2001). *Living Philosophy: Reflections on Life, Meaning, and Morality.* Edinburgh: Edinburgh University Press.

Lazarus, Richard, and Lazarus, Bernice. (1994). *Passion and Reason: Making Sense of Our Emotions.* New York: Oxford University Press.

Solomon, Robert. (1999). *Wicked Pleasures: Meditations on the Seven "Deadly" Sins.* Lanham, MD: Rowman & Littlefield.

ENDNOTES

[1] Emmett Barcalow, *Moral Philosophy: Theories and Issues* (Belmont, CA: Wadsworth, 1998), p. 99.

[2] Ibid.

[3] Ibid.

[4] Cf. Emmett Barcalow, *Moral Philosophy*, p. 107.

[5] Judith A. Boss, *Ethics for Life* (Mountain View, CA: Mayfield, 2001), p. 402.

[6] Emmett Barcalow, *Moral Philosophy*, p. 99

[7] Ibid., p.107.

[8] Philippa Foot, "Virtues and Vices." In Joram Haber, *Doing and Being: Selected Readings in Moral Philosophy* (New York: Macmillan, 1993), p. 301. Originally published in Philippa Foot, *Virtues and Vices and Other Essays in Moral Philosophy* (1978).

[9] Aristotle, *Ethics*, J. A. K. Thomson (trans.) (New York: Penguin, 1976).

[10] Ibid, p. 63.

[11] Gerald Hughes, *Aristotle: On Ethics* (New York: Routledge, 2001), p. 23.

[12] Paul Kurtz, *Embracing the Power of Humanism* (Lanham, MD, Roman & Littlefield 2000), pp. 25–34.

[13] Erich Fromm, *Man for Himself: An Inquiry into the Psychology of Ethics* (New York: Fawcett, 1965), p. 55.

[14] Jean-Paul Sartre, *No Exit* (New York: Vintage Books, 1955), p. 47.

[15] Emmett Barcalow, *Moral Philosophy*, p. 111.

[16] Carliss Lamont, *The Philosophy of Humanism* (New York: Humanist Press, 1997), p. 273.

[17] Emmett Barcalow, *Moral Philosophy*, p. 109.

[18] Aristotle, *Ethics*, p. 101.

[19] Ibid., p. 102.

[20] Ibid., p. 101.

[21] Ibid., p. 94.

[22] Donald Palmer, *Visions of Human Nature: An Introduction* (Mountain View, CA: Mayfield, 2000), p. 56.

[23] Ibid.

[24] Ibid.

[25] Aristotle, Ethics, pp. 91–92.

[26] Lawrence Hinman, *Ethics: A Pluralistic Approach to Moral Theory* (Fort Worth, TX: Harcourt Brace, 2003), p. 280.

[27] Judith Boss, *Ethics for Life*, p. 402.

[28] Ibid., p. 403.

[29] Ibid., p. 426.

[30] John Fuller, *Criminal Justice: Mainstream and Crosscurrents* (Upper Saddle River, NJ: Prentice Hall, 2006) p. 538.

[31] M. Kay Harris, "Moving into the New Millennium: Toward a Feminist Vision of Justice." In H. Pepinsky and R. Quinney (Eds.) *Criminology as peacemaking* (Bloomington, IN: Indiana University Press, 1991), p. 89.

[32]Ibid.

[33]Ibid.

[34]Lawrence Blum, "Compassion." In A. Rorty (ed.), *Explaining Emotions* (Berkeley: University of California Press, 1980), p. 511.

[35]John Fuller, *Criminal Justice: A Peacemaking Perspective* (Boston: Allyn & Bacon, 1998).

[36]John Fuller, *Criminal Justice: Mainstream and Crosscurrents,* (Upper Saddle River, NJ: Pearson Prentice Hall, 2006), p. 553.

[37]Ibid., 552.

[38]John Fuller, *Criminal Justice: A Peacemaking Perspective.*

[39]John Fuller, *Criminal Justice: Mainstream and Crosscurrents*, p. 555.

[40]Ibid., pp. 556–559.

[41]Ibid., p. 558; see also, Dennis Sullivan and Larry Tifft, *Restorative Justice: Healing the Foundations of Our Everyday Life*, 2nd ed. (Monsey, NY: Criminal Justice Press, 2005).

[42]Ibid., p. 558.

[43]Ibid., p. 553.

[44]Gordon Bazemore and Mara Schiff, *Restorative Community Justice: Repairing Harms and Transforming Communities* (Cincinnati, OH: Anderson, 2001).

[45]Michael Braswell, John Fuller, and Bo Lozoff, *Corrections, Peacemaking, and Restorative Justice: Transforming Individuals and Institutions* (Cincinnati: Anderson, 2001).

[46]John Fuller, *Criminal Justice: Mainstream and Crosscurrents*, p. 561.

[47]Ibid., p. 561.

[48]D. Van Ness and K. Strong, *Restoring Justice* (Cincinnati, OH: Anderson, 1997).

Chapter 11

THE EXAMINED LIFE: A GUIDE TO MORAL THINKING AND DECISION-MAKING

Morality is ultimately about the choices we make and the actions we undertake (or fail to take) as a result of our decisions. Whether our choices are informed by our character, our commitment to moral duties and principles, our obligations, or a rational consideration of the potential consequences of our actions, moral goodness is ultimately reflected in morally-good choices. Yet what makes a choice "good"? For example, on what grounds can we say that one's decision to support the death penalty, to endorse racial profiling as a legitimate method of policing, or to promote the waiver of juveniles to the adult criminal justice system is, indeed, morally justified or "sound"? On what grounds can we say that one's decision to "rat on" a fellow police officer, to "look the other way" when stopping a friend for driving under the influence, or to accept bribes from drug dealers is morally unjustified? On what grounds can we claim that our choice to be truthful with a friend or colleague even though in doing so considerable harm comes to a third party was the "right" one? What *conditions* make decisions morally right or wrong, good or bad?

Recall from Chapter 1 that while "morality" has to do with *people's beliefs about right and wrong, good and bad, and the choices they make and the actions that they take as a result of those beliefs,* "ethics" has more to do with *critically reflecting on moral values, beliefs, choices, and actions.* As a process of critically reflecting on morality, ethics should not simply describe moral issues and present moral perspectives; rather, ethics should also offer us some *strategies* that can be *used* to determine what position we should take on moral issues and what choices we should make in given moral contexts. Determining what position to take on moral issues such as capital punishment, racial profiling, or abortion requires a thorough analysis of the issue, utilizing principles of reasoning as well as whatever evidence we have available. Determining how we should choose or what we should do in a given situation requires the same sort of analysis—in this case, not of the issue, but of the situation, its circumstances, and how moral values and principles might be *applied* in that situation.

In this portion of *Ethics, Crime, and Criminal Justice*, we outline a number of concerns with specific relevance to moral decision-making. In a way, we hope that readers will understand what follows as a collection of "tools" that can be used as aids in moral choice-making. Though admittedly not exhaustive, our aim is to assist crime and justice professionals as they confront any number of possible moral issues and dilemmas in their everyday personal and professional lives. The observations that follow might be thought of as a practical "guide" for ethical choice-making and behavior. The types of skills and tools emphasized are *essential* components of morality. They help us make sound moral judgments, and these judgments or choices become the basis for undertaking right actions. Arguably, if these skills and tools become a part of how the criminal justice professional approaches moral dilemmas, they help to ensure that the person will lead a life built on character, integrity, and virtue.

JUSTIFYING BELIEFS AND DECISIONS

This is perhaps the most important point to be made about moral beliefs and ethical decision-making. The ethical life requires that we make good decisions, and good decisions are *justified* decisions. To say that a particular choice, decision, belief, action, law, policy, practice, punishment, or sentence is "justified" is to be able to show that *there are good reasons for it*. Beyond this, justification also requires that we be able to show that our "good reasons" are better than those for alternative decisions, policies, and so forth. While you may be able to produce good reasons for being dishonest at a court appearance, if there are better reasons for being honest, we cannot claim that dishonesty is a justified choice.

- *We cannot simply seek to develop reasons for our decisions; rather, we must assess reasons for all possible alternatives, choosing the alternative that is supported by the best reasons.*

Moral Reasons Are Different from Personal Reasons

Personal reasons for decisions are those that appeal to our personal needs, desires, emotions, and interests. Most of the everyday, nonmoral decisions we make can be justified by appealing to personal reasons. One might have chocolate ice cream for dessert rather than chocolate cake because it sounds more pleasurable, because it has fewer calories, or perhaps because it is the middle of summer and ice cream seems more refreshing.

- *What reasons can you provide for your position on gun ownership, abortion, or flag burning? How many of those reasons appeal to self-interest? Emotion? Personal needs and desires? How many of them are reasons you have adopted from parents? Friends? Religious teachings?*

Personal Reasons Are *Not* Sufficient Reasons for Moral Decisions

While perhaps justifying everyday (nonmoral) sorts of decisions, *personal reasons are not sufficient to justify decisions with moral implications.* We might support equal treatment of women because we recognize that equality is an important part of a just society, not because we are trying to impress our parents, pastor, or a romantic interest.

Good Reasons Are the Result of Careful, Rational, and Unbiased Consideration

While most of us can offer a variety of reasons for our beliefs and decisions, closer examination oftentimes reveals that our reasons are flawed in one or more ways. More often than not, this is a result of our tendency to accept beliefs and make decisions without having fully and carefully scrutinized them. Good ethical decision-making and sound ethical actions require that we spend some time considering *where* our beliefs and opinions come from, *how* and *why* we believe certain things or have certain opinions, and, most importantly, whether we are *justified* in having them.

Ethical Frameworks Can Serve as Bases for Thinking About Reasons

Moral reasons often stem from ethical frameworks. Over the course of this text, we have been exposed to a variety of ethical frameworks, all offering reasons for moral decisions. Moral reasons may appeal to the consequences of our actions for other people, to moral duties or principles (e.g., it is wrong to take an innocent life), or to the value of virtue. The frameworks outlined in Chapters 8, 9, and 10 are good starting points for developing good reasons for moral decisions.

UTILIZING OUR CAPACITY TO REASON

The ethical life is not simply about "doing the right thing," it is about *doing the right thing for the right reasons.* When we talk about good or right reasons, we are stressing the importance of human *rationality* and the *capacity for reasoning* which it provides. Reasoning skills are and have always been considered an important—indeed necessary— part of the pursuit of the ethical life. When making choices in both personal and professional contexts, we must utilize our uniquely human capacity to *reason.*

Reasoning Generally Refers To

any *process whereby we apply available information such as evidence or principles (i.e., reasons) to a question, issue, or dilemma in the interest of reaching a conclusion.* When we think critically about whether we should support capital punishment, whether we should lie to a friend when telling the truth could be harmful, or about what we should believe or do with regard to any issue or in any situation, we are engaged in reasoning.

Broadly Speaking, There Are Two Basic Types of Reasoning

These include *theoretical or pure reasoning* and *practical reasoning*. Though there is some considerable overlap between the two, for our purposes they can be described as follows:

- *Theoretical or pure reasoning* involves *deciding what we should or <u>ought to believe</u>. When we reason theoretically, we are not figuring out what we should do in a given situation, but attempting to reach conclusions about morally responsible beliefs. Thus, theoretical reasoning is what <u>guides our thinking</u>.*
- *Practical reasoning* involves *deciding what we should or <u>ought to do</u>. We involve ourselves in practical reasoning anytime we deliberate an action. Thus, practical reasoning is what <u>guides our actions</u>.*

Theoretical Reasoning Assists Us in Developing Good Moral Beliefs

As we will see shortly, an important part of becoming a moral person is critically reflecting on the values and beliefs we hold, the principles we follow, the policies and practices we support and uphold, and the ends toward which we strive. We do so in the interest of identifying desirable values and principles, distinguishing justified from unjustified beliefs, and determining good policies and practices.

- *Should the value of life outweigh the value of choice? Should the virtue of loyalty be held in higher esteem than that of honesty? Are the consequences of our actions more important considerations than our moral duties? Is the overriding goal of our system of punishment and corrections to deter would-be criminals? To rehabilitate convicted criminals? To exact vengeance? Are nonviolent strategies of conflict resolution more desirable than violent ones? How can we use ideas from moral theory (e.g., utilitarianism, Kantian ethics) to justify our answer?*

Practical Reasoning Assists Us in *Applying* Values, Beliefs, and Principles to "Practical" Issues or Situations

Practical reasoning is crucial when we are facing an issue or situation about which *something needs to be done*. It guides our choices and actions by aiding us in determining how best to achieve ends that we have determined to be good, how we should choose when faced with conflicting ends, and most generally how the insights we gain from theoretical reasoning can be *used* over the course of our everyday personal and professional lives.

- *If rehabilitation is determined to be a desirable end or goal for our system of punishment and corrections, practical reasoning is necessary to determine the best method(s) by which to achieve this outcome.*
- *Law enforcement officers are sometimes forced to choose between being loyal to a fellow agent versus telling the truth in a court of law. This sort of ethical dilemma can materialize when concerns are raised about an officer's investigative techniques or respect for the constitutional rights of suspects. Reasoning helps to clarify and evaluate the options we possess, enabling us to make more informed (and hopefully "better") decisions.*
- *If nonviolent strategies of conflict resolution are more desirable than violent strategies, we need practical reasoning to tell us how to apply nonviolent strategies in a given situation or with regard to a given issue.*

The Ethical Life Thus Requires That We Make Good Use of *Both* Theoretical and Practical Reasoning Abilities

Morally, some "ends" are better than others, and some means are better than others for achieving those ends. Theoretical reasoning aids us in contemplating the goodness of ends, while practical reasoning assists us in determining what to do in the interest of attaining those ends. Assuming that equality, for instance, is a desirable end, theoretical and practical reason together may help us determine: (1) *that* equality is a desirable end or state of affairs; and (2) *what means* (e.g., laws, policies, personal or institutional practices, character traits) are best—practically and morally—for achieving the end-state of equality.

Effective Reasoning Requires That We Have *Skills and Tools* with Which to Work

Reasoning about ethics is not something we simply "do"; rather, it is something that requires knowledge, skills, tools, and a good bit of critical reflection. These skills and tools of reason are often discussed as those of *critical thinking*.

THINKING CRITICALLY

The ethical life certainly involves making good decisions and performing right actions on the basis of those decisions. Good decision-making in ethics, in turn, has much to do with being a good *critical thinker*. To be a good critical thinker is to clearly *possess and routinely use the knowledge, skills, and tools necessary to work through ethical dilemmas, and to effectively analyze laws, policies, practices, and other concerns of moral significance.* Knowing *how to think* provides us with a foundation for being ethical people, for making morally good choices, and for reaching justified conclusions on complicated moral issues. As we come to incorporate critical thinking strategies into various facets of our personal and professional lives, practicing them with regularity, this tendency to think critically and to make sound decisions becomes almost second nature.

Critical Thinking Is the "Activity of Reason" or "Reason in Action"

It is the process by which we actively use our innate capacity for rational thought to make good choices or decisions, as well as to justify and carefully assess beliefs, principles, laws, policies, and the like.

The Goals of Critical Thinking Include

(1) *understanding and evaluating reasoning,* including existing and proposed laws, policies, and court decisions; (2) *making well-reasoned choices* and decisions, both in our personal lives and in professional contexts; and (3) *being fair-minded, avoiding the traps or pitfalls of emotion, convention, and other problematic—though common—influences on moral judgments and decisions.*

Accomplishing These Goals Requires a Good Mindset Coupled with an Understanding of How Reasoning Works and Where It Can Go Wrong

While we cannot hope to consider even most of what needs to be said in this context in a short chapter, we have identified some of what we believe are the most important points to be considered as you embark on the journey that is the ethical life. Attaining a good ethical mindset and making good ethical decisions requires, in part, that we: (1) recognize uncritical thinking in ourselves and others; (2) be willing to explore ways unseen; (3) recognize and seek to avoid common errors in reasoning and judgment, including *assumptions, errors of relevance,* and *errors of evidence;* (4) be able, on at least a basic level, to evaluate our own reasoning and that of others; and (5) be able, on at least a basic level, to *apply* moral principles and ethical frameworks to issues, situations, and dilemmas of ethical relevance.

RECOGNIZING UNCRITICAL THINKING

In *The Republic,* Plato asks us to envision an underground cave with the mouth open toward the light of a fire. Within the cave are cave dwellers (i.e., prisoners) who are chained such that they are unable to move, seeing only the cave wall directly in front of them. The light from the fire illuminates the wall so that shadows of people and objects can be seen, but not the people and objects themselves. Because it is all they know—all they can see and experience—the cave dwellers come to equate these shadows with truth and reality, naming them and talking about them as if they were real. In other words, truth and reality for the prisoners are merely shadows of what is.

Plato suggests that if one of the cave dwellers were to escape or be allowed to leave the cave, he would realize that the shadows were merely reflections of a more complex reality. He would realize that what had been truth and reality for him and his fellow cave dwellers—what they had taken to be knowledge of the world—was flawed and distorted. Having experienced what exists outside of his imagined world, our escaped prisoner would never be able to live the old way—having seen the world outside, he would never be able to return to the cave and the world of images that he once took to be real. He would no longer be able to accept his confinement, and he would pity the ignorance of his fellow dwellers. If he were then to share his new-found knowledge with his fellows, he would be met with ridicule, derision, and mockery. To the prisoners, the images of the cave wall are a meaningful reality—far more meaningful than a world they had never experienced. Furthermore, because our once-released prisoner would be unable to resume life in the imagined world, he would be perceived by the others as dangerous. Consequently, they would come to believe the world outside to be dangerous, favoring their world of images only that much more. What lessons can we learn about critical thinking and ethical decision-making from Plato's "allegory of the cave"?

It Is Easy to Become Imprisoned by *Favored Ways of Seeing the World*

We too easily slip into *habits of thought, belief, opinion, preconception, prejudice, stereo-type*, and the like. If we are not careful, we can become "trapped" in certain ways of thinking about or seeing the world, unable or unwilling to recognize alternative possibilities. When challenged, rather than critically assessing the value of alternative thoughts, opinions, policies, and so forth, we tend only to become even *more strongly attached* to our favored ways of thinking. Our thoughts come to take on a power of their own, exercising *control over us* and shaping—if not determining—the way we perceive, experience, and interpret the world.

We Think "Uncritically" When We Accept Ideas, Opinions, and Beliefs Without Carefully Assessing Their Merit

Plato's cave demonstrates the need to *think* rather than accept things as they appear or are given/taught/preached to us. For Plato, this kind of critical reflection is the path out of our metaphorical "imprisonment"—the means by which we escape the state of being confined in a "cave" of ideas and opinions that we have accepted but left unexamined.

Socialization and Experience Tend to Provide Us with a *Limited and Incomplete* Portrait of Ourselves, Others, and the World in Which We Exist

Beginning at a very young age, we unknowingly absorb the ideas and opinions that are presented to us. We are largely passive products of our socialization and environment, digesting almost everything our parents, teachers, religious leaders, and others tell us. As we mature, we are bombarded by the advertising industry, mass media, political officials, and other assorted "experts" telling (or "advising") us as to how to think, what to know, and how to be. This extended process, in conjunction with the personal experiences we have along the way, shape and largely determine the way we perceive and understand the world. Consequently, our understanding is often *limited* and *incomplete,* subsequently making it difficult to engage in objective, unbiased, careful, and critical examination of moral concerns.

The Ethical Life Requires That We Develop Our *Own Reasons* for Beliefs, Opinions, Decisions, and Actions

The value of socialization and experience is not to be altogether dismissed. Much of what we are taught or exposed to, as well as that which we learn from personal experience, can have value. We should first simply recognize that we come to accept a good many ideas, beliefs, and opinions without ever having decided their merits ourselves. Whether we continue to accept them or decide to reject them after critical reflection is less important than developing our *own reasons for accepting or rejecting* them. Developing our own reasons is what thinking critically is all about. The ethical life requires that we objectively weigh ideas, opinions, and arguments when presented to us and, *through this process,* reach sound conclusions.

Ways of Seeing Can Become *Ways of Not Seeing*

When we think in exclusive ways—as "Christians," "liberals," "women," "environmentalists," etc.—no matter how attractive those ways might seem and how much easier it makes understanding the world, we can be prevented from considering new methods of understanding or new ways of seeing existing problems. When this occurs, the process of intellectual growth and moral development is inhibited, and efforts to find desirable solutions to ethical dilemmas and moral issues are hindered. In short, our *"ways of seeing" become ways of not seeing.*

- *Think, for instance, of how absorbed people can become in the beliefs and opinions of their political party or religion when discussing current issues such as crime or poverty. When trapped in such favored ways of seeing, they become unable (or simply unwilling) to consider alternative perspectives. Rather than talking with one another and engaging in reasoned discourse in the interest of a desirable and agreeable resolution, they simply talk past one another.*

Critical Ethical Thinking Requires That We Approach Issues in Unbiased, Unprejudiced, and Open-Minded Ways

When we engage an issue by *starting with a conclusion* or answer that is consistent with our feelings, politics, religious sentiments, etc., we trap ourselves into not seeing. Oftentimes, we make the critical mistake of *seeking out evidence or justifications to support our preestablished conclusion.* In so doing, we are likely not to see beyond the limits of our own point of view.

■ *If we strongly believe that executing juveniles under the age of 16 is a morally acceptable criminal justice response to offender behavior and then proceed to search only for evidence that supports our position, we will never "get to the bottom" of the issue. More than likely, there are many important points to be considered and not all (or even most) of them will necessarily be consistent with what we already believe. What is important is that we consider all of these points, arguments, and sources of evidence. Only by approaching complex crime and justice issues in unbiased, unprejudiced, and open-minded ways can we hope to be good ethical thinkers and make sound, informed, and morally responsible decisions.*

Sometimes, Traps of Not-Seeing Can Have Their Basis in the Beliefs and Norms of Entire Cultures, Communities, or Organizations

Sometimes the traps of not-seeing are much broader in scale than we realize. They can stem from traditions that have existed for hundreds or thousands of years; they can stem from the largely shared beliefs or norms of entire countries or cultures. In these cases, ways of seeing or doing can seem perfectly "natural" and "normal." What is regarded as natural and normal, in turn, is often presumed to be the "right" or "correct" way of seeing or doing.

■ *Consider, for instance, the ways in which the tradition of **patriarchy** impacts the organization and practice of law enforcement. Patriarchy is a form of social organization in which men and typically masculine values are granted priority over women and values that are customarily defined as feminine. Under these conditions, patriarchy becomes a cultural force that can serve as a conceptual prison. For instance, without our conscious awareness of it, patriarchy can encourage us to regard masculine values as somehow better, more important, or more desirable that feminine ways of knowing, being, and doing. One of the*

*practical effects of patriarchy in law enforcement is that this profession has
tended to structure itself around masculine values, with the majority of senior
positions within precincts and departments occupied by men. Values such as
aggressiveness, control, and forthrightness are deemed more desirable
within law enforcement than the values of human relating, compassion,
and reconciliation. Interestingly, however, most police work is not physically
demanding. In fact, aggressiveness is seldom a necessary characteristic for
successful performance. Instead, the skills that are most useful to police officers
include communication, negotiation, and nonviolent problem-solving. In
many important respects, these skills are consistent with feminine ways of
knowing, interacting, and being.*

EXPLORING WAYS UNSEEN

We noted earlier that good (justified) decisions require not that we develop reasons
for our decisions, but that we assess reasons for all possible alternatives, choosing the
alternative that is supported by the best reasons. As ethical thinking requires exploring and considering all possible ways of seeing an issue or situation, it requires that we
always make a point to seek out and consider various explanations, reasons, forms of
evidence, and the like. Doing so can go a long way toward helping us overcome the inevitable prejudices or selfish interests that often shape our reasoning about difficult
moral issues. Problematically, many of us put up a good bit of resistance to this
necessity. How willing are we to *explore ways unseen*?

> ■ *Think of a moral issue that you feel quite strongly about (e.g., abortion, sexual
> abuse, murder, flag burning, or police use of lethal force). First, identify 3 rea-
> sons to support your position (some people have trouble even with this). Next,
> identify 3 reasons in support of the* <u>opposing</u> *position. When asked to do so,
> many people eventually realize that they are so committed to their own perspec-
> tive that they cannot cite many (if any) reasons to support the contrasting view-
> point. Most often, what this indicates is a failure to adequately consider
> alternative possibilities.*

Living the "Examined Life" Requires That We Regularly *Take a Step Back* in Order to See What Is in Front of Us

The ethical life entails subjecting our beliefs, opinions, and ideas to critical scrutiny.
Making ethical choices and undertaking ethical action (i.e., being moral) entails examining and continually reexamining these crucial elements of ourselves. Living the examined life means that we take a step back from our experiences, socialization, feelings,
and other influences that are potentially bias-inducing, in order to assess thoughtfully
the issue right in front of us. Failure to do so can result in making poor choices, including the support of laws, policies, and practices that are largely ineffective and, worst, directly harmful or counterproductive. Ethics helps not only to *clarify our thoughts and*

feelings on many of these matters, but also enables us to *work through* those thoughts and feelings in the interest of critically evaluating their merit. In this respect, the ethical life is about carefully reviewing moral values, principles, and arguments that form the basis of our opinions and beliefs, as well as our decisions and actions.

The Examined Life Requires That We Maintain a Healthy Degree of *Skepticism*

Skepticism is the *willing suspension of belief pending investigation of reasons*. Thus, skepticism is an *attitude*. To be "skeptical" of something is not to deny its validity, truth, value, or desirability. Rather, to be skeptical is to *doubt* and to *maintain that uncertainty* until we have *sufficiently investigated* and reflected on reasons that support or fail to support the validity, truth, value, or desirability of that which is at issue.

- *It may be helpful to think of ethical reasoning like the process of critical thinking that occurs during a legal proceeding. In proceedings like a criminal trial, there are standards of proof, burdens of proof (that attach to the defense or the prosecution), and judges and/or juries who weigh the evidence presented to them. The evaluation of the evidence is undertaken in the interest of determining whether the relevant standards and burdens of proof have been successfully met. Thus, when thinking critically about ethical issues, a healthy amount of skepticism should be maintained until such time as we are confident that we have sufficient information or evidence enabling us to believe, choose, or act a certain way.*

The Examined Life Requires That We Keep an Open Mind

Narrow-minded persons avoid thoroughly considering all possibilities or courses of action, often because they limit their considerations to preformed ideas about what is worthy of consideration. Narrow-minded persons are sometimes dogmatic and often adopt a defensive posturing—almost instinctively defending their preformed ideas rather than thoughtfully considering alternatives and challenges to their ideas. In all cases, the defining feature of narrow-mindedness is simply an unwillingness to open oneself to new ideas, learn from those new ideas and, where appropriate, *change one's own ideas*. Remember, as soon as we believe we have found *the* answer or the *correct* way of being or doing, we close ourselves off to other possibilities and make growth and development nearly impossible.

- *Willingness to change—particularly in light of new evidence—is central to keeping an open mind. The ethical life should be thought of as a work-in-progress. We regularly have new experiences, attain new knowledge, and are exposed to new evidence and new alternatives. The ethical state of mind is one in which we demonstrate a willingness to incorporate these new experiences, knowledge, and alternative possibilities into our ways-of-thinking about the world.*

- *Clearly, it would be impossible—and detrimental—to be open to every idea and every possibility. The ethical life requires that, to some extent, we be discriminate. As a general rule, <u>be judicious and use reasoned judgment</u> when determining which ideas and alternatives may be valuable in a given context or with regard to a given issue. We run into problems, of course, when we discriminate against new ideas and possibilities simply because they are different from ideas we have already formed.*

The Examined Life Requires That We See Beyond Categories, Labels, Stereotypes, and Other Preformed Ways of Sorting and Separating

When we categorize people or ideas, we attach generalized and stereotypical characteristics to them *before* considering them on their own merit or as unique entities. Specifically, we (often subconsciously) attach the stereotyped qualities of the category to the individual idea or person, thus seeing the person or idea *through* the category. Categories such as race, gender, social class, ethnicity, and nationality are common ways of limiting our perspective on people and, consequently, preventing ourselves from seeing unique characteristics, circumstances, and possibilities. The same happens when we see people through labels such as "criminal," "convict," or "sex offender." At other times, we see ideas through categories, whether these be political, religious, theoretical, philosophical, or otherwise. Doing so prevents us from seeing ways unseen in the fullest light.

AVOIDING ERRORS IN REASONING AND JUDGMENT

The first point we made at the outset of this chapter was that the ethical life requires that our beliefs and decisions be *justified*. Justifying beliefs, opinions, decisions, laws, and policies, in turn, requires that two conditions be met: (1) that we have *good reasons* for them; and (2) that the beliefs, decisions, etc. *follow from* those reasons. Decisions and judgments "go wrong" when they are made on the basis of any of a number of errors in reasoning. Over the course of the next several segments of our guide to ethical thinking and decision-making, we catalogue several of the more common types of these errors. Before doing so, we need to look briefly at the two above-mentioned conditions for justification.

Conclusions and *Reasons* Are the Basic Units of the Reasoning Process

Though reasoning is a complicated process, on its most basic level it consists of two units of analysis: reasons (sometimes called "*premises*") and *conclusions*.

- A *conclusion* is the "point" of the reasoning process. Conclusions can be *beliefs or opinions* that are upheld or adopted; they can be *laws or policies* that are implemented; they can be *decisions* that are reached or *actions* that are taken. In short, the conclusion is whatever it is that is the point, aim, or purpose of the reasoning process. If you decide, through critical reflection, that "honesty is the best policy" in a given situation, you have *concluded*—through reasoning—that telling the truth is the best moral choice. Ultimately, the process of *reasoning aims at reaching a conclusion*—ideally, one supported by good reasons.

■ *Premises* are another way of referring to the "reasons" that justify or lead to a conclusion. Though philosophers use the term "premise," we can just as easily substitute the more common term "reason." If we decide or "conclude" that being honest with a co-worker is the right choice in a particular situation *because* we would want her or him to be honest with us if we were in that same situation, we have offered a reason to support our decision. If we determine that capital punishment is a desirable practice *because* it deters future crime, we have offered a reason in support of our belief or opinion.

■ *In the argument, "Abortion is always wrong because taking a human life is always wrong," the conclusion "abortion is always wrong" is supported by the premise or reason "taking a human life is always wrong."*

■ *In the argument, "It should be legal to own handguns. I saw a poll in this morning's newspaper that said 83% of Americans believe that we should have that right. How can you argue with 83% of Americans?," the conclusion ("it should be legal to own handguns") relies on the fact (reason) that 83% of Americans believe that we should have the right to own handguns to support the argument.*

Good Beliefs and Ethical Decisions Require That Two Conditions Be Met

As a *rule*, good beliefs and decisions require that: (1) the *reasons that lead us to have the belief, make the decision, etc., are good, true, or acceptable* and (2) the *conclusion follows from the reasons*. When these two conditions are met, we can say that a belief, opinion, law, policy, decision, etc. is good and justified.

Inference Is the Process of Connecting Reasons to Conclusions

When conclusions are reached on the basis of reasons, we say that we have made an "inference"—we have "inferred" a conclusion from our reason(s). Making decisions, justifying beliefs, and choosing actions all involve the process of inference. Good reasoning, however, requires not only good reasons for the decisions we make and beliefs we hold, but also that the inferences we make that lead us from reason to conclusion be good.

■ *Criminologists, for instance, often infer conclusions on the basis of scientific research. If, on the basis of research on serial murder, we find that 80% of serial murderers were sexually abused as children, we might infer that childhood sexual abuse has a causal influence on later criminal behavior. In this case, the research data serve as the reason for reaching the conclusion.*

Not All Inferences Are Good Ones

Think of a detective having good evidence, but "misreading" that evidence and being led to the wrong suspect. In this analogy, we can think of the evidence as the "reason" (or pieces of evidence as reasons), while the suspect to whom the detective is led as the "conclusion." Even when we have good reasons, we do not always reach the right conclusion based on those reasons. These types of errors are *errors of inference.*

- *"On average, men are physically stronger than women. Therefore, men make better leaders than women." For this conclusion to be acceptable, we need both good (true, acceptable) reasons and a good inference. The reason offered in this argument is, in fact, true. On average, men are physically stronger than women. The inference, however, is faulty. While inferences can go wrong in a number of different ways, the fault of this inference is that <u>there is no connection between the reason and conclusion</u>. It would be difficult to claim that physical strength has any connection to leadership abilities. The conclusion is poor not because the reason is false, but because the inference made assumes a connection between the reason and conclusion that is absent.*

Not All Reasons Are Good Ones

While problems of inference commonly plague reasoning, equally problematic are errors that involve reaching a conclusion on the basis of poor reasons. Because good reasons are such an important part of ethical decision-making, we will have more to say on this subject in a moment. For now, it is worth noting that just as a detective might have good evidence but arrest the wrong suspect because of a faulty inference, in other cases she or he might arrest the wrong suspect on the basis of faulty or poor evidence. Reaching a good conclusion begins with having good evidence or reasons.

Evaluating Beliefs and Decisions

Because two conditions are required for a belief, decision, etc., to be an instance of good reasoning, the evaluation of our own beliefs and decisions and those of others (including the reasoning underlying laws, policies, etc.) involves two basic strategies. These include the following: (1) assessing the truth or acceptability of the reasons; and/or (2) assessing the quality of the inference that is made. As a good starting point, when assessing beliefs, decisions, and the like:

- *Identify the main <u>conclusion</u> (e.g., the belief, decision, law)*
- *Identify the <u>reasons</u> being offered in support of the conclusion*
- *Identify any problematic <u>assumptions</u> embedded in the reasoning (see below)*
- *Determine whether the reasons might not be <u>true or otherwise acceptable</u> (see errors of relevance, evidence, etc., below)*
- *Determine whether the reasons <u>support the conclusion</u> (i.e., does the conclusion follow from the reasons)?*

AVOIDING ASSUMPTIONS

In addition to reasons and conclusions, most of the reasoning that we do also involves *assumptions*. We make assumptions when we leave things unsaid or take things for granted. While this may not always be a problem, in some cases the assumptions we make are themselves sources of debate or are otherwise problematic. In most cases, assumptions are *implicit* or not specifically considered in the reasoning process. We may not even be aware that we are making use of assumptions in our reasoning. In other cases, we may be aware that we or others are making assumptions. Either way, we should consider assumptions problematic if we do not have sufficient reasons for accepting them.

- *Always be aware of assumptions that we or others may be making. Assumptions are not always a problem in critical thinking and ethical decision making. They may be correct, true, acceptable, etc., elements of forming sound beliefs and reaching good decisions or conclusions. In other cases, however, it is the things we take for granted that cause decision-making to go wrong. Always consider whether you or others are making assumptions and, as a general rule, if the assumption might not be true or otherwise acceptable, it is likely a problem that should be addressed or issue that should be taken into consideration.*
- *In the argument, "Abortion is always wrong because taking a human life is always wrong," there is an important assumption. What is assumed or taken-for-granted that may not be acceptable to all people? Hopefully, you identified the assumption as embedded in the premise; namely, this argument assumes that unborn children (i.e., human fetuses) are human beings. It is argued that abortion is wrong because taking human life is wrong. The problem created by the assumption is that we can accept the conclusion if and only if we accept the assumption that unborn children are, in fact, human beings. Of course, this belief is a source of considerable controversy and would need to be supported by a separate argument.*

AVOIDING ERRORS OF RELEVANCE

One of the more common errors in reasoning occurs when we use reasons that are not or should not be considered relevant to the issue or situation. There are a variety of types of errors of relevance. We have chosen to explore only several that seem common in criminal justice: those that rely on authority, popular opinion, expertise, tradition, and emotion as sources of justification. We should note upfront that these sources are not necessarily problematic in all ethical thinking and decision-making. In many instances, however, they lead to problems rather than good solutions.

The Use and Abuse of Authority

Authorities are common sources of belief, and authority is a common justification for decisions and judgments. We routinely make appeals to the U.S. Constitution, the

Bible or Koran, public opinion polls, books, teachers, or politicians when engaging in ethical arguments or even when making decisions about what to do in our personal and professional lives. Unfortunately, authorities are not always *good* sources and authority is not always a *good* supporting reason for moral judgments. This is not to suggest that authority is without place in ethics; rather, it is to recognize that beliefs held and decisions made on the basis of authority are only as good as the authority itself.

- *Appeals to authority occur when we justify a belief, decision, etc. by appealing to the word of a presumed authority. Appeals to authority typically rely on social institutions (e.g., laws, constitutions), public opinion, social and cultural customs and conventions, religious teachers, scientific and moral "experts."*
- *When we use authority, we need to carefully assess: (1) the reliability of the source; (2) whether other sources can corroborate the word of the authority (e.g., do other authorities in the field tend to agree); (3) whether the authority is sufficiently trained/educated on the subject matter in question to be regarded as an authority; and (4) whether the authority her-, him-, or itself has good reasons for making the claims that it does.*
- *Be aware of unknown or unnamed authorities. Though we sometimes make such appeals for the sake of simplicity, claims such as "experts agree that . . .," "research demonstrates that . . .," or "people in the know say that . . ." may be problematic. Ask yourself, what experts? What research? What people? Apply the same guidelines listed above.*

The Use and Abuse of Tradition

Tradition refers to an established way of doing things. When we make an **appeal to tradition,** the reason that we offer in support of a belief or decision appeals to the longevity of the belief, law, practice, and the like. Appeals to tradition are beliefs or decisions based on the fact that something has "always been that way" or "always been done that way." While tradition is not always problematic, it is not a good reason for ethical decisions and moral judgments. In other words, appealing to tradition is not sufficient grounds for ethically-good decisions. That women have "always been" regarded as inferior to men, for instance, is not by itself a good reason for continuing to regard and treat women as inferior; because the United States of America was founded as and has always been a democracy is not by itself sufficient reason for claiming that democracy is the best form of government for the United States. If we were to hold tradition to be an adequate justification of policies and practices, we would have to concede that *slavery* was morally-acceptable up to the point at which it was abolished.

- *In some cases, there may be good reasons that a tradition exists. Where this is the case, identify and utilize those reasons rather than simply appealing to the tradition itself.*

The Use and Abuse of Majority Belief

Contemporary culture barrages us with statistics everywhere we look—from the front page of the daily paper, to the evening news, political speeches, and scholarly journal articles and books. Problematically, these statistics are often presented in such a way as to appear as authoritative voices. The more we become accustomed to hearing or seeing them, the more we may begin to believe that they are, in fact, authoritative. We may begin to believe that public opinion carries weight of some significance when it comes to current issues and events—that the "majority" must be right. If 73% of Americans favor the death penalty, then the death penalty must be morally right or, at least, acceptable. What makes 73% of Americans "experts" on capital punishment, war, abortion, or any other contentious issue? We can use some of the same criticism outlined above to judge public opinion: does the public have sufficient knowledge of and education about the subject matter?; does the public itself have good reasons for beliefs?

- *The **democratic fallacy** occurs where we appeal to majority belief to justify a decision or belief. Simply because 88% of the population believes X, does not mean that X is good, right, just, etc. Public opinion polls offer us interesting pieces of information about what the public thinks and feels, but not a good reason for our own beliefs, decisions, and judgments. Like other sources of authority, the majority can be wrong (remember, the "majority" of people once believed that the earth was flat!).*

The Use and Abuse of Emotion

Many philosophers and nonphilosophers alike have held a deep distrust of emotion. Emotions and feelings have been and are commonly regarded as belonging to that part of our psychological makeup which disposes us to poor judgment, uncritical belief, and harmful behaviors. Emotions are often discussed as irrational forces—collectively, the antithesis of reason—impeding our capacity to think rationally and make sound choices. Because emotions are such powerful forces, they can be powerful influences on our decisions and actions. Many of the beliefs we hold and the choices we make are likely informed in part by emotion. While emotions have many positive functions—even within ethics—they do not always incline us to do the right thing. For every moral action motivated by sympathy, there is likely an equally immoral action motivated by vengeance, hatred, or fear.

- *When approaching ethical issues and decisions, we want to do so in a way that demonstrates what Anne Thomson discusses as "__moral fair-mindedness.__" This requires that we: (1) be <u>self-critical</u>, judging ourselves by the same standards we judge others; (2) judge and decide <u>without reference to prejudices and biases, likes and dislikes;</u> (3) judge and decide <u>without reference to self-interest</u> (or those of our race, class, gender, group or organization); and (4) assess moral issues and make decisions <u>without reference to our own feelings.</u>*
- *As a compromise between eliminating emotions and being driven by emotions, we might consider the ethical need to make assessments as to <u>whether our feelings are appropriate responses to the situation.</u>*
- *Emotions must be governed by the rule of fair-mindedness as well. We must be able not only to assess the appropriateness of our own emotions, but also to make an effort to <u>understand the emotions of others.</u>*

AVOIDING ERRORS OF EVIDENCE

Much of the reasoning we do in the social sciences is *inductive* in nature. **Inductive reasoning** involves making inferences about a population based on known properties of a *sample* of that population. We assume that the properties of the whole population in question will be more or less similar to the properties of the sample about which we know something. Good inductions require a sample that is *similar to the population*. The more similar the sample is to the population as a whole, the more valid and reliable our inferences will be. On the other hand, if our sample is dissimilar in significant ways to the population, our inferences will be poor ones. Several common errors in reasoning result from our making a poor inference about a population based on a sample that is dissimilar in one or more ways. Though there are others, these include: hasty induction, forgetful induction or unrepresentative sample, slothful induction, and exclusion.

Hasty Induction

Hasty inductions are conclusions about a population based on an *insufficient number of cases*. In other words, the size of the sample is too small to make a good inference about the entire population.

- *Research on twenty convicted murderers demonstrates that each of them has an underdeveloped frontal lobe of the brain. On the basis of those twenty cases, we attribute the characteristic of an underdeveloped frontal lobe to all (or most) murderers, claiming that this characteristic is a causal factor in murder. Because there are thousands of convicted murderers around the world and throughout history, we cannot justifiably attribute this characteristic to all (or even most) of them on the basis of twenty cases. Our conclusion was reached on the basis of a hasty induction.*
- *The state of Oregon implements a ban on handguns and, two years later, its crime rate has dropped by 10%. We conclude that crime rates can be lowered in all states by implementing bans on handguns. We have committed an error of hasty induction because, even if we could show that Oregon's reduced crime rate was a result of the ban, one state's experience is not sufficient to claim a general rule that would apply to all states.*

Forgetful Induction

While hasty inductions reflect a failure to observe a sufficient number of cases, forgetful inductions fail to observe a *sufficient variety of cases*. This is sometimes referred to as an *unrepresentative sample*. The problem is not that we have observed too few cases, but that the cases we have observed are not sufficiently diverse to reflect the diversity of the population.

- *On the basis of interview research with three hundred women who have had abortions, we determine that only a small handful of them had good medical reasons for doing so. As it turns out, all three hundred women in our sample were between sixteen and twenty years of age. If we would have interviewed women in other age categories (e.g., under 14, over 35), we may have found significantly more cases where good medical reasons existed for the procedure.*

- *Instructors typically have students do course evaluations near the end of the semester. In a particular class, the instructor has exempted all students who have over an 80% in the class from taking the final examination. The course evaluations are handed out on the last day of class—a day which is to serve as a review session for the final examination. Problematically, all of the "A" and "B" students in the course—a good number of whom found the course interesting and enjoyable—are not present to do the evaluations. The evaluations ultimately reflect the opinions of those students who struggled with the material or the instructor.*

Slothful Induction

In some cases, we refuse to reach a conclusion (accept a belief, reach a certain decision) even though there is sufficient evidence leading us to that conclusion. We induce "slothfully" when we deny the "correctness" or value of a belief or opinion even when all available evidence tells us that we should accept it.

- *Joey has been convicted of child molestation four times. He has just been released on parole. As Joey's parole officer, he has assured us that "this time is different," and we are inclined to believe that he is rehabilitated. Each time he has been released from prison in the past, he has committed a sex offense within two months. Each of those times, he swore that he was "better" and would not re-offend. While we should not discount the possibility that this time is different, all of the evidence we have should lead us to conclude that Joey will commit yet another offense in the near future.*
- *Dr. Jenks hypothesizes that low serotonin levels cause aggressive behavior in adults, oftentimes leading to violent actions. Over the years, numerous studies have failed to confirm this hypothesis. Many violent persons did not have low serotonin levels, and many people with low serotonin levels did not act aggressively or violently. Nevertheless, Dr. Jenks continues to maintain that a strong relationship exists.*

Exclusion

In some cases, we ignore or exclude important evidence that would have a bearing on the conclusions we reach or the decisions we make. The most problematic instances are those where we refuse to acknowledge evidence because the conclusion to which it leads is undesirable or challenges our accepted and comfortable ways of thinking and doing. Good reasoning requires that we consider *all* available evidence, no matter what implications that evidence may have for the beliefs we hold and decisions we reach.

- *Over the past month, the "Wild Hearts" gang has been linked to thirty-two of thirty-eight crimes committed in the neighborhood. Earlier today, Mrs. Robinson was robbed at gunpoint. Chances are, the "Wild Hearts" had something to do with it. Without any other information, this induction might not be entirely objectionable. However, if we consider that none of the thirty-two crimes linked to the "Wild Hearts" were robberies and none of them involves the use of handguns, our induction becomes poor. With this information, our conclusion would likely be that this crime is not connected to the "Wild Hearts" gang.*

- *One of the more common types of exclusion in social science occurs when we ignore evidence that is contrary to our hypothesis, explanation, etc. Suppose that, in justifying the merit of a theory of crime, we refer to the twelve studies that support the theory, while ignoring or failing to include the fourteen studies that either did not support or effectively refuted the theory. These types of exclusions become especially likely when we become attached to favored ways of seeing and doing.*

AVOIDING OTHER COMMON ERRORS

Errors in reasoning are numerous. Those of evidence and those of relevance represent only two of a variety of categories of faulty thinking. Rather than providing a comprehensive treatment of the remaining categories, we have chosen to single out several additional types of reasoning errors that may be especially useful for thinking about and making decisions within criminal justice.

Two Wrongs Don't Make a Right

This common saying has much validity. Two wrongs always make two wrongs. If, for instance, a suspect assaults a police officer while she or he is in the process of making an arrest, the suspect has committed a wrong. If, in turn, the officer assaults the suspect in retaliation, the officer's actions are no less wrong than the suspect's and certainly do not magically (or morally) make the situation right. Simply because our motive is revenge or retaliation does not mean that actions so motivated will somehow rectify, remedy, or "fix" the initial wrong.

- *Many proponents of <u>restorative justice</u> argue that punishing criminals is an attempt to make two wrongs equal a right. Instead, they argue, if we wish to remedy the initial wrong, we should focus on utilizing restitution, reconciliation, and other strategies designed to restore well-being rather than add harm to harm.*

Stay Focused on the Issue and Relevant Circumstances

There are several common errors in reasoning that involve allowing ourselves to become distracted or attempting to distract others from the real issue at hand or the relevant circumstances as they apply to that issue. At times, we "attack" the source of a claim rather than the ideas offered by that source. Commonly, this attack is of a person's politics, religion, race or gender, groups or organizations to which she or he belongs, her or his character or personal habits and preferences, or the person's situation.

- *If we are politically liberal, we should not dismiss the ideas of a political candidate or commentator because she or he is politically conservative. Alternately, disregarding a person's argument against capital punishment because she or he is a "bleeding heart liberal" is similarly problematic. In each case, we should seek to refute <u>the ideas themselves</u>, rather than attempting to discredit the ideas by discrediting the person offering them.*
- *If we are interested in whether prisoners should be allowed to train with weights, we should not dismiss the claims made by prisoners simply because they are in prison and have a vested interest in the issue. In such a case, we should consider not the person, but the reasons the person is offering in support of her or his position.*
- *It has recently been discovered that an ethics professor, married with children, has been having an affair with a student and, further, that he lied about the affair when formally questioned. Simply because the professor does not "practice what he preaches," we should not discredit the value of the ideas he taught in his courses.*

Lack of Proof Does Not Disprove and Lack of Disproof Does Not Prove

This statement is self-explanatory. Simply because we have no proof that something is the case, does not mean that it is not the case; similarly, simply because we cannot prove that something is not the case, does not mean that it is. As a general rule, it makes good sense to err on the side of the majority of evidence; however, in so doing we should not exclude alternative possibilities.

Avoid Black-and-White Thinking

Black-and-white thinking relies on *binary* or *either/or logic*—thinking in terms of right/wrong, good/bad, or black/white with no consideration for what lies in between. This type of thinking occurs when we give or are given a limited number of options with respect to a complex issue when, in fact, there are more options available. A recent U.S. president made such a claim with regard to the "war on terror," offering something to the effect of, "either you're with us or you're against us." This type of either/or logic fails to consider that most issues are not "black or white." While commitment is an important part of moral character, we should not forget that good answers and good decisions are sometimes—if not usually—to be found in the gray areas. Always ask whether there are additional alternatives. Can a compromise be reached? Is there room for a creative solution?

- *The defendant is either guilty or innocent*
- *The defendant is either mentally-healthy or mentally-ill*
- *The defendant was either sane or insane at the time of his offense*

Strive for Consistency in Moral Beliefs and Decisions

Anthony Weston calls this "judging like cases alike." One of the key features of the examined life and of good moral character more generally is consistency in beliefs, decisions, and actions. If a moral belief or decision in a given situation is based on a certain moral value or principle, the same principle should apply to all other similar beliefs and situations. Sometimes we fail to see the similarities between issues or situations; other times, we don't want to see the similarities, as doing so might require us to change our belief or decision with regard to one of them. Valuing loyalty over honesty in one situation, and honesty over loyalty in a different but similar situation, may indicate a failure to thoroughly examine one's value priorities. As well, it may simply indicate a failure to see the two situations as similar and, thus, as requiring similar choices. Good ethical thinking and decision-making demands that we be clear about our own values and principles and that we seek to apply them regularly and consistently.

- *The **principle of universalizability** holds that if we judge a practice or behavior to be morally right, we must also judge all morally-similar practices to be equally right. If we judge an action to be morally wrong because it causes suffering, then all other actions that cause suffering must be regarded as equally wrong.*
- *To believe, for instance, that abortion is wrong because it is wrong to take a life while simultaneously believing that capital punishment (i.e., taking a life) is desirable or acceptable would likely constitute <u>inconsistency of belief</u>. If you are morally opposed to acts of killing, consistency demands that you oppose all acts of killing (or change your principle).*
- *When inconsistency is an issue, we have only two options: (1) we can <u>determine ways in which what seem to be similar issues or situations are actually different</u>, thus requiring different principles, decisions, etc.; or (2) we can <u>change our minds</u> about one or the other issue or situation. In the above example about capital punishment and abortion, you might determine ways in which abortion is different in <u>morally significant</u> ways from execution. Your guiding principle may not be "it is wrong to take a life," but "it is wrong to take an innocent life." This, in turn, might have implications for whether you support or oppose war, whether you hunt for sport, eat meat, and engage in other practices that involve taking innocent lives. Ask yourself what makes taking life in a time of war morally different from executing criminals; what makes killing animals for food (or sport) different from abortion or execution? To hold different positions on these matters, we must be able to identify exactly how one is different (in a morally-relevant way) from the others. If we cannot, then our positions are plagued by inconsistency.*

PUTTING IT ALL TOGETHER: A SUMMARY OF GUIDELINES FOR THE ETHICAL LIFE

- In making decisions about what to believe or what to do, make sure your decisions are justified (i.e., are backed by good reasons).
- Avoid making decisions based on self-interest or the interests of a group to which you belong (e.g., race, gender, religion, political affiliation).
- Avoid becoming trapped in favored ways of seeing the world.
- Recognize that many of your existing beliefs, ideas, and opinions are likely limited and incomplete.
- Seek to develop moral autonomy, developing your own reasons for beliefs and decisions.
- Practice "taking a step back" to see what is in front of you.
- Maintain a healthy, but selectively employed, amount of skepticism.
- Keep an open mind, avoiding dogmatism and defensive posturing.
- Avoid making assumptions.
- Avoid relying on authority as the sole reason for ethical beliefs and decisions.
- Avoid relying on tradition or convention as the sole source of ethical beliefs or reason for decisions.
- Avoid making too much of public opinion.
- Avoid making decisions solely on the basis of emotions, passions, and desires.
- Before making generalizations, make sure you have observed a sufficient number and variety of cases.
- Follow, do not dismiss, good reasons and evidence.
- Do not exclude important sources of information or evidence simply because it does not support preformed ideas.
- Do not add harm or evil to already existing harm or evil by responding to a wrong with another wrong.
- Stay focused on relevant information.
- Keep in mind that lack of proof does not disprove, and lack of disproof does not prove.
- Avoid black-and-white thinking, thinking dichotomously, and seeing through categories and labels.
- Finally, strive for consistency in moral beliefs and ethical decisions.
- Making an effort to "know thyself" and live an "examined life" will go a long way toward ensuring that you adopt and maintain good moral beliefs and that you make good and consistent ethical decisions.

SUGGESTED READINGS

Baggini, Julian, and Fosl, Peter. (2003). *The Philosopher's Toolkit: A Compendium of Philosophical Concepts and Methods.* New York: Blackwell.

Blackburn, Simon. (2003). *Being Good: A Short Introduction to Ethics.* New York: Oxford University Press.

Fisher, Alec. (2001). *Critical Thinking: An Introduction.* Cambridge, MA: Cambridge University Press.

Hindes, Steve. (2005). *Think for Yourself: An Essay on Cutting Through the Babble, the Bias, and the Hype.* Golden, CO: Speaker's Corner Books.

McInerny, D. Q. (2004). *Being Logical: A Guide to Good Thinking.* New York: Random House.

Ruggiero, Vincent. (2003). *Thinking Critically About Ethical Issues.* New York: McGraw-Hill.

Ruggiero, Vincent. (2004). *Beyond Feelings: A Guide to Critical Thinking.* New York: McGraw-Hill.

Solomon, Robert. (1984). *Ethics: A Brief Introduction.* New York: McGraw-Hill.

Thomson, Anne. (1999). *Critical Reasoning in Ethics: A Practical Introduction.* New York: Routledge.

Weston, Anthony. (2001). *A 21st Century Ethical Toolbox.* New York: Oxford University Press.

INDEX

T

U

V